PROLIFE FEMINISM

Photo Credits

ProLife Feminism

Yesterday and Today

Expanded Second Edition, 2005

Mary Krane Derr, Rachel MacNair,
Linda Naranjo-Huebl

Contents

PART TWO:
1960S TO THE PRESENT

Preface and Acknowledgments—Second Edition

A bumpersticker from the National Organization for Women (U.S.) reads: "Feminism is the radical notion that women are people." Prolife feminism is the even more radical notion that *both* women *and* unborn children are people. This volume documents the living, evolving tradition of prolife feminists—and in some cases sister travelers—that now spans at least three centuries and arises into many nations, cultures, and religions. We coeditors readily acknowledge our activist intent. Our purpose is to offer a largely untapped but nonviolently powerful resource for healing and preventing the personal, familial, and societal wounds surrounding abortion and other forms of lifetaking.

To respect contemporaries whose standpoints differ from our own, we generally use their preferred self-designations: "prolife" and "prochoice." We have not, however, edited individual writers' own terminology. Nor have we covered over historical usages of outmoded, offensive words, such as noninclusive language and terms like "defectives" (i.e., disabled persons). While opposing current use of such offensive language, we cannot presume to go back and change the past. Wherever possible, we have foregrounded substantive text in the voice of each activist—although the organic shape of some stories could not be crammed and lopped into this format. We want to caution some prolifers: please quote early feminists responsibly. Please don't use our work in an uninformed, sloppy way—let alone present it alongside indifference or hostility to present-day women's real-life struggles. We also ask skeptical prochoice feminists: please accord us the same hearing you would like for yourselves, and dialogue with us over your responses.

Mary Krane Derr wishes to thank the following individuals and organizations: her life partner Jonathan Derr; their daughter Sarah Derr; all whose voices are heard through this book; her clients and colleagues in her previous work as a pregnancy and adoption counselor; her many friends, both prolife and prochoice, from the Bryn Mawr College alumnae community, particularly Sidney Callahan; Jen Roth, Laura Ciampa, Felecia Thompson, Jeff Donels, Rose Evans, Geoff Goodman, Nat Hentoff, Laurie Ramsey Jaffe, Kelly Jefferson, Evelyn K.S. Judge, Rachel MacNair,

Frederica Mathewes-Green, Linda Naranjo-Huebl, Marvin Olasky, Charlotte Paris, Suzanne Schnittman, Richard Stanley, staff at Americans United for Life, the Library of Congress, the Schlesinger and Countway Libraries of Harvard University, the University of Chicago Library, the Newberry Library, Chicago Historical Society, the Dorothy Day Library on the Web, the Dorothy Day Archive at Marquette University, the Women's Christian Temperance Union, the Coleman Library of Tougaloo College, the University of Illinois at Chicago Library Special Collections, Tsering Tashi of the Office of Tibet, London, England, Vasu Murti, Ruth Enero, Jean Bethke Elshtain, Joan Baranow, the late Wayne Teasdale, and anyone else she may have failed to mention. Mary dedicates her portion of the work to all her foremothers who have moved to the other side of the veil, especially her mother-in-law Joan Turner Derr (1938-1998), aunt Patricia Dix (1940-1990), and grandmother Sylva Lathrop Dix (1916-1991). The word "midwife" means "with-woman," and these three women were certainly with Mary and Sarah through and beyond an unplanned, utterly challenging pregnancy nearly two decades ago.

Rachel MacNair and Linda Naranjo-Huebl would like to thank Cindy Osborne, Pat Goltz, Catherine Callaghan, Jessica Pegis, Martha Crean, Pam Cira, Paulette Joyer, Mary Meehan, Sharon Richardson, Mary Bea Stout, Gail Grenier-Sweet, Juli Loesch-Wiley, Kay Castonguay, Carol Crossed, Barbara Willke, Penny Salazar Phillips and others for their help in providing historical and biographical information on the contemporary feminists included in Part Two. Linda would particularly like to thank Scott, Micaela, and Maura for their lifelong support in helping young pregnant women in need by sharing their home and family; the Alternatives Pregnancy Center in Denver for their more than twenty years service to pregnant and post-abortive women; the wonderful women with whom Linda has labored for social justice; all those heroic women who have chosen life under difficult circumstances; and their children, who prove every day that their mothers' choice is worth celebrating. Rachel MacNair would like to especially thank her mother, Dorothy MacNair, whose practical and emotional support made it possible for her to spend all those years as president of Feminists for Life of America.

All of the editors thank the numerous contributors to *Sisterlife* (1973-1995), the predecessor to Feminists for Life of America's current journal *The American Feminist*. These writer-activists laid a solid foundation for contemporary prolife feminist theory and practice, frequently before learning about the weight of *herstory* behind them.

PART ONE
1790-1960

Elizabeth Cady Stanton and
her daughter, Harriot.
from a daguerreotype 1856.

Introduction to Part One, Second Edition

If we live in a society where women's knowledge and theories are notable by their absence, in which women's ideas are neither respected or preserved, it is not because women have not produced valuable cultural forms but because what they have produced has been perceived as dangerous by those who have the power to suppress and remove evidence . . . So while men proceed on their developmental way building on their inherited tradition, women are confined to cycles of lost and found, only to be lost and found again—and again . . . We can see that what we are doing today is not something new but something old: this is a source of strength and power.

—Dale Spender, *Feminist Theorists: Three Centuries of Key Women Thinkers* (1983)

Prolife feminism is a "new but old" approach to abortion. It is well summed up by this 1868 headline over an article in Elizabeth Cady Stanton's and Susan B. Anthony's newspaper *The Revolution*: "Man's inhumanity to woman, makes countless infants die."[1] Admittedly, the term "prolife feminism" was in not in use at that time. Before the early twentieth century, women's rights supporters generally called themselves "the woman movement." Antiabortionists did not term themselves "prolife" until the late twentieth century. We simply use the term "prolife feminism" as apt, convenient shorthand for the historical thread traced in this book. [2] Since the 1960s, this once prevalent view has been reduced to an overlooked, dismissed, and even suppressed stance, but it has persisted. Indeed, its renaissance over the past decade, its encounters with already like-minded people of diverse backgrounds, along with the cultural diversification of women's studies, and the return to consciousness and print of many feminist classics make necessary this expanded second edition.

We do not know when and where prolife feminism originated; the question lies beyond this volume's scope. We have had enough challenge squeezing in the wealth of materials from "modern" feminism, often defined as starting with Mary Wollstonecraft. As Americans whose shared tongue is

16

English, we focus primarily on English-language, although multicultural, activists and documents from the United States, while presenting materials that show the international character of abortion discourse. Our respective biographies disclose further the identities and experiences that have shaped our individual and shared standpoints. We do *not* in any way deny the value of other possible standpoints. We are simply starting with the parameters most familiar and accessible to us—not trying to have "the last word." May there be many more standpoints and words to come!

Despite the usual ardor for recovering lost herstory, many contemporary prochoice feminists have denied, minimized, or neglected feminism's enduring prolife strain.[3] Is this because for the past four decades the majority of white, middle- to upper-class, industrialized-world feminists have defined a moral and legal right to abortion as a necessary condition for women's equality, even of women's very right to life? Knowing that a profound ethical concern for women's sufferings—*not* some "selfish" desire for "convenience"—moves prochoice feminists, we can fathom their disbelief and outrage at us. At the same time (we believe), such resistance denies feminism a "lost source of strength and power" that still promises much deeper, more constructive solutions to women's problems than abortion ever can. At the very least, it is unwise for feminists to turn away from any facet of herstory, palatable today or not.

With time, more prochoice feminists have acknowledged the existence of prolife feminists, today's and yesterday's. Some even recognize us as genuine—not merely "self-described"—feminists.[4] These are most welcome changes. To our sadness and frustration, the assumption that we deceptively, manipulatively wrench early feminists' words out of context to impose an "ultra rightwing" agenda still thwarts dialogue and cooperative action. Some prochoice activists do acknowledge early feminist anti-abortion sentiment, but attribute it to the procedure's illegality and danger to women; "regular" (allopathic) physicians' drive to eliminate "irregular" (alternative) doctors and midwives as competition; a restrictive motherhood mystique; prudery; and/or patriarchal religious dogma.[5]

Delving into primary sources shows that early feminists *were* quite concerned about abortion's physical and psychological dangers, but their response was to eliminate abortion itself, not seek legal and ethical sanction for it. Prochoice historian Carl Degler honestly acknowledges that endangerment to women was not their only or even primary objection.[6] Nor was abortion's illegality *per se* the reason. Many feminists committed nonviolent civil disobedience: sheltering runaway slaves and abused wives, refusing to pay taxes, entering polls and attempting to vote, picketing, marching, hunger striking, providing sexual/reproductive health education and services.[7] In contrast, they supported laws against abortion while being very clear that thorough relief of its root causes mattered most of all. Not all sought to suppress "irregular" doctors and midwives; many early feminists *were* such practitioners or their enthusiastic clients and advocates.

The early feminists did celebrate motherhood as a uniquely female power and strength that deserved genuine reverence, while exposing the motherhood mystique as a cover-up for real-life degradations.[8] Recognizing that women had creative capacities other than the womb's, early feminists fought for women's entrance into higher education and the professions, resisting the dictum that female physiology inherently prevents public achievement. Their perspectives on motherhood led naturally to their outspoken criticisms of prudery and the sexual double standard. Many affirmed the value of sex for pleasure and communication, not just procreation, for both sexes.[9] Even as they "bemoaned the horrors of abortion," they "nevertheless insisted upon limitations upon fertility" and upon guarding women "against the deceit, exploitation, and conflict that inevitably ensued from sexual ignorance."[10]

Indeed, they actively promoted sexual and reproductive health education and "voluntary motherhood" as urgently necessary alternatives to abortion, along with direct service and public policy aid to pregnant women and other mothers—including single ones, often condemned as "undeserving" of support. Some addressed these issues through the forerunners of today's socially conscious businesses. All agreed that abstinence was a valid means of exercising the right to voluntary motherhood, also called the "right over one's own body." A number extended that right to withdrawal, coitus reservatus, douches, condoms, and pessaries (which evolved into diaphragms). Some also sanctioned "Alphaism," "Dianaism," "Alpha-Abstinence," "Non-procreative Love," or resort to sexual practices other than penis-vagina intercourse.[11] Some openly chose "Boston marriages," life partnerships between women.[12] Many spoke up for women's right to choose pain relief during labor; trained, skilled midwifery services; and avoidance of unnecessary, overly aggressive surgical and medical interventions.[13]

Feminist advocacy of nonviolent choices intensified as abortion rates escalated. Abortion and postnatal infanticide were hardly unknown in colonial Anglo America, where nonmarital pregnancy was indeed made into a social ordeal. Yet a single expectant mother could claim *some* community aid, however rudimentary and moralistic, for herself and her child. By the nineteenth century and into the twentieth, such community assistance had disappeared, rendering nonmarital pregnancy an even greater crisis. Indeed, aid was actively withheld because "bad women" and their "bastards" purportedly did not deserve it. Of course not all aborting women were unmarried, but as Jane Addams and other feminists insisted, justice for single mothers was closely tied to justice for all women.[14] Tragically, U.S. culture on the whole never took such wisdom to heart. Despite its illegality and peril to two lives at once, abortion became even more entrenched and desperate a recourse, even as voices of "Christian morality" denounced it.

For their courageous, plainspoken advocacy of nonviolent choices, many early U.S. feminists ran afoul of Anthony Comstock (1844-1915), the anti-vice crusader and book burner behind the Comstock Law, the federal anti-obscenity statute equating sexual/reproductive health education with pornography, family planning with abortion, and abortion with "sexual immorality" instead of lifetaking. Comstock adopted a child without the foreknowledge, let alone consent, of his wife, whom he extolled as an ideal—that is, passive and self-effacing—woman. [15] His misogyny was equally evident in public. A famous cartoon shows Comstock hauling a bedraggled woman before a judge: "Your Honor, this woman gave birth to a naked child!"[16] Along with the maternal and fetal deaths he caused, he boasted of driving at least fifteen "enemies" to suicide, especially Ann Lohman, the New York City abortionist known as Madame Restell. She was not the last.[17]

Patriarchal, sectarian religious dogma was not an early feminist motive, either.[18] The activists in Part One were spiritually diverse: Unitarian, Haudenosaunee (Iroquois), Quaker, Spiritualist, Congregationalist, Methodist-Episcopal, Episcopalian, Presbyterian, Evangelical Protestant, Jewish, Roman Catholic, and Baha'i. Some were "freethinkers," who identified themselves as atheists, agnostics, Theosophists, or persons seeking spirituality outside of organized religion. Rather than submitting blindly to their respective traditions, early feminists critically questioned and challenged injustice-promoting doctrines as an integral part of their devoted service to womankind, humankind, and (in many cases) the Divine.[19]

What motive might be left for early feminists' opposition to abortion? They repeatedly called the procedure "ante-natal murder," "child murder," "ante-natal infanticide," or simply "infanticide." They spoke of *two* lives being lost in any abortion that killed both woman and fetus. They regarded abortion as a violent wrong against *women* as well, one arising from the violent wrong of denying women authentic sexual and reproductive choices. Their approach was shaped by scientific discoveries about prenatal development; the egalitarianism of the Haudenosaunee Six Nations;

abolitionism; the brave, groundbreaking life and work of Mary Wollstonecraft; and women's "heart-histories" around sex and reproduction. Pioneering women physicians prided themselves upon the healing nature of listening with deep empathy to patients and drawing out their heart-histories, the inner experiences and emotions of their own lives. [20] Perhaps inspired by the many physicians among them, and by the genre of slave narratives, early feminists—like feminists today—often appealed to and mobilized these personal stories to foster societal healing. Thus our conclusion that earlier prolife feminists were motivated primarily by a broad ethic of respect for lives and their interdependence. This ethic was (and still is) one that people of diverse faiths and none could adopt and practice. Degler's work lends credence to our conclusion regarding the recognizably humane, nonsectarian/ interfaith motives of prolife feminism.

> Seen against the broad canvas of humanitarian thought and practice in Western society from the seventeenth to the twentieth century, the expansion of the definition of life to include the whole career of the fetus rather than only the months after quickening is quite consistent. It was in line with a number of movements to reduce cruelty and to expand the concept of the sanctity of life. The reduction, in the course of the nineteenth century, in the use, or the elimination of the death penalty, the peace movement, the abolition of torture and whipping in connection with crimes all represented steps in that centuries-long movement. The prohibiting of abortion was but the most recent effort in that larger concern. [21]

Feminism, of course, was and is an essential part of that "broad canvas of humanitarian thought and action," like other movements that have long drawn feminists. Feminism has always been a multi-issue movement for life and liberty on many fronts. Early feminist opposition to abortion was interwoven with concern for women's overall conditions; already-born children's rights and welfare; healing from substance abuse; the abolition of slavery, genocide, and other racist institutions; peace and anti-imperialist advocacy; labor reform and revolution; disability rights; environmental conservation; animal welfare; and vegetarianism. Yesterday's prolife feminists practiced what today is called "a consistent life ethic," or respect for lives before, during, and after birth. A prolife feminist, consistent life ethic approach resonates with values that people of many faiths and none already share. [22] We do *not* renew and build upon this approach out of blind obedience to the past, let alone to exclusively sectarian religious beliefs. We do acknowledge that yesterday's feminists (like today's) sometimes fell short of their ideals in matters like religious tolerance, disability, race/ethnicity, and class. We hope to do better than this as we pursue a feminism-grounded consistent life ethic—because it still matters and still applies, in ways both foreseen and unforeseen by our foremothers.

Mary Wollstonecraft (1759-1797)

Anglo-Irish intellectual and writer Mary Wollstonecraft is often credited with inspiring the First Wave of American and European feminism. Her *Vindication of the Rights of Woman* (1792) validated many women's intuitions, rousing them to action. The Quaker abolitionist Lucretia Mott, a mother of organized US feminism, enshrined a copy of the book in her living room.[1] Surprising as it may seem today, neither Wollstonecraft nor her admirers argued for the general morality and legality of induced abortion. The first modern "Westerner" to do so was the Marquis de Sade (1740-1814), who repeatedly inflicted sexual violence upon nonconsenting women and girls he deemed socially inferior.[2] The word "sadism" derives from his name.

In his *Philosophy of the Bedroom* (1795), deSade argued that abortion was necessary for women's sexual fulfillment—thus he invoked the stereotype of sexual women as murderous, that ancient, enduring projection of misogynist violence onto its victims. Yet he insisted that abortifacients "did no more harm" than laxatives. If unborn humans were akin to excrement, then what, in de Sade's reckoning, did that make the already born, particularly people from groups he devalued? He praised the ancient Greeks for immediately killing disabled newborns judged incapable of future military use, as opposed to "maintain[ing] richly endowed houses for the preservation of this vile scum." If the state gave its warriors the right to kill, he reasoned, the individual had the right to dispose of unwanted children. DeSade's novel *Juliette* (1797) culminated with the disembowelment and killing of a poor pregnant woman and her unborn child on an altar, as a kind of sacrifice.

DeSade's views on abortion, infanticide, and the exploitation of women contrast tremendously with Mary Wollstonecraft's.

> Women becoming, consequently weaker, in mind and body, than they ought to be have not sufficient strength to discharge the first duty of a mother; and . . . either destroy the embryo in the womb, or cast it off when born. Nature in every thing demands respect, and those who violate her laws seldom violate them with impunity. . . . Contrasting the humanity of the present age with the barbarism of antiquity, great stress has been laid on the savage custom of exposing the children

whom their parents could not maintain . . . [M]en ought to maintain the women they have seduced . . . one means of stopping an abuse that has an equally fatal effect on population and morals. (*Vindication of the Rights of Women*, Chapter Eight)

Wollstonecraft approved of a *nonviolent* family limitation method, now called the Lactational Amenorrhea Method and considered up to 98% effective.[3]

For nature has so wisely ordered things that did women suckle their children, they would preserve their own health, and there would be such an interval between the birth of each child, that we should seldom see a house full of babes. (*Vindication*, Chapter 13)

Would de Sade have dismissed the disabled Wollstonecraft as "vile scum"? Her disability, bipolar disorder, helped her envision new, expanded human possibilities, ones that did not bode well for the Marquis's lifestyle and the hierarchies he depended upon.[4] Born in Spitalfields, London, Wollstonecraft came from an Anglo-Irish, Anglican Church-affiliated textile craft family. At 19, Mary escaped the household, which was dominated by her father's alcoholic rages. She sheltered her sister Eliza, who fled a violent husband. Dissatisfied with women's limited educational opportunities, the two ran a girls' school together until realizing their students had already internalized negative views of women.

After joining the Rational Dissentist minister Richard Price's chapel, Mary Wollstonecraft entered London's welcoming literary, intellectual, and activist circles and began her career as a writer. William Blake and William Godwin applauded Wollstonecraft's critique in *Vindication of the Rights of Man* (1790) of English social fixtures like the monarchy and slave trade. Tom Paine was inspired to publish his *Rights of Man*, and Price and Joseph Priestly to form the Unitarian Society. Wollstonecraft then published *Vindication of the Rights of Woman* to further argue against gender, marital, governmental, military, and religious hierarchies. She was widely jeered as a "hyena in petticoats" for this book, which was promptly parodied as *Vindication of the Rights of Brutes*. As Edmund Burke began to suppress the civil liberties of Unitarians and other radicals—"loathsome insects," in his words—Wollstonecraft fled to France.[5] There she critically documented Robespierre's atrocities and lived with American adventurer Gilbert Imlay. In 1794 she bore their daughter Fanny, named for her dear friend who had died in childbirth. Despondent at Imlay's abandonment and the vitriol surrounding "illegitimacy," Wollstonecraft grew ill and attempted suicide.

By 1797, she had regained health, returned home, and become happily involved with her old friend William Godwin. When she became pregnant, they agreed to marry, despite their philosophical objections; Wollstonecraft wished to protect herself and her children from further hostility. She began gestation also of her novel *Maria, or the Wrongs of Women* (1798).

Wollstonecraft never finished the book. Her spouse recounts that, just as she had at Fanny's birth, "she determined to have a woman to attend her in the capacity of midwife . . . sensible that the proper business of a midwife, in the instance of a natural labour, is to sit by and wait for the operations of nature . . ." After delivering a girl, Wollstonecraft retained the placenta and hemorrhaged. An obstetrician, or "man-midwife," was called in: the very personage she had wanted to avoid, with his view of pregnancy as a disease mandating aggressive mechanical intervention. He cut up the placenta and extracted it, declaring it entirely removed. He was wrong. Ten days later, in the presence of her husband and friends, Wollstonecraft died of placental sepsis. The infant was named after her. Both Wollstonecraft's daughters inherited her bipolar disorder. Fanny also struggled with her biological father's rejection, her mother's death, and a society that did not heed her mother's vision of welcoming every child and woman. At 22, she committed suicide. Her unsigned note read, "The best thing I could do was to put an end to the existence of a being whose birth is unfortunate." Mary Godwin (later Shelley) became a radical, visionary writer whose best-known work, *Frankenstein*, written when she was a mother of 19, warns of exclusively male-controlled reproduction: the very subject that Wollstonecraft explores, although differently, in *Maria*, whose unfinished manuscript Godwin published after her death.[6] In these passages, men and male-defined institutions drive wedges between women and their own bodies and lives, women and their own children, and women and each other.

"I Never Had A Taste of Human Kindness"
by Mary Wollstonecraft *[Summaries by Editors]*

[Maria, a middle-class woman, has been institutionalized for "madness" by her husband—i.e., for challenging his brutality. His retaliation has forcibly separated her from her nursling.]

Her infant's image was continually floating on Maria's sight, and the first smile of intelligence remembered . . . She heard her half speaking half cooing, and felt the little twinkling fingers on her burning bosom—a bosom bursting with the nutriment for which this cherished child might now be pining in vain. From a stranger she could indeed receive the maternal aliment, Maria was grieved at the thought . . .

The retreating shadows of former sorrows rushed back in a gloomy train . . . Still she mourned for her child, lamented she was a daughter, and anticipated the aggravated ills of life that her sex rendered almost inevitable, even while dreading she was no more. To think that she was blotted out of existence was agony . . . yet to suppose her turned adrift on an unknown sea, was scarcely less afflicting . . .

[Maria takes solace in friendship with Jemima, a servant who brings her books. Jemima, conceived outside marriage and motherless and abused from birth, eventually shares her life story.]

"I shudder with horror, when I recollect the treatment I had now to endure. I never had a taste of human kindness to soften the rigour of perpetual labour . . . I was despised from my birth, and denied the chance . . . of being considered as a fellow-creature . . .

"At sixteen, I suddenly grew tall, and something like comeliness appeared on a Sunday, when I had time to wash my face, and put on clean clothes. My master had once or twice caught hold of me in the passage; but I instinctively avoided his disgusting caresses.

"One day however, when the family were at a Methodist meeting, he contrived to be alone in the house with me, and by blows—yes; blows and menaces, compelled me to submit to his ferocious desire; and, to avoid my mistress's fury, I was obliged in future to comply, and skulk to my loft at his command, in spite of increasing loathing.

"The anguish which was now pent up in my bosom, seemed to open a new world to me: I began to extend my thoughts beyond myself, and grieve for human misery, till I discovered, with horror—ah! what horror!—that I was with child. I know not why I felt a mixed sensation of despair and tenderness, excepting that, ever called a bastard, a bastard appeared to me an object of the greatest compassion in creation.

"I communicated this dreadful circumstance to my master, who was almost equally alarmed at the intelligence; for he feared his wife, and public censure at the meeting. After some weeks . . . I in continual fear that my altered shape would be noticed, my master gave me a medicine in a phial, which he desired me to take, telling me, without any circumlocution, for what purpose it was designed. I burst into tears, I thought it was killing myself—yet was such a self as I worth preserving? He cursed me for a fool, and left me to my own reflections.

"I could not resolve to take this infernal potion; but I wrapped it up in an old gown, and hid it in a corner of my box.

"Nobody yet suspected me . . . a creature of another species. But the threatening storm at last broke over my devoted head—never shall I forget it! One Sunday evening when I was left, as usual, to take care of the house, my master came home intoxicated, and I became the prey of his brutal appetite. His extreme intoxication made him forget his customary caution, and my mistress entered and found us in a situation that could not have been more hateful to her than me . . . She tore off my cap, scratched, kicked, and buffeted me, till she had exhausted her strength, declaring, as she rested her arm, 'that I had wheedled her husband from her.—But, could any thing better be expected from a wretch, whom she had taken into her house out of pure charity?' What a torrent of abuse rushed out? till, almost breathless, she concluded with saying, 'that I was born a strumpet; it ran in my blood, and nothing good could come to those who harboured me.'

"My situation was, of course, discovered, and she declared that I should not stay another night under the same roof with an honest family. I was therefore pushed out of doors, and my trumpery thrown after me, when it had been contemptuously examined in the passage, lest I should have stolen any thing.

"Behold me then in the street, utterly destitute! Whither could I creep for shelter? . . . This night was spent in a state of stupefaction, or desperation. I detested mankind, and abhorred myself. In the morning I ventured out, to throw myself in my master's way, at his usual hour of going abroad. I approached him, he 'damned me for a b—, declared I had disturbed the peace of the family, and that he had sworn to his wife, never to take any more notice of me.' He left me; but, instantly returning, he told me that he should speak to his friend, a parish-officer, to get a nurse for the brat I laid to him; and advised me, if I wished to keep out of the house of correction, not to make free with his name.

" . . . [R]age giving place to despair, [I] sought for the potion that was to procure abortion, and swallowed it, with a wish that it might destroy me, at the same time that it stopped the sensations of new-born life, which I felt with indescribable emotion. My head turned round, my heart grew sick, and in the horrors of approaching dissolution, mental anguish was swallowed up. The effect of the medicine was violent . . ."

Maria took her hand, and Jemima, more overcome by kindness than she had ever been by cruelty, hastened out of the room to conceal her emotions . . .

—From Chapters 1 and 5, *Maria, or The Wrongs of Woman*,
Preface by William Godwin, 1798.

Ganeodiyo (Handsome Lake) (c. 1735-1815)

Many early European American suffragists had significant ties with upstate New York, including the great "suffrage triumvirate" of Elizabeth Cady Stanton, Susan B. Anthony, and Matilda Joslyn Gage, and their beloved elder Lucretia Mott. One critical reason was the profound influence of the area's Native Americans, the Haudenosaunee or "People of the Long House" (called Iroquois by the French). The Haudenosaunee were and are a confederacy of six nations: Mohawk, Onondaga, Oneida, Cayuga, Tuscarora, and Seneca. The 1848 Seneca Falls Convention marked the start of organized American feminism—at first chiefly an Anglo, Protestant, and middle—to upper-class movement. This event bears the name of the upstate New York town where it was held—a town named after a Haudenosaunee nation. Yet European American historians have often overlooked the woman movement's original connection to the Six Nations—a connection much stronger and deeper than this secondhand coincidence of names would suggest. Sally Roesch Wagner helped to uncover this hidden-in-plain-sight story.

> For 20 years I had immersed myself in the writings of early United States women's rights activists . . . Yet I could not fathom how they dared to dream their revolutionary dream . . . living under conditions they likened to slavery . . . My own stunningly deep-seated presumption of white supremacy had kept me from recognizing what these prototypical feminists kept insisting . . . They believed women's liberation was possible because they knew . . . women who possessed rights beyond their wildest imagination: Haudenosaunee women.[1]

The Haudenosaunee suffered severe cultural upheavals following the arrival of Europeans: war, coerced displacement from ancestral lands, violated religious liberties, the proliferation of alcohol abuse, depression, accusations of black magic, and interpersonal violence. Even so, Haudenosaunee women fared better within their own society than white women in theirs. The Six Nations, envisioning the Divine as double-gendered, accorded women critical responsibilities in religious rituals and ruled by consensus, not gender-restricted majority. No man could assume leadership unless innocent of theft, murder, wife abuse, and failure to provide for his family. ("*There goes Congress!*" thought Wagner when she learned this.) Six Nations women had an equal part in government; clan mothers were integral to it. Loose-fitting, comfortable Haudenosaunee tunics and leggings inspired the "bloomer" outfit that a Stanton relative later devised as an alternative to corsets and other excruciatingly uncomfortable, unhealthy fashions. When other women were denied satisfying, truly honored work, Haudenosaunee won great respect for their productive, ingenious, ecologically sound farming methods, especially the "Three Sisters" method of cultivating corn, squash, and beans together. Family descent was traced through the mother. "Illegitimacy" was an unknown concept before the Europeans arrived. Pregnancy and birth were not considered terrifyingly pathological. Women had their say in matters of childrearing, property, marriage, and divorce. Domestic violence and rape—still comparatively rare—were treated as truly grave offenses. Thus Haudenosaunee women were remarkably free to enjoy voluntary motherhood.[2]

As traditional ways disappeared, some Haudenosaunee assimilated and accepted Christianization. The Seneca prophet Ganeodiyo, or Handsome Lake, sought both preservation of old ways and survival alongside the white world. Son of a clan mother and half-brother of a military leader, Ganeodiyo fought in battles and took part in treaty negotiations and signings between the Six Nations and the U.S. government. General Sullivan's invasion of Haudenosaunee lands dislocated Ganeodiyo's family to a reservation. He became severely depressed and alcohol-addicted. Around 1800, Ganeodiyo fell into a coma and was feared dead. Upon awakening, he described visions of divine messengers entrusting him with prophecies and revelations. Despite opposition from Christian missionaries, the visions became the heart of the Long House religion and were orally transmitted down the generations as The Gaiiwo ("Good Message"), also called the Code of Handsome Lake.

The Gaiiwo predicts the world's end if environmental destruction continues. Haudenosaunee are thus active local and global environmentalists.[3] The Gaiiwo also resonates with past and contemporary social movements in its counsels against alcohol abuse, lack of hospitality to the poor, and abuse and neglect of women and children—including pregnant women and their unborn children. The Seneca Arthur Caswell Parker (1881-1955), anthropologist, museum director, acquaintance of Susan B. Anthony, and a feminist himself, extensively documented Haudenosaunee cultures in the early twentieth century.[4] His translation from the Gaiiwo follows. Here may lie one origin of another hidden-in-plain-sight story: that of early feminists and abortion.

From *The Gaiiwo* ("Good Message" or Code of Handsome Lake)
Translated from the Seneca by Arthur Caswell Parker

["They," the main speakers, are the messengers of Ganeodiyo's vision. "He" is Ganeodiyo himself.—Eds.]

"Now another word. It is sad. It is the fourth word. It is the way Yondwi'nias swa'yas ['she cuts it off by abortion'].

"Now the Creator ordained that women should bear children.

"Now a certain young married woman had children and suffered much. Now she is with child again and her mother wishing to prevent further sufferings designs to administer a medicine to cut off the child and to prevent forever other children from coming. So the mother makes the medicine and gives it. Now when she does this she forever cuts away her daughter's string of children.[5] [The Seneca and Onondaga belief is that every woman has a certain number of children predestined to them and that they are fastened on a stringlike runner like tubers, or like eggs within a bird.—Parker's note]

"Now it is because of such things that the Creator is sad. He created life to live and he wishes such evils to cease. He wishes those who employ such medicines to cease such practices forevermore. Now they must stop when they hear this message. Go and tell your people." So they said and he said. Eniaiehuk .... ['It was once that way.']

"Now another message.

"Go tell your people that the Great Ruler is sad because of what people do.

"The Creator has made it so that the married should live together and that children should grow from them.

"Now it often happens that it is only a little while when people are married that the husband speaks evil of his wife because he does not wish to care for her children. Now a man who does that stirs up trouble with his wife and soon deserts her and his children. Then he searches for another woman and when he has found her he marries her. Then when he finds her with child he goes away from her and leaves her alone. Again he looks for another woman and when he has lived with her for a time and sees her growing large, he deserts her, the third woman.

"Now this is true. We, the messengers, saw him leave the two women and the Creator himself saw him desert the third and punished him. Now a sure torment in the after life is for him who leaves two women with child but the Creator alone knows what the punishment is for the man who leaves the third."

So they said and he said. Eniaiehuk . . . .

"Now another message to tell your people.

"The married often live well together for a while. Then a man becomes ugly in temper and abuses his wife. It seems to afford him pleasure . . . Now because of such things the Creator is very sad. So he bids us to tell you that such evils must stop. Neither man nor woman must strike each other."

So they said.

Now furthermore they said, "We will tell you what people must do. It is the way he calls best. Love one another and do not strive for another's undoing. Even as you desire good treatment, so render it. Treat your wife well and she will treat you well."

So they said and he said. Eniaiehuk . . . .

"Now another message.

"Tell your people that ofttimes when a woman hears that a child is born and goes to see it, she returns and says in many houses where she stops that its mother's husband is not its father. Now we say that it is exceedingly wrong to speak such evil of children. The Creator formed the children as they are; therefore, let the people stop their evil sayings."

So they said and he said. Eniaiehuk . . . .

—Sections 4, 6, 10, and 18 in Arthur Caswell Parker, *The Code of Handsome Lake, the Seneca Prophet*, New York State Museum at Albany, 1913.

[During the early twentieth century, the Euro-American woman movement turned for inspiration to a well-known member of another First Nation:[6] the Lemhi Shoshone teen mother Sacajawea (ca. 1787—ca. 1812), who expertly guided

and interpreted for the Lewis and Clark expedition. Six months pregnant when she joined the expedition as its only female member, Sacajawea birthed her son Pomp en route and carried him on her back in traditional Shoshone fashion. During the 1990s, another predominantly female social justice movement also turned to Sacajawea. Prolifers saw in her a strong, intelligent, capable woman who mothered and otherwise made compassionate use of her gifts in arduous circumstances. They joined the campaign for an image of Sacajawea carrying Pomp to be engraved on the U.S. dollar coin, which Susan B. Anthony has also occupied. As anthropologist Faye Ginsburg has concluded, prolifers—just like suffragists—belong to a living American tradition of female-led reform movements.[7] —Eds.]

Slavery: Violence Against Lives and Choices (Nineteenth Century)

For centuries, European colonization of North and South America depended heavily on millions of enslaved human beings—some of First Nations but mostly of African or mixed heritage. Their captivity was enforced through systematic violence against their lives and their reproductive rights. To stave off the contradiction between this reality and the humanitarian ideals of their newly independent country, Anglo Americans salved their consciences with false images of benevolent, upright slaveholders and happy, well-tended slaves. Although they were not the first New World (so-called) residents to protest slavery, members of a remarkable Anglo family were among the first Americans of any race to unmask an inherently violent institution and widely challenge public opinion. They were Upstate New Yorker Theodore Weld (1803-1895), his spouse Angelina Grimké Weld (1805-1879), and her sister Sarah Grimké (1792-1873). The three lectured, organized, and wrote pamphlets for the American Anti-Slavery Society, with public unrest dogging them, the sisters especially, wherever they traveled. Convinced the Bible forbade public speaking by women, outraged mobs threatened to burn down churches where the Grimkés preached. Public officials in their home state set the sisters' pamphlets on fire, threatening them with arrest if they came back.

Daughters of a plantation-owning South Carolina Supreme Court justice, both sisters were revolted by slavery as very young children. They moved to Philadelphia, joined the Society of Friends, and worked all their lives for progressive causes. After Emancipation, they discovered that their late brother Henry had conceived two sons with his slave Nancy Weston. They unconventionally welcomed their destitute biracial nephews into their own home and paid for their educations. Francis James Grimké (1850-1925) attended Howard University Law School and Princeton Theological Seminary, then became an outspoken minister and civil rights activist. Archibald Henry Grimké (1849-1930) became one of Harvard Law School's first Black graduates, U.S. consul to the Dominican Republic, editor of a newspaper for Black Republicans, and an early leader of the National Association for the Advancement of Colored People (NAACP). As we shall see, his daughter Angelina Weld Grimké became a noted Harlem Renaissance writer.[1]

The nephews' way to emancipation was paved in part by a book their abolitionist aunts and uncle published in 1839: *American Slavery As It Is: Voice of a Thousand Witnesses*.[2] Theodore was named as the author, but Angelina and Sarah helped to compile its eyewitness accounts and contributed their own. They documented, among other atrocities, the sexual and reproductive traumas inflicted on African slaves. Writing under the pseudonym Linda Brent, Harriet Ann Jacobs (c. 1813-1897) was one of the few slave narrative authors to speak out about her own "indelicate" experiences. She validates *American Slavery*'s observations that white men regularly subjected African women to sexual harassment, rape, and forced breeding. Women who resisted were flogged or killed—even if they were infertile from malnutrition, exhaustion, and poor health. At the same time, slaveholders interfered at will with Black women's right to choose their own partners. Black women and their babies were denied essential care before, during, and after birth. Women in the perils of labor might be compelled to go it alone, and, if they survived, to return soon to work in the fields, where they were often not allowed to nurse their babies as needed—that is, if the babies survived.[3]

Women's child care "choices" were strapping their babies on their backs as a protection against poisonous snakes, laying the babies alone on the ground or in a basket, or enlisting the aid of children too young for fieldwork—i.e., four to six years old. If a baby died from illness or accident, the master punished the mother for depriving him of valuable property; no matter that *he* was the one who made it so difficult for slave children to live in safety and good health, and that he was often the biological father. Yet if a child managed to live through the enforced neglect, the mother knew the sorrows she or he was bound to experience as a slave. For example, disabled and/or elderly slaves were routinely discarded and neglected until they died. Only medical experimenters deemed them "useful." The mother also knew she had no power to stop the master from selling "his property" at his whim. He even had the legal right to whip her during pregnancy until he killed her unborn child—that is, to commit a forced abortion, with impunity.[4]

The relentless "Dr. Flint," her mistress's father—actually Dr. James Norcom, a physician of high social standing in Edenton, North Carolina—sexually harassed Harriet Jacobs from age 15 onward. Desperately trying to resist, Jacobs became involved with another white man, the future U.S. Representative Samuel Treadwell Sawyer ("Mr. Sands"), whom she "at least did not despise." When Jacobs became pregnant, Norcom angrily reminded her that he had the power of life and death over her and her unborn child:

> He talked of the disgrace I had brought on myself . . . He intimated
> that if I had accepted his proposals, he, as a physician, could have
> saved me from exposure. He even condescended to pity me. Could
> he have offered wormwood more bitter? . . . He clinched his teeth,
> and muttered, "Curse you!" He came towards me, with ill-suppressed
> rage, and exclaimed, "You obstinate girl! I could grind your bones to
> powder . . . You are blinded now; but hereafter you will be convinced
> that your master was your best friend. My lenity towards you is a proof
> of it. I might have punished you in many ways. I might have whipped
> till you fell dead under the lash. But I wanted you to live . . ."[5]

More than once, Jacobs contemplated death for herself and her children,
never imagining the freedom they would someday win.

While slaveholders were quite directly responsible for most killings of
Black fetuses and neonates, captive Blacks did sometimes engage in abortion
and infanticide out of the same situational pressures and despair that
sometimes led them to suicidality. In January 1858, some fugitive Kentucky
slaves, including Margaret Garner, her husband, and her four children,
crossed the frozen Ohio River near Cincinnati, hoping to enter the
Underground Railroad. Officers pursued the fugitives, who barred
themselves up in a house and fought back with guns. When the officers
battered down the door and dragged her spouse out,

> Margaret Garner, seeing that their hopes of freedom were vain, seized a
> butcher knife that lay on the table, and with one stroke cut the throat of
> her little daughter, whom she probably loved the best. She then
> attempted to take the life of the other children and to kill herself, but
> she was overpowered and hampered before she could complete her
> desperate work. The whole party was then arrested and lodged in jail . . .
> Margaret Garner for murder, and the others for complicity in murder.
>   . . . While in the court-room . . . [t]he babe she held in her arms was
> a little girl, about nine months old, and was much lighter in color than
> herself . . . During the trial she would look up occasionally, for an
> instant, with a timid, apprehensive glance at the strange faces around
> her, but her eyes were generally cast down. The babe was continually
> fondling her face with its little hands, but she rarely noticed it, and her
> general expression was one of extreme sadness. The little boys, four
> and six years old, respectively, were bright-eyed, woolly-headed little
> fellows, with fat dimpled cheeks . . . [sitting] on the floor near their
> mother, playing together in happy innocence, all unconscious of the
> gloom that shrouded their mother, and of the fact that their own future
> liberty was at stake . . . Those who came to speak words of comfort and

cheer felt them die upon their lips, when they looked into her face, and marked its expression of settled despair.[6]

The court remanded all the fugitives to the slave master. On the return boat, Garner jumped into the river with the infant.[7] Levi Coffin, a veteran Quaker leader of the Underground Railroad, noted that "no case attracted more attention and aroused deeper interest and sympathy."[8] Garner's story and others like it may have influenced early feminist portrayals of abortion and infanticide as desperate, violent acts to escape the enslaving conditions imposed on mothers of all backgrounds.

Many early feminists were abolitionists who discerned parallels between gender and race oppression. Sarah Grimké was not the first or last feminist to identify men's property claims over women as a prime cause of abortion.

> Has [woman] not, too often, when thus compelled to receive the germ *she could not welcome*, refused to retain & nourish into life the babe which she felt was not the fruit of a pure connubial love? . . . And yet the Times is horror-struck at the idea of woman's claiming "A supreme sovereignty over her own person & conduct." Is it not time that she should? Has not man proved himself unworthy of the power which he assumes over her person & conduct? . . . Let us now look at the results of such a recognition. A right on the part of woman to decide *when* she shall become a mother, how often & under what circumstances. Surely as upon her alone devolves the necessity of nurturing unto the fullness of life the being within her & after it is born . . . she *ought* to have the right of controlling all preliminaries.[9]

Margaret Garner was largely forgotten until the African American writer Toni Morrison imaginatively reconstructed her story in the novel *Beloved* (Knopf, 1987). Given the extreme pressures upon slave mothers, how much of a distinction existed between coerced and "voluntary" abortion/infanticide? Dorothy Roberts states, "Slavery could only exist by nullifying Black parents' moral claim to their children." Roberts discusses the contemporary feminist notion of the "maternal-fetal conflict," "the way in which law, social policies, and medical practice sometimes treat a pregnant woman's interests in opposition to those of the fetus she is carrying," a conflict widely thought to originate with twentieth-century fetal imaging technologies. Roberts believes it started when "slaveholders forced women to lie face down in a depression while they were whipped" so that the women could be injured, but not their fetuses.[10] However, isn't abortion (so often obtained, past and present, under exigent circumstances) an example of the maternal-fetal conflict, too—and one that predated this form of whipping?

Dr. Elizabeth Blackwell (1821-1910)

Remembered as America's first female physician, Blackwell was more accurately the first to earn the allopathic medical degree. Although dismissed as "irregulars" by many allopaths, many nineteenth-century doctors practiced with "alternative" credentials in such fields as homeopathy and hydropathy—and, of course, throughout history midwives have practiced healing arts without any official sanction. Blackwell, a Unitarian, came from a prosperous, reform-minded English immigrant family. Her sister Emily followed her into medicine. Their sisters-in-laws were suffragist Lucy Stone and writer Antoinette Brown Blackwell (the first woman minister ordained by a U.S. congregation); their niece was second-generation suffragist Alice Stone Blackwell.[1] Elizabeth's occupational choice was clinched by a *New York Herald* item on Madame Restell, who built up a well-known, openly advertised business from the 1840s on. Blackwell wrote:

> The gross perversion and destruction of motherhood by the abortionist filled me with indignation, and awakened active antagonism. That the honorable term "female physician" should be exclusively applied to those women who carried on this shocking trade seemed to me a horror . . . an utter degradation of what might and should become a noble position for women. Being at that time a reader of Swedenborg, and strongly impressed by his vivid representation of the unseen world, I finally determined to do what I could "to redeem the hells" and especially the one form of hell thus forced upon my notice.[2]

After rejections from over a dozen medical schools, Geneva Medical College in Syracuse finally admitted her in 1845—as a prank. Despite relentless harassment, she graduated at the top of her class. After further training in Europe, she returned to New York City. Initially, other doctors shunned her and potential landlords refused to rent to her, mistaking her for an abortionist. (In the 1970s, a Philadelphia abortion clinic apparently mistook her for one, too, naming itself Elizabeth Blackwell Center.)[3] Undaunted, in 1854 Blackwell adopted a seven-year-old orphan, Katharine ("Kitty") Barry, a remarkable choice for a woman who had opted to remain single. Her sister Emily later adopted a daughter, too. Along with Emily and Polish-German midwife/physician Marie Zakrzewska, Elizabeth started the New York Infirmary for Women and Children, the first entirely female-staffed American hospital, later chartered as a women's medical college.[4] Elizabeth courageously hired Dr. Rebecca Cole, the nation's second African American female physician (after Rebecca Lee Crumpler), as a hygiene and prenatal care educator to their indigent patients.[5] Dr. Elizabeth Cushier (1837-1932), their coworker and Emily's life partner, recalled that the Infirmary was the only safe haven at the time in New York City for single pregnant women.[6] In this spirit of welcome and respect for the dispossessed, Elizabeth Blackwell also openly challenged the Restell business,[7] and taught that life began at conception, contrary to the popular belief that it commenced with "quickening," the woman's first detection of fetal motion.

Leslie Reagan presents the life-begins-at-conception view as misogynist and expert-imposed, and the quickening doctrine as woman-centered and democratic.[8] Is the matter so clear-cut? After all, even before (or without) modern medical innovations like the pregnancy test, women have detected earlier signs of pregnancy than quickening. The quickening theory also has historical ties to Aristotle, who defined the womb as a passive receptacle for the sperm, i.e. the animating, active male principle that alone became the fetus. It shaped the common male Victorian fear of sperm loss as a horrid disease, "spermatorrhea," that could lethally bankrupt men's bodies. Elizabeth Blackwell reassured the panic-stricken that nocturnal emission (like menstruation) was a "natural healthy action of self-balance." The notorious womanizer Frank Harris feared it so much, he slept with a whipcord tied to his penis and shrank in horror from masturbation and contraception. On the other hand, he did not mind impregnating a lover and performing an abortion on her, which, he wrote, *"got rid of the intruding semen"* (emphasis added).[9]

The early nineteenth-century discoveries of mammalian ova and of conception as a union of maternal cell with paternal cell, actively nurtured by the pregnant woman's body, must have been quite empowering for early feminists. The health professionals among them, including Blackwell and her colleagues, were eager to democratize this information, and nonmedical women and girls were eager to learn it (see Densmore French and A Teacher, Stockham, and Duffey, Part One).

"Look at the First Faint Gleam of Life"
by Dr. Elizabeth Blackwell

Look at the first faint gleam of life, the life of the embryo, the commencement of human existence. We see a tiny cell, so small that it may be easily overlooked; the anatomist may examine it with scalpel or microscope, and what does he discover? Nothing but a delicate, transparent membrane, containing one drop of clear water; the chemist may analyze it with the most scrupulous care, and find nothing but the trace of some simple salts. And yet there is in that simple germ-cell something wonderful—life!—it is a living cell; it contains a power *of progressive growths according to laws, towards a definite type*, that we can only regard with reverent admiration. Leave it in its natural home, tended by the rich life of the healthy maternal organism, and it will grow steadily into the human type; *in no other by any possibility.* Little by little the faint specks will appear in the enlarging cell, which mark the head, the trunk, the budding extremities; tiny channels will groove themselves in every direction, red particles of inconceivable minuteness will appear in them—they move, they tend towards one central spot, where a little channel has enlarged, has assumed a special form, has already begun to palpitate; finally the living blood in the small arteries joins that in the heart, and the circulation is established. From every delicate incomplete part, minute nerve-threads shoot forth, they tend invariably towards their centres, they join the brain, the spinal marrow, the ganglia. The nervous system is formed. The cell rapidly enlarges, its attachments to the maternal organism becomes more powerful, for increasing amounts of fresh nourishment must be conveyed to the growing being, the work advances to perfection, each organ is distinctly formed, placed in the cavities of head, chest, and abdomen, that are now completely closed; the human type is surely attained, and after a brief period of consolidation the young existence, created from that simple cell, will awake to a further development of independent life. Throughout this period of early life we remain spectators merely of the wonderful growth; it would be impious folly to attempt to interfere directly with this act of creation; but even here, in this early stage of existence, we have *important aid* to render . . . Such favoring influences are found in the daily life of the mother, during the early period of the embryonic existence, in the cheerful sunshine of the spirit that should so naturally enfold the new centre of many hopes, in the observance of those important rules of hygiene, regular habits, early hours, periodic exercise, cold bathing, plain wholesome food, and loose comfortable clothing; these rules are simple, easily understood, not difficult to be observed, yet they are of *immense importance*—they are the *favoring circumstances* of growth, they are *our part* in the work of creation. Then, surely, they never can be neglected by the wise mother who has once clearly recognized their use.

—*The Laws of Life,* New York: Putnam and Sons, 1852, 70-73.

Henry Clarke Wright (1797-1870) and an Anonymous Correspondent

At Spiritualists' 1858 Rutland (Vermont) Free Convention, the reformer, itinerant lecturer, and American Anti-Slavery Society activist Henry Clarke Wright presented pacifism, "nonresistance" (now called "nonviolence"), and women's and children's rights as interconnected causes. In the same breath, he opposed slavery, war, and the death penalty, and affirmed "the most sacred and important right of woman . . . to decide for herself how often and under what circumstances she shall assume the responsibilities and be subjected to the cares and suffering of Maternity."[1] The same year, Wright bolstered his case for voluntary motherhood by publishing women's tales of abortion.

"My Womanhood Rose Up In Withering Condemnation"
by Henry Clarke Wright and an Anonymous Correspondent

Dear Friend:

The following experience of a woman, given in her own words . . . is the cry of anguish from woman's riven heart to man to save her from the revolting alternative of killing her child before it is born or of giving life to one whose very existence is loathed by her . . .

"How did I feel? I felt that I was committing a damning sin. My soul shrank from the deed with intense horror and loathing. The remonstrances of a guilty conscience I could not silence. I had submitted to the relation in which maternity originates, thinking it my duty, as a wife, to do so whenever my husband demanded. I told him that my very soul shrank from maternity; that I was not yet prepared for its responsibilities and agonies, and begged of him not to impose that burden upon me till I could joyfully welcome it, which I felt that I should, in due time. But he heeded not my prayer. He insisted on the relation. Conception and maternity ensued.

"My soul died within me. An ever-present loathing of the new life that was being developed within mine was in my heart . . . The spirit of murder, towards the unconscious child in embryo, was ever present to me; yet my

---

40

soul shrank with horror from the deed. Shall I kill my child before its birth, or give existence to one whose birthright inheritance is, *a mother's curse?* was the question I found myself debating continually; for my curse was on its very life.

"I consulted a woman, a friend in whom I trusted. I found that she had perpetrated that outrage on herself and on others. She told me it was not murder to kill a child any time before its birth. Of this she labored to convince me, and called in the aid of her 'family physician' to give force to her arguments. He argued that it was right and just for wives thus to protect themselves against the results of their husband's sensualism—told me that God and human laws would approve of killing children before they were born, rather than curse them with an undesired existence. My only trouble was, with God's view of the case. I could not get rid of the feeling that it was an outrage on my body and soul, and on my unconscious babe. He argued that my child, at five months, (which was the time,) had no life, and where there was no life, no life could be taken. Though I determined to do the deed, or get the 'family physician' to do it, my womanly instincts, my reason, my conscience, my self-respect, my entire nature, revolted against my decision. My Womanhood rose up in withering condemnation. And after the deed was done, I felt that I could never respect myself again . . . [and] all that was pure and true in manhood and womanhood would shrink from me as a polluted, disgusting object.

"I tried to cast the blame on my husband, who had imposed the necessity upon me. I tried to feel that the outrage and the guilt were all his own; that had he heeded my prayer, and dealt justly by me, I should have never been driven to the dread alternative of ante-natal murder, or of giving birth to a child I did not want. But I saw and felt, that however great the wrong he had done to me, the fact still remained—my nature was outraged, if not by my consent, yet by my sufferance . . . I had no right to add to the outrage by killing my child. I felt myself to be a crushed, prostituted, abandoned woman . . ."

—from *The Unwelcome Child,* Boston: Bela Marsh, 1858, 101-104,
courtesy of the Department of Special Collections,
University of Chicago Library.

Susan B. Anthony (1820-1906)

Susan Brownell Anthony's heritage was rooted in the Society of Friends (Quakers). During the 1840s, while supporting herself as a teacher, she became involved in abolition, including the Underground Railway, and temperance. Temperance was a feminist issue because male alcohol abuse led to domestic violence, child abuse, and family destitution. Anthony's enduring, selfless devotion to women's rights grew from her frustration over the male-dominated power structures of the abolition and temperance movements, and from her close friendship with Elizabeth Cady Stanton. Over five decades, they joined together to lead national suffrage organizations, conduct numerous speaking tours and women's rights conferences, publish the fearlessly outspoken newspaper the *Revolution*, and write the first three volumes of the monumental *History of Woman Suffrage*.

In 1872 Anthony was put on trial for illegally attempting to cast a ballot. While she focused on suffrage, she sought to link women—and men—across class, cultural, and religious differences, sometimes successfully, sometimes not. For example, she and Stanton alienated African Americans by prioritizing white women's suffrage over that of Black men. Yet she spoke out against legalizing prostitution, concerned that this would legitimate the economic discrimination compelling women into this trade. Remembering the female laborers in her father's upstate New York mills, she founded the Working Women's Association. She illegally sheltered the abused wife and child of a wealthy and prominent man. Prefiguring the modern contention that "sisterhood is global," she organized the International Council of Women during the 1880s.[1]

Anthony was happy with her personal choices not to marry a man or have biological children, to sustain and be sustained primarily through closeness with women, and to channel her considerable life energies into "the cause." She spoke of her passionate devotion to women as sacred: "I pray every single second of my life; not on my knees but with my work. My prayer is to uplift women ... Work and worship are one with me."[2] Anthony honored women's different choices and life courses. She praised egalitarian marriages and remarked that sex "is not coarse or gross, it is simply the answering of the highest and holiest function of the physical organism."[3] She did sometimes chafe at Stanton, her beloved friend, and other suffragists whose domestic responsibilities limited their activism time. When Stanton was perhaps three months pregnant with her seventh child, Anthony wrote to Antoinette Brown Blackwell, "I only *scold now* that for a moment's pleasure to herself or her husband, she should thus increase the *load* of *cares* under which she already groans—but there is no remedy now . . ."[4]

Anthony accepted and loved children who had already been conceived. Though well aware that some women, even in her own family, considered abortion a "remedy," she clearly did not.[5] She helped raise Stanton's seven children, and doted on her biological nieces, writing that "a child one loves is a constant benediction to the soul." She regarded younger feminists as her "nieces" too, and they called her "Aunt Susan." Anthony supported one "niece's" choice to adopt a baby while single.[6] A male friend told Anthony, "With your great head and heart, you, of all women I have met, ought to have been a wife and mother." She replied, "I thank you, sir . . . but sweeter even than to have had the joy of caring for children of my own has it been to me to help bring about a better state of things for mothers generally, so that their unborn little ones could not be willed away from them."[7]

In nineteenth-century America, if a child were still unborn at the father's death, she or he could be forcibly taken from the mother at birth and given to a guardian previously appointed by the father. This traumatic arrangement (for both parties) often led to the baby's death. It only made sense that Anthony opposed abortion.

Further evidence of her opposition appears in the *Revolution*, which debuted January 8, 1868, with Anthony as manager/proprietor, and Elizabeth Cady Stanton and Parker Pillsbury (and later Paulina Wright Davis) as editors. The masthead boldly declared the *Revolution's* refusal of "Quack or Immoral Advertisements" i.e., ads for thinly disguised patent medicine abortifacients, a major revenue source for periodicals.[8] This policy could not have been adopted without the approval of Anthony, who was charged with the already difficult task of fundraising for a controversial political newspaper. "Marriage and Maternity," the article excerpted below, expressed her wish to get at the root causes of abortion.

Despite its enthusiastic subscribers, the *Revolution* went bankrupt in 1870. Anthony personally assumed responsibility for the $10,000 debt, paying it off through six years of lecturing. One especially straightforward speech from those years was "Social Purity," which enlarged upon the themes of "Marriage and Maternity" and praised Sister Irene Fitzgibbon

(1823-1896), the Catholic nun who created the New York Foundling Hospital because there was no public provision for the city's thousands of abandoned infants. At the same time, Anthony noted that the 1300 babies whose lives it saved and tended in its first six months meant "thirteen hundred mothers' hopes blighted and blasted." Fortunately its services soon expanded beyond institutional care of the babies to not only foster and adoptive family placements, but to shelter, health care, and job training for the numerous single, homeless, and/or poor mothers who often wish to parent.[9] In 1895, while president of the National-American Woman Suffrage Association, Anthony received a letter from Dr. Sarah Hackett Stevenson (1841-1909), outspoken abortion opponent and first woman member of the American Medical Association. Stevenson requested "a word of encouragement" for her gestating creation, the Chicago Maternity Hospital. This would serve single pregnant women and their babies, so often denied health care and other services. Dr. Harriet Alleyne Rice (1866-1958), the first African-American graduate of Wellesley and a resident of Jane Addams' Hull House, was medical director. Anthony responded: "I trust the day will come when there will be no such unfortunate mothers, but until then, it is certainly the duty of society to provide for them."[10]

"A Dreadful Volume of Heart-Histories"
by Susan B. Anthony[11]

In a late REVOLUTION is an extract from the New York *Medical Gazette* rebuking a practice common among married women, and demanding a law for its suppression.

Much as I deplore the horrible crime of child-murder, earnestly as I desire its suppression, I cannot believe with the writer of the above-mentioned article, that such a law would have the desired effect. It seems to be only mowing off the top of the noxious weed, while the root remains.

We want *prevention*, not merely punishment. We must reach the root of the evil, and destroy it.

To my certain knowledge this crime is not confined to those whose love of ease, amusement and fashionable life leads them to desire immunity from the cares of children; but is practiced by those whose inmost souls revolt from the dreadful deed, and in whose hearts the maternal feeling is pure and undying. What, then, has driven these women to the desperation necessary to force them to commit such a deed? This question being answered, I believe we shall have such an insight into the matter as to be able to talk more clearly of a remedy.

Women are educated to think that with marriage their individuality ceases or is transferred to their husbands. The wife has thenceforth no right over her own body. This is also the husband's belief, and upon which he acts. No matter what her condition, physical or mental, no matter how ill-prepared she may feel herself for maternity, the demands of his passion may never be refused.

He thinks, or cares nothing, for the possible result of his gratification. If it be that an immortal being, with all its needs, physical, mental, and moral, shall come into the world to sin, to suffer, to die, because of his few moments of pleasure, what cares he?

He says he is ready to provide for his children, therefore he feels himself a kind father, worthy of honor and love. That is, he is ready to provide for them food and clothing, but he is not willing to provide for them, by his self-denial, sound bodies, good tempers, and a happy ante-natal existence. He gives his wife wealth, leisure, and luxury, and is, therefore, a devoted husband, and she is an *undutiful*, unloving wife, if her feelings fail to respond to his.

Devoted husband? Devoted to what? To self-gratification at the expense of the respect of his wife. I know men who call themselves Christians, who would insist that they are *gentlemen*, who never insult any woman—but their wives. They think it impossible that they can outrage them; they never think that even in wedlock there may be the very vilest prostitution; and if Christian women are *prostitutes* to Christian husbands, what can be expected but the natural sequence—infanticide?

Women who are in the last stages of consumption, who know that their offspring must be puny, suffering, neglected orphans, are still compelled to submit to maternity, and dying in childbirth, are their husbands ever condemned? Oh, no! It was only his right as a husband he claimed, and if maternity or death ensued, surely he could not be blamed for that. He did not desire it. The usual tenor of men's conduct in this respect seems on a par with that of Henry VIII, who when asked if the life of his wife or of his child should be saved, as it seemed needful that one should be sacrificed, answered, "O the child, by all means. Wives are easily obtained."

Women whose husbands are habitual drunkards and whose children are therefore idiotic, deformed creatures, and who feel assured that such must be the case with all their offspring, must yet submit. And if such a woman as the dying consumptive, rather than bring into the world such miserable children, rather perhaps than give life to a daughter to suffer all that she has endured, destroys the little being, so she thinks, before it lives, she would be punished by the law, and he, *the real murderer*, would go unrebuked, uncondemned.

All the articles on this subject that I have read have been from men. They denounce women as alone guilty, and never include man in any plans proposed for the remedy of the evil.

It is clear to my mind that this evil wholly arises from the false position which woman occupies in civilized society. We know that in the brute creation, the female chooses her own time, and . . . among Indians . . . yet what Christian woman, wife of a Christian husband, is free to consult her own feelings even in these most delicate situations?

Guilty? Yes, no matter what the motive, love of ease, or a desire to save from suffering the unborn innocent, the woman is awfully guilty who commits the deed. It will burden her conscience in life, it will burden her soul in death; but oh! thrice guilty is he who, for selfish gratification, heedless of her prayers, indifferent to her fate, drove her to the desperation which impelled her to the crime. It is very fine to say:

> My Author and Disposer, what thou willst
> Unquestioned I obey—Thus God ordains,
> God is my law, thou mine.[12]

But God has never given woman's individuality into the hands of man. If He has, why hold her responsible for this crime? If man takes her individuality he must also take her responsibility. Let him suffer.

No, I say, yield to woman her God-given right of individuality. Make her feel that to God alone is she responsible for her deeds; teach her that submission to any man without love and desire is prostitution; and thunder in her ear, "Who so defileth the body, defileth the temple of the Holy Ghost!" Let maternity come to her from a desire to cherish love and train for high purposes an immortal soul, then you will have begun to eradicate this most monstrous crime.

Teach man to respect womanhood whether in the person of his own wife or the wife of another; teach him that as often as he outrages his wife he outrages Nature and disobeys the Divine Law, then you will have accomplished still more.

Oh, there is a dreadful volume of heart-histories that lies hidden in almost every family in the land! It tells of trust betrayed, of purity violated under sanction of law, of every holy feeling outraged and purest love turned to fear and loathing. If the moral feeling in the heart of woman was not stronger than death itself, the crimes we now chronicle against them would be virtues compared with the depths of wickedness and sin into which they would be driven. But God is stronger than man and he holds us true to our higher natures, martyrs though we be. If, on the other hand, women were not so weak and disgracefully submissive, they would rise to the dignity of womanhood and throwing off the degrading touch, would say, "I am free. And to God alone will I unquestioningly yield myself."

I believe all that is needed is for the eyes of men to be opened up to the true state of affairs. They have received without a thought the faith of their fathers. The misery and degradation have not been personally felt by them. But let every wife dare to be honest, let her open her heart freely to her husband, and I know there are few whose better natures would not be touched, few who would not be awakened to a nobler life, to a more exalted view of marriage.

Then would marriage assume its high and holy place. Then would our children be truly olive plants, types of peace, lovingly desired, tenderly cared for, body and soul. Then the wife, looking with love and respect upon the husband, who has never caused her to fear his manhood, could say: "I am thine, and these are they whom God at our desire has given us."

—*The Revolution*, 8 July 1869.

Elizabeth Cady Stanton (1815-1902)

Observing her father's upstate New York legal practice, young Elizabeth Cady Stanton resolved to overturn the laws denying women control over their economic and family lives, even their bodies. The common-law doctrine of *femme couvert* defined a married woman's personhood as incorporated into her husband's and thus civilly dead. Stanton married an abolitionist merchant. Like Lucretia Mott and others, she became inspired by Mary Wollstonecraft and disaffected by the anti-slavery movement's hypocritical failure to include women as equals. Out of their discontent came the 1848 Seneca Falls Convention. Even while raising her seven children, Stanton fought for "the Cause"—as an editor of the *Revolution*, a traveling lecturer, a leader of the National Woman Suffrage Association, coeditor (with Susan B. Anthony and Matilda Joslyn Gage) of the *History of Woman Suffrage* (Volumes I-III), and author of the controversial *Woman's Bible.*[1]

Stanton decidedly rejected the notion that maternity was women's *only* creative power and that every woman *had* to be a mother.[2] She exulted in her subversive vitality throughout pregnancy and labor, particularly when she had her first daughter:

> I have never felt such sacredness in carrying a child as I have in the case of this one. She is the largest and most vigorous baby I have ever had, weighing 12 lbs . . . And yet my labor was short and easy . . . What refined, delicate, genteel, civilized woman would get well in so indecently short a time? Dear me, how much cruel bondage of mind and suffering of body poor women will escape when she takes the liberty of being her own physician of both body and soul![3]

To women-only groups, she insisted, "We must educate our daughters that maternity is grand, and that God never cursed it, and the curse, if there be any, may be rolled off."[4] For this she was called a "savage," a charge she found ridiculous; among Haudenosaunee, childbirth was not deemed impossibly painful and debilitating.[5] In the hope of "rolling off the curse," Stanton addressed many subjects considered unfit for public consideration:

the unfair denial of child custody to divorced women, the limits of patriarchal religion, the desirability of family planning, the suffering that the disease model of pregnancy inflicted upon mothers, and the dire economic and social conditions that compelled so many women to resort to prostitution and to such equally "degrading" (her word) practices as abortion and infanticide. As early as 1854, Stanton publicly called for women's right to a trial by jury of their own peers in such situations.[6]

In 1868, Stanton led the feminist defense of Hester Vaughan, an English immigrant servant thrown into the street by the employer who impregnated her, and then unjustly accused of infanticide after she delivered her dead baby alone in an unheated garret, the only lodgings she could afford. Stanton, Susan B. Anthony, Eleanor Kirk, Dr. Clemence Lozier, Dr. Charlotte Denman Lozier, and Ernestine Potowski Rose visited Vaughan in prison. They successfully petitioned Pennsylvania's governor to lift her death sentence and release her from prison. After Vaughan's pardon, they helped her back to England. Stanton lamented, "What a holocaust of women and children we offer annually to the barbarous customs of our present type of civilization!"[7] She found it "appalling to the highest degree" that "infanticide is on the increase to an extent inconceivable" not only in cities but rural areas like Androscoggin County, Maine, where "there were *four hundred murders annually produced by abortion* alone . . . There must be a remedy for such a crying evil as this. But where shall it be found, at least where begin, if not in the complete enfranchisement and elevation of woman?"[8]

Infanticide[9]

> The remarkable mortality among natural or illegitimate children is a topic agitating the Press very largely just now . . . The system of boarding them out for slow murder . . . is alarmingly on the increase among the well-to-do . . . It is impossible to shut our eyes to these facts . . . Where lies the remedy?
>
> —*NY Times*

In the independence of woman. "Give a man a right over my subsistence," says Alexander Hamilton, "and he has right over my whole moral being." When the world of work is open to woman, and it becomes as respectable as it is necessary to happiness for women of the higher classes, as well as others, to have some regular and profitable employment, then will woman take her true position . . .

The strongest feeling of a true woman's nature is her love for her child; and the startling facts in the above extract, multiplying as they are on every side, warn us that all things are inverted. Objectors cry out to us who demand our rights, and the ballot to secure them, "Do not unsex yourselves." It is against this wholesale unsexing we wage our war.

We are living to-day under a dynasty of force; the masculine element is everywhere overpowering the feminine, and crushing women and children alike beneath its feet. Let woman assert herself in all her native purity, dignity, and strength, and end this wholesale suffering and murder of helpless children. With centuries of degradation, we have so little of true womanhood, that the world has but the faintest glimmering of what a woman is or should be.

—*Revolution*, 29 January 1868.

Infanticide and Prostitution[10]

Social Evil Statistics
The annual inspection report of . . . New York City and Brooklyn, gives the number of houses of prostitution as 523 . . .

—*Sun*.

Child Murder
. . . The murder of children, either before or after birth, has become so frightfully prevalent that . . . were it not for immigration the white population of the United States would actually fall off . . .

—*Tribune*.

Scarce a day passes but some of our daily journals take note of the fearful ravages on the race, made through the crimes of Infanticide and Prostitution. For a quarter of a century, sober, thinking women have warned the nation of these thick coming dangers, and pointed to the only remedy, *the education and enfranchisement of women;* but men have laughed them to scorn. Let those who have made the "strong-minded" women of this generation the target for the jibes and jeers of a heedless world repent now in sackcloth and ashes, for already they suffer the retribution of their own folly at their own firesides, in their sad domestic relations. Wives sick, peevish, perverse; children deformed, blind, deaf, dumb, and insane; daughters silly and wayward; sons waylaid at every corner of the streets and dragged down to the gates of death, by those whom God meant to be their saviors and support. Look at these things no longer as necessary afflictions, sent to wean us from earth as visitations from Providence; but as the direct results of the violation of immutable laws . . .

We ask our editors who pen those startling statistics to give us *their* views of the remedy. We believe the cause of all these abuses lies in the degradation of woman . . .

Wonder not that American women do everything in their power to avoid maternity; for, from false habits of life, dress, food, and generations of disease and abominations, it is to them a period of sickness, lassitude, disgust, agony and death.

What man would walk up to the gallows if he could avoid it? And the most hopeless aspect of this condition of things is that our Doctors of Divinity and medicine teach and believe that maternity and suffering are inseparable.

So long as the Bible, through the ignorance of its expounders, makes maternity a curse, and women, through ignorance of the science of life and health find it so, we need not wonder at the multiplication of these fearful statistics. Let us no longer weep, and whine, and pray over all these abominations; but with an enlightened consciousness and religious earnestness, bring ourselves into line with God's just, merciful, and wise laws . . .

—*Revolution*, 5 February 1868.

Dr. Anna Densmore French (fl. 1860s) and a Teacher

Hospital reformer and physician Anna Densmore (later French) was a founder of Sorosis, the New York City professional women's group. She requested use of public school property for a novel health initiative—to hold classes for women educators in how to teach girls and young women about their bodies. The school board gave unanimous consent, and one enthusiastic participant gave the testimonial below.[1] The next year, Sorosis resolved to investigate whatever public resources were available to relieve "the homeless and unprotected condition of those upon whom, by misfortune or crime, is laid the burden of unlegalized motherhood . . ." If public commitment was lacking, the organization would then

> consider the question of the erection of such asylums and hospitals with the hope that the divine 'quality of mercy' might be extended to the erring woman no less freely than to the erring man, and that the desolate and despairing, through whom society has dishonored the holy office of maternity by degrading its entire significance, and negating its most imperative and sacred claims, may be rescued from misery and vice, and her offspring saved to fill an honorable place in our great, intelligent, and virtuous commonwealth . . .[2]

"Much Delighted With The Valuable Instruction"
by a Teacher

New York, March 18, 1868
Editors of the *Revolution:*
    . . . [P]erhaps you might not be aware that there is a movement now in successful operation in our own city that is destined to do more for women in the way of widespread physiological knowledge among them than has ever been accomplished.

Dr. Anna Densmore, of our city, delivered a course of lectures to ladies, at Bunyan Hall, in the month of January last, which were more largely attended than any course of scientific lectures on medical topics ever given in this city.

Many of the teachers in our public schools were present, and both principals and subordinates were much delighted with the valuable instruction afforded them . . . Dr. Densmore proposed to form a class for teachers exclusively, to qualify them to instruct young women and girls in those departments of Physiology and Hygiene, that are specially important to their future as wives and mothers . . .

Further assuring us that it is only in the light of such knowledge that young women can expect to cope with temptation successfully under all the various forms in which it is disguised, and that it is only necessary for women to know themselves *thoroughly*, in all that pertains to the varying attributes of girlhood, wifehood, and maternity; for true morality to attain a sound enduring foundation, against which the artifices of past times can make but a light impression. And that to ignorance of the laws that govern her life in all these particulars, are due to the sad advances that Frivolity, Invalidism, and Crime, have made in all communities of women.

I can assure you that we were deeply touched, as well as interested, by the earnest appeal made to us as teachers to improve the large and valuable opportunities that our position and extensive intercourse with the young and others of our sex can command, to carry on the work of Physiological training on a large and successful scale.

Every woman physician, she said, should herself be a teacher, and make it a cardinal rule to spread the knowledge she has gained, in reference to the prevention of disease and the possibility of imparting better constitutions to our children than is now done. But, from the nature and multiplicity of our professional duties, they could not as a class be as largely useful in this direction as they ought and desire to be, *unless* they could make available the talent and energy of some other class of women that could carry on the work continuously, after suitable preparation, from the point where the woman physician was compelled by circumstances to relax her efforts.

She then demonstrated to us in a forcible and happy way that we were the great connecting link between woman physicians and the vast numbers that were perishing from want of instruction, and the only class of women that could make such knowledge readily and extensively available.

The class was formed in a few days, and we number from one hundred and fifty to two hundred, I do not know the exact number.

The Board of Education granted us the use of the main hall of the Twelfth Street Public School by a unanimous vote, and we are progressing rapidly, to say nothing of the engrossing interest with which the entire subject is invested by Dr. Densmore.

All teachers are cordially imparted to partake of these advantages without money and without price, and I will add that the hall will not seat more than *two hundred.* In reading the article on "Child Murder,"[3] I could not repress the wish that the whole world could have heard Dr. Densmore's remarks at Bunyan Hall upon that theme. Those who had the privilege will never forget the startling effect of the truths that she revealed relative to the primitive and ever present vitality of the developing embryo, as evidenced by the fainting of several self-convicted participators in the crime of premeditated child destruction before birth . . . I am *sure* that women would rarely dare to destroy the product of conception if they did not *fully believe* that the little being was devoid of life during all the earlier period of gestation.

This was my own impression, and I know that the majority of women have never had any other opinion. In fact, we have been taught it from our mothers.

But Dr. Densmore demonstrated to us fully and clearly that the fulfillment of life processes were going on from the very beginning of embryonic development, and showed us how, step by step, was added bone, muscle, and nerve, and that even before any intimate connection was made between the little structure and the parent, that by the process of endosmosis an albuminous product that was furnished by the mother was absorbed and nourished the embryo to the extent of adding to its substance, and forming distinct enveloping membranes that continued to develop and remain as permanent structures till the child was born. And that even before the mother could assure herself that she was to wear the crown of maternity by realizing the movements of the child, that the educated ear of the physician could often distinguish the beating of its heart. These are the facts that women need to know.

We have not such an amount of inherent depravity, nor such a degree of reckless daring to our composition, nor such a deficiency in the motherly instinct and other elements that go to make up the true woman, as to lead us into the commission of this most *deadly* crime *realizing it to be so.*

Give us *knowledge* before accusing us of crime, and do not forget to gauge the calibre of our sins by the light furnished to guide us.

Do not tell us that it is indelicate for us to know ourselves, and then ask us to discharge our responsibilities to ourselves and our children in a manner creditable to us and them and acceptable to the Almighty!

Let every God given function be stripped of the mysterious mantle with which the darkened mind of man has enshrouded it, and we shall no longer, wittingly or unwittingly, stain our hands with the blood of the innocent.

A Teacher

—*Revolution,* 19 March, 1868.

Matilda Joslyn Gage (Ka-ron-ien-ha-wi) (1826-1898)

Matilda Joslyn Gage led the suffrage movement for decades while coping with recurrent ill health and a visual disability. Her parents deemed her as worthy of education as a son, and she felt that that "the grandest training given her was to think for herself."[1] Her family of origin's home in upstate New York had been a gathering place for radicals and a part of the Underground Railroad. The home she established with her merchant husband and four children became an Underground Railway station as well. Barred from medical school on the grounds of her sex, Gage turned to societal healing. At the 1852 Syracuse National Convention, the unknown Gage bravely rose up and gave an impressive speech on women's historical accomplishments. Lucretia Mott immediately reprinted and distributed it. Gage maintained, as she did throughout her whole career, that men had often robbed women of their creative accomplishments. Gage helped to organize the National Woman Suffrage Association, served as one of its officers, and edited its paper, *The National Citizen and Ballot Box*. She linked a variety of issues to women's lack of voting power, from prostitution to judicial punitiveness towards rape victims to the mistreatment of Native Americans. While many whites endorsed or tolerated the slaughter and forced removal of First Nations peoples, Gage resisted. She pointed out the equality, including freedom from rape, that Haudenosaunee women enjoyed, as well as the Iroquois Six Nations government's profound influence on American democracy's structure and as-yet unrealized ideals.[2] Gage lamented:

> How completely demoralized by her subjection [woman] must be, who does not feel her personal dignity assailed . . . when she finds that which should be her glory—her possible motherhood—treated everywhere by men as a disability and a crime![3]

In 1893, she published her magnum opus *Woman, Church, and State,* dedicating it to her mother. It shows her interests in freethought and Theosophy, and her reclamation of the systematically persecuted, often executed women called witches or *wicca* ("wise woman"). Gage observes

---

that many were advanced, skilled healers who could relieve childbirth pain. A century before today's feminist spirituality movement, she postulated an ancient age of "Matriarchate, or Mother-Rule":

> All life was regarded as holy . . . Even the sacrifice of animals was unknown. The earliest phase of life being dependent upon [woman], she was recognized as the primal factor in every relation . . . It is through a recognition of the divine element of motherhood as not alone inhering in the great primal source of life, but as extending throughout all creation, that it will become possible for the world, so buried in darkness, folly, and superstition, to practice justice towards woman.[4]

Out of respect for her wisdom and spiritual power, the Wolf Clan of the Mohawk Nation adopted the Anglo Gage as a member and gave her the name "Ka-ron-ien-ha-wi" ("Sky Carrier")—even as some Anglos feared and derided her so-called "unbelief." Anthony Comstock threatened to arrest the school board in Gage's hometown if they accepted her donation of *Woman, Church, and State* to the school library. Nineteen years after Gage's death, when the book went out of print, "respectable" suffragists were already writing her out of movement history.[5] Lynne Spender comments:

> To read Matilda Joslyn Gage is in many respects to be shocked . . . that this powerful and perceptive analysis of society should have been formulated a century ago, and not built upon . . . that in the late 1960s we had to begin again without benefit of those valuable insights which she herself forged over a lifetime . . . It is time this remarkable woman was reclaimed as she herself reclaimed so many women before her. She must not be lost again.[6]

These remarks seem applicable to Gage's perspectives on abortion and the killing of "deviants."

Is Woman Her Own?
by Matilda Joslyn Gage

The short article on "Child Murder" in your paper of March 12 touched a subject which lies deeper down into woman's wrongs than any other . . . the denial of the right to herself. In no historic age of the world has woman yet had that. From the time when Moses, for the hardness of his heart, permitted the Jew husband to give his unpleasing wife a letter of divorcement—to Christ, when the seven *male* sinners brought to him for condemnation the woman taken in adultery—down through the Christian centuries to this nineteenth, nowhere has the marital union of the sexes been one in which the women has had control over her own body.

Enforced motherhood[7] is a crime against the body of the mother and the soul of the child.

Medical jurisprudence has begun to accumulate facts on this point, showing how the condition and *feelings* of the mother mould not only the physical and mental qualities of the child, but its moral nature.

Women keep silence upon many points, not breathing their thoughts to their dearest friends, because of their inner reticence, a quality they possess greatly in excess of men.

And, too, custom has taught them to bear in silence.

But the crime of abortion is not one in which the guilt lies solely or chiefly with the woman. As a child brings more care, so also, it brings more joy to the mother's heart.

Husbands do not consult with their wives upon this subject of deepest and most vital interest, do not look at the increase of family in a physiological, moral, or spiritual light, but almost solely from a money standpoint. It costs. Tens of thousands of husbands and fathers throughout this land are opposed to large families. And yet so deeply implanted is the sin of self-gratification, that consequences are not considered while selfish desire controls the heart.

Much is said of the wild, mad desire of the age for money. Money is but another name for power, it is but another name for bread, it is but another name for freedom, and those who possess it not are the slaves of those who do.

How many states in the Union grant the wife an equal right with the husband to the control and disposal of the property of the marital firm? But two. [Which two?—Eds.]

How long is it since a married woman in this state had the right to control of her own separate property? Barely twice ten years.

How long since she could control her own earnings, even those of a day's washing? Not yet ten.

History is full of the wrongs done the wife by legal robbery[8] on the part of the husband. I need not quote instances; they are well known to the most casual newspaper reader. It is accepted as a self-evident truth—that those "who are not masters of any property, may easily be formed into any mould."

I hesitate not to assert that most of this crime of "child murder," "abortion," "infanticide," lies at the door of the male sex.

Many a woman has laughed a silent, derisive laugh at the decisions of eminent medical and legal authorities, in cases of crimes committed against her as a woman. Never, until she sits as a juror at such trials, will or can just decisions be rendered.

This reason and that reason have been pointed to by the upholders of equal rights, to account for the oppression of women during past ages, but not one that I have ever heard offered has looked to the spiritual origin of that oppression.

If my health and eyes enable to me to do so, I shall be glad to write occasionally as you request. Perhaps a series of short articles upon the above point will be timely. Individual freedom is emphatically the lesson of the nineteenth century.

—*Revolution*, 9 April 1868.

"No Compassion"
by Matilda Joslyn Gage

In looking at the history of witchcraft, we see three striking points for consideration:

First; That women were chiefly accused.

Second; That men believing in women's inherent wickedness and understanding neither the mental nor the physical peculiarities of her being, ascribed all her idiosyncracies to witchcraft.

Third; That the clergy inculcated the idea that woman was in league with the devil, and that strong intellect, remarkable beauty, or unusual sickness were in themselves proof of this league . . .

[Martin] Luther said: "I would have no compassion for a witch; I would burn them all." He looked upon those who were afflicted with blindness, lameness, or idiocy from birth, as possessed of demons and there is record of his attempt to drown an afflicted child in whom he declared no soul existed, its body being animated by the devil alone. But a magistrate more enlightened or humane than the great reformer, interfered to save the child's life. Were Luther on earth again today . . . he would regard the whole community as mad. Asylums for the blind, the dumb and idiots, curative treatments for cripples and all persons naturally deformed, would be to him a direct intervention with the ways of providence. The belief of this great reformer proves the folly of considering a man wise, because he is pious . . .

—From Chapter V, "Witchcraft," in Matilda Joslyn Gage, *Woman Church and State*, Chicago, IL: Charles Kerr, 1893.

Eleanor Kirk (1831-1908)

New Yorker Eleanor "Nellie" Maria Easterbrook Ames supported herself and her children by writing under the pseudonym Eleanor Kirk. Kirk became involved in the struggle for women's rights after leaving an abusive marriage. At an American Equal Rights Association celebration in Steinway Hall, she took the platform with Ernestine Potowski Rose, Matilda Joslyn Gage, Frederick Douglass, Amelia Bloomer, Paulina Wright Davis, and Lucy Stone.[1] A member of the New York Working Women's Association,[2] Kirk profoundly sympathizes with female laborers in *Up Broadway*, her novel about the moralistic discrimination that almost drives an indigent single mother to kill herself and her child. Her only other "choices" are domestic work for sexual harassers, or prostitution.[3] Kirk visited Hester Vaughan in prison, helped run a large public meeting on her behalf,[4] and took on a common objection to feminism.

What Will Become of the Babies?
by Eleanor Kirk

From every quarter is wailed this cry—and wherefore? Only because women are waking up to a sense of their position as wives, mothers, and members of society, and insist on their right to have a hand in the management of all public affairs appertaining, however remotely, to their interest, socially and financially. Why is it that a great many cultivated, intelligent men and women, too (that's where the rub comes), persist in ignoring the fact that female equality and suffrage mean more love, more tenderness, an occasion of respect and thoughtfulness for our companions, and better sense in molding the characters of our children. Said a lady to me yesterday:

"Why should I lift up my voice for this Revolution in social affairs you so strongly advocate? Religiously and politically my husband and myself are one; and our love for each other is such that *his* wish is my law, and vice versa."

Now, just that little sentence caused every nerve in my body to quiver painfully. No true woman can shut herself up in a little Paradise of her own, and never look out into the great thoroughfare of life. Why, woman alive, or woman asleep, where there is one wife happy and contented in the love of a noble man, there are thousands of wretched ones who are driven to feebleness, moral destruction, and the grave. Think a moment. Suppose death, inexorable and strangely exacting, should claim his own; what then? Your husband's salary, which now nicely supports you, you would receive no longer. Your three babies fatherless, and you a widow, educated, refined, and fitted by numberless graces to adorn a little niche in society, undisturbed by want or the necessity of labor; our opinion is, that you would be glad to take into consultation even Revolutionists under such circumstances, and be very happy to welcome any educational or philanthropic movement whereby you could walk out into the world, and demand as an equivalent for your work a comfortable living for yourself and your babies. Then, at the conclusion of that heartless speech, to have her look so sweetly and wisely into our face, and remark:

"But Frank and I have been thinking should women turn to politics and literature entirely, what will become of the babies?"

What will become of *your* babies, madam, should you be suddenly deprived of the means of their support? Have you the courage, stamina, ay, *ability*, to fight the world single-handed? "A fellow-feeling makes us wondrous kind." We have been there, thank you, and know all about it. Every heart-throb, every blush in indignation, every dastardly attempt to change the wages of labor for the wages of sin, we are familiar with; and it makes us *sick* when we see an intelligent female looking at so great a subject through so small a glass, and dirty at that. What will become of the babies? Why don't somebody ask—what *has* become of the babies? Ask Restell and thousands of physicians, male and female, who have been engaged in their work of destruction for years. Physicians who have graduated from our first medical colleges, whose elegant equipages stand in front of Fifth Avenue mansions, who pocket a big fee and a little bundle of flesh at the same time, and nobody's the wiser; not even the *husband* in hosts of instances. What will become of the babies—did you ask—and you? Can you not see that the idea is to educate women that they may be self-reliant, self-sustaining, self-respected? The wheel is a big one, and needs a strong push, and a push all together, giving it an impulse that will keep it constantly revolving, and the first Revolution must be female suffrage. After this, the ponderous affair will move regularly, and perhaps slowly; but education, moral, physical, and intellectually practical, will as surely follow as dawn follows the darkness of night. Then marriages of convenience will not be necessary; men and women will come together, attracted by mutual respect; namby-pamby, doll-faced, wishy-washy, milk-and-water feminine bundles will be unmarketable. God speed the time, for the sake of the babies. Little ones will then be welcome, and mothers will know enough to instruct them sensibly, with a view to the practical side of life. Men, if you desire healthy, intelligent, economical wives, do not oppose this new movement; for in this way *only* can you and yours, and subsequent generations, be saved from degeneracy. Will somebody please tell us why women who pay taxes (we will leave out the rest just at present) should not be allowed a voice in the management of the laws decreeing taxation? Don't be afraid to speak; come out squarely. This is the time for free, earnest discussion on all points of general interest; but please do not take for your final syllogistic premises the foolish idea that women who are self-reliant must necessarily be unlovable. It is no such thing, we assure you, and we know. My dear fellows, this is quite as much for your benefit as for ours. What we propose to do, is so to arrange things that should you ever become sick or poor, we can put our hands to the plough and run the machine, nursing, sympathizing, attending to the finances, and loving you to distraction at the same time. How do you like the picture?

—*Revolution*, 28 May 1868.

Mattie H. Brinkerhoff (fl. 1860s)

Missouri native and suffrage lecturer Martha (Mattie) H. Brinkerhoff toured Kansas in 1867 with Susan B. Anthony, Elizabeth Cady Stanton, and Universalist minister Olympia Brown, the first denominationally ordained woman reverend in the U.S. In her 1868 tour of Illinois and northern Iowa, Brinkerhoff "roused great interest and organized many societies, canvassing meanwhile for subscribers to *The Revolution*," which described her as "modest and lady-like in her deportment, earnest and candid in her reasoning, interesting and entertaining as a speaker." The *Dubuque Herald* expressed pleasant surprise that this suffragist was not "the extravagant scold" of stereotypical fame. Brinkerhoff was an ardent, effective activist who had time to accept only half the speaking invitations she received. Yet when she left her husband and married another man, she was deliberately written out of suffragist history.[1]

Woman and Motherhood
by Mattie H. Brinkerhoff

... [T]he boldness with which many men blame women for the crime of infanticide without assuming themselves, in the case, a shadow of responsibility, I should think would rouse every *mother*, at least, to utter words in self-defence. That American women are more guilty of this practice than women of any other nation, I do not doubt; but is there not a reason for this?

Knowledge and slavery are incompatible. Teach a slave how to read, and he wants to be his own master—and as the masses of American women not only know how to read and write, but so much of the "tree of knowledge" have many of them eaten, that they have learned it should be for them to decide when and how often they shall take upon themselves the sacred duties of motherhood, but as law and custom give to the husband the absolute control of the wife's person, she is forced to not only violate physical law, but to outrage the holiest instincts of her being to maintain even a semblance of that freedom which by nature belongs to every human soul.

When a man steals to satisfy hunger, we may safely conclude that there is something wrong in society—so when a woman destroys the life of her unborn child, it is an evidence that either by education or circumstances she has been greatly wronged. But the question now seems to be, how shall we prevent this destruction of life and health?

Mrs. Stanton has many times ably answered it—"by the true education and independence of woman."

Our German writer seems to think that the whole aim of a woman's life should be motherhood. Suppose this were true, is the mission of so little importance that no preparation be required to fill it? If, to be a first class artist, or lawyer, it requires years of thought and culture, what preparation should be made to carve the outlines and justly balance the attributes of an immortal soul. Are little children, the germs of men and women, of so little importance that it matters not whether their mother be physically healthy or unhealthy, cultivated or uncultivated in mind; expanded or dwarfed in soul? Some or no culture must be desirable in the mother. If some culture, then how much? Shall she have strong arms but weak legs, strong stomach but weak lungs, keen imagination but devoid of reason, large perception but no reflection? We are forced to ask, by what law shall we decide when woman is sufficiently developed in body and mind to be a good mother? Before what tribunal shall she be judged? Does not reason answer, the council chamber of her own being?

... If we would make woman free, let us teach her the alphabet of human *life*, make her understand and value true womanhood. Then she will scorn to be man's petted slave. She will scorn his smiles and courtesies, when they are proffered only as an excuse for justice.

Oh motherhood! which our opponents say is woman's holiest mission. We cannot have true mothers without having true womanhood first. Let us see that our daughters are developed into true women, and the office of maternity will take care of itself . . . Then, and not till then, will man's shackles fall, for noble manhood must be the legitimate fruit of free and exalted womanhood. Brothers, 'tis for you, as well as ourselves we plead. Will you neglect so great a salvation?

—*Revolution*, 2 September 1869.

Dr. Charlotte Denman Lozier (1844-1870)

Millburn, New Jersey native Charlotte Denman Lozier was the oldest of five children in a family that moved west to the prairie town of Winona, Minnesota. She graduated from the homeopathic New York (City) Medical College for Women, which outraged conservatives because of its students' gender and its hygiene curriculum. Dr. Augustus K. Gardner raged that the College sinfully exposed women to "the horrors and disgusts of life . . . accustomed [as they are] to softness and the downy side of life."[1] As a student, Charlotte successfully protested Bellevue Hospital's refusal of clinical privileges to women. After graduation, she joined her alma mater's faculty, held office in the Working Women's Association, and married the physician son of College founder Clemence Lozier.[2] When Charlotte was six months pregnant with her third child, the popular and feminist press alike praised her for her aid to a pregnant woman in the spirit of the care she gave Hester Vaughan, as the article below shows.[3]

Preparing for a New Year's 1870 party, Charlotte fell off a ladder and began to hemorrhage uncontrollably. Three days later, she died of peritonitis. Her two-months premature daughter survived through the Lozier family's diligent care. This baby, so tiny she slept in a shoebox, grew up to have her own family and become an acclaimed journalist with the *Brooklyn Daily Eagle* and a successful matchmaker for American expatriates in Europe. Jessica Charlotte Lozier Payne lived to be 81.[4] At Charlotte's death, *Revolution* editor Parker Pillsbury sadly noted that "an earthly career of the very brightest promise has been arrested . . . . Her funeral was very largely attended, the [Methodist Episcopal] church being nearly full, and a more sorrowing audience is seldom seen . . . How large was the loss both in a private and domestic and in a public view."[5]

Restellism Exposed
by the Staff of the *Revolution*

Dr. Charlotte Lozier of 323 West 34th Street, of this city was applied to last week by a man pretending to be from South Carolina, by name,

Moran, as he also pretended, to procure an abortion on a very pretty young girl apparently about eighteen years old. The Dr. assured him that he had come to the wrong place for any such shameful, revolting, unnatural and unlawful purpose. She proffered to the young woman any assistance in her power to render, at the proper time, and cautioned and counseled her against the fearful act which she and her attendant (whom she called her cousin) proposed. The man becoming quite abusive, instead of appreciating and accepting the counsel in the spirit in which it was proffered, Dr. Lozier caused his arrest under the laws of New York for his inhuman proposition, and he was held to bail in a thousand dollars for appearance in court.

The *[New York] World* of last Sunday contained a most able and excellent letter from Dr. Lozier, in which she explains and most triumphantly vindicates her course in the very disagreeable position in which she was placed. It is certainly very gratifying and must be particularly so to Dr. Lozier, to know that her conduct in the affair is so generally approved by the press and the better portion of the public sentiment, so far as yet expressed. The following are only extracts from extended articles in the New York *World* and Springfield *Republican* relating to it:

> The laws of New York make the procuring of a miscarriage a misdemeanor, punishable by imprisonment for not less than three months, nor more than a year; they define the committing of an abortion resulting in the death of either child or mother to be manslaughter in the second degree. It was this latter crime that Dr. Lozier was asked to commit, and she insists that as the commission of crime is not one of the functions of the medical profession, a person who asks a physician to commit the crime of ante-natal infanticide can be no more considered his patient than one who asks him to poison his wife. Thus Dr. Lozier makes out her case, and seems to prove conclusively that neither law nor professional honor forbids physicians handing over to the police persons who apply to them to commit murder; but that law, professional honor, moral obligation, and social duty all unite in compelling them to thus aid in the punishment of these attempts to procure the slaughter of the innocents. This being so, how does it happen that it has been left for this woman to be the first to perform this duty? The pulpit and the press for months have been ringing with declamations against the frequency of the offence of ante-natal infanticide among the most respectable classes of American society. Has there been no cause for these accusations; or do physicians

generally hold opinions of their duty in this matter wholly different from those entertained and acted on by Mrs. Lozier?

And the Springfield *Republican* says:

> A woman physician at New York, Mrs. Dr. Charlotte D. Lozier, took the very unusual step, on Saturday, of having a man and a woman, who had applied to her to assist in procuring an abortion upon the latter, arrested and committed to jail for trial, under the New York statute, which has long been practically a dead letter, but which makes the bare solicitation or advising to commit this crime a state prison offence.

The woman, whose name is Caroline Fuller, first went alone to the office of Doctress Lozier, and on stating her purpose was kindly warned of the sin and danger of such a course, and allowed to depart. But the next day she returned with her paramour, Andrew Moran of Anderson Court House, S.C., and he boldly demanded that the operation should be performed, offering to pay roundly and to shield Mrs. Lozier from any possible legal consequences, should there be a fatal termination. Upon this Mrs. Lozier promptly sent for a policeman, who arrested both Moran and Miss Fuller, though the latter was discharged when brought before the justice for examination. Moran is held for trial, having failed to bribe Mrs. Lozier not to appear against him by offering her $1,000. Moran and Miss Fuller came all the way from South Carolina to have the abortion performed, and Moran's wife made a third in the party, though one would hardly suppose she would enjoy a trip to the metropolis under such circumstances. May we not hope that the action of Mrs. Lozier in this case is an earnest of what may be the more general practice of physicians if called upon to commit this crime, when women have got a firmer foothold in the profession? Some bad women as well as bad men may possibly become doctors, who will do anything for money; but we are sure most women physicians will lend their influence and their aid to shield their sex from the foulest wrong committed against it. It will be a good thing for the community when more women like Mrs. Lozier belong to the profession.

—*Revolution*, 2 December 1869.

Paulina Wright Davis (1813-1876)

Soon after Pillsbury's remembrance of Charlotte Denman Lozier, another *Revolution* staffer published hers. Paulina Kellogg Wright Davis, as a girl in Western New York, was stung by her church's refusal to allow women to speak in mixed (i.e., male-female) assemblies. Although the prevailing culture justified slavery on supposedly Scriptural grounds, Davis outspokenly opposed it. In 1835 a mob threatened to torch her house. As early as the 1840s, Davis and Ernestine Potowski Rose, a Polish rabbi's freethinking immigrant daughter, agitated together for married women's property rights, denied under *femme couvert*, the common-law and clerically reinforced doctrine that a wife's personhood was incorporated into her husband's. In the 1850s, Davis published the Providence, Rhode Island-based *Una*, an important public forum for feminists' newly developing critiques of ownership-based marriage and enforced domesticity.[1]

Davis's work, which "commenced before the woman's rights conventions were held," addressed women's crying need to learn about their bodies:

> As early as 1844 she commenced the study of anatomy and physiology, and gave lectures on these subjects. She sent to Paris and imported the first *femme modele* that was ever brought into the country. She has told many amusing anecdotes of the effect of unveiling this manikin in the presence of a class of ladies. Some would leave the house, others faint in their seats, others draw their veils, and a few only had the moral hardihood and scientific curiosity to appreciate it and examine the fearful and wonderful manner in which they were made. In course of time, however, these natural "weaknesses and disabilities" were overcome, and many of Mrs. Davis's classes are today professors and pupils in our medical colleges, hospitals, and dissecting-rooms, the result of her early efforts in urging the medical education of women. Many who are now comfortably supporting themselves in that profession gratefully acknowledge her influence in directing the whole course of their lives.[2]

Davis was, then, a fitting person to memorialize Lozier. Davis compares her to Elizabeth Garrett (later Anderson) (1836-1917). Elizabeth Blackwell's lectures in England had inspired Garrett to become the first Englishwoman in official medicine.[3] Of all Lozier's admirable actions, it is interesting which one Davis, an adoptive mother of two, found most commendable.

"A True Woman"
by Paulina Wright Davis

Miss Garrett has founded two scholarships for women who wish to study medicine in London. When will some of the rich women of our country go and do likewise, instead of endowing Professors' chairs in theological seminaries for "poor but pious young men"?

How many fairs have been held? how many poor eyes tortured almost to blindness, doing fancy work to support students in theological seminaries, and aid young men to get a liberal education, we will not attempt to ascertain—suffice it to say, that when women became strong enough to demand admission to colleges, theological seminaries, and medical schools, and found that there was no place for them, they saw that they must do their own work, that no college would ever voluntarily open its doors to them, and again fairs, with all their petty toil of pincushions, furbelows, raffles of doubtful morality, post-offices and clap-traps of all kinds, in order to make money, were resorted to; but now, that they are chartered and endowed and it is a fixed fact that women are in the professions, and are successful in practice, nothing more is required except to enlarge and to give till they have all the means and appliances that young men have.

It is certainly complimentary to their genius, capacity and power for grasping questions so intricate and lumbered with technicalities, that they have been able to succeed at all, with the meagre opportunities, which they have had. They claimed the right as theirs by divine adaptation, and they have proven that the claim was true. Custom and prejudice said, No, it is not your sphere. Spiritual intuition said, Go on, study when, where, and how you can; and when you have acquired give to others.

We have been led to these reflections by the unexpected death of Mrs. Charlotte Lozier, who was one of those richly gifted women who seized instinctively medical science, so far as there is any settled principles, and imparted as freely as she received.

Her steady, persistent, unwavering integrity, and her high sense of duty were strongly marked. Her recent action, prompt and decisive, against a high-handed crime cannot be too much commended. She chose to bear reproach and bitterness, rather than a stain upon her conscience. The impression will long remain with us of her pure, womanly grace and sweetness. Her real strength did not reveal itself in the brief interview we had with her; it was not till she came out firmly to stay the prevalent sin of infanticide that we knew the woman in all her greatness.

Her sense of justice would not allow her to let the wrong-doer escape the penalty of the law, while at the same time she pitied and tenderly cared for the victim. We have been amazed to hear her denounced for this brave, noble act on the ground of professional privacy. It is said she had no right to expose the outrage of having one thousand dollars offered her to commit murder.

The murder of the innocents goes on. Shame and crime after crime darken the history of our whole land. Hence it was fitting that a true woman should protest with all the energy of her soul against this woeful crime.

—*Revolution*, 20 January 1870.

On the Same Page: Dr. Juliet Worth Stillman Severance and A Mother (c. late 1860s)

In her teens, Wisconsinite Juliet Worth Stillman Severance, a relative of Lucretia Mott, started as a schoolteacher and a well-known orator at women's rights and anti-slavery conventions. After recuperating from a sickly childhood, she became a greatly successful hydropathic doctor despite harassment from enemies of women in medicine. Her three children became well-known theatrical or musical performers. Her second husband supported her healing work.[1] Severance rejected confining fashions for simple, comfortable dress. She held leadership positions in several Spiritualist, anti-death penalty, and labor organizations, including the Knights of Labor. Anticipating late twentieth/early twenty-first-century ecofeminists like Carol Adams, the vegetarian Severance remarked, "All kinds of brutes are eaten by man. Even little singing birds do not escape his rapacity."[2]

In 1883, the Woman's Social Science Association recommended castration for sexual offenders to prevent them from reproducing. Deeply troubled by the rise of punitive eugenics, within and outside feminism, Severance protested:

> I cannot see that the destruction of any organ that executes the perverted will of badly regulated minds can be other than an interference with the chances for development of the individual, which should be the grand consideration and aim, not their destruction.[3]

In 1902, Severance publicly decried Anthony Comstock's persecution of the elderly Ida Craddock, a sex reformer/educator he drove to suicide. Soon afterwards, Craddock's attorney, Theodore Schroeder, started a forerunner of the American Civil Liberties Union.[4]

Severance wrote to a Spiritualist paper that marriage

> should be a soul-union, not a curse . . . not a merging of one life into another; but . . . two individuals uniting their lives for mutual good and the good of humanity—it may be in reproduction, or it may be in

giving birth to higher, nobler ideas, and outworking them in noble deeds and grand achievements . . . . As the present marriage system makes man the owner of woman—her legal master—she is expected to submit to his gratification . . . . When the marriage system is what it should be, and woman controls in these matters, instead of man . . . Restellism shall cease, because there will be no demand for it . . . [5]

On the same page, literally and figuratively, "A Mother" anonymously concurred.

. . . I'm sick of hearing women berated for foeticide, when, seven cases in ten, the husbands and prospective fathers are more to blame than are the mothers . . . . When the hapless mother shrunk from the crime . . . he would laugh at her fears, and quiet her conscience by saying there was no life in the fetus until a certain number of months gestation had passed. Women have told me, with streaming eyes, that their husbands have insisted that they should destroy the life of their unborn babes . . . . [6]

Dr. Rachel Brooks Gleason (1820-1905)

Because no college admitted women at the time, Vermonter Rachel Brooks educated herself with textbooks at home. She taught school until her marriage at 24 to Silas O. Gleason, an allopathic and hydropathic physician. She assisted him with his practice. Silas was appointed hygiene professor at Rochester, New York's Central Medical College, an "eclectic" school teaching both allopathic and alternative skills. At Silas's urging, the school began to admit women, including Rachel, who in 1851 became the fourth American female allopath. The couple founded a nationally renowned sanitarium at Elmira, New York. It endured until World War II, mostly as a family-run establishment. The Gleasons' daughter Adele and Rachel's sister Zippie Brooks Wales both became eclectic physicians and worked there. In addition to providing clinical training, Rachel personally paid for the medical school tuition of at least 18 women, most of whom chose the profession after suffering their own health problems. Rachel generously supported schools for free African Americans and gave laywomen's groups "parlor talks" on physiology and hygiene.[1] In her sixties, Gleason wrote a book that went through at least nine editions: "a simple compend of such motherly hints as seem to be needed . . . from my long care of the sick"—including post-abortion women.[2]

"The Mental and Physical Misery Entailed"
by Dr. Rachel Brooks Gleason

There are conditions when it seems as if pregnancy should be avoided. Remember, I say avoided, *not* interrupted. Once begun, go if possible to the close; that is the only safe way for body or spirit . . .

[A] young wife called; she had a sick face, and eyes expressive of great mental agony. "I have done wrong," she said, "and am very sorry; I have come to you for counsel. I had excellent health until a few months ago, when my monthly period not coming so soon as expected, I began to be fearful I was pregnant, and as we had two little children, and my husband's means are moderate, I did not want any more just yet; so I sent to the doctor to give me some medicine to bring on my menses, thinking if I was in a family-way it would do no harm, as it was only a few days over my time. The doctor said he thought I was pregnant, and it was a pity to have another baby when this one was so young, and that he would use an instrument to bring me around all right, which would do no harm; that there was nothing wrong in so doing. I yielded, and have never been well since. I have had a bad leucorrhea, a weak back, pain and pressure in front, and I am so afraid that terrible instrument has done some harm which can never be cured; that I shall never have any more children, and then I should be so sorry. Besides all this, I have such remorse that I can not eat or sleep as I used to, and have lost my flesh, strength, and cheerfulness of spirit."

I assured her that she could be cured, and that though she had done wrong, the dear Lord forgave all the truly penitent; that she could not get well if she continued thus to worry about the injury done, or the sin committed. During this conversation hope dawned in her darkened countenance, and she said, "You have done me good, and I will try to get well, and will welcome the little ones, few or many."

I have given you this instance to illustrate what I have so often seen, that the fear of injury done, and remorse for the deed, drives women almost or quite to despair. There is a peculiar look in the eye which I note, and dread the confessions of such patients when they come for consultation . . .

With advancing years, I find myself the mother-confessor of many who have done mischief, and now want to be absolved of the mental and physical misery entailed.

Many are victims of a melancholy which amounts to monomania. When children die, or troubles come, they think they are being punished . . .

—From the "Intentional Abortion," in *Talks to My Patients*, New York: Wood & Holbrook, 1870.

Sarah F. Norton (fl. 1860s-1870s)

Sarah F. Norton, a writer and traveling lecturer, addressed economic topics like "Woman's Equal Place, Pay, and Opportunity" and "The Rag-Pickers of New York." As a leader of the New York Working Women's Association, she maintained that the capital-labor relationship of capital to labor was a most appropriate topic for "any Woman's Rights Convention." She spoke out against marriage as a form of male property ownership, challenged Cornell University to admit women, and pointedly analyzed the social and economic contexts of abortion and infanticide.[1]

Tragedy—Social and Domestic
by Sarah F. Norton

A young woman, scarcely twenty years of age, of good family, well educated, having amiable manners and enjoying the esteem of a wide circle of friends and acquaintances, alone and unattended, during the gloom of midnight, gives birth in a bath-room to an illegitimate child, which she immediately strangles and throws out of a window into a neighboring yard.

She makes her way as best she can to her own bedroom, and awaits the revelation of the coming dawn. Sick at heart, delirious in mind and exhausted in body, her friends find her in the morning beyond the reach of medical or surgical skill; and, while they are learning the shocking details of that horrible night, her lips are sealed by death, and the secret is told which the sacrifice of two lives could not conceal.

Here are the outlines of a crime at which society shudders, and for a moment stands appalled. In another moment it is put aside with a wave of the hand . . . and the affair is forgotten.

Society would have avenged the murder of the child by making a victim of the unhappy mother, but death prevented that, and now, since the grave hides them both, let the social revel go on.

Sad and tragical as all this is, there is another fact still more sad and tragical, which society utterly ignores.

. . . [T]here is somewhere a *man*, who, if he had been modestly honorable, might have saved both lives, and who, in the last analysis, is responsible for both, if there be personal responsibility for anything whatever.

Who is he? where is he? and what is the name of and penalty for *his* crime. These questions, however pertinent, society does not ask. Its war is against the woman and the child, and as they are both beyond the reach of its revenge, it is entirely willing the man should receive its protection.

In their social aspect it is clearly the use of force that made these murders shocking; for society has made child-murder a fine art, and strangulation, though good enough for a guilty man, is entirely out of place when applied to a babe guilty of being born without the sanction of that law which provides no punishment for the father's share in its conception, holds him to no account for its premature death if it happen, nor to any responsibility for its support and protection, if, perchance it persists in living, despite all efforts to destroy it.

Society has come to believe it an impertinence in children to be born at all. It is even difficult for a family with children to find a home; and throughout the entire city there are few landlords who do not stipulate for childless couples when renting their property. This partiality explains why people in cities might not want children, but is totally inadequate as a reason for the murder of them without a combination of other and greater reasons to lead it; and it cannot be considered at all in relation to the fast increasing crime of foeticide throughout the country, where space is ample, rents low, and provisions comparatively cheap. It is safe to conclude, however, that the prevailing causes are the same in both city and country. What these causes are can only be guessed at by the stray scraps vouchsafed to us through such accidents as this recent one at 94 Chatham Street, and which occasionally happen to open the doors of these dens of death and reveal their secrets.

Here we find that a husband had been procuring poison for his wife and prospective offspring! not with any wish to kill the wife perhaps, but as the chances are as five to one against every women who attempts abortion, he could not have failed to realize the danger. Had the scheme been successful in destroying only the life aimed at, what could have been the man's crime— and what should be his punishment if, as accessory to one murder he commits two?

Instead of expressing satisfaction at the non-success of his attempted crime, he writes with a sort of mournful cadence to his infamous coadjutor that it, "the potion," "had about as much effect as a glass of soda-water. Just as I expected." In this incident we find the proof of two facts: First, that professional child-murders are supported by the married as well as the single; and, second, that the husbands are equally implicated and guilty with their wives.

These, however, are no new facts; for it is generally understood, among women at least, that in such cases the husband approves if he does not instigate. Usually he does the last; as the evidence of weakly wives and their confidential physicians would amply prove, could they be induced or compelled by any means to reveal the truth.

The servants in a house where such cases occur are not to be deceived; and these self-same servants form the greater proportion of the unmarried who patronize such dens as that in Chatham Street. They get an example from their mistress, or if not that, learn from the common gossip in the house about other wives, that child-murder is an easy and every-day affair.

The pernicious effect of all this is to make the seduction of the unmarried an easy matter, and murder an accepted contingency. If the married, to whom maternity is accepted and an honor, have reason to destroy their offspring, how much more reason have they to whom it would be a life-long dishonor; and if the first sets the example, why should not the last follow it?

No returns are made of premature or illegitimate births, and we can only judge of the number by the daily accounts given in the newspapers of some woman dying or dead from the effects of an abortion or premature birth, and newly-born, cast-away infants; and as efforts at concealment are in the main successful, we can very justly determine that the cases which come to notice are mere indications of what remains unknown.

Any business self-supporting enough to become a recognized fact by the people must, of necessity, be on the increase; and the single fact that child murderers practice their profession without let or hindrance, and open infant butcheries unquestioned, establishing themselves with an impunity that is not allowed to the slaughterers of cattle, is, of itself, sufficient to prove that society makes a demand which they alone can supply.

Scores of persons advertise their willingness to commit this form of murder, and with unblushing effrontery announce their names and residences in the daily papers. No one seems to be shocked by the fact; the papers are taken into the family without hesitation, and read by all the members thereof without distinction of age or sex. The subject is discussed almost without restraint; circulars are distributed broadcast, recommending certain pills and potions for the very purpose, and by these means the names of these slayers of infants, and the methods by which they practice their life-destroying trade, have become "familiar in our mouths as household words."

. . . Is there no remedy for all this ante-natal child murder? Not any, is the reply to the question so frequently asked. Is there, then, no penalty for the crime? None that can be inflicted, for the crime has become an art, and society cannot punish those who serve it so skillfully and well.

Perhaps there will come a time when the man who wantonly kills a woman and her babe will be loathed and scorned as deeply as the woman is now loathed and scorned who becomes his dupe; when the sympathy of society will be with the victim rather than the victimizer; when an unmarried woman will not be despised because of her motherhood; when unchastity in men will be placed on an equality with unchastity in women, and when the right of the unborn to be born will not be denied or interfered with . . . .

—*Woodhull and Claflin's Weekly,* 19 November 1870.

Victoria Woodhull (1838-1927) and Tennessee Claflin (1845-1923)

Victoria Woodhull and Tennessee Claflin, sisters from a poor, chaotic Ohio family, became the first female stockbrokers on Wall Street after a stint as Spiritualist mediums (ministers). In 1870, Woodhull declared herself a candidate for the presidency—the first woman ever to do so. The next year she presented a speech to the U.S. Congress, arguing that women already had the vote under the fourteenth and fifteenth amendments, which had recently enfranchised Black men. Some feminists welcomed the sisters; others found them unpalatably outrageous. The sisters' notoriety came from their colorful personal lives and the views they expressed on their speaking tours and in their flamboyant newspaper, whose motto was, "Progress! Free Thought! Untrammeled Lives! Breaking the Way for Future Generations." *Woodhull and Claflin's Weekly* (1870-1876) advocated Spiritualism, alternative medicine, and radical economics. The first American periodical to run a translation of the Communist Manifesto, it promoted woman suffrage and "free love." "Free lovers" wished for sexual relationships to be based on personal, mutual choice, respect, and affection, rather than the man's legal ownership of the woman. They attacked the sexual double standard, especially as practiced by nineteenth-century counterparts of today's sexually abusive clerics. *Woodhull and Claflin's Weekly* broke the news of the Beecher-Tilton scandal after the Reverend Henry Ward Beecher excoriated the sisters for their "free love" views. Anthony Comstock, an adulating member of Beecher's congregation, was incensed by the sisters' accusation that Beecher was a hypocrite who had had an affair with Elizabeth Tilton, another congregant. Comstock arranged for the sisters' arrest on obscenity charges.[1]

Among their published "obscenities" was their repeated observation that the prime cause of "so much murder of unborn children, is that to have them is to make a slave of the mother." Community responsibility for child care and education would "result not only in increased benefit to such children as escape ante-natal death," but "decrease the desire ... to commit this class of murders" and "relieve the worn-out mothers of the country."[2] So, too, would the exposure and abolition of clerical sexual abuse and hypocrisy.

Press Justice
by Victoria Woodhull and Tennessee Claflin

We have a new sensation of the free lust kind, in the case of Rev. A.B. Carter of the Church of the Holy Saviour. Before we proceed we want it distinctly remembered that we did not bring this social scandal to light, and owe all we know to the pure daily press. The Rev. Holy Parson is accused of seducing a young lady and procuring an abortion, as well as with putting his victim into a house of assignation.

The *Star* asks, which is the sinner? If the charge be true, the man is the greater sinner, because of his age, calling, education, his wife and children; these are arguments against him; it is barely possible she waylaid and seduced him; and if she did, the facts still stand against him. It was his business to save her *soul*, not prostitute her body, ruin her reputation, murder the fruits of their joint act, and send both to hell, if he was not a hypocritical ranter as well as a lecherous divine.

The *Tribune* in harmony with its vulgar and brutal instincts, without hearing evidence further than the charge and denial, at once denounces the woman as attempting to blackmail the innocent *soul maker* as well as *soul saver.* We prefer to wait the hearing of the evidence. The frequent occurrence of those Rev. monogamic free *lust* digressions, as furnished in the columns of the *Tribune*, shows as a class, the per cent of Rev. seducers as very fair; and the inference at first blush against the cloth.

So far as this particular case is developed, the impression is against Mr. Carter. The lady would hardly risk the exposure and loss of standing in the community, where she was thoroughly protected, unless, indeed, there is a necessity for another abortion, which may explain the fact of her desperation and imperative demand for the remaining $30,000.

That he met her in the vestry is conceded. That that was a convenient place to conduct such a transaction, immediately under the droppings of the sanctuary—who will question?

We suspend judgment, and await with patience this piece of pious scandal. We hope the Rev. gentleman will not charge his little misdemeanor to our paper and its doctrines. The *Weekly* was not in existence when this little affair was said to have commenced. Meantime we are curious to know, if it be total depravity or the special depravity of those particular sinners, or monogamic, permanent legal marriage without regard to fitness; or is it a false public opinion begotten of all these.

Here legal motherhood is creditable, hence illegal motherhood begets disgrace, and hence suicide and murder. When the day comes that motherhood is deemed the right of all healthy women, and no disgrace attaches to the manner of it, then murder and abortion will cease, and not until then . . . .

The right of motherhood is founded in nature, and is before, above and beyond all human legislation. There is neither vice nor virtue in it, except as it agrees or disagrees with the natural justice of the case.

In the eyes of the world this woman's confession forever bars her from respectable society. If this man is proven guilty, it will seriously mar his standing—ordinarily it would soon be forgotten.

After marriage, this obligation rests lightly on him, heavily on her. Few men are strictly faithful—few women unfaithful.

The *Times* is as unjust as the *Tribune;* it saddles all the blame on the woman. We think it more reasonable to judge after the evidence; that it is mean, unmanly, and libelous to use the power of the press to manufacture public opinion against either, even if both are guilty, which is just as probable as that the woman *alone* is guilty; and in this case even more so. But the press is willing to accept the denial of the man—but not the affirmation of the woman. The woman loses her social position by her confession—the man retains his and his salary. Let any honest mind compare the cases, and the injustice of the press is apparent. And yet we do wrong to demand justice for women, in the eyes of such creatures!

The fact that the girl is willing to retire, and that the reverend gentleman is inexorable, does not prove her guilt or his innocence. This spirit of persecution is illy in keeping with the life and precepts of the Master; and however innocent he may be of this particular charge, he has proved one thing beyond a doubt—and that is, that he is unfit to be a Christian minister. He cannot endure persecution without resentment—vengeance; and this adds strongly to the suspicion that he is not free from blemish in the affair.
—*Woodhull and Claflin's Weekly,* 23 March 1872.

The Slaughter of the Innocents
by Victoria Woodhull and Tennessee Claflin

If there is one fact in modern society more horrible, and at the same time more sorrowful than any other, it is that one which relates to the death-rate among the young from the time of conception up to five years of age. It is one of those things against which almost everybody willfully shuts his eyes and professes to think that it does not exist: and everybody pretends to everybody else that he knows nothing about it; while on every hand—in every household—the young drop off like leaves before the autumn wind . . .

But this enforced ignoring of one of the horrible facts of modern society is engendering in society itself a morbid condition of mind regarding children which, if not speedily checked, will prove fatal to civilization itself . . .

[Humanity] . . . is seemingly indifferent to the life or death of the young. Its practices cut them down like grass before the scythe. Parents deposit one-half of their young in the grave-yards before they reach the age of five years. What a commentary this is on the social condition! . . . Childhood ought to be the healthiest period of life, but in our condition it has degenerated until it is ten times more fatal than any other period. And yet we talk of the sacredness of human life as if it were so regarded at all! A human life is a human life and equally to be held sacred whether it be a day or century old; and that custom which cuts off one-half of the young almost in infancy, is as virtually murder as would be the same death-rate among adults resulting from compelling them to the use of life-destroying food. Children die because they are not properly cared for. If adults received equally improper treatment as children received, they would die at the same rate; but adults, being capable of judging for themselves as to what is proper and what is improper, by choosing the former, decrease the death-rate ten times below that which obtains among the classes who depend upon others for their treatment . . .

But this fact regarding the indifference to life that exists among parents is not perhaps the worst feature of modern society. It is not only a fact that this terrible death-rate persistently continues among children, but that there is still another death method not included in its horrible details, which, if possible, is still more revolting, and which is nonetheless a slaughter of the innocents . . . .

Wives . . . to prevent becoming mothers . . . deliberately murder [children] while yet in their wombs. Can there be a more demoralized condition than this? . . . Why should the birth-rate decrease as the people become more enlightened? . . . Simply because with increased knowledge comes increased individuality; and with increased individuality, increased repugnance to submission to the slavery that child-bearing almost necessarily entails in our society as at present organized; and with these also the knowledge that pregnancy can be broken up, sometimes with little present evidence of evil to the, otherwise, mother . . . If this practice prevail so widely among wives, who have no need to resort to it "to hide their shame," but merely to prevent an increase in the number of their children, how prevalent it must be among the unmarried class who have social death staring them in the face when they become pregnant without the consent of the canting priest or the drunken squire? . . .

... Is it not equally destroying the would-be future oak, to crush the sprout before it pushes its head above the sod, as it is to cut down the sapling, or cut down the tree? Is it not equally to destroy life, to crush it in its very germ, and to take it when the germ has evolved to any given point in its line of development? ...

We ask the women of this country to consider carefully the subjects thus hastily presented, and see if they do not find in them an unanswerable argument for sexual freedom for themselves ... We speak of these things in connection with the subject of child-murder, because originally they are the foundation for it.... And yet there are still to be found apparently intelligent people who seem honestly to think that the social question ought not to be discussed publicly! ... For our part, so long as the terrible effects of our unnatural sexual system continues to desecrate humanity, there is no other question to be considered in which the health, happiness, and general well-being of the race is so intimately involved.

—*Woodhull and Claflin's Weekly,* 20 June 1874.

Laura Cuppy Smith (fl. 1870s)

Laura Cuppy Smith is practically unknown today because, as Victoria Woodhull's biographer Emanie Sachs has observed, she was "a serious romantic" "too sincere" and "too faithful" "to win fame or fortune" for herself. Smith stood by Woodhull throughout the Beecher-Tilton scandal, serving as a character witness at the trial, bringing her food in jail, and defending her on the national lecture circuit. Smith, the daughter of a British naval officer, emigrated by herself to the United States at fourteen. She fell back on her own resources again when money problems occasioned her first husband's suicide. She and her children moved to San Francisco, where she worked as a lecturer and Spiritualist minister. The *San Francisco Chronicle* proclaimed her "the acknowledged leading champion of Radicalism on the West Coast." She helped to organize suffrage societies and was part of the delegation that presented the first woman suffrage petition to the California legislature. This presentation "was without a parallel in the history of the State. The novelty of women addressing the legislature attracted universal attention, and the newspapers were filled with reports of that important meeting." Later Smith took part in labor agitations. When free lover Ezra Heywood was prosecuted under the Comstock Law, she won a presidential pardon for him.[1] At Woodhull's prompting, Smith disclosed the motives for her dedication to human liberty.

How One Woman Entered the Ranks of Social Reform, or, A Mother's Story
by Laura Cuppy Smith

Will a page torn from a woman's heart—a mother's heart—help other women, other mothers, to be strong? If it will, the world shall hear it, come what may. In the year 1865 I found myself a worker on the Pacific coast, a dweller in that sunny land toward which my heart turns ever with wistful longing, not alone because it is the home of my beloved daughter and sons, and the abiding-place of dearly-cherished and fondly-remembered friends, but because to me it will ever seem the land of richest possibilities, holding the germ of grander, freer, more complete lives than can be lived elsewhere. I worked hard, unceasingly, as one who loved work for its own sake. I threw my whole heart and soul into the words I uttered, and found my reward in the knowledge that they penetrated sometimes the armor of custom and conventionalism and reached the inner consciousness of those addressed. But ever, in public and in private, I cherished the dear hope of bringing my little children across the two broad oceans, to a home in the "thousand-masted bay and steepled town" of San Francisco. Every day my heart leaned over the space that divided us, and listened for the echo of my children's voices. My labors were crowned with success. Never did I love gold before; but as with beating heart I touched the shining coin with which I was to pay for my little daughter's passage and I kissed them with almost childish glee. She must come first, as I could not send for all; then my boys should come later. How I watched the aspect of the sky; how in thought, I traversed the ocean till the tardy waves bore my "one little ewe lamb" safely to her place in my heart. At last my boys came; and then, a united family once more, I said: "Now I will shelter my darlings; now no harm can come to the nest over which a mother's watchful love shall brook with ever-waking vigilance and tenderest solicitude." Each day developed my little girl into a woman. The child's somewhat awkward angles rounded into a young maiden's fair proportions and winsome grace. One day I was startled to observe a young man pause, for a second look, at the sunny-haired girl, and to note that her blue eyes drooped and her cheek blushed beneath his ardent gaze, and with a sudden pang such as mothers alone can know, I said: "My child has grown into a woman, she is no longer all my own." Need I tell any mother who reads this page of heart-history what hopes I cherished for my fair young daughter; how I dreamed of a future for her that should realize my dream of a happy and perfected womanhood; and, since I could not keep her a child, sweetly dependent on her mother, pictured her grown into a grand and noble woman, a happy wife and mother, safely shielded from all the storms that had made shipwreck of my peace, in the quiet haven of a perfect home? I suppose all mothers have some such dreams for their beloved. It only remains then for me to relate how infinite wisdom saw fit to thwart these hopes founded on ignorance and weakness and take my child's life into different channels, educating us both for a higher and broader sphere than we otherwise should have occupied by an experience that seemed to us very bitter, very cruel, but for which we now thank God, glad of the thorny pathway that led up to light.

I do not wish to enter into details regarding the events that changed the currents of our lives; suffice it, a mature but young and brilliant man unconsciously, I think, at first, won the heart of this young girl. I warned and counseled; but when did young impassioned love ever listen to the warning and counsels of experience? The interference only estranged the child's heart for a time . . . for had I not found flaws in this idol of her dreams? But one day I penetrated the secret of the change that had descended upon the girl's joyous spirit. This young maiden who was not a wife would soon be in the world's sight, as she was now in mine, a mother. I thank God in the bitterness of the revelation that then dawned upon me, nothing save an agony of tenderness filled my heart, a passion of love for my child that revealed depths of devotion unknown, undreamed of in the relations of our past. Strange still, I did not hate her lover; he had not deliberately, wickedly seduced a young and trusting person; circumstances threw in his path a fresh, lovely, girl, who loved him, undisguisedly and engrossingly from the first moment she saw him. Society had made him what he was. I deeply deplored it, but realizing his education, his impulsive, passionate temperament, I dared not judge and condemn him. Circumstances—among them considerations of a complicated nature, into which religious scruples entered that have no place in this relation and belong to him personally— forbade marriage; and my daughter and myself would have proudly rejected the hand that was not spontaneously offered, under any circumstances. What was to be done? was the question pondered over, as I lay on my sick bed, holding to my aching heart my infant daughter only two weeks old, for I had been married a year before. Friends said—well-meaning friends— "There is a way, hide this thing from sight, send her on a journey, destroy this evidence of youthful folly, all may yet be well." I was proud; I loved a good position in society for myself, how much more for my children; my daughter in her youth and grace and beauty, how could I bear that the world should point its finger at her and utter its mocking laugh? how could I save her? should I accept this "one way" suggested? If I wavered—and I might as I wrestled in that Garden of Gethsemane—God knows it was but a second. I made my resolve. I said, "This child of youth and love! this child of my child has a right to live, and *shall live*—has a right to love, and shall have that also; has a mission to its mother and shall perform it. This girl-mother has a right to all tenderness and the society of her lover; while she is solving the divine problem of maternity—learning the sacred lessons which the new life stirring beneath her heart whispers to her awakened nature—and she shall have them (for I think that the children, born of mothers deprived of the sweet and tender magnetism of the father in that fateful period prior to birth, come into the world orphaned in part). No dark secret shall dog my child's footsteps through life; she shall enter no man's home with a lie on her lips. I know that her soul is pure, her heart stainless. Love, not guilt, has made her what she is. If the world calls her 'wicked,' 'outcast,' the world lies, and we will live the lie down." I told my child how I had resolved, and she answered: "Mother, you are right, and I am not afraid since you love me still." And accordingly, we entered upon our future. That we struggled through it alone; that kindest friends shook their heads doubtingly, is not wonderful. I think all souls are alone in their direst extremities. The heart upon which I leaned most, could not indorse so strange a course, could only coldly tolerate it; doors that would have opened to one—gladly to him, and for hire to her—utterly refused to shelter both, and his society I insisted she should enjoy.

A woman of questionable repute, so the world said, opened her door when all respectable people closed theirs, and there I, in time, went also, to welcome my little grandson into existence, a child as bright and fair and pure as if all the priests and bishops in Christendom had given him permission to be born and live and aspire. When his young mother was able to walk out, I took the baby in my arms and we walked the whole length of the principal street, running the gauntlet of curious eyes; then I felt the worst was over, the world could not wound us much after that; we had "grasped the nettle," it could sting us no more.

Some of the purest souls I have ever known gave us their hands at last, our nearest and dearest who had been sorely tried by our unusual course, acknowledged, with tears, the wisdom that sustained us. My daughter came out of the ordeal and took up her new life, a matured woman: girlhood had flown in the trial, but had left a sacred boon in its stead; my hair showed a frost it had not shown before, but my soul had gained strength, my whole nature a divine consecration. My little grandson bears his mother's maiden name, as she does; his father loves and cherishes both mother and child. Quietly and with growing self-reliance and with complete self-respect, she lives her life, and with a smile sad but sweet, meets the averted faces of summer friends. In a recent letter she says: "Mother, when I see how lightly some women who frown on me take the obligations of marriage, I am so thankful my 'little mother' helped me live a truer and purer life . . ."

For myself, do you wonder that my whole life is consecrated to the cause of freedom? that I have sworn that I will never permit myself to brand as outcast, prostitute, or fallen, a sister woman, while men standing erect, knee deep in vice, look God and man unblushingly in the face, and are received into our best society without a protest? Do you wonder that I trample underfoot, in indignation and loathing, that shallow mockery you call, with a reverence born of ignorance, "The Marriage Law," a law obligatory upon woman but ignored by man, and that says to the woman who has gone down into the valley of the shadow of death to win the boon of motherhood, "You have no legal right to the child you have purchased by months of suffering, culminating in mortal agony?"

I have transcribed this page of heart history, not wholly without pain, because I am mortal, and hold my inner life as too sacred for the careless gaze of strangers; but if I can help in any sense some sorrowing mother to be strong, some young girl to be brave, I have not written in vain; I can truly look back on my stormy past and thank God for every agony endured, for every weakness conquered, for every bitter experience that has brought me into closer sympathy with human suffering, and above all for this crowning trial that led me out of the land of bondage and prejudice, through the Red Sea of pain, into the perfect liberty of the children of God. It has been my privilege to stand by the priestess of social reform, Victoria C. Woodhull, in the present crisis, and, while I honored her as one chosen of God, as a leader in this great reform, to possess the dearer right of drawing near to her in the sacred association of close and intimate friendship. She has often urged me to write the above, and now my own soul has prompted me to obey.

—*Woodhull and Claflin's Weekly*, 1 March 1873.

Isabella Beecher Hooker (1822-1907)

Isabella Beecher Hooker's siblings included Harriet Beecher Stowe, author of *Uncle Tom's Cabin*; Catharine Esther Beecher, a women's education and domestic science pioneer; and Henry Ward Beecher of the aforementioned Beecher-Tilton scandal. As trying as the scandal was for the family, Isabella came to believe that Henry was guilty as charged. She defended the Claflin sisters' freedom of speech and their attack on the sexual double standard. For her loyalty to women, Isabella paid dearly. Henry called her insane. Other relatives and more conservative suffragists denounced her. Historians neglected this engaging, important figure until quite recently.

At 19, before marrying abolitionist and constitutional lawyer John Hooker, she insisted upon an affectionate, egalitarian relationship. The Hookers had a small family for their time: four children, three of whom survived infancy. The couple likely made a joint decision to limit their reproduction.[1] In a letter to her friend John Stuart Mill, Hooker articulated the reverence for the maternal-fetal bond behind her advocacy of voluntary motherhood.

> [O]f late I have been impressed more and more with the close likeness to the divine nature which woman seems to bear, in that she is more sensibly, if not more truly, a creator than man is. Add to this her more intimate fellowship with the child of her womb during the antenatal period, and the power of sympathy that comes through this, and you have given her a moral advantage that man can never have, and for which he has no equivalent or compensation.[2]

Although she took a lively interest in public affairs and assisted her husband in his legal and political activities, Isabella had little respite from household responsibilities, except for a stay at Rachel Gleason's sanitarium for treatment of gynecological ailments. Hooker delighted in her children's unfolding personalities, while chafing at the limits of domesticity and envying her sisters' public achievements. In 1868, when only her youngest child was left at home, she debuted as a suffragist lecturer and writer. Frances Willard and Mary Livermore characterized her career as "one of ceaseless toil, heroic endurance of undeserved abuse, and exalted effort." She served as vice-president of the National Woman Suffrage Association's Connecticut chapter. In 1878 she spoke before Congress, and in 1888 to the International Council of Women. In her only book, Hooker defends woman's right to challenge the double standard on all fronts. Published during the Beecher-Tilton scandal, this book occasioned much of the "undeserved abuse," bringing Hooker "many earnest expressions of gratitude from intelligent mothers."[3] Here she gently, firmly confronts a nemesis of nineteenth-century feminists.[4]

"My Mother's Heart Stirs Me to Immediate Reply"
by Isabella Beecher Hooker

The subjoined letter, addressed to the Rev. Dr. Todd, was written in April, 1867 . . . . A very serious and earnest article from his pen appeared in the *Boston Congregationalist* of April 19, entitled "Fashionable Murder," in which the crime of foeticide was severely condemned, and the claim made that the chief causes of it were the desire of women to live in ease and fashion, and an unwillingness to undergo the pain of childbirth . . .

The injustice done to women in this article, and the superficial manner of treating a most profound subject drew from me a reply, which was immediately forwarded to the *Congregationalist*, in which a second article by Rev. Dr. Todd had then appeared . . . The editor declined to publish the reply, and soon after these two articles of Dr. Todd were published as a pamphlet [that] . . . and had a wide circulation. In the mean time the reply has been privately circulated among the writer's friends, and especially among mothers, with an increasing interest in the subject, and an often-expressed desire for its publication . . .

And if any one, in all the world, should be allowed to speak on these subjects, who so much as we who are mothers and grandmothers, who can speak from our own happy or sad experience, and to whom no unworthy motive can, for a moment, be imputed? In looking upon my own children and grandchildren, I see in them the representative of all humanity, and my heart reaches out in sisterly sympathy to all mothers, and in motherly yearning toward all the children of the earth . . .

April 20, 1867
Rev. John Todd, D.D.

Dear Sir:

I have just read in the *Congregationalist* of April 19 your impressive words in condemnation of mothers who criminally relieve themselves of unwelcome offspring, and my mother's heart stirs me to immediate reply . . . I shall be giving you the result of many years of observations and reflection upon the subject.

You have spoken of two great laws of our race that came with transgression—excessive labor for man, suffering and subjection for woman . . . It is no less true, however, that both men and women have all along been rightfully striving to ameliorate their condition in these respects, and to come into a condition of perfect liberty of choice, even the liberty wherewith Christ doth make us free.

That some women have mistaken the way to this personal freedom, and been led into deadly sin and into the fearful suffering which inevitably follows the serious transgression of even physical law, is true . . . and such need warning; and I, for one, cannot but rejoice when the sin and danger of their evil ways are plainly set before them; but I rejoice also in the whole truth, and the fair statement of a vital question, and in this respect your article seems to me very defective . . . .

Is it not time, then, that these vital questions, which do, in fact, underlie all social moralities, were examined and discussed under all the light which science and religion can impart, and be handled by mothers as well as by fathers, and more especially by the former, since they chiefly are the watchful observers and guardians of those young days when right habits and beliefs may be taught to children of both sexes?

And now permit me to say that a great part of the physical and moral deterioration of the present day arises, it seems to me, from the fact that children are not conceived in the desire for them, and out of the pure lives of their fathers, as well as their mothers; and that far worse misfortunes might befall our race than decreasing families . . .

To my conception, one generation of *instructed* mothers would do more for the renovation of the race than all other agencies combined . . . Under such guidance as this, would there be need, think you, of the warnings of your article? . . . Do we not simply lop the branches and leave the sturdy trunk, when we criticize this and that practice of human parents, and overlook their fundamental misconceptions of the nature of their being?

You have spoken of ministers' families illustrating by their size the piety of the parents; but it does seem to me the quality of offspring is far better testimony than the quantity... At all events I have heard of one New England minister, the father of many children, whose word to his daughter and her approaching marriage was, "You must instruct your husband, my dear, that he do not allow you to have children too often. If I had known what I now know earlier in life, your mother, of blessed memory, might be living to this day." And then he went on to state to her his deep convictions on the general subject, which were in accordance with the views I am urging, and which he had reached, not through the medium of science, but through the promptings of a great and noble heart and a courageous will, which led him to the truth even at the cost of self-condemnation and a great and perpetual sorrow.

By this do I feel encouraged to suggest to all young parents that there is a more excellent way of bringing happiness to their households than by seeking to escape the suffering and care, the toil and privation, that children may bring... [Y]our whole life will be chilled if you wilfully shut out these sunbeams. But you must not invite these little ones to your homes any oftener than you can provide for them in body and in spirit, and for the health and the strength of the mothers who are to bear them...

With sincere respect,
A Mother
— From "Motherhood," in *Womanhood: Its Sanctities and Fidelities*,
Boston, MA: Lee and Shepard, 1874.

Elizabeth Edson Evans (1832-1911) and Six Anonymous Women

From youth, New Hampshire native Elizabeth Edson Gibson Evans was an artist and writer of verse, novels, essays, and books, including *The Christ Myth* (1900). This last work declared her "joy and peace" in acknowledging and following her doubts about Christian church authority and doctrine and becoming a freethinker dedicated to "the pursuit of truth and benevolence towards all human beings."[1] She was the spouse of Edward Payson Evans, a noted modern languages and literatures scholar and animal concerns activist.[2] His 1898 treatise *Evolutional Ethics and Animal Psychology*, which was dedicated to her, stated,

> We have happily rid ourselves somewhat of the ethnocentric prepossessions . . . to regard all other peoples as barbarians; but our perceptions are still obscured by anthropocentric prejudice which prevents us from fully appreciating the intelligence of the lower animals and recognising any psychical analogy between these humble kinsmen and our exalted selves.[3]

As the prochoice historian Carl Degler notes, Elizabeth Evans was "certainly a friend of women."[4] Consciously building on Gleason's work, she documented post-abortion experiences in *The Abuse of Maternity*. Because this book asserted the right of voluntary motherhood, the *Albany Law Journal* lambasted it as dangerously "obscene literature" whose ideas were dismissable as the suspect products of "long-haired men and short-haired women."[5]

"I Have Lost A Child"
by Elizabeth Edson Evans

And now let us listen to the regretful complaint of one whose early feelings [about overextending herself in others' care—Eds.] were not so kindly consulted . . . "In my childhood," she says, "I was remarkable for an

---

over flowing and unselfish affection for every living thing that was smaller and more helpless than myself; dogs, cats, chickens, birds, and all other household pets were the delight of my heart; and as for babies, I loved them to idolatry. And so it came to pass that not only were my services called for in season and out of season by all members of the family in behalf of the little ones of our own nursery, but my visits to neighbors and friends were made use of in the same way; while the children of any guests who might be staying with us were given over almost wholly to my loving and patient care.

"This distinction was rather a pleasure than a trouble to me so long as I remained myself a careless, playful child, but as years went on and my mind began to expand with a desire of knowledge, and I longed for silence and solitude in order to carry on the ponderings and questions of an active intellect and an earnest soul, I became impatient of the restraints which had so long bound me; I felt that I ought to be allowed more individual opportunity, instead of being so completely involved with the younger lives that were developing around me. But circumstances were too powerful for my resistance, and the only result of my struggle was, that I gradually lost, through my perceptible discontent, the reputation for amiability which I had hitherto enjoyed, and which had tempted others to impose an unjust share of their responsibilities upon me. At last I became free through my marriage, but when, soon afterwards, the prospect of a nursery of my own dawned upon me, I turned away in utter weariness, and would have none of its once so fascinating fatigues. I imagined that I hated children, and believed that the instincts of my early years had not sounded the real key-notes of my character. Now, when I recall the tender love I used to feel for my dolls, and the still-more exquisite enjoyment I formerly took in the contemplation and care of infants, I am wild with regret at my folly in rejecting the (alas! only once-proffered) gift of offspring. My only comfort is in the fact that my crime has not lost me my rare power of attracting the affection of dumb animals and speechless babes—the dogs of strangers still turn gladly to meet my caressing hand, and I can always woo the cherished child from the arms of its doting mother."

... Said a woman who has never ceased to regret an early sin against her motherhood, "While I was debating the subject in my own mind—being tempted to the crime chiefly through the fact that my sister had suffered extremely during childbirth, and the corresponding fear that I, who was even more slight and delicate than she, would surely lose my life in the struggle—my mother-in-law—who had not yet overcome the natural jealousy caused by seeing another holding the first place in the affections of a favorite son—took occasion, one day, while talking with a neighbor, to expatiate with all the eloquence of truth upon the frightful agonies she had suffered during parturition; saying, by way of climax, that, old as she was, it made the cold sweat start at every pore only to recall that long-past experience. What possessed her to speak in this manner, suspecting, as I think she did, my situation at the time, I cannot imagine; at all events, in my then excitable state, her words were daggers to my heart, and I left the room fully resolved to take speedy measures to spare myself the full measure of the tortures I could not expect entirely to avoid."

. . . Said one of these victims of early [physiological] ignorance, "During the first years of my repentance, when I was almost insane with unavailing sorrow, I became acquainted with one of the purest and loveliest specimens of my own sex that I have ever known. From the first she manifested a preference for my society, and soon showed a disposition to select me as a confidential friend. But this distinction I felt myself unworthy to accept, and I finally resolved to confess the secret to her and be guided concerning my future estimate of myself, by her judgment as to my sin. She listened to the story with surprise and pity, but without any signs of aversion, and, in trying to lighten my evident despair, she begged me to consider the fact as a mistake; sad and eventful certainly, but by no means indicative of my real character, nor decisive as to its power to blast my future career. This true woman, true wife, true mother, true friend, saved me from myself at a terrible crisis, and her unabated confidence and affection have since been as a strong shield against the keen darts of remorse which, ever and anon, have threatened to overcome my courage."

. . . Said a woman who, after many years of despondency, had begun to realize the truth of Madame De Stael's vigorous maxim—"*Repeated penitence wearies the soul—it is a sentiment that can but once regenerate us*"—and to feel that atonement could best be made through diligent and useful endeavor— "From the moment when I began to appreciate my irreparable loss, my thoughts were filled with imaginings as to what might have been the worth of that child's individuality; and, especially, after sufficient time had elapsed to have brought him to maturity, did I busy myself with picturing the responsible posts he might have filled, the honors he might have won, the joy and comfort he might have brought to his suffering fellow-creatures; nor, during the interval, have I read of an accident by land or by water, or of a critical moment in a battle, or of a good cause lost through lack of a brave defender, but my heart has whispered, '*He* might have been there to help and save; *he* might have been able to lead that forlorn hope; *his* word or *his* deed might have brought that wise plan to successful issue!"

... Said one: "I think I was for a long time as near being insane as one can be without really going mad. Although much debilitated through the physical consequences of my sin, I often took long walks, much longer than I could have borne in health; and though going at a rapid pace, and without any pause for rest, I was as unconscious of fatigue as unimpressed by the features of the landscape, or by the persons and objects I passed. I had an idea that I had lost, through that unnatural deed, the normal powers and qualities of a human being. I no longer ate and drank with the old hunger and thirst, nor slept the quiet sleep of innocence; I took no heed of the passage of time, and all that I saw and heard seemed to be the occurrences of a dream, as though life were already finished for me and I was observing it from another state of existence. The first ray of hope that dawned upon me was when, during an illness succeeding to this dangerous excitement, I found that the remedies prescribed for my feverish restlessness and excruciating headache affected me as they would have affected another person. From the moment of that discovery I began to amend in health, and have since recovered sufficient energy to interest myself in the work that seems to belong to me especially to do, though the strange feeling of having set myself apart from the rest of my sex, through that sin against my motherhood, will probably always remain to increase the bitterness of my childless and lonely condition."

Said another: "I envy a mother who goes to weep beside her baby's grave; because she knows where it is laid, and remembers how it looked in life, and is not ashamed to say, '*I have lost a child.*' And when I hear mothers lamenting over such a loss, I pity them indeed; but I feel like saying to them, 'You think you are deeply afflicted, but your trouble is really light, because it is not mingled with remorse, and you are not to blame for the infant's death.' Truly all sorrow that I have ever known or heard of is not to be compared with my sorrow ..."

—From *The Abuse of Maternity*, Philadelphia, PA: J.B. Lippincott, 1875.

Eliza Bisbee Duffey (d. 1898)

Eliza Bisbee Duffey penned spirited etiquette and advice books. She entered the feminist uproar over Dr. Edward H. Clarke's book *Sex in Education*, which insisted that women's biology precluded academic success and physical health in a coeducational setting. Duffey's *No Sex in Education* responded that prejudice, not physiology, hampered women.[1] And because women were impaired by *ignorance* of their physiology, Duffey wrote her sex education manual *What Women Should Know* (Philadelphia: JM Stoddart, 1873) along with *Relations of the Sexes*, excerpted below. While the Comstock Act thwarted her from describing particular methods, Duffey boldly presented voluntary contraception as an ethical good, referring her readers to the concrete advice in Robert Dale Owen's *Moral Physiology*.[2]

The Limitation of Offspring
by Eliza Bisbee Duffey

I think women should be left free to accept or reject motherhood. I now say that they should only accept it when their hearts go out towards it, and they feel that it will prove a blessing. They should reject it, when the circumstances which attend it are likely to turn it into a curse in many ways. But the great cry of suffering women is, "How shall we refuse it?" Could this question be answered satisfactorily to them, I *know* that to an overwhelming majority of women life would suddenly be flooded with a light and a beauty that for long years has been absent from it; that a weight of fear and trouble would be lifted from their hearts, that has bowed them down, and made them feel helpless and hopeless... And I know, if they dared to speak, there would come to me as with one voice, the words of hosts upon hosts of women in corroboration of my assertion...

Sufficient practical means have been discovered to make it possible for a whole nation to modify the size of its families... Women should have knowledge of these means in order to save them from the terror and dread which, if they would admit the truth, four out of every five would confess, overcloud and destroy the happiness of all their child-bearing years—

embittering affection and killing passion. They should have it, that there may be light, and hope, and love, in their homes—and even conjugal delight; for I cannot conceive that that which is so eminently desirable and honorable in a man, should be valueless and shameful in a woman. They should have it that they may not have offspring forced upon them before they are ready for them; that the little ones may be welcomed with love, and desire, and joyful expectancy.

I know there is a feeling in every woman's heart—a feeling which goes down deeper than prejudice even—which tells her that the constant fear of offspring, and the burden of large families, are more grievous troubles than ought to be thrown upon her. She *knows* I am right in what I have been saying in these chapters, for there is a response—let her try to stifle it as she will—to every word, in her own breast. But she has been taught that she must not harbor this feeling, because she was born to be a mother, and a mother without any limit to her duties. Men have taught her this, though her own nature, while it admitted the former, has rebelled against the latter clause. This might be right, if her capabilities were also limitless. But she knows, alas! too well, that they are not, and there is where I have touched the key-note of her feelings. She is willing to do all she can, poor foolish woman; she counts the sacrifice of her strength and life as nothing, in her tireless efforts to cope with impossibilities . . . [I]t was for men's interests . . . to make [women] believe that it was their duty to accept unlimited maternal cares, because their acceptance *implied* unlimited sexual gratification on the part of the men; and partly because men are as ignorant and blinded as women themselves. The women of the present day . . . feel the heavy drawbacks in this respect under which they are laboring, yet dare not speak one word of the bitterness and reproach which are welling up in their hearts . . .

. . . "Children have a right to be born!" . . . [No one] is justified in interfering with this most sacred and indubitable right, or in any way to lessen the certainty of their being born . . . After a child *is*, no one has a right to tamper with its existence. But, returning to the statement . . . let us decide whether it can be appropriately applied to the prevention of conception. By what possible twist of imagination can any one suppose something, which is not something at all—which is nothing, because it is nowhere, and has no existence—to be a child? A being which does not exist, has no rights, to be either granted or withheld. If it has, how about those children which numberless married couples might have had, if they had but married a few years earlier, or if the mothers had weaned their babies a few months sooner? How about the might-have-been children of those who never marry? Are there no qualms of conscience about these potential offspring?

When we talk about children having a right to be born . . . I mean that no one has a right to jeopardize a life which has already begun ever so brief an existence . . . . My meaning shuts at once and forever the door of abortion. But before that existence has commenced, we have a right—nay, it is a sacred duty, unmistakably delegated to us by God—to consider whether we shall assume the responsibility of evoking such an existence, and whether we can insure it happy conditions . . . . Abortion, intentionally accomplished . . . should be regarded as murder. Yet women have been taught to look lightly on this offence, and to consider it perfectly justifiable up to the period of quickening. "The embryo has no life before that period," they will say in justification of the act. I have even heard a woman, who acknowledged to several successful abortions, accomplished by her own hands upon herself, say, "Why, there is no harm in it, any more than in drowning a blind kitten. It is nothing better than a kitten, before it is born." I was a young girl myself when I heard this, and I accepted the statement as a true one. Nor did I dream of questioning it, until, in later years, I became thoroughly acquainted with sexual physiology, and comprehended the wonderful economy of nature in the generation and development of the human germ.

The act of abortion which I had hitherto regarded as a trivial thing, at once became in my eyes . . . the most aggravated crime . . . Consequently, the surest preventive against this crime will be a thorough teaching to women, even before marriage, of the physiology, hygiene, duties and obligations of maternity. Men may preach against this act as a sin; but knowing as women do, how one-sided it is possible for men to feel and talk about other matters of a similar nature, in which the sexes are equally concerned, it is not strange that these sermons produce no effect. The strangeness is still further decreased when the sermonizers are not infrequently themselves guilty of the no less heinous offence of forcing motherhood upon a woman against her will. The two offences go together, and neither legal enactment nor social reprobation can ever divorce them. The woman knows instinctively that if her husband is justified in the one, he has no moral right to interfere with her in the accomplishment of the other . . .

From the moment of conception, the embryo is a living thing, leading a distinct, separate existence from the mother, though closely bound to her. The mother's blood courses through its veins, and she nourishes it, and gives of her physical substance the material for its bones and muscles. From almost the earliest stage, the form of the future being is indicated, and it has its separate heart-beats, distinctly perceptible through the intervening tissues of the mother's body, which cover it. It is a human being to all intents and purposes. The period called quickening is merely a fictitious period, which does not indicate the first motion of the embryo. These first motions are not usually detected—unless the woman is very observant, and knows just what feeling to expect—until they have acquired considerable force.

Nature has put this little creature—this small man or woman, as yet all undeveloped—in a place of seeming security, and has placed every guard around it to keep it safely until the hour shall come when it is fully prepared to make a complete change in its mode of existence. If by intent or accident it is disturbed before that period, the whole of nature's plans are thwarted, and nothing is in readiness. A hundred bleeding wounds remain, when the child, with its accompanying membranes, is torn untimely from the womb of the mother; mouths that would have closed themselves at the appropriate time, but now remain open to bleed away the mother's life . . .

. . . Do not be content to tell women it is wrong, and then stop there. Women are impatient of being treated like children, or like unreasoning beings; nor do they like to be dictated to. Tell them the how and the why of the whole matter, and they will discover the wrong themselves, and *feel* the full force of it, far more than they ever can by taking it merely on the say-so of men.

Then the laws which are already upon our statute books should be strictly enforced, not only on the occasion of bursts of indignation, when some unfortunate girl endeavors to get rid of the evidence of her shame; but whenever the fact of a wilful abortion comes to the cognizance of community. And *husbands and seducers should be made to share the punishment as accessories to the crime,* since if they had not forced an undesired motherhood upon the women, there would have been no occasion for the abortion.

Not only every maker, advertiser and seller of patent medicines, warranted to "remove female obstructions," should be subjected to prosecution and punishment, but every publisher who prints an advertisement of this sort should be held equally guilty. Community will not be injured in the least by the suppression of these advertisements . . . no matter how innocent may be the intent of the person using them . . .

No; the evils attendant upon large families may be manifold; but they must not be averted by any such criminal means as this; for the remedy is as bad as the disease . . .

—From *The Relations of the Sexes,* New York: Wood and Holbrook, 1876,
Chapter 13.

Dr. Alice Bunker Stockham (1833-1912)

Alice Bunker Stockham married, raised a son and daughter, and eventually became "a proud grandmother, but is not inclined to diminish her efforts on that account, as she is yet in the prime of life." As the *Chicago Tribune* declared, this most productive physician was "an enthusiastic worker in reform movements" and "above all, a loyal friend to her sex."[1] Born of Ohio Quaker parents, she taught school, then earned degrees from both eclectic and homeopathic medical colleges. Her persistent gastrointestinal disorder shaped her interest in medicine. While maintaining her busy Chicago practice, she operated a free kindergarten and became involved in suffrage and "Social Purity," the feminist campaign against the sexual double standard. She personally met with novelist Leo Tolstoy in Russia and wrote a book extolling his philosophy of nonviolence. Stockham and her daughter printed and distributed this book through their publishing house, which specialized in social change literature. Stockham's *Karezza* (1898) gave birth control advice, asserted that sexuality was *not* a matter of "man's necessities and woman's obedience to them," proclaimed the healthfulness of sexual pleasure for its own sake, and indicated that women were just as capable and deserving of it as men.

By the 1890s, Stockham's writings, global travels, and warm personality had gained her national and international praise from evangelical Christian temperance workers as well as anarchist freethinkers. They applauded her for employing vulnerable women at risk for prostitution to sell her books door-to-door. In 1905, when she was 72, Anthony Comstock machinated her arrest on obscenity charges. Despite feminist support and Clarence Darrow's legal defense, Stockham was fined, her writings banned, the publishing house forced to close. The Chicago suburb of Evanston, where she had been an honored longtime resident, effaced her name from a street and park.[2]

Comstock could not erase the positive changes that Stockham had already catalyzed in her readers—especially those who devoured the information about female physiology and prenatal self-care in the multiple editions and translations of *Tokology* (Greek, "obstetrics"). This popular book insisted that female bodily functions were not inherently pathological. Pregnancy was not naturally the painful and debilitating disease so many women experienced it to be; rather, it was made into one by an improper diet, a lack of exercise, the wearing of corsets, and by a general societal failure to treat it as a normal, healthy state of being. Stockham directly linked the disease model of pregnancy to the practice of abortion:

> This period is transformed from one of hope, of cheerfulness, of exalted pleasure, into days of suffering, wretchedness, and direful forebodings. It is one long nightmare, and childbearing is looked upon as a curse and not a blessing. Motherhood is robbed of its divinest joys ... Ordinarily pregnancy is classed by both physicians and women among the diseases. Physical sufferings and mental agonies are the common accompaniments of the condition. Murderous intent fills the mother's heart, and the fearful crime of feticide is daily committed.[3]

"Two Wrongs Cannot Make a Right"
by Dr. Alice Bunker Stockham

Feticide is a produced abortion, whether by drugs, intentional shocks, electricity, or by instrumental interference, either by one's own hand or by the hand of a surgeon.

Many women have been taught to think that the child is not viable until after quickening, and that there is no harm in arresting pregnancy previous to the feeling of motion; others believe that there is no *life* until birth, and the cry of the child is heard ...

When the female germ and male sperm unite, then is the inception of a new life; all that goes to make up a human being—body, mind, and spirit, must be contained in embryo within this minute organism. *Life must be present from the very moment of conception.* If there was not life there could not be conception. At what other period of a human being's existence, either pre-natal or post-natal, could the union of soul and body take place? Is it not plain that the violent or forcible deprivation of existence of this embryo, the removal of it from the citadel of life, is its premature death, and hence the act can be denominated by no more mild term than murder, and whoever performs the act, or is accessory to it, is guilty of the crime of all crimes?

The life of the babe in her arms is to the mother more precious than all else; her heart is thrilled with a pang of agony at the thought of the least danger to its life. By what false reasoning does she convince herself that another life, still more dependent upon her for its existence, with equal rights and possibilities, has no claim upon her for protection? More than this, she deliberately strikes with the red hand of murder and terminates its existence with no thought of wrong, nor consciousness of violated law.

The woman who produces abortion, or allows it to be produced, risks her own life and health in the act, and commits the highest crime in the calendar, for she takes the life of her own child. She defrauds the child of the right to its existence.

By a wise provision we are placed in this world for growth, development and preparation for another life. As we leave this life, we must enter the other. In so far as a human being is deprived of this existence, to that extent he is deprived of schooling and preparation for the other life. Pause for one moment and think of the thousands of stunted, dwarfed beings that are prematurely ushered into an existence that can not be normal and designed. Were infants to have been born into spirit life, provision would have been made to that effect. That they are born into this life is proof that this world is best adapted for their growth and education.

There may be no harm in *preventing* the conception of a life, but once conceived it should not be deprived of its existence in that world which in all its appointments is specially adapted to its development.

What are some of the incentives to produce abortion? An unmarried woman, seduced under false representation by a man who feels no responsibility for his own offspring, suffers alone all the shame and con-tumely of the act, and is tempted to cause miscarriage to shield her good name.

Married women who fear that maternity will interfere with their pleasures, are guilty of forcibly curtailing embryonic life. Others again, who are poor or burdened with care or grief, or have licentious or drunken husbands, shrink from adding to an already overburdened existence . . . .

Two wrongs cannot make a right . . . When girls are given proper instruction upon the relations of the sexes and understand how to govern and guard themselves; when young men are taught that virtue has as high a meaning for one sex as for another, that the protective chivalry of which they boast does not imply that they shall force the woman with whom they associate to the defensive; and that the *paternal* interest in, and responsibilities for a child are equal to the *maternal*, then the temptation to produce abortion for the purpose of shielding one's character will not exist.

Of the second class, who produce miscarriage . . . for selfish interest, there is little to say in extenuation. They may be victims of ignorance or of a false education . . . Of the last class, who have an apparent need to limit the size of the family, what can be said in extenuation of their committing this crime? Shall not the mother who already has many children, who is herself sick, nervous, and prostrated, or else has a husband who is diseased or a drunkard, leaving her the support of the family, save herself additional care by arresting the life of the embryo? The heart goes out in sympathy for all such, but even the most aggravating circumstances cannot atone for the crime. The whole nature of every true woman revolts against forced maternity.

Thoughtful minds must acknowledge the great wrong done when children are begotten under adverse conditions. Women must learn the laws of life so as to protect themselves, and not be the means of bringing sin-cursed, diseased children into the world.[4]

The remedy is in the prevention of pregnancy, not in producing abortion. When men and women have learned the wise control of the procreative functions, then may we hope that children will be begotten in love and unselfishness. It is the undesired and undesigned maternity that is revolting to the nature of woman. As long as men feel that they have a right to indulgence of the passions under law, no matter what the circumstances, what the condition of the wife, or the probabilities of maternity, so long will the spirit of rebellion take possession of women and the temptation enter their souls to relieve themselves of this unsought burden. May the day soon arrive when men will learn that even passion should serve reason, and that gratification at least should not be sought at the expense of conjugal happiness and *unwelcome children.*

—*Tokology,* 2d ed., Chicago, IL: Sanitary Publishing Company, 1887, 245-51.

"The Courage to Assert the Right to Her Own Body": Lucinda Banister Chandler (1829-1911)

As a baby in Potsdam, New York, Lucinda Banister incurred a painful, lifelong disability from a severe spinal injury in a fall. When she entered school at age nine, "her teacher registered her as two years older because of her advancement in studies and seeming maturity of years." At 13, however, she was forced to end her formal education: "her first great disappointment." At 20, she married John H. Chandler. Their only child, a son, drowned at age three. Fortunately, "Mrs. Chandler's marriage was a happy one, and the tender, devoted care and provision for her relief and benefit by her husband was no doubt the providence that made it possible for her to enjoy a period of usefulness in later life."[1]

When bedridden, Chandler studied politics and wrote works like the acclaimed booklet *Motherhood: Its Power Over Human Destiny*. A passage from it ran in some editions of Stockham's *Tokology*.

> Every mother from the moment the new life commences, is overshadowed by the Most High. Could she understand her needs and powers, and secure to herself respect due to her sacred office . . . very rapidly would disappear . . . the discordant spirits now blotting the fair proportions of mankind.[2]

Whenever her health permitted, Chandler traveled, lectured, chaired meetings, and organized. She was vice president of the National Woman Suffrage Association and cofounder of Chicago's political education-focused Margaret Fuller Society.[3] Yet she considered women's legal equality only "*one* feature of the adjusting process." The "purpose of her heart" was creating the Boston Moral Educational Society, which quickly inspired others elsewhere. Like the consciousness-raising groups of the 1970s, moral education societies offered women an opportunity to "safely, fully, and openly discuss . . . without intimidation from men" the intimate, essential matters of sexuality, marriage, and birth control.[4] Moral education, Chandler believed, was necessary to achieve feminism's most vital end: "Woman must have the courage to assert the right to her own body as the instrument of reason and conscience, and the fulfillment of the function of motherhood subject to no authority but the voice of God in her soul."[5]

The broad-spirited Chandler was a progressive Spiritualist, "Free Religionist," contributor to *Woodhull and Claflin's Weekly*, adviser to Elizabeth Cady Stanton's *Woman's Bible,* and much-valued worker with the Women's Christian Temperance Union. Her issues of moral education, voluntary motherhood, and "enlightened parenthood" united feminists across the religious and political spectrum.[6]

Chandler encouraged nonviolence in all spheres. A decade before Upton Sinclair and Caroline Hedger exposed the horrors of the Stockyards, the Chicago Vegetarian Society published Chandler's tract on "non flesh eating."

> [T]he evil is the most serious to the one who kills . . . The abattoir and the shambles cannot promote the fraternal sentiments nor a high order of morals. Familiarity with the slaying of animals and their struggles cannot promote fine and human feelings.[7]

The previous year, Chandler had made, according to the radical paper *Lucifer*, "an important addition to the anti-death penalty literature" with her leaflet for the Chicago Moral Educational Society. "Woman, who pays the costly price of a human life, may fittingly and wisely enjoin men to cease the destruction of *the children of women* either by warfare or judicial murder."[8] Chandler joined with pacifist Jane Addams, also white, and African American anti-lynching feminists Ida B. Wells-Barnett and Anna Julia Cooper to oppose U.S. war on the Philippines, including sexual exploitation of Filipinas. The anti-imperialist Chandler considered this war the "killing of people who had committed no wrong to this country, and who only were seeking their inalienable right to liberty and self-government."[9]

Chandler strongly advocated peace in the womb, too. Carroll Smith-Rosenberg notes that feminist sexual and marital advice writers—"figures as disparate" as Alice Bunker Stockham, Elizabeth Blackwell, Victoria Woodhull, and Lucinda Chandler—"bitterly" opposed abortion because it

> did not symbolize an increase in personal and sexual freedom for these women, but its reverse. The vaginal penetration the male abortionist perpetrated upon the unwillingly pregnant wife replicated her husband's initial uninvited penetration . . . Abortion, in this way, doubly violated women's physical integrity.[10]

This analysis is sound but incomplete. These feminists believed that abortion violated personal integrity in still another sense: by destroying the unborn child's body, literally severing her/his close interconnection with the mother's. Even when pregnancy resulted from apparently consensual sex, and/or abortion was not performed surgically by a man, Chandler and her peers equated abortion and rape. As Elizabeth Cady Stanton observed of wrongs against women in general, "Society as organized today under the man power is one grand rape of womanhood."[11]

Reproductive Wrongs Unto Death: Eugenic Strictures (Late Nineteenth – Early Twentieth Centuries and Beyond)

Early feminists believed that voluntary motherhood and birth control would safeguard both women and children in ways beyond preventing abortion. They believed that if the power imbalance in sex was not righted, any children conceived might be sickly, mentally ill, or developmentally delayed. This fear derived from the reality of syphilis, often transmitted to women, whether wives or sex workers, and thus to unborn children by male devotees of the double standard.[1] This was a eugenic argument, but one meant to safeguard individual rights and wellbeing, not to advance a broad reactionary agenda—at first. As early as the 1870s, Elizabeth Cady Stanton called for legal restrictions on the right of disabled people to marry, and said that women committed infanticide to avoid bearing "moral monsters."[2] By the 1890s, Victoria Woodhull, the mother of a developmentally delayed daughter, began to inveigh against "the rapid multiplication of the unfit," namely "imbeciles, criminals, paupers" who "must not be bred."[3]

However, such wide-scale eugenic agendas had far more to do with racial/ethnic, ableist, and class prejudices than feminism. From the arrival of the Great Hunger refugees onward, the Anglo-Saxon Protestant ruling class of the U.S. felt under siege. The Mexican American War and the subsequent Treaty of Guadalupe Hidalgo (1848) brought thousands of Mexicanos/as under U.S. occupation. Urbanization made crime more concentrated and visible and catalyzed labor unrest and political radicalism. The emancipated African American population was growing. Despite their forced displacement onto barren reservations, the First Nations refused to die out. Puerto Rico and the Philippines were seized through American imperialist schemes. New waves of predominantly Jewish and Catholic Southern and Eastern European immigrants arrived on U.S. shores, stirring up fears that an influx of Asian laborers on the Pacific Coast heralded an Asian "yellow peril." The efficiency—and profit-oriented values of large-scale industrial capitalism increasingly defined disabled persons as "useless burdens." Non Anglo racial/ethnic identities—including the Scotch-Irish heritage of poor Southern and Appalachian whites—and disabilities of all kinds were conflated with "feeblemindedness," rapacious and perverse sexual impulses, reckless breeding, criminality, and the poverty of the "undeserving poor."

Eugenics falsely assumed that all these traits—which, incidentally, lacked precise scientific definitions—were hereditary. For decades, it allowed the ruling class to "scientifically" justify defense of its status as promoting the "survival of the fittest" necessary to human evolution, a crude mapping of Charles Darwin's biological theories onto the human social domain called Social Darwinism. This warping of genuine science rationalized already entrenched forms of competition, domination, and bigotry—including racial, gender, and disability discrimination—as necessary and natural to human social order. As Lara Foley notes, eugenics was (and is) tightly linked to an ultraconservative conviction that "social reforms were useless because problems did not reside in the social system, but in the genes of the 'unfit' . . . Any theory that some people are genetically superior or inferior to others poses a powerful potential threat to reproductive rights."[4]

Eugenics did indeed assault reproductive and other crucial civil rights—including, as discussed below, the right underlying all others: the right to life itself. It became a strong movement in England as well as in Scandinavia, where wide-scale sterilization abuse took place. Yet eugenic goals were actually realized the most in the U.S. and in Germany. American eugenicists were often prosperous, highly educated Anglo men who envisioned womankind as either "pure" or "impure." They urged the former group to turn out large numbers of children as a social duty but were more obsessed with deliberately, punitively curbing the reproduction of the latter. Not surprisingly, given their rigid gender role expectations and their horror over "deviants" of any variety, eugenicists also led the early twentieth-century "scientific" charge against men and women who experienced same-sex attractions and/or displayed the manners commonly associated with the "opposite" sex.[5] The first federal immigration restriction, the 1875 Page Act, banned Asian, particularly Chinese, women suspected of entering the U.S. for "immoral purposes." The few Chinese prostitutes in the U.S. often creatively resisted their near-enslavement, yet mass hysteria turned them into menacing symbols of America's "moral and racial pollution." The Page Act spawned further immigration bans on Asians, Latin Americans, and Southern and Eastern Europeans. These laws would eventually damn many Jewish refugees during the Holocaust. Immigration laws also staved off two other "deviant" groups: political radicals and disabled persons. Anti-miscegenation laws—bans on marriage between whites and people of color, especially African Americans—proliferated as guards against "race suicide" and "mongrelization." The standard criterion for defining a person of color was "one drop" of other-than-white blood. These laws were not overturned until the U.S. Supreme Court's *Loving* decision (1967).[6]

Persons with a wide range of disabilities were legally barred from marrying *anyone*. The mass coercion of disabled persons into sexually segregated institutions for life was designed precisely to prevent their marriage and reproduction. Before long, eugenicists pushed compulsory sterilization of "defectives" as more cost-effective. Without proper consents, the Eugenics Records Office conducted intrusive genealogy research on the U.S. population to identify candidates for eugenic intervention. It concluded that one-tenth of Americans had to be stopped from reproducing. From the 1900s through the 1970s, at least 70,000 disabled or dislabeled U.S. citizens—mostly women—were subjected to sterilization abuse. By the early 1980s, 42% of First Nations and 24% of African American women had undergone sterilization, compared to 15% of white women. While some procedures were no doubt voluntary, stories from many women, such as the Black civil rights leader Fannie Lou Hamer (Part Two), indicate widespread coercion.[7]

Like the blitz of immigration restrictions, the rapid multiplication of compulsory sterilization laws began with the scapegoating of "bad" women, as symbolized by an indigent white family. In 1920, a Virginia commission declared widow Emma Buck "feebleminded" after pressing her to divulge a history of prostitution charges and syphilis. She was involuntarily, permanently committed to a "Colony for Epileptics and Feebleminded," that is, a public trash heap for social outcasts. During her marriage, Emma had birthed a daughter, Carrie. Carrie was taken from her and placed with a middle-class foster family without any formal legal proceedings. In 1924, eugenicists selected the 18-year-old, single, pregnant Carrie as a test case for a new compulsory sterilization law. Carrie was herself decreed "feebleminded" and sent to the Colony. Carrie's baby Vivian was forcibly taken away at birth and placed with the same foster family—even though Carrie had conceived from a foster relative's rape! The test case, *Buck v. Bell*, went all the way to the U.S. Supreme Court, which ruled in favor of state compulsory sterilization laws, representing a *second* rape against Carrie. Judge Oliver Wendell Holmes, Jr., decreed, "Three generations of imbeciles are enough." Never mind that all three Bucks—including Vivian, before her death at eight of an infectious disease—actually were good students. Open season on disabled/dislabeled persons' reproductive organs ensued.

In 1979 and 1980, just a few years before her death, a Virginia disability rights activist and some journalists found the elderly Carrie Buck Metamora working as a housekeeper and tending her ill husband. It turned out that in 1928 her sister Doris Buck Figgins too was forcibly sterilized, under the ruse of an "appendectomy." Doris "broke down and cried" when she finally learned the truth: "My husband and me wanted children desperate—we were crazy about them." Carrie herself asserted: "They done me wrong. They done us all wrong." Although some states have apologized to victims of sterilization abuse, others have never removed the laws permitting it from the books.[8]

When sterilization abuse wasn't enough to "weed out the unfit," institutions could intentionally deny lifesaving medical treatment to inmates, even those far from the end stages of terminal illness—and institutions did. Edwin Black pointedly notes, "murder was always an option." Some eugenicists publicly rejected "the lethal chamber, the permission of infant mortality, interference with [pre]-natal life, and all other synonyms for murder." Others were quite smitten by the "lethal chamber," an 1880s invention for euthanizing animals with carbonic acid gas. The "lethal chamber" concept in eugenic discourse inspired the U.S. government to form the Chemical Warfare Service and the use of the gas chamber for executions, starting with a Chinese-born man in Nevada. If the state could dispose of its enemies and criminals, why not permit it to dispose of *all* the "unfit"?[9]

And if eugenic execution was desirable after birth, why not before? Dr. William Josephus Robinson recommended chloroform or potassium cyanide gas for the already-born "children of the unfit." He referred to the prenatal entity as merely "a few inanimate cells." Echoing the Marquis de Sade, he called abortion—which he performed himself—"cleaning out uteruses." In Robinson's view, the abortionist deserved gratitude for being a "real benefactor" who rescued young women and families from nonmarital pregnancies. Robinson evidently was not interested in discerning any value in those who questioned him. He dismissed antivivisectionists as "hard-hearted fanatics . . . deliberate prevaricators, and impudent ignoramuses, who deserve no consideration and are to be handled without gloves." Incidentally, most were outspoken feminist women whose love of animals was part of an overall aspiration to supplant cruelty with mercy.[10] As this book has already shown, that mercy embraced both the pregnant woman and the unborn child and thoroughly questioned the vilification of single mothers and their babies.

Socially respectable American eugenicists actively cooperated with and financially supported the government-based German movement, even after the full extent of Nazi atrocities was known—and they were never *unknown*, contrary to popular American belief. Following its humiliating defeat in World War I, Germany became increasingly obsessed with racial "health" and "purity." Even before coming to power, Adolf Hitler eagerly absorbed American eugenic ideas. U.S. anti-miscegenation laws inspired Nazi bans on sexual relationships and intermarriage between Jews and Aryans. Jews were even defined according to a "one drop" standard. The Nazis directly modeled their forcible sterilization of the "unfit" on American precedents, even as they forbade voluntary contraception and sterilization to healthy Aryans. Healthy Aryan women with nonmarital pregnancies were sent to the state-run *Lebensborn* facilities, which provided funds for childrearing or adoptive placements in certified Aryan families—not out of authentic respect for maternal and fetal lives, but out of a view that "racially pure" women had a public duty to breed. Abortion was not only legal for pregnant undesirables, and pressured on them by social circumstances, medical personnel quite directly forced it. Women with unapproved pregnancies eventually were gassed in the lethal chambers that the Nazis had perfected through the T4 euthanasia campaign. Capitalizing on the mass segregation of disabled persons, known as "useless eaters," into institutions, T4 began with lethal injections of children. The gas chamber was soon adopted as a more efficient, cost-effective means for eliminating 275,000 disabled persons of all ages, including World War I veterans. T4 methods and technology were then moved to the concentration camps and used to systematically kill nearly twelve million other "undesirables": Jews, Sinti and Roma ("Gypsies"), GLBT persons, Jehovah's Witnesses, pacifists, Communists, and other radicals. The Nazi government located many victims through unethical genealogy research modeled after the Eugenic Record Office's, using IBM data processing systems.[11]

Meanwhile, the U.S. federal government essentially ignored the citizenry's widespread, Depression-heightened desire for voluntary, pre-conception family limitation methods. During the 1930s, the government pushed for legalized contraceptives and rolled out a wide-scale program in only one place: Puerto Rico, whose impoverished, overcrowded residents had recently begun leaving for mainland cities. This program overrode the protests of both the Catholic Church and Puerto Rican nationalists like J. Enamorado Cuesta. The problem, he objected, was not a sheer excess of Puerto Ricans, but the American occupation's systematic robbery of their farmlands and food security. Cuesta did not oppose birth control *per se*; he simply wanted his people to decide their own fate, and was confident they would rally behind *voluntary* family limitation.[12] The occupation refused to listen. Indeed, the coercive Puerto Rican program served as a pilot for domestic and foreign population control measures to come. Puerto Riqueñas were guinea pigs for the original, unsafe hormonal contraceptives. By the early 1980s, 35% of Puerto Rican women had been surgically sterilized.[13]

It was no coincidence that a few American professionals began expressing an abortion rights position with the Great Depression. American and Western European leftists often romanticized the Soviet Union, which had legalized abortion in 1920, and some wondered if that particular measure should be duplicated elsewhere (see Pankhurst, Part One). In the absence and in lieu of adequate voluntary pregnancy prevention and maternal/child welfare services, not to mention a just and humane economic system, the violence of sterilization abuse had already become a sanctioned response to social problems. Some simply, understandably despaired over difficult-to-enforce antiabortion laws and continuing maternal deaths and injuries; others had far darker motives.

The Holocaust gave eugenics the bad name it should have had all along, but it did not disappear. To this day, it has simply taken other names and guises. For example, many eugenics organizations remade themselves into population control groups obsessed with cutting the numbers of certain oppressed social groups. Like any closed ecosystem, the Earth cannot support an endless number of living beings; thus her actual carrying capacity for humans and the role of voluntary pregnancy prevention in maintaining it are not matters to be dismissed, as some antiabortionists unfortunately do. However, population control organizations have traditionally failed to address the tremendous role of prosperous countries' overconsumption in degrading the environment and in perpetuating the deprivation of the targeted groups—preferring instead to lay the blame on poor women of color's fertility.[14]

It was no surprise that abortion openly, officially became a weapon in the population control arsenal. The wealthy Missouri industrialist Joseph Sunnen took it up following a 1957 visit to Puerto Rican *favelas*. His foundation boosted the legal and clinic-level agendas of the population control and abortion-rights movements. Particularly after 1966, abortion-rights supporters knew he would finance their cause. That year, nine California doctors went up before the state medical board for aborting rubella-infected women who had feared prenatal disabilities. Sunnen said he would pay their defense fees if they agreed to become a legal test case. They declined, but Sunnen soon got the chance to finance the legal efforts culminating in the 1973 *Roe v. Wade* ruling. His money then helped to found and sustain Reproductive Health Services in St. Louis, soon one of the Midwest's largest abortion providers.[15]

Public attitudes towards abortion had begun to shift in Sunnen's favor in the early 1960s when the births of disabled babies exposed *in utero* to rubella or thalidomide had stirred up revulsion towards "imperfect" humans. The cause of disability abortion even had its own media darling in Sherri Finkbine, who had unwittingly taken thalidomide while pregnant. Declined an abortion in the U.S., she traveled to Sweden for one. The doctors, discovering that her fetus indeed had the limb impairments associated with thalidomide exposure, told her not to think of "it" as a "baby" but "a growth."[16]

This was not the first time the very existence of "undesirable" humans— whether on the individual or mass scale—was perceived as some kind of horrific, out-of-control, cancerous disease process that had to be stopped promptly, aggressively, without question. Nor was it the last.

Mostly Missed Opportunities:
The Woman Movement and Irish Catholic America
(Mid-Nineteenth – Early Twentieth Centuries)

In the wake of An Gorta Mor, the Great Hunger of the 1840s, nearly two million Irish Catholics came to the U.S.: the original large wave of immigrants whose culture, religion, and material poverty the Protestant Anglo majority deemed alien and suspect. These refugees established many institutions of the U.S. Roman Catholic church—its parish buildings, religious orders, hospitals, and charities. Their descendants have remained a large, vital presence in American Catholicism and social justice movements ever since. The accumulated small donations of "ordinary" Irishers made these organizations possible. Among the most generous contributors were young women who immigrated—frequently by themselves—to labor as domestics in prosperous Yankee households. In an often hostile new country, they found strength in female-based social networks, enjoyed an unprecedented degree of economic independence, and behaved assertively in their own as well as others' interests. Even as they aspired to material prosperity, they fiercely sustained their Irish ways, including their identification with the dispossessed. Irishwomen like Mother Mary Jones, Elizabeth Gurley Flynn, Leonora O'Reilly, and unnamed thousands of others flocked to the labor movement.

With some notable exceptions like Flynn and O'Reilly, these progressive, independent-minded women kept a highly critical distance from the organized "woman movement." Why this distrust? The most visible, numerous feminists were well-off Anglo Saxon Protestants—many Irishwomen's employers. Too many of them publicly and privately derided Irishers as dirty, stupid, lazy, impractical, drunken, violent, recklessly reproductive, disloyal to America, and blindly submissive to Vatican dictates. No matter how much some of them professed to champion labor and Irish home rule, their obvious bigotry did not endear them to the women who cleaned their houses, cooked and served their meals, and sewed their lavish textiles. Thus any shared gender concerns went by the wayside. Nor did it help that Irishmen were as prone as any to the ancient, slanderous equation of female liberation with the unleashing of destructive forces. Irish men feared that their women would completely betray their culture and religion. Just like reactionary Anglo Saxon Protestant men, they equated female independence and feminism with abortion. While treasuring their independence, Irishwomen, too, concluded—inaccurately—that the woman movement sought "the slaughter of the unborn innocents."[1] Perhaps this was because of whispered secrets in their employers' families, along with the enduring custom of throwing out domestics "guilty" of nonmarital pregnancy, and the heartbreaking levels of induced abortion among underpaid, overworked laborers and their families.

In a Protestant, Anglo-dominant country, Irish Catholics of both sexes drew much of their identity and sustenance from their religion. This does not mean their stance on abortion was exclusively sectarian. Another source was the collective experience of oppression in the new country and in the old. An Gorta Mor (Irish, "The Great Hunger," known popularly as the "Potato Famine") which killed or drove into exile a third of Ireland's population, was a genocide inflicted by the English occupation, not purely a natural disaster. Irishers knew this long before late twentieth-century academic historians marshaled and argued the evidence.[2] The dispossession of the unborn child—and frequently of the mother—thus resonated deeply with them. For example, the New York Foundling Hospital, created by Sister Irene Fitzgibbon and run by her order, Saint Elizabeth Ann Seton's Sisters of Charity, offered maternity as well as children's services. Donation drives among Irish Catholic women raised large sums for this agency. They understood the poverty, desperation, prejudice, and exploitation that could make pregnancy and mothering feel like an unbearable nightmare, especially for single women. This letter of December 1, 1875 was pinned to a three-week-old baby girl entrusted to the nuns' care.

> Dear Sister,
>   Alone and deserted, I need to put my little one with you for a time. I would willingly work and take care of her but no one will have me and her too. All say they would take me if she was 2 or 3 years old, so not knowing what to do with her and not being able to pay her board, I bring her to you knowing you will be as kind to her as to the many others who are under your care, and I will get work and try hard to be able to relieve you of the care when I can take her to work with me . . . No one knows how awful it is to separate from their child but a mother, but, I trust you will be kind and the only

consolation I have is if I am spared and nothing prevents and I lead
an honest life that the Father of us all will permit us to be united.

A Mother[3]

Irish Catholics already felt so alienated from Anglo Saxon Protestants,
they did not on any wide scale engage with the woman movement's shared
opposition to abortion and creation of lifesaving options. They might,
however, have been able to find common ground with at least one feminist
contingent: the women who started the early twentieth-century movement
to legalize contraceptive education and access. These birth control activists
were primarily working-class, labor-oriented, often socialist and/or Jewish
women who argued and organized for voluntary birth control as part of a
woman's multifaceted right, whatever her socioeconomic status, to secure
her own life and well-being and protect her children's. Like many Irish
Catholic women, this group sought to alleviate women's reproductive
miseries and the social and economic conditions that gave rise to them.
Emma Goldman became an impassioned birth control advocate because of
her midwifery among Irish and Jewish tenement dwellers, who desperately
inflicted abortion on themselves: "[W]hat fantastic methods despair could
invent: jumping off tables . . . drinking nauseating concoctions, and using
blunt instruments, generally with great injury . . ."[4]

Unfortunately, any window of opportunity for dialogue was abruptly
shut. The wealthy, heavily Yankee, male-dominant eugenics establishment
rapidly co-opted the birth control movement, reframing "undesirable" human
beings rather than social conditions as the problem.[5] One person involved
in this shift was Margaret Sanger, nee Higgins. She must have appeared the
embodiment of Irishmen's fears about independent-minded, upwardly mobile
Irishwomen turning on their heritage. Her immigrant father was an indigent,
freethinking stonecutter; her second-generation mother a TB-afflicted
Catholic housewife who died young after eleven live births and seven
miscarriages. Sanger was moved to get an education, work as a nurse in
New York City's poor immigrant neighborhoods, and become involved in
the socialist, feminist, and birth control movements. She awoke to women's
need for legal sex education and pregnancy prevention when her patient
Sadie Sachs died from yet another abortion. Sanger bore witness also to the
regular Saturday-night "groups of from fifty to one hundred with their shawls
over their heads waiting" for the "five dollar abortionist."[6] Like others
who sought to heal the reproductive sufferings so unnecessarily imposed
on women, Sanger saw maternity as a sacred process that should not be
desecrated: "Birth to me has always been more awe-inspiring than death.

As often as I have witnessed the miracle, held the perfect creature with its tiny hands and tiny feet, each time I have felt as though I were entering a cathedral with prayer in my heart."[7] Sanger too sought a better way than abortion, "an abhorrent operation which kills the tenderness and delicacy of womanhood, even as it may injure or kill the body."[8] She lamented "the most barbaric methods" of family limitation, namely "the killing of babies— infanticide—abortion."[9] However, with her rise in the birth control movement, she sought out wealthy eugenicists for funding and began to sound more and more like them. The feminist-sounding assertions about reproductive self-determination in Sanger's books *The Pivot of Civilization* (1922) and *Woman and the New Race* (1920) are overwhelmed by eugenic, victim-blaming disregard for the reproductive and other human rights and needs of the poor, immigrants, racial/ethnic minorities, disabled persons, parents with a preference for large families, and unplanned children.

According to her granddaughter, Sanger always was ashamed of her background; she felt she "made it" only after gaining entrée to wealthy Anglo circles.[10] She downplayed her history of ties to anyone poor, immigrant, non-Anglo, or radical (a word sometimes used to mean "disreputable" or as derogatory code for "Jewish"). Sanger spoke as if she were the first ever to defend birth control, as if Emma Goldman had never mentored her.[11] She made short shrift of Dr. Aletta Jacobs, a Jewish woman, who founded the world's first birth control clinic in Holland and taught her about the diaphragm she introduced into her own clinics.[12] According to Kathleen Tobin, Sanger trumpeted pro-birth control sentiment from Protestant clergy, while saying curiously little about Jewish activism, even when Reform Judaism became the first American religious body to doctrinally accept contraception (1927).[13] If this was how Sanger treated non-Anglos who *agreed* with her about legalizing contraception (though not always for quite the same reasons), her open hostility towards Roman Catholics, especially the predominantly Irish hierarchy, should be no surprise. Contraception was a matter of debate within, across, and among *many* religious denominations, but Catholicism hit too close to home for Sanger. Not only did it have a more evident, vocal anti-contraception tradition than some other faiths, Catholicism had been the religion of Sanger's tubercular mother, whose frequent pregnancies contributed to her early death. Although the animosity went both ways, Sanger baited Catholics with Anglo stereotypes of them, thus doing her part to close off any opportunities for dialogue. In fact, she encouraged birth control advocates to target and antagonize Catholics as "the enemy," a strategy appealing to nativists, who feared that Catholic hordes would outnumber them. By contrast, the Yankee

Congregationalist Mary Ware Dennett respectfully encouraged Catholics to frame the birth control issue as one of according others the same freedoms of speech and religion they wished for themselves.[14]

Many Catholic contraception opponents did agree with Sanger and Dennett that preventing a new life was not the same as interrupting a life already begun. Such Catholics often advocated voluntary family limitation through celibacy within marriage.[15] Irishers already had their own customs that in effect prevented some pregnancies: comparatively late marriages and extended family structures with places for lifelong bachelor uncles, aunts, and cousins, as well as relatives who were priests, brothers, and nuns. Another culturally and religiously compatible method became available during the Great Depression, after Kyusaku Ogino of Japan and Hermann Knaus of Germany separately and accurately sequenced the female cycle's fertile and infertile phases. Chicago physician Leo Latz energetically publicized the Ogino-Knaus findings to eager lay Catholics as "natural birth control" or "the rhythm." One of Latz's motives was to prevent *both* fetal and maternal deaths through abortion, which he attributed to female disempowerment, not degeneracy: "[U]nless we are confirmed pessimists, we must hold that every last woman from whom the fruit of her womb was criminally removed would a thousand times rather not have that occur." After some controversy, including Latz's dismissal as a Loyola medical school professor, church officials began deferring to the laity's enthusiasm for the rhythm. As Kathleen Tobin observes, "No denomination recommended incessant childbearing, especially in a condition of poverty. Rather, the conflict centered primarily on the method of preventing pregnancy."[16]

At least one birth control advocate, Carl G. Harman, praised Latz's effort to educate Catholic laity, concluding that the rhythm was, "if followed closely," almost as effective as methods used in contraceptive clinics.[17] Sanger testified before Congress: "If I picked up that book and read it and believed as a Catholic . . . I would follow it to the letter." Feminist voluntary motherhood ideas had not only worked their way into supposedly hostile territory; Catholics had already aspired towards their own means of family planning. Unfortunately, Sanger's recognition of possible common ground with Catholics over the rhythm never went any farther; indeed, she mocked it. To keep her "establishment" support, she sought for family planning to be more in the hands of doctors than women. She thus objected to the rhythm's largely "do-it-yourself" character. She also found it expedient to keep portraying Catholics as enemies of progress; never mind that many Catholics were much closer to the street-level feminist empathy for everywoman that she had shed for the sake of "respectability," and that so many members of the Anglo ruling class had never had to begin with.[18] So many opportunities for respectful dialogue and cooperative action between the American woman movement and the majority of Irish (and other) Catholics had already been missed for decades. The consequences endure into the present.

The Nonviolent Power of the Maternal Body Politic: Jane Addams (1860-1935) and Hull House (founded 1889)

Jane Addams' astoundingly fruitful life included a Nobel Peace Prize—the first ever to an American woman—and founding or early leadership roles in the professions of sociology and social work, the Women's International League for Peace and Freedom, American Civil Liberties Union, National Association for the Advancement of Colored People, and National American Woman Suffrage Association. She was the guiding spirit of Hull House, Chicago's globally famous settlement.[1] The settlement house movement fostered mutual understanding, artistic pursuits, and cooperative social action among urban dwellers of diverse ethnicities, classes, and religions. Some conservative Christians objected that settlements were "secular" or "anti-religious" because they did not proselytize. Addams pointed to the basic value of settlements: "one of the tenets of all the great ethnic religions . . . the permanent dignity and value of human life" (a tenet of many freethinkers, too).[2]

Hull House originated partly in Addams' life crisis as a young woman. She came from the north-central Illinois town of Cedarville. Her father was a prosperous miller and state legislator whose Quaker background shaped his abolitionist, pro-feminist stances and his preference for a spirituality that "upheld universal mystery and personal morals over particular dogmas or creeds."[3] When Jane was two, her mother died of pregnancy complications. At six, Jane lost an elder sister to typhoid fever. At eight, she gained a stepmother and two stepbrothers. Under her stepmother's doting influence, Jane cultivated her enduring love for aesthetic accomplishments. Her father shaped her early interest in history and politics. Addams attended Rockford (IL) Female Seminary (now Rockford College). She was bewildered to be perceived as a charismatic, popular leader, even as she resisted the institution's calls to evangelical conversion and domesticity or missionary work. Here too she met her close friend Ellen Gates Starr.[4]

Addams briefly attended the Women's Medical College of Pennsylvania until her father's death, family responsibilities, and a disabling back condition intervened. Addams grew deeply depressed until 1888 when she and Starr visited the world's first settlement house, Toynbee Hall, in London's East End. They decided to found a similar institution in Chicago and align it with the city's well-established circle of female reformers, clubwomen, and philanthropists. From its experimental, tenuous beginnings, Hull House became a wellspring for practically every Progressive-Era social justice movement and a vigorously empowering, woman-centered space. Men were welcomed and valued in the work of Hull House, even as its heart was formed from close friendships among some remarkable women, including Addams; her life partner, the quietly generous philanthropist Mary Rozet Smith; physician Alice Hamilton; and social worker and reformer Julia Lathrop. Addams led Hull House until her death, just one year after Smith's.[5]

Addams skillfully melded "feminine" compassion and "masculine" science in addressing social problems. Though she found the theory of evolution persuasive as biology, Addams could never accept *Social* Darwinism. As Jean Bethke Elshtain notes, Addams "glimpsed . . . a form of power that doesn't have as its means violence and doesn't have as its end total control and command." Her vision of the body politic was not the classical king's dominion, but "the maternal female body" as "the central image of social generativity and fecundity." This was not a demand for compulsory biological motherhood, but an invitation to community-building fruitfulness of all kinds.[6] This image of the body politic may explain Addams' responses to abortion, infanticide and other disability-related discrimination, cruelty to single mothers, the death penalty, war, and any other use of violence to "resolve" social problems.

Around the turn of the twentieth century, death penalty proponents argued for electrocution as a supposedly instantaneous, painless, humane alternative to hanging. Electrical shock had already been used as an abortion technique, as it is today in Chinese-occupied Tibet (Stockham, Part One; Introduction, Part Two). This pro-death penalty argument rationalized a major U.S. electric company's drive to upstage its main competitor. Despite his professed personal opposition to the death penalty, Thomas Edison oversaw the invention of the electric chair for Westinghouse, selling the press on it by lethally shocking dogs and cats. In 1903, he filmed his electrocution, billed as an "execution," of Topsy, a Coney Island elephant, before a crowd of 1500. The neglected, abused animal had rampaged and killed three men, including a trainer who deliberately threw a lit cigarette into her mouth. The same year, a Michigan legislator and businessman proposed electrocution upon birth for disabled babies—as an amendment to the budget for the state's home for the "feebleminded." Addams, a death penalty abolitionist, responded:

> The suggestion is horrible. It is not in line with the march of civilization nor with the principles of humanity. The Spartans destroyed children physically infirm. Are we to go back to the days of Sparta? Feeble-minded children are one of the cares of a community. It is our duty to care for them.[7]

She would reiterate this position with the 1915 killing of a disabled baby, Allan Bollinger (see Lathrop and Hamilton, Part One). The perpetrator and other male critics denounced her stance as irrational, "false and sickly sentiment"—that age-old strategy to dismiss women's cries for justice.[8]

Against the growing push for permanent mass institutionalization, Addams argued for what the disability rights movement now calls independent living. She saw disabled persons as a normal, expectable part of the human spectrum, entitled as anyone to grow up in their own families and communities, with the public supports and accommodations—in education and work training, for example—they needed to realize their potentials. Above all, it was necessary to "consider the problem of the special child . . . from the point of view of the child," or, as present-day disability advocates would say, "Nothing about us, without us." To overwhelmed parents, Addams offered,

> You think you have a child unlike other children; you are anxious that your neighbor not find it out; it makes you secretive; it makes you singularly sensitive; it places you and the normal children in your family in a curious relation to the rest of the community; but if you find out there are many other such children in your city and in . . . the United States, and that a whole concourse of people are studying to help these children, considering them not at all queer and outrageous, but simply a time of child which occurs from time to time and can be enormously helped, you come out of that particularly sensitive attitude and the whole family is lifted with you into a surprising degree of hopefulness and normality.[9]

In 1908, Hull House and the Chicago Medical Society (CMS) formed the Joint Committee on Midwives: Doctors Rudolph W. Holmes, Charles Sumner Bacon, Caroline Hedger, and Alice Hamilton; the Visiting Nurses Association; and public health nurse F. Elizabeth Crowell. Previously, as heads of the CMS Committee on Criminal Abortion, Holmes and Bacon had assisted public officials in prosecuting those who performed "the crime of feticide," temporarily persuaded newspapers to ban "criminal advertisements," and discovered "the relatively great frequency of the crime of abortion among midwives; at the same time . . . the deficiency of these practitioners in learning and ability . . ." The midwifery committee was charged to explore these problems further with Hull House promising "to defray all cost." Jane Addams' commitment of Hull House's hard-won, always precarious funds evinced her personal support of the study's goals. With contentious issues, Addams had an admirable skill for taking action yet keeping herself in the background so that things could simply get done without public uproar getting in the way.

The midwifery committee did not categorically oppose the existence of midwives or seek to drive them out of business. They recognized immigrants' marked preference of midwives over physicians. Forty-seven percent of reported Chicago births at that time—mostly among German, Slavic, and Italian immigrants—were midwife-attended. The committee did seek improved midwifery education/training requirements and deterrence of "feticide" in any profession, including medicine. They found that diplomas from European training programs correlated with skillful practice. Many American midwifery schools, however, were

> veritable diploma mills run for revenue only, usually by some conscienceless physician who receives lucrative returns for a minimum outlay of time and trouble. In the majority of cases, the woman who takes such a course does so in entirely good faith . . . One physician, whose school seems to be well-patronized . . . offered for an additional fee to instruct the supposed candidate privately as to the *modus operandi* of successful abortion work, assuring her that it would bring in large returns, that it was a perfectly safe business and that the midwives who were caught were fools . . . [T]he school of midwifery also seems to have been a school of crime . . . [10]

The Committee observed that members of other, male-dominated occupations, especially medicine and pharmacy, were involved in abortion. Some midwives had standing arrangements to refer abortion seekers to particular doctors, whom, the Committee noted, "were willing to prostitute their profession." Some midwives called certain physicians into their unlicensed "abortion shops" or "lying-in hospitals" to falsify death certificates as needed. Yet only a third of the study sample evidenced any involvement in abortion work, meaning that two-thirds were probably *not* engaged in "feticide," contrary to an ancient stereotype about midwives.

The committee further observed,

> [T]he practice of abortion in the United States . . . is no longer regarded as a crime, rather as a perfectly justifiable, even laudable method of limiting the increase in population. And yet the law recognizes the right of the unborn child to life and to property, and endeavours to safeguard these rights by making criminal abortion a felony. In addition . . . many abortions are self-induced . . . [sometimes] because the pressure of economic conditions is so great that the possibility of one more mouth to feed becomes a tragedy to be averted at any cost. We have the testimony of many a poor tenement-house mother to support this last assertion . . . When such interference [with Nature] creates a pathologic condition which renders the patient peculiarly liable to infection we have an added danger the seriousness of which can not be overestimated. Unfortunately, actual statistics of disease and death . . . can never be written.[11]

The midwifery investigation occasioned a public uproar whose exact nature awaits further research. Addams simply asked, "Were these oppositions so unexpected and so unlooked for merely a reminder of that old bit of wisdom that 'there is no guarding against interpretations'?"[12] Did Holmes touch upon one possible reason for the uproar when he lamented most doctors' lack of interest in challenging abortion? "It is not possible to get twelve men together without at least one of them being personally responsible for the down fall of a girl, or at least interested in getting her out of her difficulty."[13] In the decades following the investigation, Addams and all four committee physicians dedicated themselves even more deeply to the very social measures that got at the root causes of abortion. (See also Hedger and Hamilton, Part One.) Bacon had already called for abundant "obstetrical asylums," safe houses for pregnant women.[14] Bacon and Holmes insisted on sex education and contraception and served as medical advisors to the Illinois Birth Control League, which became Illinois Planned Parenthood, an organization that probably maintained its founders' general opposition to abortion "rights" until the 1960s. In addition to its day nursery, infant care clinic, mothers' club, and other maternal-child programs, Jane Addams involved Hull House in sex education and the direct provision of family planning.[15] For her international readership, Addams wrote more than once of the need, at the personal and policy levels, for compassionate acceptance and aid of all those involved in nonmarital pregnancy.[16]

Concern with crisis pregnancy spanned Addams' entire tenure at Hull House. During the first, highly improvisational year, Addams and Julia Lathrop were surprised with an initiation into midwifery.

> [A] young woman rushed through the door quite breathlessly to tell us that a girl in her tenement house was having a baby all by herself; she was "hollering something fierce; my mother says it is disgracing the whole house she is!" . . . [N]one of the women would go into help because the girl wasn't married and anyway none of them would call the doctor because the girl had no money . . . [and the women were] afraid to be the one who paid him . . . There seemed nothing for it but to go ourselves . . . We found the poor girl alone in her agony . . .

By the time another Hull House resident had summoned a sympathetic doctor and the girl's mother arrived home from work, Addams and Lathrop were cleaning the girl's bed and bathing her new son. The girl gratefully named Julius John in his midwives's honor. Sadly, at only four months, the baby died. Near the end of her own life, Addams described his birth.

> I vividly recall through the distance of forty-five years that as we walked back . . . stirred as we were by the mystery of birth . . . I exclaimed: "This doing things that we don't know how to do is going too far. Why did we let ourselves be rushed into midwifery?" . . . [Julia Lathrop answered:] "To refuse to respond to a poor girl in the throes of childbirth would be a disgrace to us forevermore. If Hull House does not have its roots in human kindness, it is no good at all." [17]

Addams had long been impressed with the power, richness, and moral imaginativeness of women's visceral recollections—that is, "heart-histories"—to enlarge human kindness past customary bounds. In *The Long Road of Woman's Memory* (1916), she observed,

> [T]hose individual reminiscences which, because they force the possessor to challenge existing conventions, act as a reproach, even as a social disturber. When these reminiscences, based upon the diverse experiences of many people unknown to each other, point to one inevitable conclusion, they accumulate into a social protest . . . Such searching and sifting is taking place in the consciences of many women of this generation whose sufferings, although strikingly influencing conduct, are seldom expressed in words until they are told in the form of reminiscence after the edges have been long since dulled. Such

sufferings are never so poignant as when women have been forced by their personal experiences to challenge the valuable conventions safeguarding family life.

Addams felt that the woman movement's success "in the direction of a larger justice has come through an overwhelming desire to cherish both the illegitimate child and his unfortunate mother." This desire arose when "respectable" women, often through personal trials, realized that laws and customs which disadvantaged and punished "harlots" and their children constrained all women and children. Addams dared to hope that

> Maternal affection and solicitude, in woman's remembering heart, may at length coalesce into a chivalric protection for all that is young and unguarded. This chivalry of women expressing protection for those at the bottom of society, so far as it has already developed, suggests a return to that idealized version of chivalry which was the consecration of strength to the defense of weakness, unlike the actual chivalry of the armed knight who served his lady with gentle courtesy while his fields were ploughed by peasant women misshapen through toil and hunger . . . [18]

Addams' vision of the maternal body politic, with its "form of power that doesn't have as its means violence and doesn't have as its end total control and command," remains one that could bring peace to the abortion war today, with its forced and lethal pitting of disempowered women against their own unborn children, not to mention other, related wars.

Frances E. Willard (1839-1896) and the Anchorage Mission (founded 1886)

A century after Mary Wollstonecraft was shunned and ridiculed for giving life to her daughter Fanny, single pregnant women continued to be socially stigmatized, denied community support, and criminally prosecuted for lewd conduct, fornication, or adultery. If they dared to claim child support, they ran the serious risk of being branded sex offenders. Often their only other economic recourse was prostitution. Under the double standard's continuing reign, their children's fathers more often than not could deny responsibility. Many "strong-minded" women in addition to Susan B. Anthony, Sister Irene Fitzgibbon, Sarah Hackett Stevenson, and Harriet Rice knew of the strong ethical responsibility to offer single pregnant mothers and their children aid. As the director of one women's refuge noted, it was literally a matter of life and death.

> A large number of those who come to us . . . are with child. They come in deep distress, not knowing which way to turn for help . . . How can we turn them away? Those suffering ones appeal to our mercy. If we do [turn them away], suicide or infanticide, a seared conscience and a downward course ending in a whirlpool of despair, is the almost certain result.[1]

Not only Catholic but Jewish and Protestant women and their charitable groups offered aid to overburdened single (and sometimes married) mothers. In her Mississippi River hometown of Quincy, Illinois, Dr. Sarah Vasen (later Frank, 1870-1944), supervised the obstetrical ward at the multidenominational Blessing Hospital, the only local facility welcoming unwed mothers. She later worked at Philadelphia's Jewish Maternity Home, founded and run by Ezrath Nashim (Hebrew, "Help of Women"). Then Vasen devoted her Los Angeles practice to maternity cases, treating poor women referred by the Hebrew Benevolent Society for free and (even more unusually) saving the life of a premature 2.5 pound baby.[2]

Among the most visible maternity aid groups was the evangelical Protestant Women's Christian Temperance Union, then the largest, most effective force for suffrage. As previously noted, many early feminists connected temperance to women's rights because they saw how frequently alcohol use led men to rape, other domestic violence, child abuse, financial irresponsibility, and abandonment of their families. Maternity homes like the WCTU's were conscious attempts to offer women both an alternative to abortion and relief for the stigma of single motherhood. Unlike Ireland's infamous Magdalen laundries, these institutions were not intended to be degrading lifetime prisons. The WCTU had already established a "Social Purity" campaign that worked for legislation to raise the age at which girls could legally consent to sex (as low as seven in one state), to prosecute rapists and customers of prostitutes, and fight child abuse. Then a wealthy New York businessman and evangelist, Charles Crittenton, gave the campaign an endowment to administer the Florence Crittenton Rescue Homes, named for his daughter who died of scarlet fever at age three.[3]

The Anchorage Mission, founded in 1886, became Crittenton's Chicago affiliate. It reached out to young single women who flocked to the city in search of a living, only to discover they had few economic opportunities other than prostitution, and that they were vulnerable to undesired pregnancies. The Anchorage offered a place to live, spiritual and emotional support, and practical job training. The Anchorage accepted women of diverse ethnic backgrounds—with the unjust exception of African Americans, who in the Crittenton system often lived with foster families or in boarding houses, rather than the central maternity home. African Africans also had their own charities, such as the National Association for the Relief of Destitute Colored Women and Children Home in Washington, D.C., where Rebecca Cole served as matron for a time. Another drawback was that the Anchorage and other maternity homes served particular "social control" purposes that residents sometimes quite justifiably experienced as being at cross purposes to their own interests and preferences. For example, staff in some Christian maternity homes had an agenda of religious conversion. At the same time, many residents resorted to and valued these facilities primarily as places where warmly concerned (if in some respects intrusive) staff offered them a temporary respite from their tremendous struggle to survive. In this sense the homes did indeed fulfill their intention of empowering women through alternatives to abortion.[4]

The WCTU and its maternity homes came to their heyday through the capable leadership of Frances E. Willard. Unfortunately, Willard tangled with Matilda Joslyn Gage over the issue of the separation of church and state, and with Ida B. Wells-Barnett over race. A Christian socialist and a vegetarian, she served as president of the Northwestern University Ladies' College in Evanston, Illinois; published a vocational guidance manual for the growing number of female college graduates; coedited the biographical encyclopedia *Woman of the Century*; interpreted the Christian Bible to contend that women deserved equal places in the ministry and church government; and wrote a delightful short book about her adventures learning to ride a bicycle, which "ladies" were not supposed to do.[5] And she fully supported the work of the Anchorage, which did, on balance, represent an advance in attitudes towards single mothers and their children.

Until after World War II, U.S. maternity homes typically discouraged adoption. Instead they sought, as the National Council of Jewish Women's Lakeview Home on Staten Island initially did, to provide a shelter for "a girl with her baby . . . where her mother love and responsibility would be awakened, where a strong moral influence would be at work, and where she could be trained industrially to make her future earning capacity meet her needs and likewise support her child."[6] But the choice between parenting and adoption belonged ethically to the pregnant woman (and still does, of course). On the other hand, this widespread philosophy quite radically recognized single mothers and their children as genuine families and tacitly recognized the loss inherent in any adoption, no matter how "successful" for all involved parties. Overall it may have more closely approximated residents' own preferences and psychosocial needs than the widespread post-WWII maternity home policy Rickie Solinger terms "the adoption mandate": the use of shaming pressure tactics to make unwilling women relinquish healthy white babies to anonymous closed adoption arrangements in which they had no say. They were then told to forget about their own flesh and blood and move on with their lives. Adoptees and adoptive families were pressured to continue the shame and secrecy by pretending that they were identical to biological ones. The adoption mandate had a flip side: children of color and disabled children were largely deemed "unadoptable" and their mothers irredeemably bad or deviant by definition, and therefore undeserving of assistance with either parenting or adoption.[7]

The complex herstory gone awry of maternity homes holds both encouragements and warnings for those who wish to aid pregnant women today. We decidedly do *not* call for a return to the sort of facility and overall cultural ethos that terrorized abortion-rights scholar/activist Rosalind Pollack Petchesky during her youth.

> The local home for unwed mothers was as shrouded in horror and hysteria as an asylum or leper colony . . . It drew my fascination by the lifelessness outside its walls and the miserable types I imagined must dwell within. The windows always seemed closed . . . Stories of unknown origin . . . circulated in our high school about a hatchet-wielding killer named "Sparky," a crazy man . . . in search of innocent girls or couples who parked on deserted roads to hack to pieces . . . Somehow the two symbols of lost innocence and the terrors of sex . . . became closely connected in the dark shadows of my mind.[8]

Consciously or not, today's woman-run prolife pregnancy centers often, in a modernized form, revive the essentially compassionate purpose early feminist aid efforts had before their takeover by abusive social agendas. Petchesky's terror over the local maternity home, so long after the feminist intent of these facilities had been discarded and forgotten, serves as a cautionary tale against imposing such agendas on young women in need.

A Plea for the Forgotten
by Frances Willard

To the Union Signal: I have this week visited the Florence Crittenton Anchorage for Girls, on Wabash Avenue, founded some years ago by the Central WCTU.

I found these thirty-five women, some of them pitifully young, and twelve with babes in their arms. It was a sight to make careless hearts thoughtful and steady eyes dim. The poor child who was deceived, betrayed, and robbed a few days ago by the man she trusted, and who tried to take her young life, was there. At last she had found those whom she could trust, and who told her they would do all in their power to help her build her wrecked young life anew on the foundations of industry, purity, and honor.

Some of us talked to these forgotten ones as helpfully and kindly as we could, and then they spoke to us with tears, of their gratitude for a home so friendly and mother-hearts so sheltering . . .

. . . I make this plea [for funds] because I feel sure that there are a sufficient number of good and true women and men to pay this sum for these deceived and defrauded ones, if only the facts are brought to their knowledge . . . Let us remember our sisters who are "in bonds, as bound with them" . . .

—*The Union Signal*, 28 November 1895, the Official Publication of the National Woman's Christian Temperance Union, Evanston, Illinois.

"Women Helping Women"
by the staff of the Anchorage Mission[9]

Another busy year at the Anchorage has passed, the Home has been filled to its utmost capacity during the entire year and we have been unable to care for all who have sought its protection.

As we come to review the work of the year we feel assured that a large measure of success has attended our labors, as we have sought to help those wronged, unfortunate and deserted girls. Many of them have gone into the world again and are making good. They are supporting not only themselves but their little ones, and are living honorable, upright lives.

When these girls come to us in their hour of perplexity and sorrow, their first thought is to find a place of refuge for themselves and when the little ones come to give them away, never thinking it would be possible to keep and care for them. And while the doors of the Home are ever open to all girls in need . . . they are taught not to shirk the responsibility of motherhood and are encouraged to keep their babies and care for them.

One of the mothers who is making a brave fight for herself and her little one, writes: "I think we at least owe it to our children to keep them; poor, little innocents! They had nothing to say about coming into the world. My boy has given me a purpose in life and keeps me good." And what is true of this mother is true of many others, the influence of the little ones on their lives to keep them good.

The nursery—the brightest, sunniest room in the Home, filled with little folks, is the center of interest. While this room is in charge of two of the mothers who take turns in day and night duty, each mother is given the care of her child and is instructed how to properly care for it, and is taught that she is the one responsible for its welfare.

As all of these mothers are assigned to various tasks in the Home, they are impressed with the fact that while babies must not be neglected, yet they must so arrange the care of the child and the work, that they will not conflict.

As many of them go to housework with the babies this training is of the greatest value to them.

Several times each week the nursery is visited by a physician to see that all is well . . .

During the year ninety-five girls, representing seventeen nationalities have been cared for; among the number one Chinese and two Greek girls. Any intelligent person can imagine some of the difficulties where there is such dissimilarities of birth, education, and character and the difficulty in securing work and homes for them.

Many of those whom we welcome to our Home are in dire poverty, destitute of proper clothing. This need has been most generously supplied by donations from the following groups:

The Needle Work Guild of America, Chicago Branch;
The Needle Work Guild of America, Oak Park Branch;
Ladies' Aid Society, First Baptist Church, Oak Park;
Ladies' Aid Society, Trinity M.E. Church. Chicago;
Ladies' Aid Society, Friends' Church, Chicago;
King's Daughters, Harvard Cong. Church, Oak Park;
Byron Conclave No. 8, Chicago.

... As we have in our State a law compelling the father of a child born outside of lawful wedlock to provide for the partial support of the child for a period of ten years, by the payment of one hundred dollars the first year and fifty dollars a year for the nine succeeding years, making a total of five hundred and fifty dollars, we urge every mother to prosecute the man who is the father of her child and will assist her in every way with the prosecution. The Court of Domestic Relations provides for the prosecution of these cases without expense to the mother...

When the time comes for the girls to leave the Home and find their places in the world again, sincere regret is manifested at the thought of leaving, and we hear many expressions such as: "This is like leaving your own home;" and "I never had such a good home as this;" and another says: "I do not know what I would have done if I hadn't heard of this Home."

Those who remain in the city are constant visitors and from those who leave the city we are constantly receiving letters expressing their gratitude for what they received at the Home and for the way in which they had been helped to make a new start in life.

A very large number of girls have been returned to their relatives; some have resumed their former occupations; for others we have found homes with their babies. Eight have been married.

Through a friendly interest in each girl and by various methods employed we have been enabled to keep in touch with seventy per cent of those cared for during the year, and know that the greater number are making good.

—From *Thirtieth Annual Report of the Florence Crittenton Anchorage, 1886-1916*, Chicago: Florence Crittenton Anchorage Mission, 1916, 101-103, Courtesy of the Chicago Historical Society.

A Businesswoman's World-Mending Invention (Early 1900s)

During the late nineteenth and early twentieth centuries, even married pregnant women were pressured into "confinement": hiding themselves from public view once visibly with child. Victoria Woodhull protested:

> To bear a child is the most sacred and honorable work on Earth. The pregnant woman is a coworker with God . . . Whoever makes so noble a deed a theme of vulgarity only proclaims the foulness of his own base nature. Mothers themselves are ashamed when they ought to be proudest.[1]

"Confinement" had never been economically feasible for working class women, and now more middle—and upper-class women were regularly venturing out for paid or volunteer work. If women wore clothing that publicly revealed their condition, they would be harassed and ostracized. Yet available fashions were often excruciating even for the nonpregnant. The Haudenosaunee and feminist dress reform lessons about comfortable, healthy clothing had not been learned. Then an imaginative, socially conscious businesswoman came up with a solution.

In 1895, Lena Himmelstein, a sixteen-year-old Lithuanian Jew, emigrated to New York City and found work in the garment industry. She proved such an accomplished seamstress that her wages quickly increased from one dollar per week to the unheard-of sum of fifteen dollars per week. She married and had a child with a Russian Jewish immigrant jeweler named David Bryant but was widowed not long after the baby's arrival. A bank teller misspelled her first name as Lane, and the error stuck. She created and sold bridal wear and lingerie from her own store. Its attached apartment enabled her to care for her son while she worked. When a pregnant client asked for "presentable but comfortable" clothing, Lane Bryant skillfully obliged. Immediately, demand for the new maternity garment grew through customer word of mouth.

In 1909, Lane Bryant and Albert Malsin became marital and business partners. She would have two more children with him. In 1911 the couple finally persuaded a newspaper that running a maternity wear ad was not "indecent." The business rapidly expanded into mail order and catalog sales of maternity clothes. The catalog juxtaposed a woman shut up at home with another in glamorous dress, walking carefree down a city street. Reassuring her that Lane Bryant would help her do the right thing, it asked the "dear mother" to choose, for her own and her baby's health, which picture she would be in. Lane Bryant, Inc., rapidly grew into one of the American clothing industry's leading mail order firms and retail chains. Its founder led the company until her death in 1951, and the business remained in family hands until the 1970s.

Lane Himmelstein Bryant Malsin pioneered in mail order sales, niche marketing, and employee benefits like disability, health, and life insurance, profit-sharing, and a pension plan. Her stores ran clothing drives for impoverished Europeans following World War II. She donated generously to charities like the Hebrew Immigrant Aid Society. We do not know what she thought of feminism or abortion. But through her innovation of comfortable, affordable, readymade maternity wear, she certainly helped to make the culture more hospitable to pregnant women. Today thousands of predominantly Christian crisis pregnancy center workers regularly sew, collect, sort, and distribute maternity clothes. They do not realize their indebtedness to a Jewish single immigrant mother's determination to exercise her gifts at sewing and entrepreneurship, support herself and her child, and help others, in accordance with her religion's ethical responsibility of *tikkun olam*—Hebrew for "mending the world."[2]

Dr. Caroline Hedger (1868-1951)

Braceville, Ohio, native Caroline O. Hedger attended Berea and Wellesley Colleges, trained as a nurse, and earned medical degrees from Northwestern and Rush. She tirelessly advocated for the Polish and other immigrant workers in the Chicago Stockyards, people like the anonymous pregnant barrel hauler and striker on the cover of this book. Stockyards owner Phillip Armour fancied himself as a generous provider of jobs, inexpensive, speedily and efficiently mass-produced meat, and charitable endowments to edifying Sunday schools, while refusing to acknowledge the consequences of his untrammeled cost cutting for his employees. Upton Sinclair's Stockyards exposé *The Jungle* (1906) led to the rapid passage of the Pure Food and Drug Act but not, to the socialist author's chagrin, a comparable outrage over the workers' plight. Hedger, however, did share his outrage: "It must be realized in Packingtown that workers are human beings."[1]

The mostly temporary laborers received tiny wages for long, strenuous days. Bullied into moving as fast as possible, they lacked time and material means for sanitary precautions. In the brutal Chicago winters, the buildings went unheated. Workers' feet became numb and frostbitten unless inserted into freshly butchered cattle. Resisters were fired without recourse and replaced by one of the hungry, unemployed people who flocked daily to the company gate. Packingtown was heavily polluted with untreated meat waste products and full of high-rent, overcrowded, dimly lit, poorly ventilated houses. Residents could access bars, but not stores with affordable, nutritious foods.

Hedger linked the neighborhood's poor nutrition to its unusually high number of developmentally delayed persons. She noted the high tuberculosis incidence, which not only compromised Armour product safety but threatened the workers and their families, before and after birth. Instead of blaming the workers, she blamed their employer's robbery of living wages and time and energy for childcare and homemaking. As a staff physician for the Women's Trade Union League, she encouraged agitation for remedies like prenatal care. Hedger disseminated her findings on Packingtown and her ideas for solutions to health and social welfare professionals and labor unionists, as she did in the presentation below to the first U.S. national conference ever on reducing infant mortality. While Social Darwinists justified inaction on baby deaths in terms of "survival of the fittest," Hedger knew this was an unconscionable excuse.[2]

The Relation of Infant Mortality to the Occupation and Long Hours of Work for Women
by Dr. Caroline Hedger

The profit that shall accrue to a man who loses his own soul is but a suggestion of the profit that shall accrue to a state that slaughters its children.

You may heap warehouses with goods, but if those goods are made by women whose babies die untimely death, your chance for future life of the state is gone.

Women work for pay—six million of them. Where do they work? Either at home or away from home. What do they work at? 295 occupations—everything but firemen, soldiers, sailors, U.S. marines, roofers' helpers, copper smelter helpers, street car drivers . . .

A certain portion of these occupations demands our attention in considering infant mortality . . . We must consider every trade condition that depletes the woman's vitality so that puny children are born; every work that so fatigues the mother that her milk is bad, whether at home or abroad; and every trade or occupation that takes a mother away from her baby longer than a normal nursing interval, whatever the conditions; or work which attacks moral standards—and we have a right to consider these—and when found, to regulate such trades.

. . . I think we can throw out of our consideration professions, and those occupations like working housekeeper in which the mother can have the child with her, and approach the arrangement of a home where things have to stop at intervals till the baby is taken care of.

. . . [T]he classes of trades that really threaten . . . are:

Beasts of Burden trades,
Physical Strain trades,
Nervous Strain trades,
Poisonous trades.

In speaking of Beasts of Burden trades, your mind reverts to women dragging cars in the mines of England, and you flatter yourself that is of the past. We have them yet. Last week we found in the stock-yards a girl who lifted barrels all day, and each barrel weighed over 30 pounds. There is a girl who assembles screw-drivers and kicks 7000 times day with one foot... How much excess nutrition would you expect in such cases for the production and nursing of children?

Take a grade of labor a shade less terrible—the Physical Strain trades—spinners, shop-girls, laundresses; the standing trades—sweated industries. You know as well as I the effects of standing...A healthy young Polish girl, whom I have known three years, went through the Christmas rush in a department store standing until eleven o'clock each night, and a few weeks later showed a marked prolapse, the uterus being within one half-inch of the vulva...Budin shows the effect on the weight of nurslings of morbid nervous states in wet nurses. If nervous states can so violently influence lactation, what effect the nervous strain trades must have on the whole nervous adjustment that has to do with nutrition and reproduction...

The complicated processes of modern manufacture demands constant watching to prevent poisoning. One case brought this clearly to mind—sub-acute poisoning from bronze powder scattered on the wet ink in a printing establishment. Turpentine poisoning and paint poisoning from can poisoning in the yard are other examples...Whatever spirit moves the young girl to go to work, the married woman [most commonly] goes to work...because she has not money enough to feed and clothe her children and pay rent...

... [F]actory work alone is but a factor, but... it acts in so many ways. It puts the baby on artificial food—that gives him about 22 chances to die to one normal chance. It may put the baby in care of irresponsible people, and he gets bad care and possibly drugging. One man in England, a mill owner, felt that the baby death-rate among the mothers in his mill was a disgrace; so he arranged for a fund to keep these women at home longer after the birth of the baby and to let them go home two times a day to nurse the baby. He reduced his death-rate one-half speedily...In France, rooms are provided in factories where the mothers can go to nurse their babies at regular intervals...

Another element in which work outside the home, among other things, has a part, is abortion. The work itself may produce premature birth. Some testimony points strongly to the fact that mill work of various kinds does this. Abortion may be practised by factory workers... [t]o cover sexual irregularities incident to mill life... [t]o keep the job without the interruption of pregnancy.[3]

Both of these factors are active, according to my belief. I am confirmed in this belief by trade union girls and by those who have chance for firsthand observations. This brings up the fifth danger in industry—the moral strain of trades. Are we imposing upon the social structure here a dangerous tension? Do we really believe in monogamic marriage? Do we believe that the best chance for a baby is in a home, and that a home implies one man and one woman? If so, we must take one of two courses: relieve the tension, or strengthen the material to save the baby's life.

We can all lift for such a distribution of wealth that the producer gets his share; then, if a man works, he can have enough to keep his wife at home to nurse the baby and care for it. If the man will not work, of if he cannot procure enough to feed his family, then the state must, in self-defense, feed that family, and especially must it feed the mother enough so that she can nurse her baby. And New York has set us a limited but shining example of what this line of treatment can do in reducing infant mortality . . .

[Hedger then calls for detailed research into women's working conditions, specific occupations, and their effects upon women's ability to conceive, lactation, pregnancy, abortion, and other infant deaths, among other needed studies. She proposes grade school classes in baby care, quality standards for day nurseries, and maternity leave legislation.—Eds.]

—Presentation to the American Committee for the Prevention of Infant Mortality, in *Prevention of Infant Mortality*, American Academy of Medicine, 1909.

Dr. S. Josephine Baker (1873-1945)

The "shining example" of infant mortality prevention work that Hedger mentions belonged to public health physician S. (Sara) Josephine Baker, a longtime Unitarian whose spiritual beliefs translated into tireless social action. The daughter of an attorney and a Vassar graduate in Poughkeepsie, New York, Baker lost her father to typhoid fever when she was 16. Despite family grumbling, she dropped her plans to attend Vassar and studied at the Blackwell sisters' creation, the Woman's Medical College of the New York Infirmary. At Boston's New England Hospital for Women and Children, she interned under its founder, Marie E. Zakrzewska. There Baker first explored the links between ill health and poverty. After beginning a private practice, she also performed medical inspections for the City of New York.

After being appointed assistant city health commissioner (1907), Baker focused on vaccination campaigns and successfully identified Mary Mallon, the Irish cook dubbed "Typhoid Mary," who had innocently spread typhoid fever. The ensuing public panic had some racist and misogynist overtones but generated support for government health interventions. New York created the first city Bureau of Child Hygiene in the U.S. and named Baker director, a post she held until 1923. Despite her repeated encounters with prejudice against medical women, Baker cut the infant mortality rate by 50%, the lowest for any large American urban area. Her innovative programs—clean milk distribution, health and baby care instruction, a widely copied school health measure, more effective prosecution of abortionists, and the establishment of Bellevue Hospital's outstanding midwifery school— soon inspired the creation of another pioneering agency, the federal Children's Bureau. In 1917, Baker became the first woman Ph.D. in public health at the Bellevue Hospital (later New York University) Medical College.[1] Baker and her life partner, the Australian writer I.A.R. (Ida Alexa Ross) Wylie (1885-1959), joined the socially engaged radical feminist club Heterodoxy (see Stokes, Part One). Baker insisted repeatedly that most health essentials could be secured only through "concerted effort" of "all citizens, both men and women," for the sake of human beings at all phases of development.[2] A National Child Welfare Association poster quoted her: "No Mother's Baby Is Safe Till Every Mother's Baby Is Safe."[3]

"The Action Should Be Equally Drastic"
by Dr. S. Josephine Baker

The practice of midwifery dates back to the beginning of human life in this world . . . Its history runs parallel with the history of the people, and its functions antedate any record we have of medicine as an applied science. To deny its right to exist as a calling is to take issue with the external verities of life. The only points upon which we may argue are the training required for its safe and lawful practice, and the essential fitness of those who follow this calling requisite for the safeguarding of the mother and child . . .

. . . [T]he average cost of a midwife's services is eight dollars. This amount almost universally includes attendance during the confinement, daily visits for at least ten days thereafter, nursing care (crude though it may be) and many housewifely duties, including sometimes the preparation of meals and general care of the household. Contrast this with the service rendered by the average physician for the same amount of money, and it is easy to see one of the main reasons why the midwife will continue to be employed, whether or not the law recognizes her existence.

. . . [T]he . . . criminal practice . . . is considered the most serious indictment of the midwife as she exists today . . . . [T]he production of abortions bears the same relation to the practice of midwifery by midwives as it does to the practice of medicine by physicians. In either case it is . . . amenable to laws which are in effect in practically all states, and directed toward the prohibition of this practice, irrespective of whether the offender be physician, midwife, or layman. That a midwife may be guilty of the illegal practice . . . is no more an indictment against her legitimate sphere of practice than it is an indictment of the practice of medicine if a physician be found guilty of the same offense . . . While medical examining boards and boards of health should refuse to issue a license to practise to any midwife found guilty of this crime, and should revoke any license already in effect for the same cause, the action should be equally drastic in the case of any member of the medical profession under like circumstances . . .

—From "Schools for Midwives," presentation to Annual Meeting, Association for Study and Prevention of Infant Mortality, November 1911; reprinted in *American Journal of Obstetrics and the Diseases of Women and Children*, February 1912.

"The Prenatal Period Is Of Such Great Importance"
by Dr. S. Josephine Baker

In health development as in character formation, the first seven years of life, including the prenatal period, are the most important.

From the moment the child is conceived until he is born, his environment is his mother, and the relation between the two is physical. At this time the provision of proper nourishment for the embryonic child is the most important thing that we can plan for his future well-being. From the moment of birth his world is extended . . . Throughout infancy and early childhood the home represents the world to the growing child . . . His health will be determined largely by the health care and the health education that he receives during this period . . .

In China, age is computed not from the date of birth, but from the day of conception. The first birthday comes when the child is born and the second a year afterward. Such a method might well enter into our attitude toward the health of the child, for the prenatal period is not only the time of greatest danger as far as his chance of existing at all is concerned, but it also has within it the possibility of making a lasting impression, whether for good or ill, upon his physical welfare for his entire life, however long it may be.

If, then, the prenatal period is of such great importance in relation to health, we may perhaps the more readily understand why the first year of life is the next most important period to consider . . .

—From Chapter One, "The Child, Parent, and the State,"
in *Child Hygiene,* Harper & Brothers, 1925.

Public Responsibility for *Both* Women and Babies: Julia Lathrop (1858-1932) and the Children's Bureau (founded 1912)

Before suffrage, female reformers started the highly innovative, largely woman-staffed U.S. federal Children's Bureau (CB). Its first director, the first woman head of any federal agency, was Julia Clifford Lathrop, the first-born of a freethinking Republican attorney/politician and a devoutly Congregationalist, suffragist mother in Rockford, Illinois. Lathrop, who never joined any church, was in Jane Addams' estimation a profoundly spiritual person whose heart "to the end . . . held the world in friendly affection."[1]

After finishing Vassar and trying to find her niche, Lathrop discovered and joined Hull House. To the groundbreaking *Hull House Maps and Papers* (1895), she contributed her investigation of all 102 Illinois institutions for homeless, chronically ill, and mentally ill persons, protesting the indignities inflicted upon them and calling government officials to accountability. During an 1898 European trip, Lathrop was pleased to witness "boarded out" systems: public care arrangements that accorded mentally ill and other afflicted, indigent persons places as valued community members. *A Mind That Found Itself*, Clifford Beers's account of his recovery from mental and physical abuse in psychiatric institutions (1908/1910), deeply moved her. Usually calm, she shed tears as she, Beers, and other activists set in motion "a national committee for mental hygiene . . . equally the friend of the physician and the patient; also the friend of the patient's relatives . . . In a word, it would be a Friend to Humanity, for no man knows when he himself would have to look for assistance." Lathrop also cofounded the Chicago School of Civics and Philanthropy (later the University of Chicago School of Social Service Administration); the Chicago Juvenile Court, the nation's first; the Juvenile Protective Association; and the Immigrants' Protective League.[2]

As CB director (1912-1921), Lathrop pioneered research and policy on child labor, juvenile delinquency, infant and maternal mortality, child welfare standards, mothers' pensions, nonmarital births, and care of disabled persons. Lathrop anticipated the disability rights demand of "universal design":

building maximum accessibility into all activities, products, and structures.[3] She also prefigured the disability rights slogan "no quality of life without equality of life." In 1915, multiply disabled Baby Allan Bollinger was born at Chicago's German-American hospital. Attending surgeon Harry Haiselden, a flamboyantly dogmatic eugenicist, refused to perform a lifesaving operation on Allan because the little boy would remain "grossly abnormal." The baby's mother, Anna Bollinger, reportedly deferred to Haiselden without seeing Allan first. Anna's friend Catherine Walsh rushed to the hospital and found Allan, "not a monster, a beautiful baby," unattended and unclothed. Pleading for the surgery, Walsh challenged Haiselden to let Anna see the baby. Haiselden laughed contemptuously at her: "I'm afraid it might get well." Walsh tried to whisk Allan away to a sympathetic doctor. Her plan was thwarted and the baby died.

Haiselden took a jury's exoneration as license to openly deny treatment to or lethally inject other disabled infants. He saw himself as more swiftly, efficiently accomplishing the function of the massive, poorly run, unsanitary institutions he called "slaughterhouses." Haiselden not only got away with murder; he was lionized, starring as himself, in a popular silent film, *The Black Stork*. As CB head, Lathrop challenged his bigotry, insisting "even a mental defective has a right to live." The public, she asserted, was responsible for assisting disabled children and their families through humane institutional care, not Haiselden's segregationist "slaughterhouses," whose degrading, lethal faults she knew far better than he, but services on the European model.[4]

Lathrop showed the same respect for human beings and their interconnections in her approach to maternal/child health.

> The bureau's . . . analysis . . . of infant and maternal deaths show in ways not commonly realized the dependence of the child upon the health and well-being of the mother before as well as after birth. Year by year some 15,000 mothers in the United States have been dying in childbirth from causes which are largely preventable . . . The loss involved is immeasurable . . . The prevention of maternal deaths involves the problem of making universally available and universally desired adequate care at childbirth and before . . . We can not rest content with a discussion of the ultimate minimum of nonpreventable deaths until we are assured that skilled care is available to every mother . . . [5]

Under the directorship of Lathrop and then Grace Abbott (1878-1939), her Hull House friend and successor (1921-1934), the CB developed and implemented the first U.S. federal maternity and infant health care program, the Sheppard-Towner Act. Margaret Sanger derided it as "dysgenic." Some Catholics feared having contraception imposed on them. The American Medical Association denounced Sheppard-Towner as socialism, like the national health plan bill it had just demolished, and as the nation-destroying work of "derailed menopausics" and "endocrine perverts" (a derogatory, pseudoscientific phrase for "lesbians"). Congressmen denounced CB staff as meddling "old maids" and "female celibates too refined to have a husband." A single, childless woman by choice, Lathrop faced continuous interrogation: "So what do *you* know about children? How many children have *you* helped to raise?" She delighted in replying "Four!"—her younger siblings.[6]

The organized push of 20 million newly enfranchised women, particularly the League of Women Voters, the WCTU, and the General Federation of Women's Clubs, ensured Sheppard-Towner's passage (1921). Sheppard-Towner benefited millions, funding a popular pamphlet on prenatal care and high-risk pregnancy danger signs, new maternity and infant welfare clinics, improved licensing and training of midwives (including those from the new nurse-midwife profession), and a birth registration system allowing for better maternal/child health data. Mothers' deaths from eclampsia plummeted. U.S. infant mortality dropped from 75 per 1000 children under age one (1921) to 64 (1929), although Sheppard-Towner funded a limited number of states.[7]

Sheppard-Towner never expanded nationwide. Its enemies scrapped it just as the Depression started and yet another CB study showed the urgency of *more* collective responsibility towards mothers and babies. It found that 12% of U.S. maternal deaths were due to puerperal septicemia ("childbed fever") following induced abortion.[8] Grace Abbott did succeed in her efforts to pass the 1935 Social Security Act, which did provide some federal maternal/child funding, including the forerunner of the late Aid to Families With Dependent Children (AFDC), but again it was not enough.[9] Trude Bennett charges the CB with imposing the maternal-fetal conflict because it never called for legalized abortion and thus caused women to die, all for political expediency.[10] Referring to the voluminous letters the CB received from a knowledge-hungry public, Anne Firor Scott also criticizes the CB stand on abortion: "Replies to questions about the morality of abortion left no doubt that staff members opposed that practice"—an opposition attributed to these largely white, educated professional women's class biases.[11]

While supporting contraception through other venues, Lathrop was politically blocked from bringing it under CB purview. Congress would have at once defunded the already controversial agency if it had broken anti-birth control laws. However, the CB's antiabortion/prolife stance does not seem a matter of political strategy, let alone *noblesse oblige*. Although CB staff *were* sometimes insensitive to class differences, their abortion stance seems more a matter of principled, inclusive compassion, a conclusion that anyone could arrive at through *her own* reflections and experiences. The CB regarded abortion as "not only dangerous to the mother," but a "taking of life." For example, an Ohio woman wrote of a pregnancy shortly after her marriage. She and her husband did not know what to do. A neighbor sent her to an abortionist who pumped air into her 3-months-gravid uterus. She felt "very weak and very dizzy" and "was sick in bed for 3 weeks."

> I have regretted the day I ever went to that doctor, since I saw the little creature that I killed, my own flesh and blood. It was just like a doll and now I am afraid I cannot ever have any more children. My hubby and I are just crazy to have a baby. But I am afraid I cannot, please tell me if I can ever be a mother or not.

A CB staffer wrote back, "I am very sorry that you should have so unfortunate an experience." She offered that "nature is usually very kind" and that women who "have destroyed only one child" might possibly still "conceive . . . Go to some good physician and have a careful examination made." [12]

The CB did not heedlessly impose the maternal-fetal conflict through callous inaction on abortion-related maternal deaths. They saw induced abortion as a species of infant mortality bound up with harm to women's health and lives, not a practice needing ethical and legal sanction. They *did* take action. They disseminated research data and pushed to create and expand abortion-reducing maternal/child health and welfare services. Though their warnings sometimes went unheeded, they urged doctors to prevent sepsis in *all* obstetrical crises by following simple, long-established aseptic precautions; refraining from overzealous, aggressive instrument use; more carefully, quickly assessing and treating women who presented with possible induced abortions; and improving the quality of obstetrical education. [13] Between 1915 and 1946, the U.S. maternal mortality rate dropped to 15.7 deaths per 1000 mothers, down from 60.8. The introduction of antibiotics and blood transfusion and banking technologies deserves credit, but so does the CB's persistent agenda. [14] Why assume, especially without first conducting a thorough, complex evaluation, that CB efforts did not preserve the lives and health of any illegal abortion recipients, or even empower some women to avoid the procedure altogether? And even if the CB did not have the impact it sought, was it necessarily the CB's fault? For example, if doctors did not observe the CB's infection control counsel—and many failed to do so—why pin the resulting injuries and deaths on the CB?

After leaving the CB, Julia Lathrop remained a nonviolent fighter for social justice as she struggled with fatiguing health problems. The last few weeks of her life, she led a nationwide appeal, with Jane Addams and Miriam Van Waters, to exempt minors from the death penalty. She had long sought commutation for Russell McWilliams, a Rockford teen on death row for shooting a streetcar motorman during a holdup. Addams noted Lathrop's "horror over the deliberate taking of life by the state . . . [S]o long identified with governmental service . . . official violence such as an execution held almost an element of complicity on her part which must have been well-nigh unendurable." A year almost to the day after Lathrop's death from goiter surgery complications, McWilliams's death sentence was changed to 99 years imprisonment.[15]

Abortion-related maternal as well as fetal mortality persisted under Americans' refusal to *fully* fund and establish nonviolent alternatives. If women and children continued to suffer harm and die from induced abortions and other preventable causes, it was not the CB's or Lathrop's doing, any more than the continued execution of minors (and adults) can be laid on their shoulders. Rather, the responsibility belonged, and still does, to all who have engaged in the violence of refusing their political, moral, financial, and clinical support to lifesaving, life-improving alternatives.

The Women's Cooperative Guild (c. 1913-1915), Margaret Llewellyn Davies (1861-1944) and Three Anonymous Guild Officers

Today feminists best remember the Women's Cooperative Guild as source of the powerful *Maternity: Letters from Working Women* (1915) and as the first British women's group to openly endorse legalized abortion, although in limited circumstances (1934). Little to nothing is said of Guild members' earlier stand: a consensus *against* abortion, one discernible in *Maternity*'s heart-histories. Along with their resilience, resourcefulness, and loving human bonds, anonymous Guild officers poignantly describe their struggles with poverty, miserable working and housing conditions, overwhelming domestic responsibilities, family violence, malnutrition, poor health, inadequate health care access, infertility, difficult deliveries, and maternal and child deaths from miscarriage, induced abortion, and other causes. Concerned for both women's and unborn children's health and survival, they framed abortion as a *symptom* of working-class women's troubles, not as a solution to them. This stance fit well with the book's mission: bringing about a genuine, comprehensive public commitment to the lives and well-being of women and children through such services as pregnancy and maternity benefits, better midwifery training, more hospitals competent in treating high-risk pregnancies, maternity rest homes, household aides, sanitary milk depots for infants who could not be breastfed, and advice and treatment centers for expectant and nursing mothers as well as children up to school age.

Only a small fragment of the Guild's proposal for a national maternity scheme was ever honored in deed. Perhaps this fact, plus the hardships of the Great Depression, brought about the Guild's call for some abortions to be legalized. They also sought amnesty for women thrown into prison for seeking abortion.[1] Of course abusive or neglectful male "partners," exploitative employers, and hypocritical clerics and politicians had never been imprisoned for inflicting situations that caused abortion. Very few feminists then agreed with Stella Browne's belief in a general right to abortion as the cornerstone of women's sexual and reproductive freedom. By the late 1960s, of course, attitudes had shifted.[2]

"The Cause of the Evil Lies in the Conditions Which Produce It"
by Margaret Llewellyn Davies (1861-1944) and
Three Anonymous Guild Officers

Opinions may differ as to the good or evil of the general limitation of families, but there can only be agreement upon the evil which results from the use of drugs to procure abortion . . . But here again the cause of the evil lies in the conditions which produce it. Where maternity is only followed by an addition to the daily life of suffering, want, overwork, and poverty, people will continue to adopt even the most dangerous, uncertain, and disastrous methods of avoiding it . . .

—From the Introduction by Margaret Llewellyn Davies (1861-1944) [second-generation suffragist and the Guild's General Secretary, 1889-1921-Eds.]

. . . My last baby was born at a time when we were really badly off. My husband was out of work . . . and I was not only obliged to work myself but often went short of food and warm clothing when I was most in need of it . . . I nearly lost hope and faith in everyone. I felt that even the baby could not make up for the terrible strain I had undergone and at that time I could fully enter into the feelings of those women who take drugs to prevent birth . . . I never dared to allow myself to think of the time when the baby would be born . . . I don't know now *how* I got through, and it is a nightmare to me yet . . . I believe that if I had felt quite comfortable as to the position of my other children during the time I would be laid up, my sufferings would not have been so great, or my dread of the labour.

—Letter writer 16 [Husband's wages 25 shillings; three children]

I believe the bad housing arrangements have a very depressing effect on mothers during pregnancy. I know of streets of houses where there are large factories built, taking the whole of the daylight away from the kitchen, where the woman spends the better part of her life. On top of this you get the continual grinding of machinery all day. Knowing that it is mostly women and girls who are working in these factories gives you the feeling that their bodies are going round with the machinery. The mother wonders what she has to live for; if there is another baby coming she hopes it will be dead when it is born. The result is she begins to take drugs . . . All this tells on the woman mentally and physically; can you wonder at women turning to drink? . . . When you see all this it is like a sting at your heart when you know the cause of it all and no remedy.

—Letter writer 17 [Husband's wages 28 shillings; six children]

I know personally of many mothers . . . I am sorry to say . . . who have felt they would not carry children, some because of bad husbands, others because they felt they could not properly feed and clothe those that they had. There are three who lost their lives, and another who has already had seven. These all took some kind of drug, and of course did the work they wanted it to do. The doctor felt sorry for this woman and could not blame her. She has had difficulty in rearing these seven . . . I saw her and talked seriously to her, but she said: "Mrs.—, I will not have any more by him, and I should not have cared if I had died." She loved her children, and has had sleepless nights with each of the seven . . . [H]ad Government awakened to its duty years ago, seeing to it that the mothers and children should have what was necessary, mothers would not have minded having the children, had they known each little one would be provided for . . .

—Letter Writer 139

—From *Maternity: Letters from Working Women*, ed. Margaret Llewelyn Davies, G. Bell & Sons, 1915.

Dr. Alice Hamilton (1869-1970)

The second daughter of a prosperous merchant family, New York-born Alice Hamilton was raised in Fort Wayne, Indiana with her four siblings, including classicist Edith Hamilton and artist Norah Hamilton, who beautifully illustrated many slices of Hull House life. Thanks to their Dutch/English Episcopalian mother, Scotch Irish Presbyterian father, and German Catholic household staff, the Hamilton siblings grew up in a culturally and religiously tolerant atmosphere. Their parents home-schooled them in Greek, Latin, modern languages, history, and literature. Hamilton earned her M.D. from the University of Michigan, then did postgraduate clinical and research work in Germany and at Johns Hopkins. While an intern at Boston's New England Hospital for Women and Children, she became close friends with Dr. Rachelle Yarros, who introduced her to Hull House. Hamilton came in 1897 and stayed for almost forty years.

At Hull House, Alice Hamilton conducted innovative scientific investigations on typhoid epidemiology, cocaine trafficking, tuberculosis prevention and treatment, and midwifery. This last project may have motivated her to join Yarros in Chicago's fledgling birth control movement. With the Women's Trade Union League, Hamilton fought for an eight-hour day, compulsory state health insurance, a living wage, decent housing, workers' compensation, and healthy workplaces. Her pioneering study of occupational lead poisoning for Illinois government led to the state's first legal safeguards against industrial diseases. She then conducted parallel studies for the federal government. During World War I, which she opposed, Hamilton traveled around the U.S. to research the horrific lack of worker safety at munitions plants. In 1919, Hamilton was appointed industrial medicine professor at Harvard Medical School, becoming its first woman faculty member, but not, she quipped, the first woman who *should* have been appointed. During the 1920s, she alerted the U.S. Surgeon General to the dangers of radium and the gasoline additive tetraethyl lead; remained active in peace, feminist, and socialist circles; and worked as a League of Nations Health Commissioner. Revisiting Germany after Hitler took power, she became an early, prescient critic of the Nazis and assisted German refugees into the U.S.[1] During the late 1940s, Hamilton and a younger colleague, Harriet Hardy, revised her textbook *Industrial Toxicology*, which covered threats to female and male reproductive health and to fetal life and well-being. *Hamilton and Hardy's Industrial Toxicology* remains a standard reference.[2]

Hamilton beautifully articulates her sense of life and death issues in this account of her visit to a New Jersey WWI armaments plant.

> For wide stretches the lowlands were blackened and lay festering in the sunlight; only in one spot rose a tiny mound covered with wild rose and morning-glory. The poison had not reached it yet, but was creeping close. A puff of wind from the west drove me, choking and gasping . . . Escaped to clear air I found myself in a great field all grown up with weeds. Corn used to grow there but now ragweed and burdock. The men who tilled that land were in behind the barrier making the poisonous stuff for the French, and as they did the kindly fruits of the earth perished and in their place were weeds and blackened stalks. It was better business to work for destruction than for life and so the farmers had left the fields for the acid sheds, and instead of yellow corn to feed men their harvest was heaps of picric to kill men.[3]

During the 1950s, Hamilton spoke out against McCarthyism and for the Equal Rights Amendment (ERA). Near her life's end, she publicly opposed the Vietnam War. These actions cohered with her previous responses to war, the killing of disabled persons, and abortion.

In 1915, Hamilton commented (below) on the Bollinger case (see Lathrop, Part One). Surgeon Harry Haiselden refused lifesaving treatment to newborn Allan Bollinger. Soon afterwards, Haiselden and Hamilton conflicted at a birth control symposium for Chicago doctors. Haiselden sensationally decreed his need to eugenically abort a specific patient "of low mentality." Hamilton calmly recalled her meetings with Dutch, English, and German birth control advocates who "emphasize always a distinction which seems to be far from clear in this country, one indeed which seems not always to have been made this evening . . . between the production of abortion and the prevention of conception."[4]

The Bollinger Case
by Dr. Alice Hamilton

Many readers of the newspapers have been amazed and even irritated by the widespread attention which has been attracted to the case of the

Bollinger baby in Chicago . . . But for once the instinct of the newsmonger was not at fault . . . Do the people who advocate euthanasia for the hopelessly sick or insane or idiotic realize what it would mean to let down that barrier which has always stood between the doctor—and the nurse also—and any action on his part which might even hasten death, which has kept him on the straight and narrow way of striving to preserve life in spite of temptations to act the part of Providence and decide the issue of life and death? . . . Physicians themselves know too well the limitations of their own judgment . . . and they know, too, that doctors in regular standing in the profession are not always men to whom one would willingly entrust the decision whether a helpless and useless member of the community should be mercifully and wastefully cared for or rationally and economically put out of the way. Our almshouses, our asylums for the mentally defective, for chronic alcoholics, for incurable dements, are not for the most part places we are proud of; but let us imagine what they would be like if the principle were adopted by doctors and nurses that those for whom there was no hope should be helped to die . . .

—*The Survey*, 4 December 1915

Poverty and Birth Control
by Dr. Alice Hamilton

It must have been some ten or twelve years after I came to live in Hull-House that I was suddenly asked one day in public whether I believe in birth control. Without stopping to think I answered at once that I most certainly did and then realized that this was the first time the question had ever been put to me or I had ever formulated my belief even to myself. The answer had been almost automatic, prompted by my daily experiences in a poor community where I came in close contact with the lives of Italians, Irish, Slavs, Germans and Russian and Polish Jewish families, and saw what unlimited childbearing meant to them . . .

The reasons that are convincing to those of us who live among and know the poor are perhaps not the same as those which seem most urgent to others . . . for instance . . . the plea that the upper classes are being submerged by the lower . . . We know that ability and character are not a matter of class and that the difference comes from the unfair handicaps to which the children of the poor are subject, and we would remedy matters by working for equality of opportunity for all children, instead of trying to encourage the propagation of one class and not of the other. The arguments for birth control which most appeal to us are based on the welfare of the women of the poorer classes and the welfare of their children . . .

Not long ago I invited a group of women to spend a Sunday afternoon with me at Hull-House, all of them married women with large families. The conversation turned very soon on abortions and the best method of producing them and I was in consternation to listen to the experiences of these women who had themselves undergone frightful risks and much suffering rather than add another child to a house too full already. These women were all Catholics, but when I spoke of that, they simply shrugged their shoulders. What could a priest know of a woman's life?

All the mistakes and crimes of society bear hardest on the children, and the greatest of all the injustices of civilized society is that which allows the children of one class to face life with less chance than the children of another class, less chance not only of health and happiness but even of life itself . . .

It is not a question of introducing among the poor an effort to prevent excessive childbearing . . . It is a question of introducing safe-and-sane methods . . . of offering to the poor who need it most, the knowledge and the power which have long been the possession of those who need it least.

—*Birth Control Review,* August 1925.

Rose Pastor Stokes (1879-1933)

Rose Wieslander Pastor Stokes was born in Augustowo, a *shtetl* in Russian-occupied Poland. Her parents divorced shortly thereafter. At three, Rose emigrated with her mother, Hindl, to London's working-class East End. There Hindl toiled for small wages, and Rose first became conscious of labor grievances and protests. Although a gifted student, Rose quit school after a year and a half because of a teacher's unjust, disabling blows to her hand. After Hindl remarried, the family went to live in Cleveland, Ohio, and the family grew to seven children. At 11, Rose was forced to enter the ranks of child and sweatshop laborers. Until age 23, she worked as a cigarmaker, acquiring the chronic respiratory ailments that periodically debilitated her till her death. When her stepfather abandoned the family, Rose's $8 per week was the only income for the eight people he left behind. It could not cover all the expenses unless her siblings were put into orphanages periodically.

Rose read and wrote whenever she could. After she contributed to the New York-based *Jewish Daily News* (*Yiddesches Tageblatt*), she was offered a staff position, and the family moved to the Lower East Side. When she interviewed the settlement house activist James Graham Phelps Stokes, the two were immediately attracted to each other, even though Graham was an Ivy League-educated Christian from a prominent philanthropic Anglo family. In 1905 they married to much public fanfare over this rare union across class, ethnic, economic, and religious boundaries. For many years, Rose and Graham were happily active together in the Socialist Party and the Intercollegiate Socialist Society. Rose, a gifted orator, went on ISS tours of college campuses. Speaking up for woman suffrage at every opportunity, she assisted with critical strikes: New York shirtwaist-makers (1909), New York hotel employees (1912), and Paterson, New Jersey silk workers (1913).[1]

Rose and Graham never had children together but they enthusiastically doted on their friends' children and expressed a wish for their own. When an unmarried Bulgarian immigrant domestic in their home became pregnant, the couple, breaking with custom, rallied around her and her baby. When Rose heard that Elizabeth Gurley Flynn was living alone in a hot, tiny New

York apartment with her newborn son Fred, she took them in at the comfortable rural island retreat she and Graham shared.[2]

Rose had long been aware of reproductive wrongs against workers: fertility-destroying labor conditions, starvation wages that drove women into prostitution, and exhaustion and ill health that killed them young, before they could even see their children grow up. By 1915, she had thrown herself wholeheartedly into birth control, likely through the invitation of friends from Heterodoxy. This influential Greenwich Village feminist discussion and social club disguised itself as a genteel ladies' luncheon club to throw off government informants suspicious of its "troublemaking elements." For all their diversity of occupations, sexual orientations, racial/ethnic, religious, and economic backgrounds, and political leanings, almost all members were radicals and reformers, including National Birth Control League founder Mary Ware Dennett, Dr. S. Josephine Baker, the Industrial Workers of the World's Elizabeth Gurley Flynn, and the NAACP's Grace Nail Johnson.[3]

Rose collaborated with Alice Guy Blaché (1873-1968), one of the first woman film directors, on a pro-birth control movie script, "Shall the Parents Decide?" It was never produced, although another pioneering woman director, Lois Weber, (1883-1939), did manage to film, release, and distribute the pro-birth control, anti-abortion movie "Where Are My Children?" in 1916.[4] Rose became financial secretary of the anti-civil disobedience NBCL, even as she espoused lawbreaking tactics in belief and action. She spoke at a Carnegie Hall celebration of Emma Goldman's release from prison for distributing contraceptive literature. There she announced her own plan, in solidarity with Goldman, to hand out typewritten leaflets describing contraceptive methods. The knowledge-hungry audience immediately mobbed her. Rose was furious that the police would not touch her, a wealthy man's wife, while they pounced upon Sanger and Goldman. In the wake of national press coverage, Rose was inundated with letters from people who wanted the leaflets, which she gladly mailed. However, when a man wrote that he needed help "enlightening" his wife so she would end her two-month pregnancy, Rose pointedly replied by special delivery: "I know nothing about abortion."[5]

Upper-class socialists tended to support and working-class socialists to oppose World War I. Rose briefly agreed with Graham, then reversed herself and joined the Women's Peace Party. Graham's virulently eugenicist uncle W.E.D. Stokes then volunteered as a government informant to bring Rose under surveillance. In his anti-Semitic tract *The Right to be Well Born*, W.E.D. had just decreed of immigrants, "We cannot forever absorb this influx of the scum of the earth, this off-scouring diseased, imported blood with its evil customs." The surveillance led directly to an espionage conviction (although Rose never served time) for a single sentence from a letter to the *Kansas City Star*: "No government which is for the profiteers can also be for the people, and I am for the people, while the government is for the profiteers."[6] Following the Russian Revolution, Rose moved further left and Graham right. In 1925, they divorced. Rose plunged into the new American Communist Party, which she helped found. She married a comrade, Jerome Romain (VJ Jerome), becoming an affectionate stepmother to his young son. At age 54, Rose died of breast cancer in Germany, where she had traveled for experimental radiation therapy.[7]

Rose's spirit of "fire and grace" comes through this excerpt from her published, never-staged drama *The Woman Who Wouldn't* (1916), which "merges her socialist commitment with an eloquent feminism."[8] Highly interested in political persuasion through literature, especially drama, Rose was even director of players for a socialist theater company. Arguably, the hero of *The Woman Who Wouldn't* expresses Rose's own views.

From *The Woman Who Wouldn't*
by Rose Pastor Stokes *[Summaries by editors]*

[Mary Lacey, a young single woman from a large family in a mill town, does piecework as an artificial flower maker. She has just confided her pregnancy in her older sister.]

MARY (Rising): The whole town'll tear me t' pieces when they get t' know. The neighbours'll have nothin' to do with me, my friends'll give me up—even my best friends . . . an' I'll lose my *job* . . . They won't give work t' marry Lacey when they c'n get all sorts o' better girls . . . My work'll last only a little while longer, then I'll have t' quit. Oh, I know, Jenn. I've been thinkin', thinkin'! All night long an' all day . . . I seem t've grown a hundred years older since yesterday . . . Why, Jenn, everythin' I ever heard came back t' me in the night kind o' realer and stronger like, jes' as if they never meant nothin' t' me before an' now they mean real big things . . . (With a burst) Ain't I got a *right* t' my baby? Ain't it got a right t' come into th' world an' be cared for when it gets here? No, they hound ye t' death until ye're glad t' hide in hell t' get away from them. An' it's race suicide they say? . . . It ain't me that wants to murder my baby—it's them that c'n help me but won't, them that would treat me like I wasn't human no more—like I was a wild beast . . . I want my baby! I want t' keep it!

[Jennie urges Mary to wed Joe, her boyfriend, as soon as possible, before the pregnancy shows. Mary stubbornly resists this conventional response to nonmarital pregnancies, explaining that she refuses to marry a man who now loves someone else.]

MARY: . . . I'll try to find a way out, somehow . . . some other way out. An' if I can't—I'll . . . But ye must keep this—this secret with me, Jenn . . . promise! Please promise! I had t' tell someone—I—I couldn't keep it t' myself—it was killin' me—an' I couldn't tell mother—she wouldn't understand at all, an', an' father—father's s' worried already an' has such a temper at times—an' it'd break him up s' terrible! . . . Then there was you . . . an' I thought ye'd understand how I feel about marryin' Joe now, an'—an' it'd be easier for me t'-t' . . . (Sinking into her seat): Oh, ye mus'n't, mus'n't ever breathe a word t' any one—never, no matter what happens. Jenn—th' doctor's comin' t' see Bennie—t'night, maybe. I'd heard once how—how . . . It was jes' some talk, how the boss's daughter was—was sick, an' how she got over it. How a doctor helped her; an' how—everybody was told it was—somethin' else—but it wasn't. I—I—I thought I'd ask th' doctor t'—t'— . . . T'—help me—- . . . (With a burst): S' I'll keep my job—an' my friends—s' father won't—won't be s' terribly angry—s' Joe won't *have* t' marry me . . . (Long pause.)

JENNIE: I see . . . I see . . . (She contemplates MARY with compassion, goes to her as she rises, and enfolds her in her arms.)

[Later, the doctor comes to tend Bennie, the sick younger brother. Before Mary can broach her intended request, the doctor notices that something is not right with her. She denies it and declines his offer of medicine.]

DOCTOR: . . . Very well, then, if you insist . . . (He . . . moves to the door.) But you're *not* well. Better not work so hard, Miss Mary!—Let's see, I'll be here on—

MARY: Doctor! Doctor! Don't go 'way! Don't leave me! I—I—I—want yet' help me! Ye *must* help me!

DOCTOR (Returning): Why—why—Miss Mary! Something *is* the matter!

MARY: Doctor, ye must help me, or I'll—I'll—(A long pause in which the DOCTOR regards her with a peculiar half-puzzled expression.) Oh, I want to keep my friends, an' my folks, an' my work . . .

DOCTOR: You frighten me!—What is it you want me to do for you?

(MARY, working her hands nervously, remains silent. The DOCTOR comes forward and looks long and earnestly into her face, while her head droops low and lower until she finally sinks with a groan to her knees and buries her face in her hands.)

DOCTOR: Why, child, is it possible! . . . *Is it possible!* . . . (Pause) But, of course he is going to marry you!

MARY: No.

DOCTOR (Rising to his feet): The scoundrel! And I've always thought him a very decent chap!

[Mary acknowledges Joe's decency but explains why she does not want to marry him. The Doctor pleads for marriage. Again Mary won't hear of it.]

MARY: An' ye must help me, Doctor, ye must—ye must! Or I jes' can't go on a-livin'—I—I—(She approaches him on her knees.)

DOCTOR: Why, Miss Mary, you talk like—What's in your mind, child?

MARY: Don't say ye won't, Doctor, don't say ye won't! Ye see what'd happen t' me—I'd lose my job—an—an' my friends'd go back on me, an' my father'd be jes s' mad!—Oh, I couldn't go on! I couldn't go on livin' like that. Doctor, I—(Turning her face from him) I—want—my—baby! But I—I mus'n't have it—I mus'n't!

DOCTOR: Miss Mary! Do you realize what it is you're asking me to do? You're asking me to commit a crime. (She starts and stares at him.) You are asking me to take a human life—You are asking me to do that which would send me to prison for a long term of years. And your crime would be no less than mine. You want to—*murder your baby!*

MARY: Ah! (She utters a sharp cry, rises and recoils.)

DOCTOR: *"Thou shalt not kill!"*

MARY: My baby—my—my—I—No, no, no! . . . But everybody'll . . . They'll jes' murder me an' m' baby every day. They'll murder us every hour in th' day. (She muses, shuddering.) Shall it be killin' all at once, or killin' every mornin', noon, an' night?— My baby! . . . (Rousing herself and with fierceness) Murder! Murder! An' they send us t' prison fer this—Who sends us— the "respectable" folk that goes t' church on Sundays an' robs us on Mondays, so's they c'n live in fine houses an' wear fine clo's,—an' be educated fine, an' keep their looks, an'—

DOCTOR: Who's been filling your head with this stuff and nonsense about our best people?

MARY: Yes, defend 'em. Is th' boss o' th' mills ever arrested fer cripplin' th' men in th' works?—Fer killin' them outright even? . . . Who's been fillin' my head—everythin'! . . . I see how it's all happened—an' how it's all been fer workin' ourselves deaf an' dumb an' blind fer th' men in th' fine houses on the hill, while we're starvin' fer real homes an' a little love, an' jes go crazy fer th' lack of them . . . Doctor, doctor, don't say ye won't help me, don't say ye won't!—

DOCTOR (Sitting): My dear child, I—

MARY (On her knees): Don't say ye won't, Doctor! Save me, save me!

DOCTOR (Springing to his feet): Child, don't ask me to do it! It's impossible!—Criminal!—Heaven help us, in my profession we kill often enough where we mean to save! Shall I deliberately take a human life! No, no, Miss Mary, it's absolutely out of the question! (He turns to get his hat and coat. MARY clings desperately to him, clutching his clothing.)

MARY: Doctor, I'll tell ye plain, I'll take my life t' get out o' this!

DOCTOR: Good God, child, what a thing to say! (Helping her to a seat on the sofa and taking one beside her) You—you mus'n't think of such a thing!. Here, now! ... Why, Miss Mary, you are out of your head—clean out of your head!

MARY: Oh God, God, God!

[The Doctor gently reminds her that her suicide would harm her parents and her siblings, that with her father on strike she is now "the one support" of the family and "at other times a great help." Mary calms down and promises him she will "go on."]

DOCTOR (Rising and taking her two hands in his own): You're a fine brave girl, Miss Mary. (A pause in which she gazes with fatherly compassion on her while she hangs her head.) I'm so glad to hear you say that ... You love children; and I'm going to tell you what doctors don't usually tell girls who come to them in trouble as you came to me ... If I'd helped you as you wanted me to, it might have meant *no* babies for you—*All your life!* (MARY gives a hushed little gasp.) You're a brave girl, Miss Mary—and—I'll do what I can to help. There won't be any charges for Bennie and I'll look after the medicine. (Taking up the satchel and offering his hand) And you won't hesitate to call on me whenever you should need me?

MARY (Shaking his hand): Ye're so kind, Doctor. I—I—*Ye're kinder than I knew* . . . .

[Despite his shortfalls of class consciousness, the Doctor does prove kinder than Mary knew. Mary's resolve to have her baby catalyzes her transformation into "Mother Mary," a charismatic, justly famous leader who fights for herself and all women, for all children as well as for her much-cherished daughter—one of the "women of tomorrow."]

—From Act One, *The Woman Who Wouldn't*, Putnam/Knickerbocker Press, 1916.

"There Is A Time Coming": Hayes, Mary, Unborn Baby Turner (d. 1918), and Angelina Weld Grimké (1880-1958)

The lynching of African Americans up to the present is too enormous a prolife concern to cover thoroughly in this reproductively focused volume. Yet we can and must note a matter that merits further research: the intersection of lynching with abortion/infanticide and other reproductive wrongs against Black women and children. The Anti-Lynching Crusaders, a Black women's organization working with the NAACP, estimated there were at least 3,465 U.S. lynchings between 1889 and 1922. Lynching, a direct outgrowth of the punishments inflicted upon slaves, was a terror tactic against *all* Black Americans, as well as Mexicans, other immigrants, First Nations people, and GLBT persons.[1] The Crusaders challenged a popular white notion of lynching as a vigilante but understandable death penalty, an act of self-defense citizens meted out to rapists: a myth borne of deep-set stereotypes of Black men as congenital sexual predators and white women as white men's property. Marshalling statistics and stories, the Crusaders showed that most lynching victims were not even *alleged* male rapists. Indeed, many were women, some with child, as the Crusaders document here:

> In May 1918, a white plantation owner in Brooks County, Georgia, got into a quarrel with one of his colored tenants and the tenant killed him. A mob sought to avenge his death but could not find the suspected man. They therefore lynched another colored man named Hayes Turner. His wife, Mary Turner, threatened to have . . . the mob arrested. The mob therefore started after her . . . She was in the eighth month of pregnancy but the mob of several hundred took her to a small stream, tied her ankles together and hung her on a tree head downwards. Gasoline was thrown on her clothes and she was set on fire. One of the members of the mob took a knife and split her abdomen open so that the unborn child fell from her womb to the ground and the child's head

was crushed under the heel of another member of the mob; Mary
Turner's body was finally riddled with bullets.[2]

The Turner lynchings haunted the Harlem Renaissance writer Angelina
Emily Weld Grimké.[3] A lesbian teacher without children of her own, Grimké
revered biological motherhood and other forms of maternal nurturance. We
are not yet aware of any direct expository statements by Grimké concerning
the ethics and legal status of abortion, yet she sorrowed deeply over the
destruction of Black motherhood, as her great-aunts Sarah and Angelina
(her namesake) had. Angelina Weld Grimké transmuted an unspeakable
horror into words. Grimké penned two versions of the short story titled
"Goldie" or "Blackness" because white editors felt that its plot, based on
the Turner murders, was implausible.

Grimké explored lynching's chilling, blighting effect upon Black women's
own reproductive desires, while suggesting self-defense through nonviolent,
if emotionally complex, means. Her drama *Rachel* (1916), staged under
NAACP auspices, concerns a young woman's decision to turn away from
heterosexual relationship and to care for others' children.[4] Grimké published
her story "The Closing Door" in the *Birth Control Review*, which had an
editorial policy of advocating contraception as a preventive for abortion
and infanticide. Grimké wished to educate the mainly white readership
about conditions that led Blacks, whether in the North or South, to want
birth control for themselves. Agnes, the story's generous, affectionate
protagonist, initially responds with guarded happiness to her first pregnancy,
which she announces as "the loveliest, loveliest thing for you to know was—
was there—close—just under your heart." When a lynch mob kills her
brother, she falls into an ominous depression, crying out that she is but "an
instrument of reproduction" to manufacture children for the blood sport of
lynch mobs, and that "there is a time coming—and soon—when no colored
man—no colored woman—no colored child, born or unborn—will be safe—
in this country."[5] That time comes tragically soon indeed for Agnes and her
child.

Ethel Sturges Dummer (1866-1954)

A philanthropist with "the spirit of an insurgent,"[1] Ethel Sturges Dummer quietly, powerfully shaped U.S. maternal-child welfare reform. She was a Chicago bank president's daughter and an 1885 graduate of Kirkland, the experimental school where Ellen Gates Starr taught her. At 22, Ethel married William F. Dummer, the vice president of her father's bank. They raised four daughters. Their son died as a baby. She never publicly linked this loss to her activism, but it was surely an important motive.

Until the mid-1890s, Dummer managed the family's household affairs and exposed the children constantly to novel educational and travel opportunities, with "Mr. Dummer's" blessing and aid. Dummer then brought her abundant maternal intelligence into Chicago's reform circles.[2] Decades later, she remarked: "My social work was in *thinking* and the sharing of thought." [3] Dummer published influential books and articles that drew on her multifaceted activism in child labor abolition, educational reform, mental hygiene, social science, and just treatment of prostitutes.[4] Her social work also encompassed philanthropy to innovative social scientists like the rehabilitation-oriented penologist Miriam Van Waters[5] and psychiatrist William Healy, who developed models for child guidance clinics and for juvenile delinquency treatment.[6] Dummer funded the visiting nurses' program that became a model for Sheppard-Towner. A conservationist, she donated the land that became Illinois's Kankakee River State Park.[7] Along with physicians Charles S. Bacon, Rudolph W. Holmes, Alice Hamilton, and Rachelle Slobidinskaya Yarros, Dummer and her ever-supportive husband signed onto a public call for contraceptive education and access:

> [U]ndesired children are born to ill-health and misery or are destroyed
> before birth by parents who feel themselves driven in desperation to
> this terrible recourse . . . [T]he knowledge which might remedy these
> evils is withheld from great numbers in the community.[8]

The Committee evolved into the Illinois Birth Control League, later Illinois Planned Parenthood.[9]

On the board of the Hull House affiliated Juvenile Protective Association, Dummer challenged the popular attribution of delinquency to "bad" heredity, not manmade social conditions.[10] She wrote that her "special contribution to the work of the JPA was to protest against *forcing* [emphasis added] marriage to make a child legitimate."[11] Dummer committed herself to finding better solutions for unwed mothers and their children. She insisted that "the finest feminism is that which seeks to solve the problem of mating and motherhood."[12] She researched the literature, then traveled to Europe (1913-1914) to personally meet with pioneer humanitarians such as Norway's first Minister of Social Welfare, Johan Castberg, author of the era's most advanced Western statute regarding nonmarital pregnancies. The Castberg Law honored the right of single mothers to financial support for job earnings lost to pregnancy and childcare, as well as state collection of child support. It recognized the equality of all children, whether conceived/born in or out of marriage. Back in the U.S., Dummer busily disseminated a translation that Julia Lathrop, her old colleague, published under Children's Bureau auspices. Although few were far-seeing as Dummer, she did put "illegitimacy" law reform and mother's pensions on the national agenda and stimulated federal interest in family welfare.

Stymied by others' fears about "destruction of the family," Dummer turned more to her private philanthropy, continuing to trust that human compassion and ingenuity could devise more life-affirming, multifaceted responses to crisis pregnancies. She funded sociologist W.I. Thomas's research on unwed motherhood and nonstigmatizing responses to it, then wrote the introduction to his report.

"Confidence in Life Force"
by Ethel Sturges Dummer

Modern psychology is throwing so much light upon human behavior that concerning delinquency one cannot do better than follow the teaching of Spinoza, "Neither condemn nor ridicule but try to understand." ...

Little girls unfortunate enough to have a sex experience called to the attention of the court, who in the past would have been confined behind bars, are now placed in the country, given good food and opportunity for free happy activity. Formerly for the unmarried mothers the psychological values of pregnancy were ignored, and in the effort to save the reputation by concealing motherhood the mind and character were often weakened.

If fear in soldiers could produce pathological symptoms both mental and physical, curable by psychiatry, might not some of this apparent feeble-mindedness be a hysteria resulting from shock? Most case histories showed early sex experience treated, especially when pregnancy resulted, with utmost scorn, contempt and condemnation. Surely the world offers to these little unmarried mothers as menacing a front as was faced by the soldiers in France ...

Doctor Healy questions whether such a constructive act as bringing a child into the world should ever be classed as a crime. Life, legal or illegal, must be respected.

One grows to love the incorrigible girl. She has many fine qualities. A protective officer was escorting to a State institution a girl thought too bad for a House of the Good Shepherd. A train wreck occurred and she thought, "Here is where my girl escapes me." On the contrary, the "incorrigible" turned to and helped as many as possible of those injured ...

The period of pregnancy should be (if the imagination be not filled with old wives' tales) one of health, exhilaration, development of psychic values and social consciousness. Any woman experiencing this wonderful functioning should be aided to as complete psycho-biological fulfillment as her personality and the social situation permit. Should the higher love and association of the father of her child be lacking, so much the greater is her need of genuine help and encouragement. Given this, she may be strengthened and stabilized whether the man desert or become disaffected before or after a legal ceremony ...

It is possible to minimize sexual blunder as unfortunate but not irreparable. Such lesson, however, should never be based on condemnation but must be linked with idealism. A wise physician said, "Nature tends toward meliorism." This accounts for the success of girls who pull themselves up without aid.

That nature has brought us up from the amoeba to man should give us confidence in Life Force. Life is not so simple as to have one "definition of the situation" solve the whole problem ...

—Foreword (excerpt), W.I. Thomas, *The Unadjusted Girl*, Little, Brown and Co., 1923.

"Bring A Little Stone": Bertha Pappenheim (1859-1936)

Bertha Pappenheim has been known to the world chiefly as "Anna O," Sigmund Freud's pseudonym for the "hysteria" patient whom, he claimed, inspired him to invent psychoanalysis, "the talking cure." We believe the evidence suggests Pappenheim invented "the talking cure," and Freud took credit for this female creativity, like those men Matilda Joslyn Gage exposed (see Gage, Part One). Pappenheim's life beyond her "hysteria" was long and abundantly generative. She was born in Vienna, Austria, to a prosperous Orthodox Jewish family. At that time, Jewish men greatly shaped the city's stimulating intellectual and artistic culture; Jewish women were educated only to prepare them for marriage and domesticity. Viennese women of all faiths were legally barred from higher education. Pappenheim fell ill between her twenty-second and twenty-ninth years, the ages considered "marriageable" in her cultural context. Here her biographer Melinda Given Guttmann echoes Gage's insight that accused witches were women punished for their extraordinary intelligence, sensitivity, and healing power.

> In the classical era, Bertha might have been described as having been in a divine frenzy and thus a prophetess, like Cassandra . . . In the Middle Ages, theologians explained these manifestations of hysteria as proof of an individual's alliance with unholy powers . . . Hysterics often became victims of the witch craze, that long and dreadful mass delusion . . . [1]

In nineteenth-century Vienna, "hysterics" were no longer executed, although "progressive" treatments had a punitive, stifling cast. Dr. Joseph Breuer (who actually treated Pappenheim; Freud never did) did respect her powerful self-healing method: spinning stories from the "private theater" of her rich imagination to express her spiritual longings and aspirations. Other psychiatrists dismissed Breuer's insistence upon the "talking cure," and subjected Pappenheim to agonizing electrical shocks and arsenic.

In 1888, Pappenheim published a short story collection and moved with her mother, Recha, to Frankfurt, Recha's birthplace. Their Goldschmidt relatives, prominent financiers and generous philanthropists, welcomed them warmly. A lifelong collector of fine laces, Pappenheim organized a sewing club. At a relative's request, she volunteered at a soup kitchen and was deeply moved by Eastern European Jewish refugees from pogroms. Some German Jews looked down on their less educated, acculturated coreligionists; Pappenheim and others aided them through the Israelite Women's Association. From 1895 to 1907, Pappenheim was the much-admired director/housemother of the Association's residence for orphaned and "illegitimate" girls.

Pappenheim thus dedicated her life to "spiritual motherhood" (her term). She published an article on Mary Wollstonecraft (1897) and (1899) a German translation of the *Vindication* and her own *Women's Right*. This play about the political, economic, and sexual abuse of women sympathetically portrays a woman abandoned to her crisis pregnancy and affirms her "illegitimate" child's right to the same care as any child. In 1902, Pappenheim founded the international Weibliche Fürsorge, or Care by Women, to assist Jews forced into prostitution ("white slavery"). Many were unwed mothers or abandoned wives whose husbands denied them a *get* (religious divorce). Through her travels, Pappenheim encountered news of "militant" English suffragists. She found their tactics distasteful and their objectives and strength of character admirable. In 1904, Pappenheim founded Germany's first national Jewish women's group, the Jüdischer Frauenbund (JFB), and served as its president and international ambassador until 1924. In 1907, Pappenheim created the Home for Wayward Girls in Neu Isenberg, near Frankfurt, a voluntary refuge for abandoned wives, pregnant young women, unwed mothers and their children, and young women at risk for prostitution or delinquency. Despite ludicrous gossip that Pappenheim was starting a brothel, she raised enough money. After World War I, the Home took in war orphans as well.

Unlike most American and English feminists at the time, many Germans sought a general right to abortion. Catholic and Jewish German women, however, were wary or outright opposed.[2] The year after Pappenheim's presidency ended, the JFB endorsed legal abortion, but only for severe medical or social hardship. After pointedly suggesting that judges should not impose death sentences they are unwilling to carry out themselves, Pappenheim wrote in the JFB journal:

> Those who oppose the death penalty must also oppose abortion. The death penalty destroys a life that has proven harmful to the community, but abortion robs the community of countless opportunities to bring up and witness the blossoming of life's precious values.[3]

Ominous political changes began to rapidly, widely shut down opportunities for "life's precious values" to blossom. In 1934, Pappenheim responded to Nazi book burnings:

> One needs human beings far more than books, and the dreaded spirit cannot be burned . . . [Yet] when I think of an unborn child, and see an infant in its crib, then everything that I want to learn, read, shape and form gathers and focuses on that developing being like a wish to God which I offer up to the spirit that lives scattered through books—a diaspora of the spirit.[4]

By 1935, the Nuremberg Laws had dispelled the last of Pappenheim's hope, not unknown among German Jews, that the Nazi regime might accord them a place. Although dying of cancer, she helped friends immigrate to Palestine (her anti-Zionism notwithstanding), escorted Jewish children to a Scottish orphanage, and joyfully celebrated a last Passover Seder with the residents of her beloved Home. The Gestapo interrogated her about rumors that a developmentally disabled former resident had made anti-Hitler remarks. Pappenheim remained unshakably calm and dignified. A month later, she died in the company of loved ones and was buried beside Recha in Frankfurt's Old Jewish Cemetery.

When the Nazis threatened to make them brothel inmates, 93 young women committed suicide at the Beth Jakob Seminary, a Krakow teacher's school Pappenheim had hoped to assist. On Kristallnacht, November 10, 1938, Nazis burned down the Home at Neu Isenberg. The staff saved their own and the residents' lives—temporarily. Many would soon perish in the concentration camps, as the JFB leaders did. In Pappenheim's memory, the few survivors began new Care by Women chapters in New York and Palestine.

Pappenheim herself had already addressed anyone who remembered her and wished to visit her grave: "Bring a little stone, as the silent promise and symbol of the establishment of the idea and mission of woman's duty and woman's joy in serving unceasingly and courageously in life."[5]

Although desecrated by anti-Semites past and present, the Old Jewish Cemetery still exists in Frankfurt, and with it Pappenheim's grave. Anyone who respects life in deed has a "little stone" she could bring, given the opportunity.

Estelle Sylvia Pankhurst (1882-1960)

Estelle Sylvia Pankhurst came from an English family known for thorny, complex personalities who threw themselves into reform. Her father Richard, an international law specialist, drafted the first British woman suffrage bill. Her mother Emmeline and sister Christabel led the "militant" or civil-disobedient branch of the suffrage movement, particularly the Women's Social and Political Union (founded 1903).[1] Sylvia first worked as an artist designing banners, posters, cards, and magazine covers for "the cause." She eventually broke with the WSPU over power struggles with Emmeline and Christabel, then took her activism to London's working-class East End. Defining pacifists as people who "rebel against the present organization of society," she vocally opposed World War I.[2] She started a toy factory that paid adequate wages to women, "Price-Cost Restaurants" serving inexpensive meals, "The Mother's Arms" day care center, and a Montessori school. Pankhurst agitated for birth control and sex education among female laborers, so often compelled to self-induced abortion. In later decades, she became so involved in Ethiopia's resistance to imperialist domination that she made her home and ultimately her gravesite there.

In 1927, at the age of forty-five, Sylvia openly and proudly became the mother of an "illegitimate" son, Richard. Motivated partly by this experience, Sylvia published her book *Save the Mothers*, arguing that high rates of maternal, infant, and fetal mortality were all the more reprehensible because they were preventable. With special attention to working-class and single mothers, she made the case for a universal, free maternity service. Condemning "vast expenditure on armaments," she "urge[d] that the money saved on engines of destruction . . . be diverted to the high service of life creation."[3] Pankhurst's biographer Patricia Romero notes with some surprise, "as progressive as she was on health, Sylvia opposed abortion." Romero attributes Sylvia's view to the illegality of abortion and to Victorian sexual "propriety."[4] Here Pankhurst speaks for herself.

"The True Mission of Society"
by Estelle Sylvia Pankhurst

. . . Abortion, a terrible and dangerous expedient, is appallingly common . . . Numerous indeed are the married women in this country who, under economic pressure and the strain of maintaining the welfare of their families, have attempted abortion, not once but many times. "When I found out I was pregnant again I tried everything!" How often the phrase slips out when a mother is telling her troubles to sympathetic ears! A woman who today is a Borough Councillor, with children already old enough to share her social work, came to me years ago in a pitiable condition; she had doubled and doubled daily doses of Beecham's pills, till she was swallowing thirty-two at a sitting, and had reduced herself to a state in which she was scarcely able to sit in a chair; yet had failed to attain her object.

"What shall I do now?" she wailed, looking to me to find some exit from her dilemma.

"Now we shall have to get you made better to have the baby," I answered. Nemesis-like, perhaps, to her ears; yet the lad has done well; she is proud and glad of him now.

Mothers vehemently defend abortion, declaring that they have resorted to it for the sake of their children. Increasing numbers . . . argue that, faced with undesired pregnancy, women will procure abortion by hook or by crook; therefore the law should permit abortion, provided it be done under State supervision, with strict aseptic precautions. Others consider that since even under the best conditions abortion is injurious to the mother, it should be avoided by preventing pregnancy and that the use of contraceptives should be publicly taught . . . Both views have received legislative sanction in Soviet Russia, which in this, as in much else, has become a field of experiment in social theories.

It is grievous indeed that the social collectivity should feel itself obliged to assist in so ugly an expedient as abortion in order to mitigate its crudest evils. The true mission of Society is to provide the conditions, legal, moral, economic, and obstetric, which will assure happy and successful motherhood.

—*Save the Mothers*, London: Knopf, 1930, 108-110.

Selectively Remembered? Alice Paul (1885-1977)

Alice Paul, a Friend (Quaker) from Moorestown, New Jersey, earned a bachelor's degree at Swarthmore, a master's in sociology at the University of Pennsylvania, and a doctorate at the London School of Economics. After hearing Christabel Pankhurst speak, Paul became a member of the Women's Social and Political Union (WSPU), adopting its "militant" tactics—picketing, prison hunger strikes—to agitate for woman suffrage. In this way she met her companion Lucy Burns (1897-1966), a Brooklyn Irish Catholic educated at Vassar and Yale. After returning to the U.S., the two founded the single-issue Congressional Union for Women Suffrage, later the National Women's Party, which introduced "militant" tactics to the U.S. Unlike the WSPU, but like Sylvia Pankhurst, the NWP refrained from arson and window-smashing. Suffragist leaders like Crystal Eastman and Harriot Stanton Blatch, Elizabeth Cady Stanton's daughter, soon joined the NWP. In 1913 they marched on Washington, D.C., and held smaller daily protests outside the White House. Upon U.S. entry into World War I, suffragists and other progressives were branded unpatriotic traitors. During the daily pickets, conservative men engaged in repeated physical attacks against Paul. Yet *she* was the one who served prison time, winning release only after a hunger strike. Paul's efforts gave the final push to the 1920 passage of the Nineteenth Amendment, which finally enfranchised women nearly a century after the Grimké sisters envisioned the possibility.

Paul unfortunately long neglected life-threatening barriers to Black women's exercise of their newfound right. Most African American women, and men, did not secure their voting rights in actual practice until the 1960s, and even today that security is not a given. Paul's exclusive emphasis on individual legal rights and legal equality also divided her from "social feminists" like the Hull House women and labor unionists, who preferred multi-issue attention to women's material circumstances. Paul and the NWP soon turned to the single issue of a constitutional Equal Rights Amendment. In 1923, Paul introduced the ERA's original version. She lobbied another half century for ERA, securing mentions of sex equality in the United Nations Charter and the 1964 Civil Rights Act.[1]

Though pleased over ERA's revival, Paul "took particular exception to NOW's 1967 endorsement of the movement to repeal abortion laws."[2] Paul insisted that abortion hurt the cause of women and that it was irrelevant to ERA and indeed eroded support for it.[3] Some explain her objections in terms of her single-issue versus NOW's multi-issue agenda. According to Baha'i feminist Evelyn Judge, Paul's colleague from the 1940s onward, this was not the full story. While Paul advocated voluntary contraception and voluntary motherhood, during the 1960s she asked: "How can one protect and help women by killing them as babies?" To her, abortion was lifetaking and "the ultimate in the exploitation of women."[4]

In 1977, feminists marched on Washington in Paul's memory. NOW's southern New Jersey chapter named itself after her and calls its clinic defense initiative Alice's Champion of Reproductive Rights. As a Quaker nonviolent resister who was harassed and assaulted herself, Alice Paul likely would not have countenanced verbal and physical abuse of abortion clinic staff and patients, not to mention arson, bombing, and shooting. What peace advocate and feminist, prochoice or prolife, would *not* object to such ugly tactics? But on what basis does the Alice Paul NOW Chapter assume that its clinic escorts usher pregnant women into a procedure their hero would endorse as a reproductive right? Has the organization questioned whether Paul shared their abortion-rights agenda? Is the memory of Paul selective?[5]

In 1992, Evelyn Judge, a wheelchair user, went to great personal trouble to attend the dedication of Paul's home as a National Historic Landmark. The organizers had reacted with hostility and indifference at her offer beforehand to share her recollections, including Paul's views of abortion. They completely ignored Judge during the event. Her only consolation was a life-size cardboard cutout of Alice Paul that kept falling over—a militant but nonviolent protest from beyond the grave?[6]

Dorothy Day (1897-1980)

Dorothy Day was co-founder and guiding spirit, with her friend Peter Maurin, of the Catholic Worker Movement, which now runs more than 140 "houses of hospitality" in the United States and seven other countries. The houses offer food, clothing, shelter, and welcome to homeless and impoverished people. Often called a saint, Day quipped she did not want to be dismissed so easily. Once when a naïve adulator asked if she ever saw holy visions, she rolled her eyes and exclaimed, "Oh, shit!" It is entertaining to imagine how she might respond to the present-day campaign for her canonization as a Roman Catholic saint.[1]

Day, the daughter of an Episcopalian journalist and homemaker, survived the great San Francisco earthquake of 1906 with her family. They then moved to Chicago. At 16, she won a scholarship to the University of Illinois at Urbana. Jewish friends introduced her to the flourishing socialist movement. Day heard Rose Pastor Stokes speak of birth control and social justice. Set on fire, Day left college to report for the radical New York City newspapers *The Call* and *The Masses*. Day covered the arrests and imprisonment of Margaret Higgins Sanger, nurse Ethel Higgins Byrne (Margaret's sister), and Yiddish translator/social worker Fania Mindell. Police had raided their Brooklyn birth control clinic, the first in the U.S. Day worked also for the Anti-Conscription League. In 1917, Day was imprisoned herself, one of 40 suffragists, including Lucy Burns, arrested for a White House demonstration. Deeply affected by World War I, Day began nurses' training at a Brooklyn hospital. There she met her first lover, Lionel Moise. As she recounts in her autobiographical novel *The Eleventh Virgin*, her happiness soon gave way to great anguish:

> And then June [Day] discovered she was about to become a mother . . . .
> She lay crying and sobbing on the bed. She was caught! . . . Dick
> [Moise] would never consent to have one. He had impressed that on
> her mind many times. If she insisted on having it, he would leave
> her . . . . She could not sacrifice her pride and go to a home to have a
> baby. She could sacrifice every vestige of pride—throw it all into the

flames to keep her love burning. Her love for a man. But not her love
for the child that was beginning to form in her . . . . Why should she
expect any help from Dick anyway? . . . She continued excusing him
for the brutality she expected he would show her . . . It was all her fault
anyway.[2]

She refused a woman friend's kindly challenge to have the baby, pleading
that she'd lose her boyfriend, that she was unmarried and "the most incapable
sort of person," that it would be "the height of selfishness" to bear a child
who wouldn't "have a fair chance at happiness." "Weeping at the thought
of the child she could not have," she underwent an illegal abortion:

> Just to lie there and endure . . . . The hours seemed an eternity, but the
> minutes sped by very fast . . . . The pain came in a huge wave and she
> lay there writhing and tortured under it . . . . She no longer thought of
> the child. That was over and done with. Although it was amazing how
> weak she was, she felt curiously clear and light-hearted . . . [3]

Her relief and denial soon evaporated. Moise broke his promise to take
her home and left a note terminating their relationship.

Day soon married and divorced another man. In 1924 she bought a
beach cottage on Long Island with earnings from her novel and began a
common-law relationship with anarchist Forster Batterham. Her newfound
joy intensified when she became pregnant again:

> For a long time now, I had thought I could not have a child. A book I
> read years ago, in school, *Silas Marner,* expressed the sorrow of a mother
> bereft of her child, and it expressed, too, my sorrow at my childless
> state. Just a few months ago I read it again, with a longing in my heart
> for a baby.

Tamar's birth ended "a harsh winter."

> My joy was so great that I sat up in bed in the hospital and wrote an
> article for *The New Masses* about my child, wanting to share my joy with
> the world . . . a joy all women know no matter what their grief at poverty,
> unemployment, and class war.[4]

Birthing and raising Tamar, chiefly as a single mother, empowered Day
to reclaim a psychological and spiritual growth process the abortion had

thwarted. Day went on to boldly found and lead the Catholic Worker Movement and resist the degradation of the poor, war, the death penalty, labor abuses, racism, and anti-Semitism. (When Tamar was young, Day had converted to Roman Catholicism, at the time a predominantly working-class, immigrant religion in America.) In 1977, Day wrote in *The Catholic Worker* newspaper of "a delightful visit" with Tamar, "now the mother of nine and grandmother of twelve!" She reprinted the birth story as "Having A Baby—A Christmas Story" and recounted a visit she and Tamar, then three, had with artist Diego Rivera in Mexico. He said: "I know this little girl . . . Your article 'Having a Baby' was reprinted all over the Soviet Union, in many languages. You ought to go over there and collect royalties."[5]

For years the abortion remained so painful to Day that she hesitated to speak of it directly. She burned as many copies of *The Eleventh Virgin* as she could, until her confessor advised her that divine forgiveness was hers if she desired and asked for it herself. Day obviously found a more constructive way to deal with her pain: through her challenges to what she called "remedies on the side of death."[6] Day witnessed and welcomed feminism's Second Wave but dissented from its unprecedented stress on abortion "rights," which she associated with its eugenic blinders to the poor, people of color, the Two-Thirds World.[7] Her anti-elitist, anti-eugenic prolife views seem to overlap with prochoice scholar Rickie Solinger's conclusion about the main reason the U.S. legalized abortion.

> By 1965 . . . the white unwed mother had been changed in the public consciousness from a species of mental patient into a sexual revolutionary. The black unwed mother was still portrayed as a participant in an aberrant culture of sexuality and as the taxpayers' nemesis . . . [and] increasingly cast as the triggering device affixed to the Population Bomb, U.S.A. The "sexual revolution" and the "population bomb" were racially specific metaphors of destruction . . . By virtue of these tropes, unwed mothers . . . were assigned apocalyptic importance . . . Abortion became an acceptable way to meet an old goal, that is, containing the social consequences of illicit female sexuality and fertility.[8]

From at least Mary Wollstonecraft on, Day and other independent-minded women sought healing, for themselves and for their sisters, from the punitive violence of abortion and its underlying causes. Still others have carried this still-vital struggle forward into times and dilemmas their foremothers did not live to see.

From Having a Baby
by Dorothy Day

... The [cab] driver breathed a sigh of relief as he left us at Bellevue, and so did we. We sat for half an hour or so in the receiving room, my case evidently not demanding immediate attention, and watched with interest the reception of other patients. The doctor, greeting us affably, asked which of us was the maternity case which so complimented me and amused [my cousin] Carol that our giggling tided us over any impatience we felt.

There was a Black woman with a tiny baby, born that morning, brought in on a stretcher. She kept sitting up, her child clutched to her bosom, yelling that she had an earache, and the doctor kept pushing her back. Carol, who suffers from the same complaint, said that she would rather have a baby than an earache, and I agreed with her.

Then there was a genial drunk, assisted in with difficulty by a cab driver and his fare, who kept insisting that he had been kicked by a large white horse. His injuries did not seem to be serious.

... My turn came next, and as I was wheeled away in a chair by a pleasant, old orderly with whiskey breath, Carol's attention was attracted and diverted from my ordeal by the reception of a drowned man, or one almost drowned, from whom they were trying to elicit information about his wife, whether he was living with her, their address, religion, occupation, and birthplace——information which the man was totally unable to give.

For the next hour I received all the attention Carol would have desired for me—attentions which I did not at all welcome. The nurse who ministered to me was a large, beautiful creature with marcelled hair and broad hips, which she flaunted about the small room with much grace. She was a flippant creature and talked of Douglas Fairbanks and the film she had seen that afternoon, while she wielded a long razor with abandon ... Thinking of moving pictures, why didn't the hospital provide a moving picture for women having babies? And music! Surely things should be made as interesting as possible for women who are perpetuating the race.

I had nothing at home to put the baby in, I thought suddenly. Except a bureau drawer. Carol said she would have a clothes basket. But I adore cradles. Too bad I had been unable to find one. A long time ago I saw an adorable one on the east side in an old second-hand shop. They wanted thirty dollars for it and I didn't have the thirty dollars, and besides, how did I know then I was going to have a baby? Still I wanted to buy it. If Sarah Bernhardt could carry a coffin around the country with her there is no reason why I couldn't carry a cradle around with me ...

An awful thing to get used to anything. I mustn't get used to that baby. I don't see how I can. Lightning! It shoots through your back, down your stomach, through your legs and out at the end of your toes. Sometimes it takes longer to get out than others. You have to push it out then. I am not afraid of lightning now, but I used to be . . . .

Hours passed. I thought it must be about four o'clock and found that it was two. Every five minutes the pains came and in between I slept. As each pain began I groaned and cursed, "How long will this one last?" and then when it had swept over with the beautiful rhythm of the sea, I felt with satisfaction "it could be worse," and clutched at sleep again frantically.

Every now and then my large-hipped nurse came in to see how I was getting along. She was a sociable creature, though not so to me, and brought with her a flip, young doctor and three other nurses to joke and laugh about hospital affairs. They disposed themselves on the other two beds but my nurse sat on the foot of mine, pulling the entire bed askew with her weight. This spoiled my sleeping during the five minute intervals, and, mindful of my grievance against her and the razor, I took advantage of the beginning of the next pain to kick her soundly in the behind. She got up with a jerk and obligingly took a seat on the next bed.

And so the night wore on. When I became bored and impatient with the steady restlessness of those waves of pain, I thought of all the other and more futile kinds of pain I would rather not have. Toothaches, earaches, and broken arms. I had had them all. And this is a much more satisfactory and accomplishing pain, I comforted myself.

And I thought, too, how much had been written about child birth—no novel, it seems, is complete without at least one birth scene. I counted over the ones I had read that winter—Upton Sinclair's in *The Miracle of Love*, Tolstoi's in *Anna Karenina*, Arnim's in *The Pastor's Wife*, Galsworthy's in *Beyond*, O'Neill's in *The Last Man*, Bennett's in *The Old Wives' Tale* and so on.

All but one of these descriptions had been written by men, and, with the antagonism natural toward men at such a time, I resented their presumption.

"What do they know about it, the idiots," I thought. And it gave me pleasure to imagine one of them in the throes of childbirth. How they would groan and holler and rebel. And wouldn't they make everybody else miserable around them. And here I was, conducting a neat and tidy job, begun in a most businesslike manner, on the minute. But when would it end?

While I dozed and wondered and struggled, the last scene of my little drama began, much to the relief of the doctors and nurses, who were becoming impatient now that it was almost time for them to go off duty. The smirk of complacence was wiped from me. Where before there had been waves, there were now tidal waves. Earthquake and fire swept my body. My spirit was a battleground on which thousands were butchered in a most horrible manner. Through the rush and roar of the cataclysm which was all about me I heard the murmur of the doctor and the answered murmur of the nurse at my head.

In a white blaze of thankfulness I knew that ether was forthcoming. I breathed deeply for it, mouth open and gasping like that of a baby starving for its mother's breast. Never have I known such frantic imperious desire for anything. And then the mask descended on my face and I gave myself to it, hurling myself into oblivion as quickly as possible. As I fell, fell, fell, very rhythmically, to the accompaniment of tom toms, I heard, faint about the clamor in my ears, a peculiar squawk. I smiled as I floated dreamily and luxuriously on a sea without waves. I had handed in my white ticket and the next thing I would see would be the baby they would give me in exchange. It was the first time I had thought of the child in a long, long time.

Tamara Teresa's nose is twisted slightly to one side. She sleeps with the placidity of a Mona Lisa, so that you cannot see the amazing blue of her eyes which are strangely blank and occasionally, ludicrously crossed. What little hair she has is auburn and her eyebrows are golden. Her complexion is a rich tan. Her ten fingers and toes are of satisfactory length and slenderness and I reflect that she will be a dancer when she grows up, which future will relieve her of the necessity for learning reading, writing and arithmetic.

Her long, upper lip, which resembles that of an Irish policeman, may interfere with her beauty, but with such posy hands as she has already, nothing will interfere with her grace. Just now I must say she is a lazy little hog, mouthing around my nice full breast and too lazy to tug for food. What do you want, little bird? That it should run into your mouth, I suppose. But no, you must work for your provender already.

She is only four days old but already she has the bad habit of feeling bright and desirous of play at four o'clock in the morning. Pretending that I am a bone and she is a puppy dog, she worries at me fussily, tossing her head and grunting. Of course, some mothers will tell you this is because she has air on her stomach and that I should hold her upright until a loud gulp indicates that she is ready to begin feeding again. But though I hold her up as required, I still think the child's play instinct is highly developed.

Other times she will pause a long time, her mouth relaxed, then looking at me slyly, trying to tickle me with her tiny, red tongue. Occasionally she pretends to lose me and with a loud wail of protest grabs hold once more to start feeding furiously. It is fun to see her little jaw working and the hollow that appears in her baby throat as she swallows.

Sitting up in bed, I glance alternately at my beautiful flat stomach and out the window at tug boats and barges and the wide path of the early morning sun on the East River. Whistles are blowing cheerily, and there are some men singing on the wharf below. The restless water is colored lavender and gold and the enchanting sky is a sentimental blue and pink. And gulls wheeling, warm grey and white against the magic of the water and the sky. Sparrows chirp on the windowsill, the baby sputters as she gets too big a mouthful, and pauses, then, a moment to look around her with satisfaction. Everybody is complacent, everybody is satisfied and everybody is happy.

—*The New Masses,* June 1928.

Laborers of Love: Midwives in Dispossessed Southern U.S. Communities (Twentieth Century)

By the 1930s most Americans were, like the Days, giving and receiving birth in medicalized hospital settings. Yet for several decades lay midwives persisted in the rural South's dispossessed, indigent communities: African American, First Nation, Latino/a, and white Appalachian. During the late 1980s, Debra Anne Susie recorded the last lay midwives' own words. They emerge as proud, skilled, profoundly compassionate practitioners of a woman-centered, life-giving art, with excellent safety records, and a willingness to accommodate mothers' financial hardships and give household help. Susie's interviewees clearly did not match the discrediting, dismissive stereotype of all midwives as abortionists.

> Not one . . . accepted the notion of illegitimate children: "They's all children to me" was a commonly shared sentiment. So when the topic of abortion came up, the answer was easy: "No." Yet their conviction was not so much a moralistic principle as an affirmation of all life as positive and legitimate, as they knew it from their intimate familiarity with birth . . . [Some] were willing to cross yet another barrier—one of race—to lend support to those choosing to go ahead with an unwanted birth . . . to not only deliver the child but *raise* it, black or white, and then turn it over to the mother if she . . . decided she wanted it back.[1]

One midwife remarked, "Lot of this abortion goin' on that shouldn't be. That ought to be lawed out—plum out. They'll be a lot of people suffer for that. They may not now, but they will later . . ." She recounted her response to one woman seeking abortion.

> I just thought she oughtn't have stepped out on her husband if it didn't belong to him, but I didn't tell her that . . . I told her, "That's murder . . . Don't destroy that little baby, this life. If you want to . . . you carry on to its time if you will. Then you come up here, and I'll deliver it for you; or at least I'll do my best . . . If you don't want it, then after you have it, just give it to me . . .[2]

Physicians pushed for regulation beyond reasonable training and safety standards, forcing lay midwives from practice. For example, Medicaid would reimburse obstetricians, but not midwives. Would-be clients were left with the "choice" between medicalized hospital birth and abortion. The 1960s did bring a revival of interest in homebirth and midwifery in the U.S. and other industrialized nations. Often this was the consciously feminist response of educated white women to the pathologizing of female bodily functions. These midwives—Ina May Gaskin, for example—have often tapped into the same nonviolent power as Susie's interviewees. Gaskin began the world-renowned midwifery service at The Farm, an intentional "hippy" community founded near Summertown, Tennessee in 1971. In *Spiritual Midwifery*, which has inspired countless women to train as midwives or seek their aid, Gaskin made a familiar-sounding offer that nearly 100 women accepted during the 1970s: "Don't have an abortion. You can come to The Farm and we'll deliver your baby and take care of it, and if you ever decide you want it back, you can have it."[3]

Elsewhere, abortion rights advocacy took firm hold. Many feminists, even those who rejected eugenics and population control as affronts to reproductive choice, saw it as a way out from the extremely limited, secrecy—and shame-ridden "options" inflicted upon women in crisis pregnancies during the era they came of age. Such options included hasty marriage, punitive and pressured closed adoption, or submission to illegal abortion. The prochoice cries "Never again!" and "Don't turn back the clock!" arise from the visceral fear that women will be caught in this setup again. Indeed, who would want that? A substantial, overlooked, even suppressed minority of feminists proposed the abolition of abortion itself, legal or illegal, because they saw it as *part* of this setup. Slowly but surely, they began to find one another and organize, reclaim and modernize feminism's consistent life ethic tradition, and join with the wide diversity of persons whose values and concerns already resonated with their own. Part Two documents this still-unfolding story.

PART TWO
1960s to the Present

Fannie Lou Hamer at Democratic National Convention, Atlantic City, N.J. Photograph by Warren K. Leffler, 1964 Aug. 22. From the U.S. News and World Report Collection.

Introduction to Part Two, Second Edition

In Part One, we heard the diverse voices of our feminist foremothers telling us that abortion is a violent and unacceptable alternative to the problem of crisis pregnancy. Beyond that, they identified and condemned those societal factors that led women to seek abortion, and they demanded and effected better possibilities for women. These early feminists hand down to us a vision of a world in which oppression has ceased, violence is rejected as a means of conflict resolution, and women's creative ability is valued and celebrated. The voices in Part Two of this volume share this vision. They, too, consider abortion an unacceptable choice that contradicts values of nurturing and interconnection and, like their foremothers, they scrutinize and denounce those aspects of a male-dominated society that have made abortion an integral part of woman's reality.

There are, however, several differences between the feminist voices of yesterday and the voices of today. Early feminist writings on the issue of abortion differ from ours in that none of our foremothers seemed to have imagined that abortion would one day be legal and promoted as a "woman's right," and they, therefore, do not address their fellow feminists in their argument. There was consensus among them that abortion is the violent taking of human life and that it arises from women's oppression. While the feminists in Part Two of this volume are in agreement with the conclusions drawn by their feminist foremothers, they are aware that much of today's culture finds feminism synonymous with abortion rights advocacy. They write with an intention to show that abortion is a human rights issue, and therefore a feminist one. Their opposition to abortion is part of a consistent life ethic regarding issues pertinent to the culture they live in.

Another difference between their writings is that earlier feminists often refer to their religious faith as informing their position on abortion. For many of them, their convictions on social issues were shaped primarily by their spiritual faith, as their writings show. In Part Two we also hear similarly diverse religious voices, including Christians—Catholics, Protestants, Eastern Orthodox, Quakers, Evangelicals—and also Jews, Buddhists, Muslims, agnostics, and atheists. In spite of this range of religious beliefs, however, we see few overtly theological arguments. For many of them, abortion is simply not a religious issue; it is a human rights issue that need not involve any discussion of religious faith. But for others, their views on abortion and other forms of violence are inseparable from their faith. And still for others, the current atmosphere of the abortion debate dictates that they de-emphasize their religious convictions. In today's society, in public debate one cannot reject abortion simply on religious grounds unless she keeps those beliefs to herself and refrains from imposing them on others— anything else is perceived as a violation of the separation of church and state. This is ironic in that such an imperative would have negated the works of most eighteenth- and nineteenth-century abolitionists as well as the accomplishments of such women as Lucretia Mott, Sarah Grimké and Angelina Grimké Weld, Susan B. Anthony, Matilda Joslyn Gage, Sister Irene Fitzgibbon, Olympia Brown, and Bertha Pappenheim. In the twentieth century, one would have to dismiss the contributions of dozens of social movements throughout the world that have espoused spiritually grounded nonviolent activism. Dorothy Day, Mother Teresa, and the Dalai Lama become suspect because they have acted on the basis of their religious convictions.

It is telling that such figures are charged with imposing misogynist sectarian morality if and when they openly express prolife views on abortion, no matter how organically these emerge from their dedication to interfaith/ nonsectarian values of nonviolence. This accusation is exasperatingly familiar to Roman Catholics, but belonging to another faith tradition does not confer immunity to it. It has been directed against the 1989 Nobel Peace Prize laureate, the Dalai Lama, Buddhist spiritual and democratically elected political leader in exile of the Chinese-occupied nation of Tibet. As a familiar, beloved presence in the global interfaith dialogue movement, the Dalai Lama has called for voluntary, "nonviolent birth control only," meaning "not abortion or killing."[1] Here he addresses Sakyadhita, an international Buddhist women's organization (www.Sakyadhita.org) whose efforts toward the full ordination of female monastics he supports:

> Mere tradition can never justify violations of human rights. Thus, discrimination against persons of a different race, against women, and against weaker sections of society may be traditional in some places, but because they are inconsistent with universally recognized human rights, these forms of behaviour should change. The universal principle of the equality of all human beings must take precedence . . . As well as being equally capable, women have an equal responsibility.[2]

If their prolife views were intended only for coreligionists, such religious leaders would not offer them to the world community as they have. Would most African American civil rights activists of the 1950s and 60s today be dismissed on the basis of their religious convictions? The Rev. Dr. Martin Luther King Jr. was constantly criticized for trying to "legislate morality," but his critics have fallen into disrepute.

The diversity of religious views represented in Part Two is also accompanied by a celebration and recognition of the importance of cultural diversity. Compared to earlier Anglo feminists, current prolife feminists possess an increased awareness of the pervasive forms of discrimination that accompany intolerance of cultural diversity. As mentioned in Part One, some of our feminist foremothers espoused or left unchallenged societal prejudices against minorities and immigrants, and some even held eugenic and racist views about reproduction. There was also a tendency to deny or ignore the important contributions of minority groups whose subcultures espoused a prolife ethic, including First Nation peoples, African Americans, and Latinos. Today's prolife feminism is more inclusive and recognizes the need to seek out and listen to the voices of women from diverse backgrounds. It is no surprise that the earliest prolife feminist voices of the second half of the twentieth century belong to women of color (Hamer and Olivarez, Part Two). The voices in Part Two speak out not only against sexism, but also against classism and racism as well as discrimination against minorities of all kinds. Fannie Lou Hamer, Graciela Olivarez, Lorraine Hansberry, Cheryl Long Feather, Cecilia Brown, Benazir Bhutto, Rus Cooper-Dowda, Mary Krane Derr, and Wangari Maathai all speak from personal experience about the difficulties marginal women face in dominant culture.

Like those feminist foremothers who were involved in various reform movements, the feminists represented in Part Two are active in social justice causes that seek to heal violence and oppression: peace/antiwar work; death penalty abolition; environmentalism; and the rights of people of color, GLBT individuals, and persons with disabilities, among others. They also enact their life-affirming beliefs through their work in crisis pregnancy centers, in battered women's shelters and other women's counseling centers, in childbirth classes, in women's studies courses, in churches, in the Two-Thirds World, in their writing and research, in the halls of government, and in their own homes. Some are vegetarians, several are pacifists, most are parents, and some include among their families so-called hard-to-adopt children. They remind us that the oppression of any group of people strikes at the very foundation of a feminism that is based upon the equality of all humans.

It would seem that there would also be distinct differences between the feminist writings of yesterday and those of today concerning woman's present condition in society—hasn't the woman's rights movements resulted in an amelioration of woman's oppression? While women have certainly made great strides, particularly in areas involving individual rights, we believe the devaluation of women in society has in some ways taken new forms since the nineteenth century. As will be seen, the articles in this second part of our volume share some remarkable similarities with those in Part One. In particular, feminist prolifers argue that those conditions our feminist foremothers identified as the underlying causes of abortion still need to be remedied.

The writings in Part One reflect a belief that as women become more educated about their own physiology, when contraceptives become safe and available, when society learns to appreciate and celebrate woman's reproductive ability, when women gain equal rights and enter into sexual relationships on an equal basis, abortion will no longer be a problem. Most people in contemporary U.S. society perceive these goals as having been attained: women certainly know more about their bodies than did nineteenth-century women; contraceptives are safer and more available; baby-boomers brought pregnancy and motherhood back into vogue to some degree; and women are certainly liberated—aren't they? So why have so many women sought abortion since the *Roe v. Wade* Supreme Court decision in 1973? And why is "abortion on demand" being globalized?

While science has provided us with much more information about our bodies, we frequently fail to effectively pass on this information to young women. Planned Parenthood often cites this lack of knowledge when promoting their sex education programs (although their position changes when the subject is informed consent for abortion).[3] But even some of the best sex education programs fail to address the social and political contexts within which the information is expected to be applied. Contraceptives, although certainly more accessible and reliable than many of the methods available to women of the nineteenth century, still are not entirely safe or practical, and the gender-based imbalance of power that is still so prevalent in intimate relationships dictates that the primary responsibility for the use (and failure) of contraceptives is put on the woman. Hormonal contraceptives operate on the principle of interrupting or sabotaging the natural processes of the female body, usually with negative side effects. Barrier methods are relatively safe and available, but, again, women are expected to bear full responsibility for their use. Our increased knowledge of women's reproductive cycles has thankfully led to a safe, effective, natural method of contraception, but natural family planning works on the premise of full equality in the sexual relationship—still uncommon. While pregnancy has become more normalized today (as long as you limit yourself to two children), there still exists a societal aversion to woman's biological processes: witness the multi-million dollar feminine hygiene industry that profits from the idea that we need constant cleaning and deodorizing.

We also see new issues—new degradations of women—that our foremothers did not have to address in the same form. While contemporary popular culture no longer embraces the tenets of nineteenth-century "True Womanhood," any young woman today who turns on the television or opens a magazine is bombarded with air-brushed photos of the ideal woman—skinny body, big breasts, and blond flowing hair—and her resulting feelings of inadequacy and inferiority can drive her to dangerous eating habits, drugs, and surgery. These images can perhaps be compared to illustrations in nineteenth-century women's magazines that popularized fashions requiring corsets and other restricting undergarments; but in today's much more visually oriented, mass-media saturated culture, the images are more pervasive and destructive. The alarming popularity of cosmetic surgery (epitomized by the rash of "reality" television programs featuring "extreme makeovers") shows how idealized images of women have become normalized. Woman's confidence and self-esteem are constantly attacked as she receives messages of her lack. In this state of mind, she is assailed with images of woman as sex object, and she comes to believe that something must be wrong, or at least undesirable, with her if she is not sexually active. To prove herself "normal," she enters into sexual relationships at a very young age, unprepared and often against her own inclination, and her self-esteem continues to deteriorate. When she becomes pregnant, she receives the clear message from society that career and pregnancy, or more accurately, affluence and pregnancy, don't mix. And the final message she receives is perhaps the most insidious. Faced with her dilemma, she seeks the socially acceptable solution. And what do we offer her? Male-dominated society has a history of attempting to solve its conflicts through violence. Is anyone surprised that women have resorted to abortion? To violence against their own children and their own bodies?

From this vantage point, our feminist foremothers might find it very difficult to comprehend modern prochoice feminists. But as their contemporary sisters, we must attempt to understand them and their motivation. A keen perception of gender oppression creates a desire in women to help other women. Like Laura Cuppy Smith, who recognized that her daughter would make it through her crisis only with much practical and emotional support, women today know that their sisters need them. Unfortunately, prochoice feminists respond to their hard-won, visceral knowledge of women's oppression by defending the socially expedient "solution" of abortion. In addition, because these women are so sympathetic to the plight of their sisters, they reject any stance they might find judgmental, and rightly so. By contrast, prolifers are perceived as sitting in judgment upon women who obtain abortions; and while for some this may be a correct characterization, today it is belied by the tens of thousands of prolifers who give of their time, their homes, and their resources to young women facing crisis pregnancies. While many prochoice feminists honorably seek to reduce abortion and expand choice through sex education, family planning, and maternal-child welfare policies, the prochoice movement offers little similar direct aid for carrying such pregnancies to term. Pregnancy and childbirth are simply not the least difficult alternatives.

Part of the problem lies with a lack of imagination or vision. Dominant American culture offers no exemplary construct under which individuals have a greater, or even equal, responsibility to the community (in which all life, including the *in utero* child, is a member) than they do to themselves. Nor does it offer—and this is significant—a paradigm for the community to continue loving and accepting members who have (consciously or in effect) betrayed other members. It is assumed that because prolifers condemn abortion, they condemn the women who resort to it; but women constitute the overwhelming majority of membership in prolife organizations in the U.S., and almost all of these women have had experiences with abortion, either personally or through their close relationships with women who have. Likewise, many of those women who have committed themselves to the prochoice movement have obtained abortions earlier in their lives, and they seek relief from their own grief by assisting other women in similar situations. The sense of loss and empathy that these women feel for their sisters is genuine, and feminists do little for the cause of women by denying this common ground between prochoice and prolife women who are dedicated to helping women.

Significantly, many prochoice feminists have reached some of these same conclusions concerning the underlying causes of abortion. Adrienne Rich considers abortion a violence inflicted by women "first of all upon themselves," and believes that "in a society where women entered sexual intercourse willingly, where adequate contraception was a genuine social priority, there would be no 'abortion issue.'"[4] Germaine Greer echoes Rich when she says,

It is typical of the contradictions that break women's hearts that when they avail themselves of their fragile right to abortion they often, even usually, went with grief and humiliation to carry out a painful duty that was presented to them as a privilege. Abortion is the latest in a long line of non-choices that begin at the very beginning with the time and the place and the manner of lovemaking . . . . [5]

Catherine MacKinnon opens the chapter on abortion in her book *Toward a Feminist Theory of the State* with Adrienne Rich's statement quoted above and makes an excellent case against the privacy argument for abortion, the basis of *Roe v. Wade*.[6] MacKinnon reveals much that is wrong with American attitudes toward privacy rights, but she imposes a scary alternative upon which to base woman's right to abortion: "The abortion choice should be available and must be women's, but not because the fetus is not a form of life. Why should women not make life-or-death decisions?"[7]

MacKinnon's words, after first sending a shudder through those who absolutely reject violence, contradict her own ensuing argument. She effectively articulates the problem of "privacy": that while protecting "individual rights," it privatizes woman's sexual oppression; but by endowing women with the right to decide death for an *other*, MacKinnon is suggesting a privatization of the violence against the *in utero* other. MacKinnon's concession that the fetus is a "form of life" seems to bear little weight with her. (We wonder what form of life she believes the fetus is. Of course, feminists recall that men have historically had a problem in identifying what kind of life form women are.) The life of the fetus, however, has proven to be more perplexing to other feminist theorists who are reevaluating their views on abortion.

Elizabeth Fox-Genovese, in her book *Feminism Without Illusions*, cannot take the life of the fetus quite so lightly.[8] In responding to Carol Gilligan's argument (*In a Different Voice*) that the appropriate way to approach the issue of abortion is not in terms of the life of the fetus but rather in terms of the woman's perception of responsibility to the quality of life for the mother, her family, and the unborn child, Fox-Genovese argues that the "repudiation of any attempt to define life in the abstract" violates that "highest standard of civilization"—the "respect for human life in all its diversity," a standard, we might add, that reflects basic feminist values. She further observes that while many view Gilligan's position as one located in the idea of empathy (many people assume that because they would not want to live a life of disability, abuse, or poverty, neither would anyone else), we all know (or are) abused, deprived, and physically or mentally challenged people who tenaciously hold on to and celebrate life. (The fetus' fierce struggle for life when threatened by the abortionist's instruments has been documented by fetal photography.) Fox-Genovese concludes: "To say, in the face of such evidence, that we have a right to decide which living being would and would not want to live under which conditions is to assume precisely that arrogant disregard for another's subjectivity for which feminists condemn men's attitudes toward women."[9]

It is important to identify the broader context within which Fox-Genovese locates her discomfort with abortion. Like MacKinnon, she sharply criticizes the casting of abortion as a privacy right not only because it privatizes male oppression, but also because it reinforces the individualistic view of society and "dismisses men's claims and dissolves their responsibilities to the next generation." "Abortion," she comments, "challenges feminists to come to terms with the contradictions in their own thought, notably the contradiction between the commitment to community and nurture and the commitment to individual right." It is within this paradigm that she posits the need for a collective definition of life, a definition based upon respect for the other's subjectivity. One can recognize the urgency of this task not only in terms of the abortion debate, but in terms of how society treats its minority members.

In Fox-Genovese's more recent book, *"Feminism is Not the Story of My Life,"* she addresses the "feminist elite" and its disconnection with women of color and working class women in America. This book foregrounds many voices that have been stifled in the abortion debate but which are essential to effective dialogue and practical resolution of women's problems. While some minority-group members have adopted an abortion-rights position, including such high profile activists as the Reverend Jesse Jackson and the UFW's Dolores Huerta (whose prochoice views are a turnaround from previously held prolife views), many others identify their community's plight with that of the unborn child and the pregnant woman threatened by a dearth of nonviolent alternatives to abortion.[10] As exemplified by Fannie Lou Hamer and Graciela Olivarez in this volume, they reject abortion as a sellout to the destructive values of dominant culture and a violation of the respect for and commitment to human rights that have empowered their communities to survive and prevail against injustice and oppression. Their insights resonate with those of their First Nations contemporaries, like the Lakota Mary Brave Bird (later Crow Dog), who birthed her first child as she took part with 200 other American Indian Movement activists in the 1973 taking back of Wounded Knee,[11] or the Cherokee-Choctaw physician

Connie (Constance) Redbird (later Uri, later Pinkerman-Uri), who organized medical supplies for the re-occupation and led vital challenges to sterilization abuse and environmental racism.[12] As Cheryl Long Feather and many others make clear, such holistic resistance to abortion is hardly a thing of the past.

Sometimes these critiques take the form of speechlessness towards dominant-group abortion rights advocates and/or oppressed-group members who have allied with them. In one such instance at the 2004 United Farm Workers Constitutional Convention, Dolores Huerta's advocacy of abortion as "the proper choice of every woman" was met with only scattered voices of support rather than the usual loud applause and shouts of "Sí" she receives.[13] The multitude of silences in the room perhaps reflected respect for and concurrence with consistent prolife views like those of UFW cofounder César Chávez (1927-1993)[14] and early UFW activist Dorothy Day. This phenomenon has been noted across diverse cultural and national contexts. Answering the question of why so few women of color around the world join the feminist movement as such, veteran Koori (Australian aboriginal) rights and health activist, writer, and educator Roberta "Bobbi" Sykes offers some clues about what silences of this nature may bear. She explains that at least in her urban Australian experience, white women tend to automatically relate to "black" (Koori) women in terms not of reciprocity, but of a superior/inferior, helper/helped dyad that the latter find demeaning. Thus, for their emotional safety, Koori women may avoid *any* sort of relationship with white women. However, Sykes insists, there is an even stronger reason for such avoidance: movement feminist goals may also directly sabotage pressing Koori survival concerns. And what specific goal does Sykes choose for her example? Access to abortion. As they have suffered this and other reproductive violence at the hands of whites—rape, sterilization abuse, deficient health care, forced removal of their children—Koori women have concluded:

> . . . Under more relaxed [abortion] legislation there would virtually be open hunting season.
>
> These concerns of the black community did not daunt the women's movement. Relentlessly it pursued its own objective . . . Few black women were heard on the subject, and those whose voices did surface were in opposition . . .
>
> In response to a newspaper article which appeared, a male interviewer organized a prominent white movement woman to debate the subject with me on television. Unfortunately, the woman used the occasion to scream at me that I wasn't the right sort of black, and that I

didn't have a dozen children and live in the creek-bed at Alice Springs. I had been asked by Mumshirl (Shirley Smith) to represent her opinion as she had recently publicly opposed relaxed abortion legislation. That I, representing an opinion of the black community, brazenly dared to confront and oppose an option of the white community, was sufficient to crack the veneer over the movement woman's racism, and through that crack spewed forth the most virulent and racist comments that I had heard publicly for some time. The interviewer closed off the program immediately, threw a chair across the set, and walked out—so it is not my intention here to say that all white people are to the same degree racist. However, the woman is a well-known mouthpiece for a sizeable segment of the middle-class section of the women's movement. This example occurred publicly and on live television and can therefore be verified. Privately, many similar events occur constantly . . . Black women realize that black community priorities will not become priorities of the white women's movement, even when something as important as attempted genocide threatens the existence of the black community . . . [15]

Sykes vividly portrays the possible consequences of attempts at honest engagement with white, middle- to upper-class movement feminists who have not faced and unlearned their own aggressive assumptions of race and class privilege.

It is no mystery that these women's experiences and perspectives go largely unheard or are miscomprehended within wealthier nations, particularly considering the limitations of Anglo feminist abortion discourse. One such example involves the Pacific Ocean island of Guam, a U.S. territory, which resisted "mainland" prochoice policy. In the wake of the 1989 *Webster* decision, Guam (wrested by the U.S. from Spain in 1898) provided one of the most serious challenges to *Roe v. Wade*. A bill banning abortion on "demand" and asserting fetal personhood was passed unanimously in the Guam Senate. While a "mainland" ACLU attorney bewailed it as a "Pearl Harbor for women," the bill's creator, Elizabeth (Belle) Perez Arriola (1928-2002) and other women senators backing the bill were acting consistently with their reputations as social progressives. A member of the Chamorro people (Guam's indigenous culture, whose population was decimated in WWII), Arriola was a Democrat, chair of the Senate Committee on Youth, Senior Citizens, and Cultural Affairs, and founder of an American Association of University Women chapter. In her activism, she proudly drew on her Chamorro cultural values, which affirm Matilda Joslyn Gage's point about an ancient "Matriarchate" that has not *entirely* died out (despite, in this case, a legal ban against matrilineage imposed by the U.S.).[16] Prolife campaigners insisted that there was not even a word for induced abortion in the Chamorro language, suggesting that it may have once been as unthinkable in the culture as the systematic degradation of women. As Vivian Loyola Dames notes, "'Saving the Fetus' became an analogue to 'Liberating Guam' and 'Saving the Chamorro People.'" Arriola, for one, expressly nested her concern for abortion-threatened fetuses within this larger social welfare context:

> Where are the lives that we are going to protect and preserve? Here we go talking about indigenous rights and self-determination. What good is all that if we don't have our followers to follow and enjoy the fruits of our labor, of this generation's labor, of your labor and my labor to fix this island and have autonomous rights to govern our people?[17]

Other Two-Thirds World feminists similarly point out how U.S. views on abortion ignore the reality of their material conditions and culture. Vandana Shiva, a distinguished ecofeminist from India, states,

> "Pro-choice" language reduces the larger issue of well-being of women to reproduction, and then it reduces reproduction to abortion. This reductionism has emerged from the peculiar history of reproductive politics of the U.S. . . . . Abortion is too complex an issue to be reduced to this crude polarity . . . The "pro-choice" movement of the U.S. fails in respecting the choice of Third World women in matters of economic survival, on having children and in saying "no" to hazardous contraceptives . . . To force them to have few children or no children, without changing the socio-economic conditions of their life that make it rational for them to have more children is not a politics of choice; it is a politics of coercion . . . [and] [t]he prolife movement is also not fully pro-life beyond the foetus because it fails in respecting the life of women and doctors.[18]

These feminists take issue with supposedly prolife U.S. administrations who oppose abortion while completely ignoring the pervasive negative effects of Western imperialism on women and children in these countries. In sub-Saharan Africa where 25 million persons are now HIV positive, U.S. HIV/AIDS assistance is compromised by U.S. economic policies. When asked about President George W. Bush's anti-abortion conditions for U.S. HIV/AIDS assistance, Irene Mureithi from the Child Welfare

Society of Kenya simply remarked that these could "help boost anti-abortion efforts in the continent." She did not then launch into praises of Bush's professed dedication to the sanctity of life. Could this be because his policies fall far short of the more expansive vision she pursues? Mureithi explicitly calls for mother-child HIV transmission prevention through antiretroviral drug access in pregnancy—*instead of* abortion. Fully 40% of all nations on Earth have almost no antiretroviral coverage for pregnant women and their unborn children. In sub-Saharan Africa, the world's hardest hit region, a mere 5% of total HIV positive persons have access to antiretrovirals.[19] American economic policies protect pharmaceutical companies instead, putting lifesaving antiretroviral drugs out of the reach of most IIIV positive persons, including expectant mothers and their babies.

Also a target of criticism from these feminists is the eugenic undercurrent of aid directed at population control billing itself as "reproductive rights." Many countries in Africa, Asia, Latin America, and Oceania are resisting efforts by Western nations to impose abortion legalization and coercive birth control as worldwide "rights." This resistance frequently comes from the strongest advocates of women's rights in the respective nations. Delegates to the United Nations World Population Conference in Cairo in 1994 raised this issue. A Kenyan physician who oversees clinics in rural Africa complained that while aspirin and antibiotics may be hard to find, there is a "ready supply of birth control pills." She continued, "How come there is money for contraceptive pills and billions more are being poured into the system, and there's no money for anything else? Isn't it genocide, really?" A Honduran delegate at the conference expressed similar sentiments: "Our countries need antibiotics, roads, electricity. Our children are dying because they don't even have re-hydration medicine for diarrhea . . . The only thing to go into my country—and there is plenty of it—is contraceptives."[20] American policy on reproductive issues has deep roots in eugenics and racism, from the "hygiene" movements of the late nineteenth century, to the eugenics movements of the twentieth century (including forced sterilization and even prenatal and postnatal killing of "undesirables," e.g., American Indians, African Americans, Latinos, the disabled, and the poor), to an emphasis on violently controlling reproduction, rather than promoting women and children's education and welfare, in the Two-Thirds World.

Additional new "voices" have informed the rapidly globalizing abortion debate. Medical science constantly provides new understanding of the issue. In particular, ultrasound technology has radically changed the experience of pregnancy in many countries. The nineteenth-century concept of "quickening" has been replaced with three-dimensional images of the active preborn child well before the mother feels any movement. These images enhance bonding with the baby long before birth. If they did not know it before, the thousands of expectant mothers who proudly display photos of their *in utero* children understand that the fetus is a human worthy of protection, regardless of philosophical arguments about when life begins. Such an understanding, however, underscores the irony that personhood is still granted based on the wantedness of the child—the perceptions of an*other*. Unfortunately, ultrasound and other prenatal diagnostic technologies have also enabled the detection of "defective" children, who all too often are then denied the chance to exist, as Jane Thomas Bailey discusses below in "Discrimination Abortion." In Britain, 95% of "affected" fetuses are selected for termination.[21] In one U.S. study, by the late 1980s nearly 90% of unborn children with Down Syndrome were being aborted.[22] Prenatally diagnosable "defects" today include an ever-expanding number of impairments as well as biological sex, and may someday include sexual orientation (see McGowan, Part Two).[23]

Scientific research has been investigating a link between abortion and breast cancer. The studies, from several different countries, provide reasonable biological explanations to match the data. Unfortunately, some breast cancer organizations are reluctant to fully investigate the matter and leap to conclusions about "antichoice bias," even though some prochoice researchers find the evidence compelling. Dr. Angela Lanfrachi, a co-director of the Breast Center at Somerset Medical Center, a teacher of residents and doctor to thousands of breast cancer patients, testified before the Massachusetts Joint Health Care Committee (June 11, 2003):

> Often when I have asked leaders in the field of breast cancer why they don't talk about the abortion breast cancer link at their meetings, they have said, "It's too political." I have come to believe that what is meant by "too political" is the growing influence of major women's medical organizations . . . [such as] the American Medical Women's Association . . . I believe they are so committed to reproductive rights and the protections of *Roe v. Wade,* as their position paper . . . clearly states on their web site, www.amwa-doc.org, that it has clouded good medical judgment . . . it would seem that allowing the information that studies clearly show an increased risk of breast cancer with abortion to be discussed in open medical forums, is perceived as endangering the *Roe v. Wade* ruling.[24]

Research suggests further physical complications of abortion that merit continued investigation.[25]

Research on the negative psychological effects of abortion continues but is frequently hampered by prolife v. prochoice politics. Nevertheless, a body of quantitative and qualitative research on the topic continues to grow.[26] Although quantitative studies are essential, the blanket dismissal of qualitative reports as "merely anecdotal" does not fit with mental health practitioners' enduring appreciation of case studies as rich, instructive sources of valid, clinically beneficial knowledge. Mental health professionals employ case-based methods of inquiry and interpretation developed through actual daily psychotherapeutic practice. Such methods may be associated with a belief on the therapist's part that experiences are best understood through the stories of those who live them, and that the therapist needs to shape and reshape his or her healing efforts in response to clients' stories. Case-based discovery thus resonates with past and present feminist methods of creating new, transformative politics from the themes that emerge from careful, respectful, continuous listening to women's sacred "heart-histories" in their fullness and complexity. We help women by listening to them share their narratives, for the sake of their own personal healing and for the sake of identifying social justice actions that will help other women prevent a procedure that has already brought so many—as *they themselves* tell it—to a place of suffering and loss. Mental health professionals who have devoted themselves to listening to these stories have produced a body of work that has proven helpful to women who have suffered the negative effects of abortion and to the therapists who work with them.[27]

There are thousands of powerful testimonies of women who, viewing abortion as woman's right, sought its relief only to learn later that it had negative, and in some cases, devastating effects on their lives. Interestingly, the plaintiffs in the two Supreme Court rulings that overturned abortion laws in the U.S.—Norma McCorvey, "Jane Roe" in *Roe v. Wade*, and Sandra Cano, "Mary Doe" in *Doe v. Bolton*—are prime examples of how abortion exploits rather than helps women. Sandra Cano says that she never wanted an abortion, that the case was the lawyers' idea, not hers. She was seeking help from Legal Aid to get her children out of foster care, and because she was pregnant, she was used in the case by lawyers who were certain she was a prime candidate for abortion. Meanwhile, Norma McCorvey ("Jane Roe") initially became a strong abortion advocate as a result of *Roe v. Wade*, occasionally speaking at rallies and writing about her experiences. Yet she had publicly admitted that the story of having been raped (one of the "facts" of the case) was a lie. *Sisterlife*, the journal of Feminists for Life, commented at the time on how this looked like a matter of exploitation by lawyers, given the kinds of prejudices that abortion advocates often have toward women in poverty. At the time, McCorvey didn't think so. Now she does. For several years now, she has been a prolife activist. Norma McCorvey and Sandra Cano, the original plaintiffs in the cases that brought the United States abortion-on-demand, both filed lawsuits to have their cases overturned on the grounds that the facts of the cases were false and have since changed. Unfortunately, in February 2005, the still male-dominated U.S. Supreme Court, consistent with its long pattern, declined without comment to hear the case.

Another form of the exploitative effects of abortion is seen in the rapid increase in reports of sexual misconduct by abortion practitioners. Rachel MacNair outlines several such cases in "Position of Mastery," including those involving Arizona abortionist Brian Finkel who went on trial in the fall of 2003 and was convicted on 22 counts of sexual abuse of women since 1986 and sentenced to 34 years in prison. He reportedly was responsible for a fifth of all abortions performed in the state and had been a spokesperson for groups like the National Abortion Federation on news programs like "20/20" and "Nightline." Yet before his convictions, he had in a newspaper interview referred to his clinic as "the Vaginal Vault" and to Filipinas as "Little Brown F[. . .]ing Machines." Clinic staff members as well as the women themselves testified against him at his trial. The doctor's attorney tried to discredit the women's courtroom testimonies by branding them "narcissistic" and "deliberately manipulative": a character assassination tactic recognizable to anyone familiar with the legal system's history of belittling rape victims.[28] This rise in reported abuse is part of an overall rise in abuse of female patients by their male doctors. What is distressing is that several women's organizations, while condemning abuse of woman by their doctors in general, fail to defend the women violated by male abortionists, frequently viewing the accusations as an attack on abortion availability and sometimes even defending the accused. Given that abortion facilities already operate with less regulation and fewer restrictions and oversight than any other type of medical facility, the position of many prochoice organizations in such cases contributes to the abortionists' relative impunity.

Perhaps it is because of a growing recognition of the negative aspects of abortion that abortion rates in the U.S. started declining in the 1990s. Abortion rates reached a plateau in the U.S. during the 1980s, with over 2,000 abortion clinics. At the beginning of 2003, however, there were only about 700. The number of doctors performing abortions has also decreased: ABC News reported on January 16, 1998, that 60% of abortion providers were above the age of 65. The rate of abortion has declined, as has the ratio of abortions to live births. Most importantly, if one looks only at the rate of women getting their first abortion, the decline is much more dramatic. In the U.S., while the decline has been steady over the past decade or so, it will become precipitous as repeat abortions decline due to age and other factors.[29] This decline in numbers, while attributable to many different factors, suggests that more and more people are recognizing that abortion is a bad idea.

For prolife feminists, however, a declining abortion rate is not enough. We share the sentiments of those prochoice feminists who complain that many anti-feminist prolifers care more for *in utero* life than life that has passed through the birth canal. Feminist prolifers for years have criticized those abortion opponents who have forgotten about the equally valuable life of the mother. Prolife feminists expend much energy speaking out against such hypocrisy and lobbying for life affirming social reform on multiple levels. And we are glad to say that such consciousness raising has had a modest effect. Like Jonah, who was astonished at the response of Nineveh to his message of repentance, we have been surprised and (unlike Jonah) delighted at much of the reaction by prolifers to our feminist prolife message. These committed prolifers, who have rarely before been involved in any type of social activism, have become more sensitive to the situation of young women. Hundreds of crisis pregnancy centers throughout the U.S. offering free services to women in need have been funded in part by these "conservatives," and it has been our further privilege to see some of them become more involved in alleviating the social problems contributing to the high unplanned pregnancy rate.[30] Many have joined us in our concern about how women are viewed by society; about how sex is sold to our youth; about how much pornography degrades women and promotes violence against them; about how men must take more responsibility for their sexual behavior; and about how employers must make better provision for parents and their children.

We claim only modest victories. There are many abortion opponents out there who are still motivated by little more than a desire to put down the "woman's movement" and whose self-righteous arguments on behalf of the fetus wreak of insincerity and total disregard for the obstacles that mothers with children face in our society. Our strongest criticism and condemnation is reserved for those abortion opponents who resort to violence to promote their cause. As death penalty abolitionists, like us, have long proclaimed, it is wrong to kill people to show people that killing people is wrong. We mourn the sacred lives of David Gunn, John Bayard Britton, James H. Barrett, Shannon Lowney, Leanne Nichols, Barnett Slepian, and Robert Sanderson, all horrifically cut short in the name of "respecting life." We also stand with Britton's stepdaughter Catherine Fairbanks who opposed the lethal injection execution of his killer, Paul Hill. We hope for the healing of all those wounded and traumatized by these attacks and killings and we call for greater prolife-prochoice dialogue and joint action on shared concerns.

Perhaps these violent zealots have come to believe prochoice rhetoric about the "liberating" qualities of abortion and are so fearful of women's full social equality that they make it their personal mission to restore some frightening notion of womanhood by violently attacking and even murdering abortionists and their clients. Violent "prolife" activism is a contradiction, insidious and perverse, that we condemn at every level; and despite our differences with some conservative prolife groups, most of them agree with us on this point. Although the media loves to feature inflammatory sound bytes from extremist groups, every mainstream prolife group in the United States has condemned the killings at abortion facilities and has responded by re-emphasizing their organizational policies against any kind of violence. It is especially frustrating when denunciations of such violence are immediately issued by prolife groups in each instance and then totally ignored by the media—and the next day, pundits criticize the groups for failing to condemn the actions! But the media prefers the dramatic to the mundane, and denunciations of violence by major prolife groups are apparently mundane, whereas violent opposition to abortion is quite dramatic.

Media practice is particularly frightening in the case of Paul Hill and causes us to wonder to what extent such irresponsible coverage contributes to the problem. After one shooting, a major network was going to feature a spokesperson from the National Right to Life Committee who would have unequivocally condemned the violence. They canceled her appearance and instead brought on the militant Paul Hill. Not surprisingly, he shortly thereafter felt the need to match his own rhetoric by killing Dr. James Bayard Britton and his bodyguard James Barrett, and wounding June Barrett, a clinic escort and James' wife. When Hill was executed for these murders, his final statements were widely quoted in the media; the prolife movement's widespread condemnations were still ignored. The media canceled a competent, professional woman, chosen as a spokesperson, in favor of a wild-speaking man with no ethical or humanitarian credibility and no accountability to anyone.

This tendency to irresponsible bias even shows up and occasions negative consequences in less obviously dramatic situations. After interviewing a Feminists for Life of America spokesperson, Natalie Nardelli, for "Choose or Lose," an election-year series directed at education of youth voters, MTV cut her words out entirely. A producer explained that they had opted instead for a "more representative" prolifer, one who emphasized abortion as fetal murder in contrast to Nardelli's "more nuanced objections." FFLA president (and contributor to this volume) Serrin Foster replied, "By refusing to include our message that *women* deserve better than abortion, MTV has chosen to make women the losers. It is very disappointing that MTV will only give voice to people who fit their simplistic, preconceived stereotypes."[31] Such stereotypes are hardly conducive to the most thoughtful, informed exercise of the right to vote, attained by and for women and minorities by tireless generations of hard-working activists.

Feminist prolifers have found common ground with more conservative prolifers who have made progress in recognizing the concept of a consistent life ethic. But they still have a long way to go, and we intend to keep challenging them. Likewise, we refuse to count prochoice feminists as our adversaries, particularly when they work toward mutual goals that will correct those societal conditions that we recognize as having created the perceived need for abortion. Our complaint has been that both prochoice feminists and conservative prolifers have focused so narrowly on the abortion issue, they have dropped the ball on those issues that contribute to what so many women perceive as a need for abortion in the first place. We have seen a few signs of recognition of this circumstance, and we have great hope that the realization will continue to grow.

The following articles reveal the richness and diversity of prolife feminist thought. They represent what we believe are both echoes of our foremothers and prophetic voices of our future, when the story becomes reality. A story of how we will come together and work for a world of peace and respect and interdependence among all peoples.

Fannie Lou Townsend Hamer (1917-1977)

Fannie Lou Townsend Hamer was the granddaughter of slaves and one of twenty children from a sharecropper family in rural Sunflower County, Mississippi. She grew up in a distinctively African-American strain of Christianity that celebrates a loving, nurturing, liberating God. Despite her obvious intelligence and curiosity, she was forced to quit school in the sixth grade and pick cotton in the fields to help support her family. Through the Black church and the example of her parents, she learned that real power was nonviolence itself.

This was a deeply radical lesson in a culture that oppressed, disenfranchised, and silenced African Americans through systematic brute force. Some white male physicians, for example, felt *entitled* to forcibly sterilize Black women like Hamer. In 1961, one hysterectomized her under the ruse that she required some other surgery. Hamer did not find out what really happened until she overheard whites gossiping in a house where she worked as a domestic. She and her husband Perry "Pap" Hamer had endured two stillbirths, then adopted two daughters—one the child of a single mother, the other handicapped by severe burns. Yet they had wished to conceive.

Fannie Lou Hamer felt both helpless and outraged over this violation of her body and her human and civil rights. Her sense of powerlessness ended when the civil rights movement rose up in Mississippi and she plunged herself into the voting rights campaign. "I'm sick and tired of being sick and tired" became her motto, and "This Little Light of Mine" her favorite sacred song. For this, she was fired from her job, arrested, severely injured in a prison beating, and stalked. Her home was shot at and firebombed.[1] The indomitable Hamer became secretary of the Student Nonviolent Coordinating Committee and the moving spirit of the Mississippi Freedom Democratic Party, a Black-initiated alternative to the state's white segregationist Democratic organization. At the 1964 presidential convention, Fannie Lou Hamer and the MFDP challenged the national Democratic Party's timid leadership to seat them as delegates.

   As an MFDP candidate, Hamer became one of the first Southern Blacks to run for Congress since Reconstruction. Hamer campaigned against the Vietnam War and fought for government health care, nutrition, and education programs for poor Americans of all races, especially children. She brought Head Start to her own community. She spoke out on behalf of single mothers facing personal, political, and economic discrimination; her own daughter, Dorothy Jean, had had a child out of wedlock. After giving birth to her second child, Dorothy Jean died of a hemorrhage that local doctors refused to treat—an outrageously common cause of death for rural Southern Blacks. After Dorothy Jean's husband returned severely disabled from Vietnam, Fannie Lou and Pap Hamer unhesitatingly adopted their two granddaughters.

   Fannie Lou Hamer co-founded the National Women's Political Caucus and backed the presidential candidacy—the first by a Black woman—of her friend, U.S. Representative Shirley Chisholm. Hamer had the respect, admiration, and cooperation of such movement feminists as Bella Abzug and Gloria Steinem. Yet like many poor women and women of color, Hamer could not accept the movement's blind spots in regard to race and class, let alone some feminists' demonization of men. She laughed about her husband's large physique, then insisted: "We are here to work side by side with this Black man in trying to bring liberation to all people."[2] "All people" encompassed unborn children and their mothers. Hamer was an early, straightforward dissenter from movement feminists'—"white do-gooders," in her view—growing fixation on abortion "rights": "If they'd been talking that way when my mother was bearing children, I wouldn't be here now." If society would only give poor Black children a chance instead, "they might grow up to be Fannie Lou Hamer or something else."[3] As a delegate to the 1969 White House Conference on Food, Nutrition, and Health, Hamer stopped two powerful white men from furthering a specific plan of reproductive violence. As head of a panel on pregnant and nursing women and infants, Dr. Charles U. Lowe from the National Institutes of Health recommended compulsory first-trimester abortion of every nonmarital pregnancy and compulsory sterilization of any young single woman who had given birth. His proposal was endorsed by none other than Dr. Allan Guttmacher, president of Planned Parenthood-World Population, which had recently shed its antiabortion stance.[4] [1]. Hamer could not envision sterilization abuse or abortion as humane solutions to crisis pregnancy; rather, mothers and children needed and deserved compassionate, respectful community aid that would allow their lives to unfold as *they* saw fit.[5]

As shown by her behavior towards and beyond her own family, Fannie Lou Hamer did not merely pay lip service to respecting all lives. In 1973, increasing health problems—some from her prison beating—forced her to retire, but not before she firmly defended single mothers' employment rights in court. In her final years, Fannie Lou Hamer felt abandoned by her former political colleagues, to whom she had given so much.[6] The very social justice movements that she benefited have often shut out her holistic vision of human life and wellbeing. She has never been wholly forgotten, to be sure. The 2004 Democratic national convention celebrated the 40th anniversary of Hamer's challenge to that very body. In the hope that Hamer's light will shine again in its fullness, we offer these two expressions of her unwaveringly prolife feminism.

The first selection is a transcript of a 1971 speech obtained from the Lillian P. Benbow Room of Special Collections at Tougaloo College, Mississippi. The second selection represents an excerpt of Hamer's testimony on behalf of the plaintiffs in the 1973 case of *Katie Mae Andrews and Lestine Rogers v. Drew Separate Municipal School District*. This discrimination lawsuit, which began in 1973 shortly after a general right to abortion became enshrined in U.S. law, was brought against the local segregated school district by young Black women who had been denied employment because they were single mothers. Sadly, while pregnant women and single mothers have a somewhat better legal status than they did 30 years ago, oppression and discrimination against them are still rampant, still causing wide scale abortions. Anyone who works with women in crisis pregnancies—as we do—can attest to this. Hamer's long ago testimony still speaks to recent and current welfare "reform" debates, with their vilification of single and especially Black single mothers.

"Is It Too Late?"
by Fannie Lou Hamer

I am here tonight to express my views and to attempt to deal with the question and topic of, "Is it too late?"

First, as a black woman, 54 years of age, a mother and a wife, I know some of the suffering and the pain mothers must feel for their children when they have to face a cruel world both at home and abroad.

In the streets of America, my home and land where my fathers died, I have taken a stand for human rights and civil rights not just for my sake but for all mankind.

I was born and raised in a segregated society, beaten for trying to act like all people should have a right to act. Denied access to the ballot until I was 50 years old, but things are a little better now.

God is in the plan; He has sounded the trumpet and have called the march to order. God is on the throne today. He is keeping watch on this nation and marking time.

It's not too late. There is still time for America to change. God have delayed destruction on this nation to test the hearts and consciousness of us all. Believe me, there is still time.

The war in Vietnam must be ended so our men and boys can come home—so mothers can stop crying, wives can feel secure, and children can learn strength. . . Women can be strength for men, women can help with the decision-making, but men will ultimately [be the ones in a position to] take the action.

The methods used to take human life, such as abortion, the pill, the ring, etc., amount to genocide. I believe that legal abortion is legal murder and the use of pills and rings to prevent God's will is a great sin.

As I take inventory of the past ten years, I see the many tragedies of this nation: Medgar Evers' death in my state (Mississippi), John Kennedy, Malcolm X, Martin Luther King, Jr., Robert Kennedy, and more recently Jo Etha Collier[7] in Drew Mississippi, and countless of thousands in Vietnam and the streets of our larger cities and towns. For these sins this country should pray. Because we have been spared a little longer. Miles of paper and film cannot record the many injustices this nation has been guilty of. But there is still time.

Maybe if all the ministers in this nation, black and white, would stand up tonight and say, "Come earth's people, it is not too late, God have given us time!" Perhaps we can speed up the day when all men can feel as I do. I am not afraid tonight. Freedom is in my soul and love is in my heart.

While here tonight I have a special message to my black brothers and sisters. As we move forward in our quest for progress and success, we must not be guilty of misleading our people. We must not allow our eagerness to participate lead us to accept second class citizenship, and inferior positions in the name of integration. Too many have given their lives to end this evil.

—1971 speech, archived in the Lillian P. Benbow Room of
Special Collections, L. Zenobia Coleman Library,
Tougaloo College, Tougaloo, Mississippi

"And That's What We Are Talking About"
Mrs. Hamer Wins A Victory For Single Mothers and
Their Children

Fannie Lou HAMER, expert witness for the plaintiffs
William C. KEADY, U.S. Circuit Court Judge
Champ TERNEY, cross-examining attorney for the school district—and
son-in-law of segregationist Senator James O. Eastland
Victor McTEER, Plaintiffs' legal aid attorney and Hamer's colleague

KEADY: Are you here today because you feel that you can speak for
           the entire black community or at least the majority of the black
           community in Sunflower County?

HAMER: Yes, I am here because I feel . . . the black community would
           agree, and all of them that I have talked with and, in fact, two
           rode over here this morning with us because they are concerned
           too, as we were, that we all agree that these young women are
           not really on trial. They are trying all of us. Because when you
           say that we are pulling ourselves up and you tell us to get off
           of welfare, and when peoples try to go to school to get off of
           welfare to support theirselves, this is another way of knocking
           them down. So we are here because we really don't like what
           is happening.

KEADY: You are here because you feel there is a racial question
           involved?

HAMER: Yes, I believe it is.

KEADY: Well, it is within the reasonable discretion of the court to allow a
           witness to testify as an expert. I am going to allow Mrs. Hamer
           to testify. Mrs. Hamer, as you heard yesterday there has been a
           great deal of talk about the morality of the black community.
           And I would like to ask you simply at this time how, in your
           opinion, does the black community feel about unwed mothers?

HAMER: Well, it's quite a few people, black people in Sunflower County,
           that have young people that's not married, with children. But
           these are still our children. And we still love these children.
           And after these babies are born we are not going to disband
           these children from their families, because these are other lives,
           they are—God breathed life into them just like He did into us.
           And I think these children have a right to live. And I think that
           these mothers have a right to support them in a decent way.

KEADY: You think, then, that the black community has one point of view about children who are the progeny of unwed parents as opposed to what the white community thinks about the children of unwed parents. Can you tell me what the difference is, what the white community thinks about unwed parents as opposed to what the black community thinks?

HAMER: Well, being a person who have built from what I would say the ground, I worked for white people for years, I worked in their house, I worked in their kitchen, and I know what's going on. And if justice was really done it wouldn't be only black women in here, it would be a whole lot of young white folk in here, too. So what I am saying is I think it is being—the people that's treated unjust— and this would be almost funny to me if it wasn't so serious.

KEADY: Well, how do people in the white community, from your experience, take care of their unwed children [sic]?

TERNEY: Your Honor, I don't believe she has been qualified as an expert—

KEADY: No, she is qualified, really . . . In the black community, is there any morality issue in having an unwed child [sic]? That is the question.

HAMER: Well, let me say this, Judge Keady.

KEADY: All right.

HAMER: After a child is born, I don't think that people should be treated like an outcast.

KEADY: No, that is not the question. But in becoming a parent out of wedlock, is that frowned upon, looked down on, or is it encouraged and approved?

HAMER: It's not encouraged.

KEADY: All right.

McTEER: What would be the effect, in your opinion, of this rule upon young black people in the Sunflower County?

HAMER: Well, it would be quite a few young people lose their jobs, because I know so many young women that after having one child go back to school, finish school and yet not marry, but try to better theirselves by getting a good job so they can support their children without becoming a ward of the welfare. And this is really going to be a blow to them.

McTEER: What do you think will be the result when young black women who have tried to get themselves back through school, suddenly—after having gotten through school, rather, and having gotten a degree—they find themselves without a job because of the fact that they have an unwed *child* [sic]? What would be the effect to these young mothers, in your understanding?

HAMER: It will be a terrible blow not only to these young women but it will be a terrible blow to all of us, not only in Sunflower County but across the state of Mississippi, across the United States where people are trying to lift theirselves out of certain things and bring theirselves up to a level where they can support theirselves and their child.

McTEER: What do you think will be the effect upon the child, the children of the unwed mother?

HAMER: Well, this is saying to the child that it, too, is not fit. And you know, when I think of this—may I say this, Judge Keady? I think about the story of Jesus Christ, I think of what would have happened to Virgin Mary if she walked into Drew Separate School, what would have happened if Christ had been born in that school. What would have happened?

McTEER: Mrs. Hamer, I know that in your own life this particular question touches very close to home. Could you tell the court about why it touches so close to home in terms of your own life?

HAMER: Well, for one thing, I will talk about my daughter. I had two children, adopted children, Vergie and Dorothy Jean. And during my traveling around, Dorothy Jean became pregnant. She was 22 years old. And one of my friends, a white friend in California, told me, me traveling, it might affect my reputation for her to have this child at home, and why didn't I send her off. And I told them I would stick as close to her as I could. So I kept her at home. The child was born on the 29th of December in East Bolivar County Hospital, 1965. She died in 1967, my daughter did. And if I had mistreated that child of my child, I would have never forgiven myself. I don't think that we have the authority to forgive man. Only God is that authority. Only God got that power. Man is not to judge man. We don't have that kind of power.

McTEER: Mrs. Hamer, in your opinion, what do you think the black community thinks about teachers who are unwed mothers teaching their children?

HAMER: It's nothing wrong with an unwed mother teaching children. Because I'm sure in Sunflower County that we have some unwed mothers teaching some of those kids.

McTEER: Mrs. Hamer, to your knowledge, what do you think the black community's views are in terms of where values are actually created? Are values created in the home or . . . in school?

HAMER: Values are created in the homes. You know, my mother and father of one marriage had 20 children. Six girls and 14 boys. And my mother and father taught me without any formal education about dignity and self-respect from the time that we were very small kids until we were grown. And I—you know, I was surprised yesterday to hear the kind of things, you know, like—that black people don't have any morals and that kind of thing. That's not true. Because they do have. They have moral values. They do care.

McTEER: Mrs. Hamer, does the black community feel that a woman has a right to her independent life, women like the plaintiffs in this matter?

HAMER: Yes. The black community feels that a woman, if she is not married and especially with a child have a right to make a decent living. That's why I am here. Because I feel that Miss Andrews and the others have a right to make a decent life for their children. The black community feel that any woman with children or with a child have a right to lift theirselves and fight. One of the people out there that's in the audience now that wanted to further her education after her child was born, we helped her go to Mississippi Valley State College.

McTEER: Who is that person?

HAMER: Miss Andrews.

McTEER: You have known Miss Andrews for quite some time, haven't you?

HAMER: Yes, I have known her for quite some time . . .

McTEER: Do you know Miss Andrews' reputation within her community for her good moral character?

HAMER: Yes.

McTEER: Do you think that Miss Andrews and the other ladies, plaintiffs, etc., who testified today, do you think the black community thinks that their actions are commendable for taking care of their children?

HAMER: Yes, I think it was good for them to try to do something to take care of their children. And everybody else in the community believe the same thing. That's the reason there's other black mothers here this morning.

TERNEY: *[beginning his cross-examination]*: Are you aware of the problem at Drew concerning the pregnancies of schoolgirls, unwanted pregnancies?

HAMER: I'm not aware of how many, no. I'm not aware of how many it is.

TERNEY: Well, as spokesman for the black community and knowing the conditions in the black community, do you see a problem of student-age females becoming pregnant and having to drop out of school? . . .

HAMER: Well, it is a matter of concern if the kids are too young. But the people we are dealing with here this morning are young women.

TERNEY: Well, I realize that. These plaintiffs are over 21. But I am talking about the children 13 to 18 years of age.

HAMER: Yes.

TERNEY: Now, it is a problem at Drew, isn't it, of school-age girls becoming pregnant?

HAMER: Well, it's a problem with school age children. That's not only with black children.

TERNEY: No, I realize that.

HAMER: It's with white children, too.

TERNEY: But it is a problem?

HAMER: It is a problem with children.

TERNEY: And it is a growing problem?

HAMER: Yes, with children.

TERNEY: Do you have any idea what the solution to that problem is?

HAMER: Well, I think maybe more that we should become more active in the schools and visit in the schools, maybe, the parent.

TERNEY: And the school leading them in the right moral conduct?

HAMER: Well, if he—this prove there's something going wrong if he keep them out and still that many people be pregnant. Then certainly he not doing what he ought to be doing.

TERNEY: Can't you foresee that if he employs people that have illegitimate children that the students will then think that this type of conduct is being condoned and think that it's all right and it may make the problem—probably would make the problem worse? Can't you see that?

HAMER: I don't believe that. . . .

TERNEY: The mere fact that the teacher has engaged in something wrong, whether she says anything about it, the fact that the child, the student, knows that the teacher in front of his or her class has engaged in sex outside of marriage and the product of that is an illegitimate child, can't you see that the child would think that that mother, if that teacher that that child respected engaged in that sort of conduct, that they would infer that it's all right for them to do it?

HAMER: You know what you have to do if that's what you are going to deal with? When you get back to Drew this evening, lock the doors. There won't be any school.

TERNEY: Why is that?

HAMER: The moral conduct. Nobody would teach.

TERNEY: All the teachers?

HAMER: All of them. It might not be two not fall out of the sack, if that's what you call moral. Two. Lock it up.

TERNEY: You don't have much confidence in the faculty?

HAMER: I'm just calling a spade a spade.

TERNEY: Well, what is your opinion as to whether—

HAMER: I think people should have a chance, not only—you know that, Mr. Terney? If this was a young white woman with this same problem, I would come here and fight you the same way, because I would fight for her rights as a woman, as a person fighting for her child, just like these young womens are fighting for their right to take care of their child. You always tell us, we go through this thing with the welfare or we have got so many kids on the welfare roll, "Why don't you get up and do something?" And then when we start doing something, "You don't have any business being that high."

TERNEY: You realize this rule is not racially motivated. In other words, it is enforced equally against whites and blacks. You understand that, don't you?

HAMER: I don't understand that. Because to save my life, is no way that I could believe that every white teacher in Sunflower County is single that a child isn't involved. I don't believe that . . .

TERNEY: Let me ask your opinion. As spokesman for the black community, do you feel that it's right or wrong for a female student between the ages of 13 and 19 to have sexual intercourse outside of marriage?

HAMER: I feel like they are too young.

TERNEY: You feel that it is wrong?

HAMER: I feel that it is wrong.

TERNEY: Do you realize the rule does not condemn the child? It is the conduct of the parent, whether it's the mother or the father, that the rule condemns.

HAMER: But what I'm saying, if this child, you know—it's wrong, and I'm going to teach this child these things before this happen. But if a child should become pregnant . . . I wouldn't cast a child out.

TERNEY: The rule doesn't cast the child out. Doesn't ask the child be cast out. It simply says that the parent, whether it is a mother or father, is not qualified to teach in the Drew public schools. Now does that, in your mind, deny that individual that would ordinarily have been teaching in that school system employment anywhere? Couldn't they apply to another school system or in another job?

HAMER: Well, I just have one question I would like to ask you. Why do they go if they can't work at home? Why do they pick up and go? . . .

TERNEY: Does the black community differentiate or draw a distinction between moral conduct of the type of prostitution, that is, voluntary sexual intercourse for pay, as opposed to voluntary sexual intercourse outside of marriage without pay?

HAMER: See, you know, Attorney Terney, this is ridiculous, to be going with this kind of questions and all that we are talking about, that women should have a right to work in schools if they have got the education to lift theirselves from certain things that are happening in their lifetime, meaning that they have got a kid and . . . they have gone to school to get a education to try to support their kids decent. And that's what we are talking about . . .

[Judge Keady ruled on behalf of the plaintiffs in this case, and his decision withstood appeal to the U.S. Supreme Court.[8]—Eds.]

—in *Andrews v. Drew Municipal Separate School Dist.*, 371 F.Supp. 27 (ND Miss. 1973), reprinted in *Drew Municipal School Dist. v. Andrews*, 425 U.S. 559 (1976).

Graciela Olivarez (1928-1987)

Graciela Olivarez, a native of Sonora, Arizona, dropped out of high school at age 15 to work as a secretary. She entered Spanish-language broadcasting when she substituted for a local disc jockey and became an immediate celebrity. Her experience hosting an "action line" call-in show brought her into the civil rights movement. Eventually she was appointed to head the Arizona branch of the Federal government's Office of Economic Opportunity (OEO). She also married (later divorced) and had one child.

In 1966, Olivarez was named to the national board of a brand-new human rights group, the National Organization for Women (NOW), headed by *Feminine Mystique* author Betty Friedan and the labor and civil rights activist Aileen Hernandez. NOW's original charter declared the full humanity of women, "who, like all other people in our society, must have the chance to develop their fullest human potential" and the "indivisible" nature of all human rights. It says nothing about abortion. NOW did not adopt abortion-rights advocacy until the next year, and then only after intense debate.

Around this time, Olivarez confided in Father Theodore (Ted) Hesburgh, Notre Dame University president, that no matter what positive changes she wished to implement, her hands were tied by legal obstacles. To the surprise of this high-school dropout, he offered her a full scholarship to law school. Olivarez earned her JD in 1970, becoming Notre Dame's first female law graduate. She then worked with and led such groups and agencies as the Urban Coalition, Food for All, the Mexican American Legal Defense Fund (MALDEF), and the New Mexico state planning office. President Jimmy Carter named her director of the Community Services Administration, making her the highest-ranking Latina to serve in any federal administration. In 1980 she began the sole Spanish-language television network in the U.S. at that time. Today two major honors commemorate her life and work: the Graciela Olivarez Award offered by the National Council of La Raza, and one granted by the Notre Dame Hispanic Law Students Association to distinguished Hispanic attorneys and judges.

Progressive-minded prolifers also recall that Olivarez quite publicly, straightforwardly dissented from the feminist movement's ossification into its abortion rights position. At the 1971 Conferencia de Mujeres Por La Raza in Houston, Texas, she pointed out that Latinos and Latinas had trouble evolving past *machismo* because they are afflicted with

> a virgin image and a mother complex . . . The young men look up to their mothers as virgins, as saints (all women worthy of marriage must be virgins). The mother is placed on a pedestal. The young man cannot face the fact that his mother had to have intercourse in order to give birth to him.[1]

Olivarez directly linked this dynamic to abortion. She observed that while feeling entitled to nonmarital sex themselves, young men expect and demand to marry virgins, putting tremendous pressure on young women to keep up the appearance of virginity. Young women cannot acknowledge any sexual activity, even to themselves. Because they do not face and plan for the chance of undesired pregnancy, they wind up having panic-stricken abortions and incurring a heavy, health-destroying physical and psychological burden.

In 1972, President Richard Nixon appointed Olivarez vice-chair of his Commission on Population and the American Future. In the Commission's report, issued the year before the U.S. Supreme Court's *Roe v. Wade* decision, Olivarez strongly disagreed with the other commissioners—including Senator Robert Packwood, later accused of sexual harassment—about legalizing abortion. She did so for reasons that *affirm* the original NOW charter.

From the Separate Statement of Graciela Olivarez to the President's Commission on Population and the American Future
by Graciela Olivarez

To brush aside a separate statement on the issue of abortion on the grounds that it is based on religious or denominational "hang-ups" is to equate abortion—a matter of life and death—with simpler matters of religion such as observance of the Sabbath, dietary restrictions, abstention from coffee and alcoholic beverages, or other similar religious observances. I believe that even nonreligious persons should be concerned with the issue of life and death as it pertains to the unborn.

My opposition to legalized abortion is based on several concerns that touch on a variety of issues, not the least of which is the effect such a law would have on millions of innocent and ill-informed persons. These concerns center around the rights of women to control their own bodies, the rights of the unborn child and the poor in our society, the safety of abortion, our country's commitment to preventive as opposed to remedial measures, and our future as a democratic society.

I fail to understand the argument that women have a right to control their own bodies. Control over one's body does not stem from a right, but depends on individual self-image and a sense of responsibility. I am not referring to the victim of rape or incest. And I am not referring to the poor for whom contraceptive services and techniques are not as accessible as we would want them to be.

With the recent advances in contraceptive technology, any woman who so desires is better able to control her fertility in a more effective way than has ever been before available. I accept the argument that aside from total abstention, there is no perfect contraceptive; but no one can argue that effective contraceptives are more available now than ever before, and are effective only if used. Personal and contraceptive failures do not give women the "right" to correct or eliminate the so-called "accident" by destroying the fetus.

Advocacy by women for legalized abortion on a national scale is so anti-women's liberation that it flies in the face of what some of us are trying to accomplish through the women's movement, namely, equality—equality means an equal sharing of responsibilities by and as men and women.

With women already bearing the major burden for the reproductive process, men have never had it so good. Women alone must suffer the consequences of an imperfect contraceptive pill—the blood clots, severe headaches, nausea, edema, etc. Women alone endure the cramping and hemorrhaging from an intrauterine device. No man ever died from an abortion.

[What] kind of future [do] we all have to look forward to if men are excused either morally or legally from their responsibility for participation in the creation of life?

Women should be working to bring men into the camp of responsible parenthood, a responsibility that women have had to shoulder almost alone. Perhaps in our eagerness for equality, we have, in part, contributed to the existing irresponsible attitude some men have toward their relationship to women and to their offspring. Legalized abortion will free those men from worrying about whether they should bear some responsibility for the consequences of sexual experience. In the matter of divorce where children are involved, for instance, very few men fight or even ask for custody of their children. It is customary to measure male responsibility in terms of dollars and cents, rather than in terms of affection, attention, companionship, supervision and warmth.

And laymen are not the only ones who reflect this attitude. Blame must also be placed on churchmen, who throughout the tumult and controversy surrounding legalized abortion, have expressed their concern only as abortion affects the moral and psychological problems of women, adroitly avoiding the issue of man's responsibility to decisions connected with his role in the reproductive process.

In relation to the rights of the unborn child, we seem to be confused as to the meaning of human life before and after birth. The fetus does not become "a life" at a specific magic moment in the process of development. Some biologists support the foregoing and I quote from one of them:

> Every one of the higher animals starts life as a single cell—the fertilized ovum . . . . The union of two such sex cells (male germ cell and female germ cell) to form a zygote constitutes the process of fertilization and initiates the life of a new individual.[2]

Neither is it a "mass of cells," as anyone who has witnessed an abortion can testify to. Having witnessed some abortions, I would ask those in favor of abortion to visit any hospital where abortions are performed and request permission to see an aborted fetus. It will not be intact unless the abortion was performed by the saline method. Then it will be pickled, but intact.

To talk about the "wanted" and the "unwanted" child smacks too much of bigotry and prejudice. Many of us have experienced the sting of being "unwanted" by certain segments of our society. Blacks were "wanted" when they could be kept in slavery. When that ceased, blacks became "unwanted"—in white suburbia, in white schools, in employment. Mexican-American (Chicano) farm laborers were "wanted" when they could be exploited by agribusiness. One usually wants objects and if they turn out to be unsatisfactory, they are returnable. How often have ethnic minorities heard the statement: "If you don't like it here, why don't you go back to where you came from?" Human beings are not returnable items. Every individual has his/her rights, not the least of which is the right to life, whether born or unborn. Those with power in our society cannot be allowed to "want" and "unwant" people at will.

I am not impressed or persuaded by those who express concern for the low-income woman who may find herself carrying an unplanned pregnancy and for the future of the unplanned child who may be deprived of the benefits of a full life as a result of the parents' poverty, because the fact remains that in this affluent nation of ours, pregnant cattle and horses receive better health care than pregnant poor women.

The poor cry out for justice and we respond with legalized abortion.

The Commission heard enough expert testimony to the effect that increased education and increased earnings result in lower fertility rates. In the developed countries of the world, declining fertility rates are correlated with growing prosperity, improved educational facilities, and, in general, overall improvement in the standard of living.

But it is not necessary to go beyond our own borders to verify this contention. Current data indicate that the same holds true for minority groups in this country. The higher the education attained by minorities and the broader the opportunities, the lower the fertility rate.

Thus, the sincerity of our concern for population growth (because of its effect on the quality of life for all people) will be tested if, in the face of incontrovertible facts, we move rapidly to utilize alternatives to abortion in order to reduce fertility.

The general public has not been given all the facts on the dangers, risks, and side effects resulting from abortion. On the contrary, we have been told that abortion is a "safe and simple" procedure, as easy as "extracting a tooth."

These are the facts. In Japan, Hungary, Yugoslavia, Sweden, England, and the United States, studies and surveys indicate that abortions are not that safe.

In Japan, for example, a survey conducted in 1969 by the Office of the Prime Minister revealed an increasing percentage of seven different complaints reported by women after abortion. These include increases in tubal pregnancies, menstrual irregularities, abdominal pain, dizziness, headaches, subsequent spontaneous miscarriage, and sterility.

Although one could argue that abdominal pain, dizziness, and headaches can be experienced by anyone, sterility, tubal pregnancy, and subsequent miscarriages are after-effects that have been reported in other countries.

Numerous other statistics on the after-effects of abortion exist, but are not included for lack of space. However, the New York experience, which is being touted as "highly successful," cannot go unchallenged.

Mr. Gordon Chase, New York City Health Services Administrator, in testimony before the Commission's hearings in New York City on September 27, 1971, reported that New York had experienced a birth decline since the advent of the abortion law. The fact is that the entire nation experienced a birth decline during the same period without legalized abortion.

The reduction in maternal deaths in New York, as reported by Mr. Chase, was credited to abortions. This is an assumption and not a proven fact. The decline in birthrates obviously, in itself, accounts for the decline in maternal mortality. Besides, maternal mortality declined throughout the country.

Recent statistics indicate that over 60 percent of abortions performed in New York were performed on out-of-state residents. Complications and deaths occurring as a result of abortions performed in New York on out-of-state women would not be recorded in New York; therefore, any New York statistics on the safety of abortion are challengeable at every level. Statistics can be categorized in different ways to support different conclusions.

Infant mortality rates are not reduced by killing an unborn child. How sad and incriminating that quality health facilities and services, denied to the poor for lack of money, are being used for performing abortions instead of being utilized for healing of the sick poor. But then, one represents a profit and the other an expense. It is all a matter of values.

Although we pride ourselves on being a nation that believes in "a stitch in time saves nine," we really do not practice it. The Commission's Report includes a section on "Methods of Fertility Control" which I consider an excellent exposé of this nation's lack of commitment to the development of safer and more effective preventive measures for fertility control. If it is true that this society does not want to see abortion used as a means of population control, then I, for one, will expect an immediate and dramatic allocation and distribution of resources into the field of research on reproductive physiology: the development of safer, more effective, and more acceptable methods of fertility control for everyone—men and women—plus wide-scale distribution of same throughout the country. The degree of swiftness this nation employs in moving in that direction will measure the extent of its commitment to check population growth through preventive measures and not with abortion.

—from the "Separate Statement of Graciela Olivarez" in *Report of the President's Commission on Population and the American Future*, U.S. Government Printing Office, 1972

Pat Goltz, Catherine Callaghan and Cindy Osborne

Active in social justice issues since her late teens, Cindy Osborne joined the prolife movement in 1983. She served as Coordinator of Community Services and head of the Speaker's Bureau for Clark County (Ohio) Right to Life before co-founding, with Rev. Deborah Wissner, the Ohio chapter of Feminists for Life in 1989. A 1993 visual communications graduate of Sinclair Community College, Osborne runs a home-based graphic design business. She and her husband, David, have 8 children, ages 1 through 22. The following account of FFL's origins is based on interviews and correspondence with Pat Goltz.

Pat Goltz, Catherine Callaghan, and the
Founding of Feminists for Life
by Cindy Osborne

In 1971, Pat Goltz and Catherine Callaghan were radical feminists, social activists, and members of the National Organization of Women (NOW). As fate would have it, they met in a Judo class and soon realized that they also shared prolife views. Theirs was not a popular position, as NOW was specifically fighting for abortion "rights" as a woman's ticket to sexual and economic freedom. Pat and Catherine saw the demand for abortion as being diametrically opposed to the goals of feminism. In fact, Pat had joined NOW specifically to fight that element.

Pat and Catherine were deeply disturbed because the women's movement was caving in to the demands of the patriarchy by allowing itself to be used by rich industrialists, the population control movement, and the playboy movement. They believed that feminist organizations were failing to provide viable alternatives to abortion for individual women and abandoning them to abortionists and abortion referral services who would exploit their misery. Because the single-minded focus of the movement was on abortion, they were not developing workable solutions to the problems of poor and minority women.

Pat and Catherine teamed up in an effort to change the emphasis on abortion rights in their local NOW chapter in Columbus, Ohio. Catherine met continual challenge by her sisters who questioned how she could call herself a feminist and oppose abortion. Catherine, always cool and logical, returned the challenge with, *"How can I not oppose abortion when half of all abortions kill our sisters?"* Despite Pat and Cathy's patient and consistent arguments, the opposition refused a dialogue on the issue. Pat was ordered by the president of the Columbus chapter not to discuss abortion with any member of NOW at any time or place. Pat was defiant and eventually paid the price.

In April of 1972, Pat and Cathy decided that prolife feminists needed a forum of their own in which to express their views. They set about forming an organization of international scope. One year later, on April 9, 1973, in Columbus, Ohio, Feminists for Life was born. It immediately took on international proportions when Pat and Cathy were joined by Jessica Pegis, Martha Crean and Denyse (Handlar) O'Leary of Toronto, Canada. At the time, Jessica, Martha, and Denyse, along with several other people, were publishing a monthly journal called *The Uncertified Human* (later shortened to *The Human*). FFL began publishing a quarterly newsletter, the *Feminists for Life Journal*, which was put together primarily by Pat with some help from Jessica. Shortly after publication began, Pat received a letter from Jessica. Instead of closing the correspondence with her usual "In sisterhood," this time Jessica closed with the unique "In sisterlife." The concept behind her closing words was a perfect frame for the goals and philosophies of Feminists for Life. The next newsletter went out under the flag *Sisterlife Journal*.

Even after founding FFL, Pat and Catherine refused to give up on NOW. They continued their outspoken affiliation in hopes that their words would fall on hearing ears. Catherine continued to work quietly behind the scenes, and Pat was bold in her criticism of establishment feminists for promoting abortion as the solution to everything from sexism to poverty. In 1974, NOW of Ohio could take no more; they wanted Pat out. Benson Wolman, the executive director of the Ohio ACLU, advised NOW Ohio that they had a *legal* right to kick Pat out, but certainly not a *moral* right. Putting law before morality, the leadership sent out notification of a hearing scheduled to oust Pat from NOW. Unfortunately, none of these letters reached Pat's supporters in the organization; NOW leadership claimed some members had been innocently overlooked during the notification process. At the expulsion hearing, Pat was given fifteen minutes to defend herself. She chose, instead, to do exactly what she had been forbidden to do. She spent the entire allotted time vigorously denouncing abortion before a captive audience who was bound, by rule, to hear her out. With only two votes of support and much fanfare, Pat was kicked out of the state chapter for daring to speak against NOW's sacred cow, abortion-on-demand.

Unlike the Ohio chapter of NOW, the national organization declined to oust Pat. It is doubtful that they were more tolerant than the state chapter as much as they were concerned about negative publicity. Indeed, by that time they had already gotten some nasty press by editorialists who had lambasted them for refusing to tolerate diverse opinions.

Our feminist foremothers of the nineteenth and early twentieth centuries had spoken out in tireless defense of the powerless within our society. Besides working for equal rights for women, feminists had been at the forefront of the abolitionist movement, the fight against child labor, as well as the effort to stop abortion (this, long before anyone dreamed it would someday be a legally protected "right"). Pat's expulsion illustrates the extent to which the establishment feminists had strayed from their noble roots. Not only was NOW, the alleged voice of the establishment feminist movement, promoting an insidious form of oppression under the guise of reproductive freedom, but in banishing Pat Goltz from their ranks, they made it obvious that they would tolerate no dissent.

Pat's expulsion from NOW punctuates an often ignored point. The prolife movement, often accused of consisting of narrow-minded and intolerant conservatives, eagerly extended hands of acceptance and friendship to Pat and Cathy. They were showered with opportunities to promote the goals and philosophies of prolife feminism. NOW, on the other hand, was promoting itself as the voice for all women, but refused any dialogue with those holding an opposing viewpoint on abortion.

NOW's loss was the prolife movement's gain. Barbara Willke, Chairperson of Right to Life of Greater Cincinnati, remembers, "We welcomed Feminists for Life. Pat and Catherine came from such diverse backgrounds and yet they had reached the same self-evident conclusions. They were way ahead of their time and I think they took the opposition by surprise." In 1974, Feminists for Life was invited to present a workshop at the National Right to Life convention in Washington, D.C. Pat, Catherine, Jessica, and Martha made the trek to the Capitol where the four of them camped together on a floor in student housing just one block from the Watergate Hotel. The workshop was a great success. For most of the audience, this was their first exposure to consistent feminism; and many who came in skeptics walked out visibly impressed. Pat has since spoken at hundreds of conferences and other public forums. The National Youth Pro-life Coalition (NYPLC) convention in New York holds a particularly fond spot in Pat's memory. Among the speakers were Connie Redbird Uri, a Cherokee-Choctaw Indian;

Jesse Jackson, who has since repudiated his politically incorrect prolife stance; Delores Huerta, and Dick Gregory.[1] Ms. Uri detailed how she considered abortion and sterilization a genocide of Native Americans. Mr. Gregory lightened up the convention with his speech in which he explained his large family. He related that the ZPG (Zero Population Growth) people had told him he should have 2¼ kids. After he and his wife had two, they kept trying for that ¼ kid, but a whole one kept popping out, and that's how he ended up with nine children.

In the travels connected with her many speaking engagements, Pat met people who were interested in starting FFL chapters in their own state or country. State chapters began popping up all over the U.S., and chapters were also formed in Canada, Australia, England, Mexico, and New Zealand. Over the years, Catherine took less of an active leadership role because of other commitments. Pat's move to Tucson in 1976 also signaled the end of her prominent role. New leadership was rising up just in time: Pat's workload was quickly becoming unmanageable, and she was fast approaching the point of burnout. In 1977, the Wisconsin chapter took over the international chapter and became Feminists for Life of America. Maggie Guenther, who had been vice-president since 1974, was elected president, and Wisconsin ran the national organization in parallel with their state chapter. In 1982 and 1983, they held several widely received national seminars on women's issues and prolife feminism. As a result, the mailing list began to swell and continues to grow. Soon there were members in every state as well as the aforementioned international chapters.

FFLA has pulled up roots and moved to new offices several times upon the election of new presidents—from Ohio to Wisconsin to Nebraska to Kansas City, Missouri, in 1984 where it found a home for ten years, and now, finally, to Washington, D.C. While it took a while for the national office to find a permanent home, the modern feminist prolife message took root and is rapidly spreading. We are still dismayed that the establishment feminists (who we define as those currently in power of such prominent groups as NOW and mistakenly seen as being the voice for all feminists) continue to promote abortion as the potion for all that ails us. We want equality. We demand liberty. But, as seekers of peace and promoters of justice, we know our road to freedom cannot be littered with the bodies of our own offspring. Having known oppression, we cannot stand by and allow the oppression of an entire class of weaker human beings. Having once been owned by our husbands, we cannot condone a position that says the unborn are owned by their mothers. Remembering a time when our value was determined by whether a man wanted us, we refuse to bow to the patriarchal attitude that says the unborn child's value is determined by whether a woman wants her. Goltz declares, "Abortion is an attack on the essence of our spirit, our very being." In the original Feminists for Life Declaration, the founding sisters state:

> We pledge ourselves to help the feminist movement correct its failures, purge itself of anti-life sentiments and practices and develop solutions to the problems that we, as women, face. We particularly want to welcome into fellowship Jews, blacks, Chicanas, Indians and Eskimos, Orientals, the aged and the handicapped, for all have suffered at the hand of the patriarchy, even as women have.

FFL co-founder Catherine Callaghan is a professor of Linguistics at Ohio State University. She opted out of NOW several years ago because "they kept adding extraneous planks to their platform that weren't women's issues." When asked how she reached her prolife philosophy, she replies, "Scientists tell us, and I have no reason to doubt them, that life begins at conception . . . the basis of my belief is on scientific evidence. Science is going to be the only useful, effective way to approach this issue." Because of this conviction, she has a problem with the mainstream prolife movement when they premise so many of their arguments against abortion on religious beliefs, which she finds unnecessary. She continues to actively support FFL of Ohio, predicating her prolife efforts on the basis of human rights.

Pat Goltz, still a maverick, lives in southern Arizona with her husband, John, and their seven children, two of whom are adopted. She holds a second degree black belt in taekwondo and continues to train. Pat's current work is in web site development and computer-generated art (landscapes and fractal images) and photography. She also remains active in the feminist prolife movement. In speaking about the current state of the mainstream women's movement, she comments, "They see no problem in trading in the chauvinist in the bedroom for the one on Capitol Hill!" She has a degree in art and has independently studied constitutional law and international treaties and declarations, particularly as they relate to abortion and human rights. Complementing her international interests, she has studied 140 languages, 15 of which she reads fluently. She has little patience with international family planning schemes inasmuch as she views extravagant Westerners as remarkably arrogant in the way they order African women to limit their families when it is necessary for them to have at least four children in order for one or two to survive to adulthood and help support them in their old age.

In the mid-seventies, Pat had the honor of speaking with Alice Paul, the author of the original Equal Rights Amendment. Ms. Paul, who had known some of our earlier feminist foremothers, made it clear that early feminists were altogether opposed to abortion. Also very much opposed to abortion, she had given her all to getting the ERA into Congress. She was grateful that others were now carrying the torch but was disturbed by the new trend of linking the ERA with abortion. She related to Pat her belief that abortion would destroy feminism if it were not stopped.

In its early years, FFL was very active in promoting the passage of the ill-fated ERA, especially in the home state of Ohio. The abortion issue was a direct contributor to Ohio's failure to ratify the ERA. One Senator who voted to keep the ERA in committee did so primarily because he felt the Supreme Court would be the final arbiter of the ERA. That court, he felt, could not be trusted since they had, in one sweeping decision, ushered in abortion-on-demand. Pat wrote, "As a prolife feminist, it galls me to know that an issue I totally disapprove of, namely abortion, caused the vote to kill the ERA in committee." As did Alice Paul and Clare Boothe Luce, Pat recognized the detrimental effect of abortion rights advocacy on passage of the ERA. The following article was written during this period of struggle for passage of the ERA.

Pat would like readers to know that she has revised some of her views as articulated in this early publication, but her commitment to women and children remains the same. We include it here for its historical importance in documenting the progression of prolife feminist thought.

—Written for the first edition, 1995

Equal Rights
by Pat Goltz

One of the goals of feminism is to see to it that women have equal legal protection: that the laws apply to women in the same way as they do to men. There are actually possible ways to do this. We are familiar, in general, with the Equal Rights Amendment, the effect of which would be to give us a legal handle by which class action suits of magnitudes heretofore undreamed of could be brought. The trouble with legislation already existing that purports to undo inequities for women is that there are so many exceptions and that it would cost a fortune in legal fees to cover bringing the exceptions into conformity with the rules. Money for pursuit of problems in court is something women are in short supply of. Whether or not women "own" more money than men, women control less of it. The other effect the Equal Rights Amendment would have is to act as an incentive to get a large number of laws changed at the legislative level with considerably less effort on the part of women.

State equal rights amendments have proved to be of considerable help. The major problem with equal rights amendments on the state level is that they don't apply to the Federal government—the largest agency of discrimination in the country. The Federal Equal Rights Amendment, even if it is eventually unratified, is having a profound effect. In the States where it has been ratified, legislators are busy modifying state laws to conform. Some of this activity is going on in states that have yet to ratify as well. The hope is that even if ERA goes unratified, it will have accomplished much of its purpose already. Perhaps changing laws in one state will exert pressure on the legislators in neighboring states. In any event, the outcome should be a distinct improvement.

Opponents of ERA often cite specific fears about what the ERA would do. Those active opponents I have talked to, to a woman, however, have refused to discuss with me exactly what they hope the laws will eventually be. This head-in-the-sand attitude, along with the small collection of misinformation which is being circulated and recirculated, is regarded as nonfunctional by this writer. In a sense, we feminists have to look out for our weaker sisters. They want the right to maintain the traditional female role but don't know how to go about it. The feminist movement, in general, has not been too helpful. If we do not help these women choose the traditional role at their own desire, we have failed them. Much more attention is needed in this area. What we want for women is more options, not a new straitjacket.

One disturbing aspect of the struggle for ratification of the ERA has been the slowdown among states electing to ratify. The big slowdown occurred during this legislative session (1973). It is probably due to two things: most of the states that would readily ratify have already done so, and a combination of gathering momentum on the part of opponents and tactical errors on the part of proponents has made the remaining states cautious. If nothing else, we have the inertia of eons of sexism to overcome.

The tactical errors can be broadly classified into several categories: abortion, lesbianism, and the breakdown of the family. It is known that in Ohio, abortion was a direct contributor to Ohio's failure to ratify this year. One senator who voted to keep the ERA in committee did so primarily because he felt the Supreme Court would be the final arbiter of the ERA and it is not to be trusted since that court legalized abortion-on-request. We talked with that senator, who was open to us because of our prolife stand, and discovered that he actually knows very little about the discrimination women face. He is willing to be educated and has agreed to work on individual legislation to help women. We are quite concerned that Ohio's failure to ratify in 1973 has irreparably harmed the ERA, since Ohio is regarded as a pivotal state by both sides. As prolife feminists, it galls us to know that an issue we totally disapprove of, namely abortion, caused the vote to kill the ERA in committee, after the successful ratification in the house by a comfortable margin of 54 to 40.

Lesbianism has mainly been a problem of timing. It is not a popular issue with the population at large. We at Feminists for Life have not taken a stand on lesbianism because we feel an insufficient case is made for lesbianism being a feminist issue. Open support of the gay movement prior to ratification of the ERA was poor timing. [Today, FFL welcomes GLBT persons and their friends and shares many members with the Prolife Alliance of Gays and Lesbians.—Eds.]

The breakdown of the family is also attributed to the ERA and feminist movement by opponents. If opponents think equal rights are causing the breakdown of the family, they are using this as a scapegoat and contributing to the problem! This writer sees the breakdown of the family as due to three causes: breakdown in religious and moral values (religion doesn't have to be sexist), permissive child rearing practices (which, incidentally, make women slaves of their children), and the breakdown of the school system (including the adoption of more ineffective methods of teaching reading and arithmetic, pressure from the teachers for students to conform to the peer group, sensitivity training, and behavior modification, all of which serve to entrench sexism in the young, and will continue to do so as long as the persons in power have sexist attitudes themselves). Although Feminists for Life's stand against abortion and involuntary euthanasia should have tipped people off that we are not a "typical" feminist group, a number of people have assumed that we favor the breakdown of the family. For the record, we support a strong, flexible family structure, and we accept men into membership and active participation on an equal basis with women.

Another way of attacking the problem of establishing equal rights for women is to work to get the Supreme Court to rule that the fourteenth amendment applies equally to women. This method of achieving the goal has been sadly neglected by our movement. We are working on this, also. It may turn out to be our only hope.

—1973

Daphne Clair de Jong

Daphne de Jong founded a Feminists for Life chapter in Aotearoa, also called New Zealand. She is a full-time writer who has won several literary awards, including a New Zealand PEN award for nonfiction. She has published poetry, anthologized short stories, and, as Daphne Clair or Laurey Bright, historical fiction and over seventy romance novels. She continues her work in her homeland (see <www.daphneclair.com>), where she lives with her husband and five grown children, one of whom was adopted as an orphan from China. During the late 1970s, she penned these two strong prolife feminist arguments for the *New Zealand Listener*, the national culture and public affairs magazine.

Feminism and Abortion: The Great Inconsistency
By Daphne Clair de Jong

In the same way that many opponents of slavery and racism have failed to apply their principles to the question of women's rights, so feminist writers have a peculiarly dense blind spot about the unborn. No argument in favour of freely available abortion is tenable in the light of feminist ideals and principles. And all of them bear an alarming resemblance to the arguments used by men to justify discrimination against women.

Principally, the arguments are that the fetus is not human, or is human only in some rudimentary way; that it is a part of its mother and has no rights of its own; that a woman's right to control her body supersedes any rights of the fetus; that those who believe the fetus is a human being with human rights should not impose their beliefs on others through the medium of the law.

Biologically, the fetus is not only human, but an individual human by virtue of its unique genetic inheritance. Six weeks from conception it looks like a very small baby, with a functioning heart, brain and nervous system. The appearance and behavior of very early fetal infants show definite individual patterns. After implantation of the fertilized ovum (and many would say from the first fusion of the parent cells), scientists are unable to pinpoint any stage at which something "sub-human" becomes a human being.

Regardless of arbitrary legal definitions, the concept of a definitive moment when humanity becomes present is simply the ancient religious theory of "ensoulment" rephrased in pseudo-philosophical jargon. Medieval theologians who postulated "ensoulment" at 40 days for boys and 80 days for girls had only recently decided after much debate that women had souls at all. Even in the nineteenth century, philosopher Otto Weininger wrote: "In such a being as the absolute female there are no logical and ethical phenomena, and therefore the ground for the assumption of a soul is absent . . . Women have no existence and no essence; they are not; they are nothing." Weininger described Jews in similar terms.[1] Eva Figes, author of *Patriarchal Attitudes,* comments on those views: "It soon becomes possible to deny such inferiors basic human rights. The implication is that these inferiors are not human at all." Women were not, of course, "nothing" because Weininger believed them to be so; neither is the fetus just a collection of matter because others do not accept its humanity. It is only the latest in a long line of human beings who throughout history have been denied human status because of their "different" appearance. They include blacks, Jews, dwarfs, the handicapped—and women.

Feminist writers clearly see the link between feminism and racism. "It should," Figes says, "teach us a valuable lesson about the dangers of attempting to categorize people on the basis of physique—whether it is a matter of sex or skin color?" Perhaps it should also teach us something about categorizing people on the basis of immaturity. Especially since alleged immaturity or "childishness" has been the excuse for sexual discrimination, too. Idealist philosopher Schopenhauer found women "in every respect backward, lacking in reason or true morality . . . a kind of middle step between the child and the man, who is the true human being." The unborn, particularly in the embryonic stage, bears little resemblance to the "norm" of adult white male. Feminists ought to be sensitive about arguing the nonhumanity of the fetus on the grounds of its physical appearance or size, or ability to function independently. Jessica Staff, preaching abortion on demand, contemptuously characterized the two-months fetus as "a thing the size of a cashew nut." She might have been wise to remember that size has always been a factor in the supposed superiority of the male. Not to mention all those careful measurements of male and female brains. Even now misogynist writers deny women the potential for genius because of "smaller brain capacity." (Fetal brains have similar configuration to adult brains, and EEG tracings have been made at less than six weeks gestation.)

Until this century, the laws of both Britain and America made women a "part of" their husbands. "By marriage, the husband and wife are one person in law . . . our law in general considers man and wife one person" (*Blackstone's Commentaries*, 1768). The one person was, of course, the husband, who exerted absolute power over his wife and her property. She had no existence and therefore no protection under the law. The only thing a husband could not do was kill her. The earliest feminist battles were fought against this legal chattel status of women. Many feminists were among those who overturned the U.S. Supreme Court decision of 1857 that considered the black slave "property" and not entitled to the protection of the constitution. Feminism totally rejected the concept of ownership in regard to human beings. Yet when the U. S. Supreme Court ruled in 1973 that the fetus was the property of its mother, and not entitled to the protection of the constitution, "liberated" women danced in the streets.

A fetus, while dependent on its mother, is no more a part of its mother than she is a part of her husband. Biology is constant, not subject to the vagaries of law. The fetus lives its own life, develops according to its own genetic program, sleeps, wakes, moves, according to its own inclinations. The RH-negative syndrome, which occurs when fetal and maternal blood are incompatible, is striking evidence of its separate life. That a woman or a doctor does not perceive a fetus or embryo as human is not sufficient reason to put abortion outside the context of morality and law. Most people find babies more attractive than embryos, as most of us prefer kittens to cats, and as Hitler found Aryans more attractive than Jews. But *to define humanity on the basis of one's emotional response is to rationalize prejudice.* To allow any person or group to define that certain human beings are to be regarded as less than fully human is to construct a basis for discrimination and eventual destruction. Women who object to being "sex objects" may not care to examine too closely their conviction that embryos and fetuses are expendable objects which become less so as they become more visually attractive.

There have always been "lawful" exceptions to the universal ban on taking human life: notably self-defense and abortion to save the woman's life. The mainstream feminist movement rejects most other exceptions, such as warfare and judicial retribution. Feminism opposes the violent power games of the male establishment, the savage "solutions" imposed by the strong on the powerless.

The feminist claim to equality is based on the equal rights of all human beings. The most fundamental of all is the right to life. If women are to justify taking this right from the unborn, they must contend that their own superiority of size, of power, or of physique or intellect or need, or their own value as a person, transcends any right of the unborn. In the long history of male chauvinism, all these have been seen as good reasons for withholding human rights from women.

The temptation to dominate is the most truly universal, the most irresistible one there is; to surrender the child to its mother, the wife to her husband, is to promote tyranny in the world (Simone de Beauvoir, *The Second Sex*).

To claim that the unique interdependence of the fetus and its mother is sufficient to give her absolute rights over its life, is to claim a right which society in general, and feminists in particular, do not concede to anyone else—the arbitrary right to terminate a human life. Women who will not accept that a woman's value be measured by how far some man wants her body or needs her services, now demand that the unborn be judged by the same standard—to be allowed to live or die on one criterion, its sentimental value to its mother.

A "woman's right to choose" (though more an incantation than an argument) implies that abortion is a matter of private morality. Perhaps because pregnancy is the result of a sexual act, the abortion question is frequently presented as a part of the same moral category as contraception and homosexuality. But questions of human life are always matters of public morality; in the category of war, capital punishment, and murder, include abortion. Since Nuremburg, the world has accepted that those who perceive the humanity of groups defined as "sub-human" have not only a right but a duty to protect their human rights. Those who are unconvinced by medical and biological science have a right to try to persuade others to their view. But they must recognize the obligation of those who believe in the humanness of the fetus, to oppose them. Not to do so would be "truly irresponsible. To abdicate one's own moral understanding, to tolerate crimes against humanity . . . ." (Germaine Greer, *The Female Eunuch*). (Greer was writing in general terms. Like other feminist writers, notably de Beauvoir, who was enraged at the callousness of lovers and society toward pregnant women, she fails to see the radical injustice of inflicting abortion on them as a "solution" to their problem.)

How many feminists would defend the right of a man who sincerely believed in the inferiority of women to beat, rape and terrorize "his" woman? Should the law allow him his right to choose who is to be regarded as fully human?

—*New Zealand Listener*, 7 Jan. 1978; repub. *Sisterlife*, Spring 1986

The Feminist Sell-Out
By Daphne Clair de Jong

The women's movement suffers from three classic defense mechanisms associated with minority group status: self-rejection, identification with the dominant group, and displacement.

The demand for abortion at will is a symptom of group self-hatred and total rejection, not of sex role but of sex identity.

The womb is not the be-all and end-all of women's existence. But it is the physical centre of her sexual identity, which is an important aspect of her self-image and personality. To reject its function, or to regard it as a handicap, a danger or a nuisance, is to reject a vital part of her own personhood. Every woman need not be a mother, but unless every women can identify with the potential motherhood of all women, no equality is possible. African-Americans gained nothing by straightening their kinky hair and imitating the white middle class. Equality began to become a reality only when they insisted on acceptance of their different qualities—"Black is Beautiful."

Women will gain their rights only when they demand recognition of the fact that they are people who become pregnant and give birth—and not always at infallibly convenient times—and that pregnant people have the same rights as others. To say that in order to be equal with men it must be possible for a pregnant woman to become un-pregnant at will is to say that being a woman precludes her from being a fully functioning person. It concedes the point to those who claim that women who want equality really want to be imitation men.

If women must submit to abortion to preserve their lifestyle or career, their economic or social status, they are pandering to a system devised and run by men for male convenience. The politics of sexism are perpetuated by accommodating to expediential societal structures, which decree that pregnancy is incompatible with other activities, and that children are the sole responsibility of their mother. The demand for abortion is a sell-out to male values and a capitulation to male lifestyles rather than a radical attempt to renegotiate the terms by which women and men can live in the world as people with equal rights and equal opportunities. Black "Uncle Toms" have their counterparts not only in women who cling to the chains of their kitchen sinks, but also in those who proclaim their own liberation while failing to recognize that they have merely adopted the standards of the oppressor, and fashioned themselves in his image.

Oppressed groups traditionally turn their frustrated vengeance on those even weaker than themselves. The unborn is the natural scapegoat for the repressed anger and hostility of women, which is denied in traditional male-female relationships, and ridiculed when it manifests itself in feminist protest. Even while proclaiming "her" rights over the fetus, much liberationist rhetoric identifies pregnancy with male chauvinist "ownership." The inference is that by implanting "his" seed, the man establishes some claim over a woman's body (keeping her "barefoot and pregnant"). Abortion is almost consciously seen as "getting back at" the male. The truth may well be that the liberationist sees the fetus not as part of her body but as part of his. What escapes most liberationist writers is that legal abortion is neither a remedy nor an atonement for male exploitation of women. It is merely another way in which women are manipulated and degraded for male convenience and male profit. This becomes blatantly obvious in the private abortion industries of both Britain and America, and the support given to the pro-abortion lobby by such exploitative corporations as the Playboy empire.

Of all the things that are done to women to fit them into a society dominated by men, abortion is the most violent invasion of their physical and psychic integrity. It is a deeper and more destructive assault than rape, the culminating act of womb-envy and woman-hatred by the jealous male who resents the creative power of women. Just as the rapist claims to be "giving women what they want," the abortionist affirms his right to provide a service for which there is a feminine demand. Offered the quick expedient of abortion, instead of community support to allow her to experience pregnancy and birth and parenthood with dignity and without surrendering her rights as a person, woman is again the victim, and again a participant in her own destruction.

The way to equality is not to force women into molds designed for men, but to re-examine our basic assumptions about men and women, about child-care and employment, about families and society and design new and more flexible modes for living. Accepting short term solutions like abortion only delays the implementation of real reforms like decent maternity and paternity leave, job protection, high quality child-care, community responsibility for dependent people of all ages, and recognition of the economic contribution of child-minders. Agitation for the imaginative use of glide time, shared jobs, shorter working weeks, good daycare, part-time education and job training, is more constructive for women—and men—torn between career and children, than agitation for abortion.

Today's women's movement remains rooted in nineteenth-century thinking, blindly accepting patriarchal systems as though they rested on some immutable natural law: processing women through abortion mills to manufacture instant imitation men who will fit into a society made by and for wombless people. Accepting the "necessity" of abortion is accepting that pregnant women and mothers are unable to function as persons in this society. It indicates a willingness to adjust to the *status quo* which is a betrayal of the feminist cause, a loss of the revolutionary vision of a world fit for people to live in.

The movement has never perceived the essential disharmony of its views on sexual oppression and its aspirations to a new social order, and its attitudes to abortion. The accepted feminist prophets of the new age have never brought to bear on the question the analytical power that they display in other directions. Typically, the subject is dismissed in a paragraph or two, the "right" to abortion assumed, without evidence or argument. (De Beauvoir came closest to recognizing the dangers, raging that women were often coerced into abortions they did not truly want—by men or by the circumstances of the pregnancy.) Within the movement, doctors and other men whose attitudes are glaringly chauvinist have been hailed as white knights of women's rights if they espouse abortion on demand, while "sisters" who oppose it are subjected to witch-hunts that could teach a thing or two to a Sprenger or a McCarthy.

The reasons for the abortion issue moving to a central position in liberation ideology are partly tactical. It is much easier to fight a statute than to overcome social attitudes. As the suffragette movement became cohesive and powerful by focusing attention on the single issue of the vote, the new feminist wave gained momentum when all its resources were thrown into overturning abortion laws. But the vote was dismissed by some feminists of the 1960's as "the red herring of the revolution." The abortion issue bids fair to be its successor.

The drive to legalize abortion on demand may be not only a red herring, but a tragic mistake which will perpetuate the politics of power and delay equality of rights for decades or even longer. Human rights are not exclusive. Any claim to a superior or exceptional right inevitably infringes on the rights of someone else. To ignore the rights of others in an effort to assert our own is to compound injustice, rather than reduce it.

—*New Zealand Listener,* 14 Jan. 1978; repub. *Sisterlife,* Spring 1986

Rosemary Oelrich Bottcher

Rosemary Oelrich Bottcher is a retired teacher of chemistry at Tallahassee Community College and environmental chemist specializing in hazardous waste problems. She was a columnist for the *Tallahassee Democrat* for six years and has contributed essays to three anthologies on bioethics. She lives on a farm in northern Florida (where the waste is not nearly so hazardous) with her husband, an environmental attorney. Her four children, one of whom is adopted, are now grown. Before retiring, Ms. Bottcher served as President of Feminists for Life of America from 1994 to 1999 after having served for ten years as Vice President and has continued over the past two decades to spread the feminist prolife message through her writing and speaking.

The second essay included here, "Abortion Threatens Women's Equality," is the text of a statement Bottcher delivered at the Washington Press Club in a joint press conference with the National Right to Life Committee at the Summer 1985 convention of the National Organization of Women (NOW). Her statement outlines prolife feminist resistance to being represented by religious conservative prolifers such as Jerry Falwell, then leader of the Moral Majority, or prochoice leaders such as Eleanor Smeal, then President of NOW.

Free Choice Can Cost Others
by Rosemary Oelrich Bottcher

One of the many innocent bystanders being wounded by the abortion brouhaha is our already beleaguered language. Not since the time of Humpty Dumpty have words been so emancipated from their definitions, so free to mean anything the fancy of their utterer wants them to mean.

A particularly annoying example of this is the corruption of the proper meaning of the concept of "choice." Pro-abortion activists like to call themselves "pro-choice" and prefer to refer to their opponents as "anti-choice." By this cleverly dishonest tactic, they simultaneously divert attention from the real issue, portray themselves as defenders of personal liberty, and misrepresent the motives of those who disagree. They also make some amazing assumptions about the moral significance of choices.

The Religious Coalition for Abortion Rights has declared, "Abortion is an individual decision. And therefore your God-given right." Yes, indeed, the modern religious thinking of the theologians of the coalition has concluded that the ability to decide to commit an act is equivalent to the right (God-given, no less) to commit that act.

It is the act of deciding that is important, valuable and worth defending; the choice itself doesn't matter much. Therefore, those who decide to abort (or murder, plunder and ravage, I suppose) have an absolute right to do just that.

This argument strikes me as a rather bizarre distortion of traditional Judeo-Christian ethics because it ignores one very important point—namely, that the consequences of choices almost always affect people other than the choice-maker. While it is good to be able to make choices, the fact remains that not all choices are equal; some are foolish, some are stupid, and some are evil.

Sometimes one person's choice results in terrible suffering or injustice for another person; for this reason, a civilized society is justified in limiting the choices of its citizens.

Most people realize this when they stop to think about it; nevertheless, the concept of "freedom of choice" has a long history of successfully blackmailing many people into tolerating situations that their instincts tell them are wrong.

People who objected to slavery on moral grounds were told that they did not have to own slaves if doing so would violate their consciences, but that they must respect the rights of those who did not share their opinion.

Integration was kept at bay for years by people who insisted that they had a right to choose how they managed their communities, ran their businesses and lived their lives.

Eventually the fallacy of these arguments becomes apparent, yet the misunderstanding of free choice continues to make mischief. For example, the liberal community, which prides itself on its championship of the weak and powerless, has offered almost no objection to the spreading practice of infanticide.

The American Civil Liberties Union is so devoted to individual freedom that it has courageously defended even the Nazi Party's right to speech, yet it has never, to my knowledge, offered to defend a handicapped infant's right to life. I suspect that this is because justification for infanticide is almost always couched in terms of the parents' "right to choose" the fate of their own child.

The word "choice" has become a magical incantation; breathe it into a liberal ear and the liberal mind becomes hypnotized. The well-meaning eagerness to be tolerant and open-minded disintegrates into moral paralysis.

Aficionados of handguns, nuclear weapons, drunken driving or baby-seal bashing could probably quash liberal opposition to their causes by patiently explaining their positions in terms of "pro-choice."

This all-purpose argument could be trimmed to fit any situation. For example: "Child abuse is an individual decision. And therefore your God-given right," or, "I am personally opposed to rape, but I believe that every man has a right to control his own body," and, perhaps, "The opinion that women are entitled to the same rights as men is not shared by all. A pluralistic society must respect different opinions; therefore each man can decide for himself if he will discriminate against women."

In the minds of many, these contentions are no more preposterous than the analogous apologies for abortion. Obviously, there must be some limits as to what choices a free society can allow; the disagreement is about the proper extent of those limits.

One of the printable things I am called by my not-always-polite opponents is "intolerant." Actually, I am eager to be tolerant if at all possible. I realize that there is always the possibility (however remote) that I could be wrong. Besides, eccentric ideas—and people—help make life interesting.

My own life is such a fracas that I would really rather not be bothered with having to mind anyone else's business, and few subjects bore me more than other people's sex lives. If I had a choice, I would rather putter than picket, but there is a point at which I feel obliged to obey certain moral imperatives. There is a point at which tolerance becomes irresponsible. The rub is in recognizing that point.

Years ago, when I still suffered from acute idealism and spent most of my waking hours fretting over some injustice or other, my mother counseled me about how to decide if a particular situation was worth all the worry. "Will little children die from it?" she asked. "If not, it's not worth working yourself into such a snit."

I still apply that test when deciding whether an issue is snit-worthy, and the answer to her question is what compels me to be especially intolerant and anti-choice on the issues of child abuse, infanticide, and abortion.

—*Tallahassee Democrat*, 8 Aug. 1982; repub. *Sisterlife*, Winter 1985.

Abortion Threatens Women's Equality
by Rosemary Oelrich Bottcher

NOW does not reflect the views and goals of most American women, and it does not reflect the views and goals of all feminists. Support for abortion is not the *sine qua non* of feminism. The term "prolife feminist" is not an oxymoron; rather, it ought to be a redundancy. Feminists for Life of America was established in 1972 by Pat Goltz and Cathy Callaghan after they were excommunicated from NOW for distributing prolife literature at a NOW meeting. NOW, which harshly criticizes the Catholic Church for not tolerating pluralism on the abortion issue, is itself utterly intolerant of heterodoxy on the same issue.

The Catholic Church reprimands, but does not excommunicate, members who disagree with the church's position on abortion, while NOW will not accept prolife feminists as members and will expunge any established member who is foolhardy enough to express wavering faith in the abortion sacrament. It is NOW's policy not to invite a speaker, on any subject, who does not share the major goals of the organization, including, of course, guarding the abortion icon.

Elise Rose is a member of Feminists for Life who attended the recent NOW convention. She attempted to contribute some comments at a workshop, but when it became apparent that she is not pro-abortion, a vote was taken on the spot—and she was not allowed to speak. Supposedly, one of the advantages of being feminist is that we get to do our own thinking; Jerry Falwell doesn't speak for us and neither does Ellie Smeal. Apparently NOW does not agree, at least on its core issues, and while they cannot control the thoughts of renegade feminists, they will try to ensure that unacceptable thoughts will not be expressed.

So the apparent solidarity of feminist thought on the abortion issue is an illusion maintained by NOW's refusal to even acknowledge that dissent exists. The abortion loyalty oath required by NOW is a major reason for its declining membership. Many women who are fervent supporters of equality for women know that they are not welcome at NOW.

Shunned—banished, really—by their pro-abortion sisters, prolife feminists have had to form their own group in order to provide a forum for their vision of feminism, a return to authentic feminism which realizes that feminism is, properly, merely a part of a larger philosophy that respects all human life. The early feminists of the late nineteenth and early twentieth centuries were opposed to abortion because they realized that abortion, and the perceived need for it, reflected the pervasive oppression of women. They understood that abortion is profoundly anti-woman and anti-feminist.

Abortion remains a number one threat to equality for women. There are four major reasons for this.

Defending abortion requires defending the concept of discrimination. By arguing for abortion, feminists are forced to sabotage the philosophical foundations of feminism. It is sheer hypocrisy to argue for equality for themselves and against equality for the unborn. Because of the recent revelations of fetology that let us see, literally see, the complex and delightful unborn child, pro-abortion feminists have been forced to abandon the tumor theory of pregnancy as an excuse for abortion.

Faced with the irrefutable evidence that the unborn child is indeed a living human being, they are reduced to arguing, "Well, yes, but he is not necessarily a person." The irony is excruciating. Establishing the personhood of women has been the ultimate goal of feminism. Gloria Steinem observes that the first 100 years of the women's movement was spent establishing ourselves as persons; before that we were ownable, like cattle or chairs. Or, I might add, like unborn children. In denying the personhood of the unborn child, feminists have borrowed the very same justifications that the patriarchs have used so successfully throughout history to deny full recognition as persons to women.

Abortion threatens women's equality by the very negative image of women that is projected by pro-abortion rhetoric. It makes no sense to argue that women are rational adults capable of reflection, self-direction and self-control, yet claim that unplanned pregnancies are inevitable and that pregnancy is frequently the result of factors beyond a women's control. How can we believe that the same women who will kill themselves, lose their minds, abuse their children, or commit a crime if denied legal abortions, can be trusted to handle distresses of adult responsibility?

Abortion surrenders women to pregnancy discrimination. Those who advocate legal abortion concede that pregnant women are intolerably handicapped; they cannot compete in a male world of wombless efficiency. Rather than changing the world to accommodate the needs of pregnant women and mothers, proabortion feminists encourage women to fit themselves neatly into a society designed by and for men. A society that tolerates 1.6 million abortions a year is under little pressure to make the changes necessary to address the needs of pregnant women and working parents.

NOW's obsession with abortion detracts from constructive feminist goals such as reformation of the work place, democratizing the family, and improving the quality of childcare. Even though NOW admits that fears about abortion helped kill the ERA, it refuses to support an abortion-neutral version of the amendment, which would have a good chance for passage. For NOW, abortion is more important than equality.

Legal abortion has harmed women as a group and has caused enormous harm to women as individuals. The phenomenal growth of Women Exploited by Abortion (WEBA) proves that for many women, abortion has been a wrenching experience. None of the wrenching stories of how illegal abortion can destroy women can match the pathos of WEBA members' accounts of how legal abortion can destroy women. Yet NOW feminists refuse to acknowledge the pain of these women, dismissing them contemptuously as "the guilt-trippers." NOW has not yet realized that any abortion, legal or illegal, harms women and contributes to the oppression of women.

—Statement, FFLA and National Right to Life Committee joint press conference, Washington, D.C., Summer 1985; *Sisterlife* Fall 1985.

Jo McGowan

A freelance writer who occasionally contributes to the independent liberal weekly *National Catholic Reporter*, U.S.-born Jo McGowan has lived for many years in Dehradoon, India with her Hindu husband, Dr. Ravi Chopra, and their children, including a daughter with cerebral palsy. Chopra is founder of the People's Science Institute (www.psi-india.org), an organization devoted to participatory, sustainable development. McGowan is founder and director of Karuna Vihar, an experimental school for disabled children. Her many experiences of living across human boundaries have shaped her views of abortion.

Since McGowan wrote her article, sex selection abortion has dramatically skewed sex ratios in some countries. As McGowan comments, some American prochoicers dismiss sex-selective abortion as a red herring, but in China and India, the world's most populous nations, comprising roughly a third of humankind, abortion of female fetuses has become so rampant—despite legal restrictions—that it is skewing overall sex ratios from a "normal" of 106:100 male to female births to 108:100 in India and 117:100 in China.[1] Critics of son preference and sex selection identify discriminatory social institutions rather than the targeted human beings as the problems that need to be eradicated. Indian and Chinese cultural traditions include practices of female infanticide, women's enforced economic and social dependence on men, poverty, the dowry system, the lack of a nationwide social security system, and the practice of having daughters care only until marriage for their aging parents, whereupon sons take over.[2] Women are overwhelmed by pressures to obey the "duty" to sacrifice their unborn daughters—and themselves as well. Asked by a German feminist journalist why she "chose" to abort her daughter, a 25-year-old woman in Gujarat State spoke of her husband's desire for a son, her duty to give him one, her fear of abortion after abortion, her concern that her spouse will reject her for another woman. Asked about the abortion itself, she replied: "I don't want to talk about it." When the journalist asks "Was it so terrible?'" the woman repeated, crying: "I don't want to talk . . . . each child is sent by God."[3] There are also reports of postnatal daughters, who, because of sex selection in their families, question their own right to exist so much that they resort to suicide.[4]

All Abortions Are Selective
by Jo McGowan

Amniocentesis, a medical procedure by which certain abnormalities in an unborn child can be detected, is fraught with moral dilemmas, the magnitude of which are only now being understood. The standard use of the test has been to provide women in high-risk categories—older women, women with a family history of genetic diseases, women who have contracted German measles in the first trimester of their pregnancies—with information about the well-being of their babies. If the test proves that abnormalities do exist, the options are to abort the child or carry it to term anyway.

The test by itself is not without risk to the child. It involves the precise insertion of a needle into the womb and withdrawing a small quantity of amniotic fluid which is then tested. There is always the chance of the needle going into the placenta or the child, causing severe damage or miscarriage. Women are advised that if they do not intend to have an abortion if the child is found to be defective, they would be better off not having the test at all. As such, it can be termed a "hunt and kill" method.

In the United States, when the first test came out, fears were expressed by many feminists in regard to one of the side aspects of the test: that, in addition to revealing defects, it could also reveal the sex of the child. They were afraid that such information would be used to abort baby girls simply because they were girls and irrespective of their physical and mental health. These fears were brushed aside by most people as unthinkable. Surely, they reasoned, we have gone well beyond the stage where the birth of a girl is a tragedy.

Not so in India. Recent reports in national news magazines tell startling stories of women undergoing the test for the sole purpose of discovering whether the child is a girl. If it is, it is promptly aborted. The reasons given are painfully familiar: the expense of marrying a daughter off, the need for sons to help in the family business and carry on the family name—in short, the age-old preference for boys over girls.

Feminists, naturally, have risen in anger. With morality and justice as their standards, they argue that it is "morally incorrect," to use the words of Dr. Kirpal Kaur who performs abortions at the Guru Tegh Bahadur Medical College in Amritsar, to allow sex to be the determining factor in the decision to abort. In effect, as Manjulika Dubey points out in a recent article in *Mainstream*, using the test in this way affirms what has long been suspected in this country: that to be born female is to be genetically defective.

Both Ms. Dubey and Anjali Deshpande, author of a second article in the same magazine, draw attention to the steadily decreasing ratio of women to men in India (from 1000:972 in 1901 to 1000:935 in 1981). "If amniocentesis is misused on a large scale to weed out female fetuses, the ratio is bound to show a further decline," writes Ms. Deshpande. Ms. Dubey goes on to decry the failures of the feminist movement if it is possible that women could "reject their own kind and worship and covet power objectified in the male to the point of participating in *atrocities* against their own daughters" (emphasis added).

"Atrocity" is her term for abortion. "Female feticide" is Ms. Deshpande's. And from Vimla Ranadive, secretary of the All India Co-ordination Committee of Working Women: "It is like the Nazi's 'final solution' of exterminating the Jews and it only adds a touch of sophistication to the brutal practice."

"Atrocity," "female feticide," "brutal practice." Apt descriptions of abortion—but they ring a bit hollow coming from people who, in the next breath, assert that abortion rights must be safeguarded so that women can "control their lives."

What are we to make of all this? Without denying in any sense the depravity of killing baby girls simply because they are girls, I submit that the position feminists have taken on this issue is morally bankrupt, without substance of any kind.

Why? Because one cannot have it both ways. Once the abortion of any child, for any reason, is permitted, the abortion of all children becomes acceptable. If it is all right to kill a child because it is handicapped, or because its mother is unmarried, or because it is the third child in a family that only wanted two, why isn't it all right to kill it because it is a girl?

This process of aborting girls when boys are wanted has been termed "selective abortion," but in fact every abortion is a selective one. What changes from case to case are only the values of the parents, determining what they select and what they reject. Parents who only value physically and mentally normal children might reject a child who was retarded or who had hemophilia. Parents who value education and want to be able to provide their children with it might reject a third child if their resources could only educate two. Parents who value their time and freedom might reject *any* children they produced. And parents who value boys might well reject a child known to be a girl.

Feminists who have been so active in assuring women of the "right to choose" can hardly complain when those same women exercise their freedom to choose something with which feminists do not agree. Choice being such a highly personal affair, one can hardly expect everyone to choose the same things. But it is tragically ironic that what has been hailed as the "great liberator" of women may turn out instead to be the means of their destruction—a tool to make them, in Manjulika Dubey's words, an "endangered species."

Perhaps, however, something good may yet emerge from this "female feticide" outrage. Perhaps people, and feminists in particular, will finally realize what is actually at stake in an abortion, any abortion. Perhaps from this undeniable truth that it is wrong to kill girls will emerge the larger truth that it is wrong to kill anyone. Perhaps it will first be necessary for a special interest group to champion the cause of each particular group of children targeted for destruction: feminists for baby girls, disabled activists for handicapped babies, would-be adoptive parents for unwanted babies.

This would certainly be the long way round, but perhaps at the end of it all we would realize that the single unifying factor in all these cases is that the child to be aborted is, first and foremost, a human child and one of us, that to kill her is to kill that which makes us human, bringing us closer to the day when the entire race—male and female—is an endangered species.

—*Indian Express*, 1982; repub. *Sisterlife*, June 1984

Grace Dermody

Grace Dermody holds an English degree from St. Elizabeth's College in New Jersey. Eager to work for women's rights, Dermody joined NOW in 1975 but soon left because of its increasing emphasis on abortion advocacy. Through prolife work, she read about Feminists for Life, immediately joined, and formed a New Jersey chapter. With co-member Judy Novak, she has spoken extensively on prolife feminism at Universities and other public forums. Her writings have appeared in the *New York Times* and other local publications.

In 1983, Dermody closely followed a highly publicized tragedy of a young single mother who was on trial for killing her son. She noted that the psychiatrist testifying on the mother's behalf, Dr. Robert Gould, connected the young mother's fatal beating of her child to the trauma of her abortion the day before. After the trial, Dermody interviewed Dr. Gould about his testimony and specifically about his opinion concerning the link between abortion and child abuse. Gould, who died in 1998 at age 73, had a history of sensitivity to the vulnerable. He campaigned for the official declassification of homosexuality as a mental illness, the civil rights of mentally ill homeless persons, and the protection of prisoners against violent, untrained guards, as well as leading the National Coalition on Television Violence.[1]

Trial and Trauma in New Jersey
by Grace Dermody

On July 29, 1983, a jury in Newark, New Jersey, convicted twenty-year-old Renée Nicely of the brutal beating murder of her son, Shawn. On the same day, her twenty-one-year-old boyfriend and father of their five children, Alan Bass, was convicted of aggravated murder in the same crime. The subsequent prison sentences were life for Nicely and twenty years for Bass.

Throughout this case, repeated references were made to an abortion Renée Nicely had the day before the crime. Both of her defense lawyers and the defense psychiatrist made a point of connecting it directly to the final act of killing the three-year-old youngster who had been a victim of child abuse most of his life.

Dr. Robert E. Gould, professor of psychiatry at New York University's Medical Center, examined Nicely during two two-hour sessions over a period of four months. In his testimony for the defense he told the jury that the ultimate act—"the stomping death of Shawn"—was prompted by "a very traumatic event," having an abortion the day before Shawn was beaten to death.

I interviewed Dr. Gould in December at his Manhattan brownstone (I had earlier disclosed my prolife leanings in a telephone call), and the results provide some enlightening and surprising second-thoughts from a man whose philosophy, in his own words, "does not coincide with the Right to Life group."

I first asked Dr. Gould why he, specifically, was selected by the defense to examine Renée Nicely, and found that he was a specialist for many years in adolescent and family psychiatry, and was at one time Director of Adolescent Services at N.Y.U. Bellevue. Then we discussed the trial.

DERMODY: Would you say she was a religious person?

GOULD: I didn't pick that up, but it may be an inner feeling. I don't think she was much of a churchgoer, but you can feel very religious anyway. She didn't stress that ever, but made that statement just one time. She expressed guilt and a feeling of great upset.

DERMODY: Did Renée say that the abortion was the reason she killed Shawn?

GOULD: No. She just expressed guilt, guilt and a feeling of great upset. And it was my interpretation then of the events of the next morning that included the abortion very strongly as a trigger.

DERMODY: The *Newark Star Ledger* quoted you as saying during testimony that Renée Nicely would "probably have killed Shawn anyway at some time."

GOULD: See, that's part of the problem with quotations. I would never say with a certainty that she would have killed Shawn no matter what. I'd have to be God to say that. [Here followed a discussion of the confluence of factors necessary to result in suicide or homicide.] . . . The same in talking about Renée. I am not at all sure, I mean, I couldn't feel any certainty of sureness that she would have killed Shawn had not the abortion been involved. It was the only time in her life she had an abortion. It occurred the day before she killed Shawn. She was very, very upset about it. So I have to think it was linked. It was not purely coincidental.

DERMODY: Sounds as if you were misquoted then.

GOULD: I think so.

DERMODY: Would you say then, without the abortion the day before, it's possible she might not have killed him?

GOULD: Yes. That's right. Absolutely. Absolutely.

DERMODY: Dr. Gould, you testified that the ultimate act—the "stomping to death of Shawn"—was prompted by "a very traumatic event," having an abortion the day before Shawn was beaten to death. Will you tell me, if an abortion can cause trauma resulting in murder, as in this case, what other traumatic behavior can result from an abortion?

GOULD: Well, with some people, and I have to emphasize that, it can cause any number of aberrations in one's behavior. I don't think it's stretching a point to say it may make killing easier. If you think that in killing a fetus, you are killing someone human and alive, I think it's fair to say that person who feels that way could then kill someone else more easily.

In spite of this startling conclusion, Dr. Gould defends abortion as the better choice in some cases, and he cites some teenagers for whom the abortion would be "less traumatizing than having a baby if they drop out of school, if they have their whole life compromised, if they have to give up the child for adoption and have to wonder all the rest of their lives what this child is doing..." He does admit, however, that he has had to change his mind about the number of women who are seriously affected by having an abortion.

GOULD: I do believe that almost every woman is traumatized by an abortion. That is the strongest position I've ever taken. I've felt that a substantial number of women could undergo an abortion as if it were a cold. Let me put it another way. I do think there are some women—I now think it is a minority—I used to think it was a larger number—who can undergo an abortion and not be strongly traumatized. But I used to think it was a much greater number than I now believe.

DERMODY: Is there any way to tell beforehand who will react traumatically to an abortion?

GOULD: Not completely, for sure. Because I think it can trigger responses that the individual was not aware existed. You hear women talk a good deal about what pregnancy means to them, which is very different from what they thought before they became pregnant. But I think there are enough unpredictable reactions that one has to be awfully careful. This is why I am willing to change my idea about it being a relatively simple and emotion-free procedure. But the creation, I guess, is really so unusual, and profound, and strange, that it can have meaning that the individual is not aware of.

DERMODY: Dr. Gould, people, like yourself, who support abortion say that it's necessary to prevent unwanted children to save women's lives—presumably, make the world a better place. But that's not what I see happening. I see more child abuse, just as many women dying from abortions, and an epidemic of teenage pregnancies and illegitimate births. Is it all worth it?

GOULD: I would reluctantly have to say, yes, we're better off because I place such a high value on an individual's rights. But I do think the larger the national abortion rate, the more it says something is wrong in our society. So I'm on the horns of a dilemma . . . But one of the reasons I'm in favor of the liberalized position on abortion is that, in the past, abortions were done in two ways that certainly are worse than legalized abortion provides today, that is, in a hospital setting with no criminal implications for having done it. In the past, one did it under dirtier conditions so that the chance of the mother being severely hurt or killed was present. And also, it increased the feeling of guilt that one was doing something wrong . . . But, on the other hand, the legalization of it and the implied permission, or the lack of it having the kind of importance that I think a pregnancy should have, diminishes one's value about life and makes it easier to become pregnant in a thoughtless way. And I think that has repercussions that are unhealthy.

DERMODY: What do you think the effect of abortion is on the whole society? Do you see a devaluation of human life?

GOULD: I guess I do. I guess I would agree there is devaluation. And it would be so much better not to have the problem at all.

DERMODY: We both agree that a healthy society should put a high value on human life. But in an abortion society, where is that going to come from?

GOULD: I guess it has to come from almost every sector of society, starting, certainly, from your parents—through laws, attitudes towards killing in general, including, for instance, hunting animals. I think there is a devaluation there.

DERMODY: Do you object to hunters shooting animals?

GOULD: I guess I do. I'm saying the more one kills, the less one values life ... I would guess killing anything makes it easier to kill in general. But the more—the closer what you kill is to a human, the easier it is to kill a human. So that an insect—a cockroach—if you kill it—would not be so life diminishing as killing a dog, a horse, a monkey. The closer you come to being human in form and thinking, the more, I think, you are conditioning yourself to kill humans.

DERMODY: Thank you, Dr. Gould.

—*Sisterlife*, June 1984

Elizabeth McAlister

Elizabeth McAlister is a dedicated activist who for all of her adult life has been associated with the Catholic resistance and peace making movement. She protested the Vietnam War and the 1970 invasion of Cambodia on the basis of her Christian faith through nonviolent direct actions of resistance such as draft board raids. In 1972, as one of the Harrisburg Eight (later Seven), she was tried on general conspiracy charges associated with the raids. Although found innocent of the conspiracy charges, McAlister was convicted of smuggling communications in and out of a federal prison. When the American military finally left Indochina, she continued to speak publicly about small resistance communities as the future of the peace movement.

McAlister and her husband, Philip Berrigan, later formed Jonah House, a Catholic resistance community in Baltimore dedicated to the principles of nonviolence, resistance, community, and contemplation (www.jonahhouse.org). They continued their nonviolent direct action largely through symbolic practices like pray-ins, sit-ins, and morality plays protesting American foreign policy. One such action occurred in September 1980 when Philip and Daniel Berrigan, along with six others, entered a General Electric plant in Pennsylvania, poured blood on documents, and hammered on the nose cones of nuclear warheads, enacting the Hebrew prophet Isaiah's words, "They will beat their swords into plowshares and their spears into pruning hooks" (Isaiah 2:4). Dozens of such "Plowshares actions" promoting nuclear disarmament have since taken place leading to even longer prison sentences than those handed down during the Vietnam War era. The price of resistance has gone up and commitment to the peace movement has had to increase accordingly. McAlister's commitment has never wavered, evinced by her subsequent numerous incarcerations on charges stemming from her nonviolent civil disobedience.

In 1983, McAlister and other resisters demonstrated on Griffiss Air Force Base near Rome, New York, damaging some equipment used for carrying nuclear bombs. McAlister served two years in prison for her actions. During this incarceration, McAlister wrote the following open letter in response to a controversial *New York Times* ad (1984) run by Catholics for a Free Choice.

Her letter also challenges antiabortionists who fail to see past the unborn child to the pregnant woman and the entire community of lives. After serving her term, McAlister returned to live with her family in the Jonah House community. In December 2002, McAlister lost Philip Berrigan, her spouse and longtime partner in peace work, to cancer. Surrounded by friends, family, and community, Berrigan spoke before his death of his concern to resist the impending U.S. war upon Iraq. With their children, family, and friends, McAlister carries on the fight for life.

A Letter From A Women's Prison
by Elizabeth McAlister

Dear Friends of Pro-Choice: A friend sent me a copy of your *New York Times* ad, "A Diversity of Opinion Concerning Abortion Exists Among Committed Catholics." I read it with interest and dismay, yet with hope. The hope is that you remain open to questions, to dialogue, to another way.

I read your words, and questions arose. The need to challenge you was intensified as I noted the list of those who signed your ad.

Like many of you, I have been religious; like some of you, I am a parent (mother of three). Like all of you, my life is animated by a struggle for peace, justice, freedom—especially for the freedom of conscience, without which freedom is an illusion.

I have been where you are, read your writings. You have helped me immensely to look hope in the face; I can never forget its physiognomy. In my bumbling way, I have tried to enflesh that hope in my life, as well as in the lives of my children.

Because I had lived 14 years in a religious community, my children were born when I was older. Allow me to write briefly of the experience of my third pregnancy; it was for me an awesome moment of clarity on the issue of abortion.

I was asked to undergo no fewer than 15 tests to determine possible defects in the fetus—our Katy Berrigan. The understanding, the insistence was that "of course one should avail oneself of all these insurances and safeguards that a good healthy baby be born; otherwise, one should abort."

Because I could not consider the abortion of even a damaged child, I refused all tests. (I was also suspicious of the safety of the tests, a suspicion, as I later learned, that was well-founded.) To protect the doctor and midwife from potential lawsuits, I was also required to sign a statement that I had been informed of all dangers, had been advised to undergo the tests and had refused for the following reasons . . .

Such an experience is enormously intimidating. I think that, through such pressures, the medical community can pollute Christ's channels of access to us and to one another. And where is the antidote? I was lucky. I had the support of my family and my community to withstand the pressures, to protect Katy Berrigan against these sophisticated gynecological methods. I have also had considerable experience in being regarded as a fool.

Still, I wonder what support other women have against pressures so formidable, assumptions so roundly shared. I wonder, further, whether the religious community does not, in its own way, abandon many women to the radical right, our concern being for something fondly named "pluralism" or "diversity of opinion" or "theological accuracy" "progressive thinking."

It seems undeniable that millions of parents are being persuaded that abortion is *the* serious, progressive option—the only one, in fact, should complications or surprise or even inconvenience occur in the course of a pregnancy. At the very least, it is constantly insinuated that one is a fool to bear a child without being shored up by all possible insurances that the birth will be normal in every respect. And I reflect on the terrible irony implied in the prayer of Christians, "My life is in your hands, O Lord?" The other obsession is to place one's fate in the omnipotent hands of Allstate, Hartford, amniocentesis, sonogram and such.

Let me say it once more: I have been where you are. I have had a small part in your own passion for justice, peace, clarity of conscience. And the search has somehow or other brought me to an entirely different geography. I am now someone whom some choose to call a prisoner of conscience; others, a convicted felon. In any case, a prisoner serving a sentence of three years. The terminology seems irrelevant, given my new life, led at the side of the poor, the marginalized, the down and out—however you or society choose to describe us. I dwell at the Federal Prison for Women, in Alderson, West Virginia, one of more than 600 women prisoners. Probably 80 per cent of the prisoners are mothers; more than 90 per cent are the poor whom you presumably represent in your statement in the *Times*.

But I have a different report, one that has the slight advantage of arising from life lived among the poorest of the poor, the prisoners.

If the Women of Alderson could understand your ad (many are barely literate), they would only be angered by it. I want to tread carefully here. Slowly, I learn that the poor do not speak with one voice. They are neither mass nor class, as one learns who lives their life, eats and sleeps and works with them—and, above all, listens to them. They evade our sociology, which is often a form of scatology, abstract and indecent. The women are individuals, proud, undefeated for the most part—as passionate as ourselves, not to be disposed of or cataloged.

Although these women are my daily bread, my friends and sisters, I hesitate to speak for them in this matter of pro-choice. But of one thing I am certain: they love their children as I love mine; they miss them with the same poignancy and gut-wrenching that afflict me at the thought of Jerry, Freda and Katy. At the hospital here, I have seen women pick up pamphlets on abortion, and invariably cast them down again with the flat phrase, "I don't care what anyone says, I think it's murder."

I have been where you are, in more sense than one. But for now, I feel shut out from your circle of concern and conscience. Your ad strikes me as the statement of a closed club, an elite with its own language, an altogether professional clarity that is at the same time highly questionable.

It is hard for me to write such words; they make me feel childish, even foolish. But I will take the plunge, nonetheless. Your statement excludes me and many others, not only the prisoners of Alderson. We are excluded by the limits you place on your concern for life; by your languages; by your exquisite concern, on the other hand, for something you refer to as "job security"; by your presumption that you speak for the poor. Please bear with me as I explain.

I am in prison because I acted in accord with my conscience, doing what I could as spouse, mother, Christian, to reduce the threat of nuclear annihilation. You write on "diversity of opinion" with regard to abortion. Do we walk any common ground? Do we stand together under the biblical mandate to protect and preserve *all* life? If indeed we do, I do not discover it in the way you limit the question of life and its endangerment.

I think you allow the politicians and so-called religious leaders to frame the question for you. But in so narrow a frame, the whole picture can scarcely be seen; one aspect is blown up, all others are shunted literally out of the picture. So we, the conscientious viewers, are divided, even deceived, as to what we see—and what we don't see.

Years ago, many of you taught me about Christ. I learned with you how he grasped the wondrous profundity of the human. He resolved conflicts and reconciled differences, placing an "and" where most of us insist on an "or." Confronted with a narrow image labeled "reality" (an image that was, in fact, inhuman or antihuman), he simply enlarged the frame, insisted on, included, all the variety and verve that is our glory—slave and free, woman and man, gentile and Jew.

There can be no single issue today even so urgent a one as abortion. The human being, the Christian, cannot so speak, or define himself or herself. The issue is, rather: "What is to become of humankind?" Such a question, so put, compels us to welcome and cherish the human in all its likely and unlikely guises and disguises, to protect our endangered human family from all that seeks to destroy it.

Bishop Joseph Bernardin spoke recently of the "seamless garment of life." I think he came closest to the "and" (in contrast to the "or")—an "and" I consider so great a gift of the Lord. The "and" beckons into unity all who struggle against the probability of nuclear annihilation, all who struggle against the mad arms buildup, all who struggle against the oppression of colonial seizures, who struggle against capital punishment, who struggle in behalf of life, for the born *and* unborn—the right of all the living to decent shelter, adequate food and clothing, good education, sensible work, the freedom to follow and form our own consciences.

This larger frame draws us into the human picture, out of sidelines and isolation and single-issue obsessions, into a common human understanding and movement. Or so I think.

Your language, I have said, excludes so many, including myself. What am I to make of, or how shall I explain to the mothers among the prisoners, words such as "polarization," "probabilism," "legitimate Catholic position," "ensoulment," "diversity of opinion"? Such colorless technical terms, such jargon, such signals to the initiated! The terms remind me of those spurious circumlocutions that have made bloodshed, violence and moral evasion such hideous commonplaces. As if "diversity of opinion," rather than sound biblical understanding, should govern conscience.

Years ago, many of you taught me about Christ. I learned from you that he took our deepest longings to heart, that he blessed them, that he hoped for us and with us, and that life might be worth the living.

And I ask myself, What are the longings of humans today, to which we should harken? What is the news we have to offer—that will be both good and new? Is there a word through which our humanity may be healed of its deep hurt? I look in the faces of my sisters in prison, and I rejoice. Christ has made all things new: a new language, an example, our liberation and our hope. Even here, in this demented world.

Let me say, even at risk of odium, I am bemused by the 75 Catholics who agreed with your statement but who were unable to sign it, out of fear for their jobs. Security? The word comes to those in prison as an irony beyond words. We Christians are, then, to hold vigorous convictions, to hold them fast, but inwardly only, *in petto*, a light under a bushel? And was it thus that the world was redeemed, an invisible, interior, pneumatic, "spiritual" crucifixion, *in petto*, the fine resolve of Christ substituting for the unpleasant, untidy public act? I seek instruction in this.

Years ago, you taught me something else. Perhaps my memory is faulty, or illusive; but the lesson remains part of my being. The lesson went something like this: We will accomplish very little unless we are willing to risk everything.

As to speaking for the poor. Because we are more literate (and more affluent), we are tempted in this direction. But I am convinced that our real need, if we but knew it, is rather to listen, to hear from, rather than to speak for others.

Years ago, you taught me that the Lord dwells in the poor and speaks through them. I think I understand why you spoke as you did, in order to provoke and organize, to oppose and question authorities, in both church and state. Many of them seem obsessed today, to prescribe, to lay down law, hard and fast, to foresee and determine everything. And the radical right, the Moral Majority, seizes upon prayer in the schools, right to life, as the godly American way (insinuating that godly *is* American). They would dictate our morality for us (invariably on the personal level only); they would politicize religious issues, would place authority above conscience in every instance.

And a number of our own bishops march in lockstep with the Ronald Reagans and Jerry Falwells in this, narrowing political choices, cherishing the unborn even while they damn the born to the Gehenna of war, violence, social and personal neglect—the expression of utmost contempt for the living.

I think our task implies something more difficult, more imaginative, than merely responding in kind. We must widen the frame. We must stretch our arms and our hearts until we include and cherish every human aspiration, every endangered or despised or expendable life. In such ways, we do great service, both to church and state. We practice in the world the sacrament of sisterhood and brotherhood. We liberate the oppressed consciences that would oppress and enslave others, all, we are told, in a good cause.

Signing these reflections with me are my husband Philip Berrigan, my brother-in-law Father Daniel Berrigan and, I may rightfully infer, the growing number of Plowshares Christians—those in prison, those on appeal, those awaiting trial. As well as those friends searching their hearts, searching the Spirit, wherever they may be led.

—1984; repub. *Sisterlife*, April 1985

Jane Thomas Bailey

Jane Thomas Bailey juggles career, marriage, motherhood, and community activism on behalf of women and children. An early editor of *Sisterlife*, she drew upon her journalism background to establish the newsletter as an important prolife feminist forum. As exemplified in the first two selections, Thomas Bailey has sought to explain prolife feminism to those in the prolife movement who have had trouble understanding it, with a special focus on feminist insight into the real causes of abortion. She has shown prolifers how to make their message more clearly understood to a much wider range of people.

The third selection included here on discrimination abortion participates in a wider body of writings exposing and protesting the targeting of "imperfect" children for abortion. Such abortions are premised on the eugenic notion that these children's "deviant" biological traits inevitably doom them to "abnormal," difficult lives, an idea that completely overlooks the role of social constructions—preventable acts of discrimination—in any problems they may face. Disability rights, feminist, and GLBT rights activists have rejected this defective assumption, pointing out its harms to the already-born and unborn alike. In doing so, they are up against the likes of Nobel laureate James Watson, co-discoverer of DNA's double helical structure. Watson has unabashedly stated that he would advocate abortions of GLBT fetuses and, had prenatal genetic screening been available at the time, he would have aborted his son, who has severe epilepsy. (No word on what the child's mother would have done, let alone the son's thoughts on the matter.) "I'm not a sadist . . . Any time you can prevent a seriously sick child from being born, it is good for everyone."[1] Watson's arguments are best countered by the very people whose lives he has dismissed. As Anya Souza, an artist and outspoken disability rights educator of Jewish and Goan heritage, said to the 2003 International Down Syndrome Screening Conference in London (which protestors nonviolently crashed after being refused participation),

I can't get rid of my Down Syndrome. But you can't get rid of my happiness. You can't get rid of the happiness I give others, either. It's doctors like you who want to test pregnant women and stop people like me being born. You can't abort me now, can you? You can't kill me. Sorry! Together with my family and friends . . . I have fought for my rights . . . to a job, to services when necessary, to a decent standard of living, to know about my medical problems, to speak my mind, to make choices about my friends, whether to have sex . . . I may have Down Syndrome, but I am a person first.[2]

Feminism 101: A Primer for Prolife Persons
by Jane Thomas Bailey

Though its committed adherents are a fairly small minority of citizens, feminism may have had more impact on our nation than any other social ideology of our day. Abortion aside, feminist thinking has affected nearly all informed Americans in the way we run our homes and raise our children, in the expectations we have regarding employment, and even in our use of the English language. Many women who would never consider joining the National Organization for Women and who may not be sure just what feminism is have reaped the benefits of better job opportunities, better pay, and more respect at home and in church because of the battles feminists have fought.

Any movement or ideology this influential needs to be thoroughly examined and understood, whether we ultimately accept its premises or not. We in the prolife movement must make a special effort to understand and speak to feminists because they are the foremost advocates and guardians of abortion-on-demand.

Some people may dismiss this goal as hopelessly idealistic. "Communicate with THEM?" they say. "We've shown them pictures of unborn children, alive and aborted, for years and they have only pushed us further away." This is true, but it is also true that in our urgency we did not take time to study their language and culture, so our message was incomprehensible to them. People who have advocated and participated in abortion will turn away from our pictures in self-defense because they cannot bear to look at the implications of their own actions. To reach them, we must know how to disarm them, and this can only be done gently and in a spirit of love.

Ideological feminism has a much broader vision of life than equal pay for equal work. It will be difficult for many of us who have wept over the carnage of abortion clinics to attempt to listen sympathetically to a feminist vision of justice and peace, but it is necessary for us to do so if we wish to appeal to the highest moral values of feminism itself. And it is wrong for us to snicker at the notion of feminists having morals. Some strains of feminism border on becoming a religion with its own vision of what the millennium will be like.

The feminist ideal posits a world in which everyone, male and female, is treated with equal respect and has a voice in its government. It rejects the oppression of any one group of people by any other group of people. Feminists view the male oppression of women as the central problem of society not because it is worse than whites oppressing blacks or the First World oppressing the Third World, but because it encompasses all the others and represents half the world oppressing the other half.

Though the feminists of the 1960s and 1970s prided themselves on being just as tough and unemotional as men, the neo-feminist movement sees women as having qualities of compassion and understanding that men would do well to cultivate. People who share the feminist vision of the millennium believe that when women receive their full share of power in the world, there will be no more war, no more human rights abuses, no more oppression.

If men appear to be identified as the root of all evil, we ought to note that among committed feminists there is a disproportionately high percentage of women who admit to having been the victims of incest, rape, wife-beating and other torments at the hands of men, while the male-dominated society did little to object and often treated the victim as the guilty party. There are also in the feminist movement many intelligent women who were denied the same educational opportunities as their brothers and women who put their husbands through law or medical school only to be left behind for someone prettier. Add to this single mothers who weren't being paid a living wage for their work, only to be condemned as freeloaders when they decided welfare gave them comparable pay plus more time with their children, plus divorced women whose husbands haven't made a child support payment in years, plus gifted women whose male bosses took valuable ideas from them and passed them off as their own. They embrace feminist ideology because it is appropriate to their experience.

Even prolifers who do not share this vision of the world can find some common ground on which to build bridges to the feminist community. Indeed, if we may be charitable for a moment and set aside the feminist campaign for abortion-on-demand, it is realistic to say that feminists have taken many positions from which unborn children may benefit.

First of all, rights for unborn children necessarily means rights for pregnant women. If a woman loses her means of making a living or is banished from society because she is pregnant, she will have a strong incentive to have an abortion. The feminist movement has campaigned for the right of a pregnant woman to keep working as long as she is physically possible and to be able to keep her job when she takes time off to have a baby. For what they have accomplished we should applaud them and, for what remains to be done on this front, we should join them.

Feminists have targeted campaigns against the medical community in an effort to make childbirth less forbidding and less expensive. In many communities they have led the fight for natural childbirth, where the woman is in control and her family is allowed to be with her to give her emotional support and aid in the delivery of the child. Feminists have also placed great emphasis on re-establishing the role of the midwife. When I was a Birthright director and the local doctors regularly turned away our poverty-stricken clients, I thanked God for the feminist midwives who provided them with competent prenatal care for a fraction of what they would have had to pay a doctor and a hospital.

Shared parenting is another common ground between feminists and prolifers. Feminists believe both children and parents will be happier, healthier people if both parents share in the rearing of the children. Those of us on the street level of the prolife movement have seen that women seek abortions because of lack of help or support from the father of the child, so we should likewise promote parental responsibility among men. Further, many prolifers who would never consider themselves feminists, such as Dr. James Dobson, have urged fathers, according to a biblical mandate, to take a much greater role in the rearing of their children.

With the number of single-parent households still on the rise, we need to think about the care of those children who are not aborted. Feminists have long been advocates of day care. No matter whether it is subsidized through the government, provided by the business that employs the parent, or made available through churches, synagogues and other non-profit organizations, we need to make a commitment to effect responsible child care.

Pregnant women need to eat properly or they risk harm to both their own health and that of their child. And once a child is born it needs to be fed and clothed. Again, in the case of many single mothers and low-income couples, this means providing either adequate public support for the woman who wishes to stay at home with her children or to help her obtain the education and training necessary to provide for her family. These have long been feminist causes; they should be ours as well.

These are just a few of the feminist issues that may provide points of contact with the prolife community, just as opposition to pornography has provided a point of contact between feminists and evangelical Christians. Perhaps some of these feminist goals and ideals sound very much like your own, and you're wondering how a movement with such high ideals could ever have become the leading proponent of abortion. It did not have to be that way.

Feminists of the nineteenth century viewed abortion as an atrocity forced upon women by men who were unwilling to care for the children they had conceived—still an apt analysis. Indeed, the modern demand for abortion did not originate with the modern feminist movement, but with a group of MEN who had formed the National Association for the Repeal of Abortion Laws (now the National Abortion Rights Action League). Bernard Nathanson, a founder of NARAL who is now a prolife activist, writes that this male-dominated group cooked up the ideology of "reproductive freedom" and convinced the fledgling National Organization for Women to take it on as a cause. Some leaders of NOW, apparently including Betty Friedan, argued that it would be a costly mistake to advocate abortion as a cornerstone of women's rights, but were overruled. It is also true that in all movements that are convinced of their own righteousness, it is nearly impossible for members to admit that they are capable of committing evil acts.

The basic argument for abortion-on-demand is that as long as a woman can be tied down with childbearing, responsibility for social decision-making will remain entirely in the hands of men. Therefore, the prolife movement is viewed as a male plot to keep women barefoot and pregnant. The truth is that abortion itself is sexist in nature. The currently accepted feminist argument holds that a woman can be free to take a full role in society only if she can free herself from childbearing. But since women are, by definition, people who can get pregnant, this means that pro-abortionists are not advocating rights for women, but for men. The basic ideal of feminism is a society in which the powerful do not deny the weak their rights, yet abortion is truly patriarchal because it is a prime example of the powerful (women) depriving the weak (unborn children) of their rights, to the point of killing them. The feminist euphemism for abortion is "controlling our own bodies," yet abortion represents a violent example of one person controlling another's body.

Feminists helped pioneer the battle against unnecessary surgery by telling women to stand up to their physicians. Yet abortion is a prime example of unnecessary surgery since the physical "problem" solves itself in nine months. And, while they have argued for women facing other types of surgery to be told of all the options available to them, feminists have argued that women considering abortion should not have to be told about the development of the baby inside them, or about the possibilities of adoption or parenthood.

Abortion does not address the basic inequalities, such as poverty and unequal pay, that make a woman believe she cannot have a baby. It's a cheap fix that leaves the woman as poor and oppressed as she ever was, while the politicians claim to have struck a blow for women's rights and the doctors go home $250 richer.

Finally, abortion perpetuates the image of women as reusable sex objects. If she gets pregnant, all it takes is $250 and she's slender and happy again. If she decides to give birth, the father feels justified in claiming it's not his responsibility to help care for the child since he offered to pay for an abortion. No small surprise that the Playboy Foundation gives generously to NARAL, Catholics for Free Choice, and other groups that lobby to keep abortion-on-demand.

A serious communication problem has developed around our arguments concerning pregnancy from incest or rape. I do not believe abortion is morally justified in such cases, but some prolife arguments I have heard have been inaccurate and so downright insensitive to rape and incest victims that it has made me angry. Yes, it is true that pregnancy resulting from rape is relatively rare, particularly when the victim seeks immediate treatment—which the majority do not. But pregnancy does happen and when it happens it is terribly traumatic for all concerned. Let us not forget that *Roe v. Wade* stemmed from a woman who had become pregnant as the result of gang rape.[3] One otherwise helpful prolife brochure states that pregnancy from incest is very rare, if not impossible. Talk to anyone who has done even limited study in the field of incest and they will tell you that not only is incest a great deal more prevalent than we would all like to think, but pregnancies resulting from it are quite common. Our prolife approach should be to stand against social attitudes that condone sexual abuse of any person and to respond to all victims, pregnant or not, with compassion and support. Let our literature reflect this.

Above all, we must realize that when men serve as our spokespersons for the prolife movement, this adds further conviction to the feminist belief that opposition to abortion is a male plot to keep women in a subservient role. It is important that women lead the prolife movement not only to contradict the feminist assumption, but because, legal or illegal, the abortion decision will forever ultimately rest in the hands of women.

—*Sisterlife*, April 1985

Prolifers Too Exclusive
by Jane Thomas Bailey

I am a faithful participant in our local March for Life each January 22. I feel it's the least I can do to walk a half-mile and listen to a few speeches so that I can be added to the body count that will appear in the next day's newspaper. But I often feel that the people who run the show aren't talking to me. What's worse, they're not talking to a lot of people like me who haven't decided yet what to believe about abortion. Mostly they're talking to themselves.

First of all, they sing a lot of songs about God—and a very Christian God at that. I am not putting them down for being religious. Nor am I saying that faith should be confined to sanctuaries. But I think a lot of people turn off their message as fast as they turn off the TV evangelists who flicker by on the TV dial. Many people do not like to have religion blared at them through loudspeakers in public squares.

The subliminal message from the songs, and from many of the speakers, is that you have to share these religious beliefs before you can become prolife. The Jew, the agnostic, the liberal Protestant, the Unitarian, walk quickly by thinking, "This cause is obviously not for me."

Worst of all, the religious language only reinforces the belief that abortion is "a religious issue," irrevocably linked to school prayer and creches on the courthouse steps. This plays right into the arguments of pro-abortionists who argue that prolifers are religious zealots who are trying to force their arcane beliefs about ensoulment down other people's throats. The prolife cause can be argued brilliantly on scientific and humanitarian grounds that appeal to people of many beliefs, including Christians. If we want to get a broad coalition of people on the side of the unborn, we must base our public arguments on those grounds.

I also feel excluded from much prolife rhetoric because I am a political liberal. I have heard speakers urge me to vote for "godly, conservative candidates." Since when did that become the criteria of the prolife movement? Jimmy Carter was a godly man but, alas, not prolife. Barry Goldwater is unquestionably conservative, but not prolife. You can tell people to vote prolife without invoking either the church or the Republican Party. I wonder how many potential prolifers have been turned away because of this ideological confusion?

I have also felt excluded because I am a woman who must work outside my home. Too many of the voices in prolife leadership are male, and I wonder, as they speak, how many of them have ever had to choose between a baby and a promotion? I, and many of my colleagues, have. I chose to delay conception; other women have chosen abortion. Yet I have heard prolife speakers frown on the first and castigate the second as if women were utterly selfish for seeking a bigger paycheck. All too often they are merely trying to keep the rent paid and food on the table. Of course it is wrong to kill an unborn baby in such a situation, but it is also wrong for the prolife movement to ignore the problems that employed women face. If these problems were addressed constructively from the public soapbox, more professional women would pause to listen to our message.

In an odd way, however, men have been excluded from the prolife message, too. I have seen a lot of teenage girls bravely tell of the baby they had, or the abortion they had. I applaud them for their courage in speaking out. I have never seen a boy (or a man) stand up in public to tell of the remorse he feels for impregnating several young women and then for denying responsibility for the babies. That message needs to be heard as much as the message of the woman who had an abortion. Those boys and men are among us, but for some reason we have put only the girls and women on the spot.

The prolife movement needs to address male responsibility for abortion. That must include the personal responsibility of men who don't want children, but impregnate women, and the corporate responsibility of a male-dominated economy that makes few allowances for babies. Then more women, and more men, will begin to take us seriously. But too often these critical issues are on a collision course with the conservative political and religious agendas that I wrote of above. Until all of these ideologies can be sorted out, my fear is that the prolife movement will remain a minority coalition of religious conservatives.

—*Sisterlife*, Winter 1987

Discrimination Abortion: Self-Interest's Fatal Flaw
by Jane Thomas Bailey

My husband is reluctantly, apologetically pro-life. He concedes that abortion is wrong, but it is not a priority issue for him. Embarrassed to be caught with a belief outside his usual left-wing orbit, he seizes every possible opportunity to sympathize with pro-choice arguments on various aspects of legislation.

I was, therefore, astounded to hear him ranting about "killing the babies" as we drove home from a meeting.

You see, my husband has Tourette Syndrome—a neurological disorder of genetic origin. Its most obvious symptom is constant, multiple tics, twitches and involuntary vocalizations. In some severe cases, people with

Tourette syndrome punctuate their speech with uncontrollable obscenities and racial slurs. It's a very dramatic disorder. You may have seen it featured on episodes of *Quincy*, *St. Elsewhere*, *L.A. Law* and *Geraldo*.

We have just left a local meeting of the Tourette Syndrome Association, where we had seen the latest educational film on the disorder. At one point the narrator instructed anyone with a family history of Tourette to get genetic counseling before having children. "Do you believe that?" my husband demanded. His objection boiled down to this: How can the organization to benefit people with Tourette Syndrome tell people with Tourette Syndrome that the way to prevent Tourette Syndrome is to kill the unborn babies that have Tourette Syndrome?

Now, for the record, there is no prenatal test for Tourette, although one will certainly be developed once the gene is isolated. Nor am I accusing the Tourette Syndrome Association of being a closet abortion-rights lobby. I support genetic research, although I oppose its abuse for prenatal search-and-destroy missions.

But my husband felt threatened by the film's clear assumption that children carrying the Tourette gene should be prevented from coming into existence. He perceived it as a judgment that he is too flawed to live. Long before we met, he and some other men with Tourette talked about whether they should have children. Their consensus was that they were glad that they had been born and expected that any Tourette children born to them would feel the same. For my part, the philosophy instilled in me by the pro-life movement enabled me to accept and see past my husband's disability.

Much has been written about abortion as a form of discrimination, whether against ethnic minorities, the disabled or the female gender. Indeed, the pro-life movement uses retroactive self-interest as one of its key arguments when it points out to some people that they might not have been born had they been conceived post-Roe. One of the more memorable appeals to retroactive self-interest appeared not in a pro-life publication, however, but in a gay-oriented periodical, the *New York Native*. Publisher Charles Ortleb reflected upon the implications of the search for a genetic basis for homosexuality:

> If a laissez-faire attitude exists concerning the rights of parents to abort fetuses because of presumed handicaps, couldn't these parents someday (if not today) deem homosexuality a handicap? Oddly then, it may turn out that one of our most vociferous enemies, the Right-To-Lifers, will end up the friend of future generations of homosexuals because they will help to ensure its existence. And, just as oddly, some of our feminist friends may end up as instruments to wipe out gay people once and for all.

But as effective as these arguments may be for catching people's attention, I believe that pro-lifers must beware of making them the philosophical basis for the movement. Retroactive self-interest alone is rarely enough to motivate people to display the courage and responsibility that a pro-life commitment often entails. Retroactive self-interest often conflicts with immediate self interest. Without a stronger ethic at work, immediate self-interest is likely to win out. My husband's self-interest, for instance, has not propelled him into pro-life activism. The author of the editorial in the gay newspaper was not arguing against abortion, but for rethinking political alliances.

Immediate self-interest causes people to defend against retroactive self-interest.

A recent issue of *The Disability Rag* contained an excerpt of the book *Past Due: A Story of Disability, Pregnancy and Birth* by Anne Finger.[4] I do not know what the author's ultimate conclusions about abortion were, but the excerpt gives an account of self-interest in conflict.

Finger, a disabled woman who had joined an abortion-rights organization, offered to lead a discussion on disability and reproductive rights. She spoke of the Nazi eugenics movement, of the Baby Doe—the Down Syndrome child whose parents and doctored starved him to death.

> And when I started talking about how the reproductive rights movement was sometimes guilty of exploiting fears about disability when it argued for abortion because of fetal defect, things really got strained. I said that we could defend women's right to have an abortion in such a situation without acting as if there were no other possible choice . . .
>
> When the discussion period began, I felt like a heretic. Wasn't it a terrible burden on women to have to care for a disabled child? Shouldn't disabled infants be allowed to escape the misery of their lives? I was glad when my daughter was born "normal"—do I have to feel guilty for that? What it all boiled down to was, did I really think that disabled people were as good as everyone else? Was I really saying that a disabled life was worth living? . . .
>
> I'd always thought that progressive people just hadn't had much of a chance to become acquainted with disability issues; that once they had a little bit of education, they'd clean up their act. I expected lip service, condescension, liberalism—but certainly not hostility.
>
> (And something else, too: deeper, not yet formed into words: these women are like the people you have lived among all your life: you always assumed those around you saw you as their equal. They are telling you no: we suffer your presence.)

Finger goes on to recount a summit meeting between feminist abortion rights and disability rights activists to try to resolve disagreements over Baby Doe, amniocentesis and selective abortion. The participants included a woman who did research on amniocentesis but who conceded that her own mother probably would have aborted her rather than marry at 17, had abortion been readily available. A Barnard professor, blind as a complication of premature birth, said she was appalled to read that some doctors now say it is better to let blind preemies die than to try to save them. Another woman in the group had had an abortion at six months because the fetus had Down Syndrome. The woman who had called the meeting, an abortion rights activist, admitted that her mother would probably not have given birth to her if she had had more choice. Her mother had six surviving children, four miscarriages, and one stillborn baby:

> I sometimes feel as if my political work is haunted by ghosts, the ghosts of those miscarried fetuses, of that child born dead . . . but I think too we do the best work politically when we're doing work that really tears us up.

Finally, Finger speaks. She explains that she had polio at age three and endured inhumane treatment in the hospital.

> Barbara says, "If you had been my child, I would have killed you before I let that happen. I would have killed myself too."
> My heart stops. She is telling me I should not be alive. It is my old fear come true: that if you talk about the pain, people will say, see, it isn't worth it. You would be better off dead.
> My heart stops. I feel violated. She has no right to say that to me, any more than I would have a right to say to Rayna, "I would never have done that, I would never have aborted a fetus with Down's."

The meeting concluded with a discussion of when a fetus/infant should be granted legal rights.

> "At birth," Janet says.
> "When at birth," Barbara asks. "Crowning? Birth of the placenta?"
> Adrienne asks Barbara, "If you say that parents of disabled children have the right to make those decisions, then don't the parents of non-disabled children have the same rights, to refuse medical treatment?"

"Yes," says Barbara.

"What about a Jehovah's Witness who doesn't believe in blood transfusions? Should their children be allowed to die?"

"Yes," Barbara says, slowly and reluctantly.

"And parents who beat their children?"

"Yes," she says, even more slowly and reluctantly.

For most, if not all, the women in this group, retroactive self-interest is not enough. They find ways of evading its implications. The haunted abortion rights activist believes her inner conflict is a sign she is doing her best work. The author, who feels violated by the inference that she would have been better off dead, nevertheless believes she has no right to pass judgment on the abortion of another handicapped child.

Some people can use prejudices of their own to evade the truth that they are being discriminated against *in utero*. An acquaintance of mine once found herself in conversation with a very famous feminist abortion rights advocate. The Famous Feminist was upset that reporters had been asking her about sex-selective abortions. "It's a non-issue. I always dare those reporters to find one case of someone who had an abortion for sex-selection," the Famous Feminist said. "Only one reporter came back to me, with two cases, and both of those were Korean."

Apparently it was okay to abort Korean girls, because they didn't count. It wasn't an issue, much less a problem, unless white, conceived in the U.S.A. fetuses were involved. Sexism is bad, unless it can be justified by racism.

Yet, some people do make the leap from retroactive self-interest to the full pro-life philosophy. In a recent issue of *Harmony* magazine, Alison Davis,[5] head of the British organization Disabled Women for Life, gave insight not only into how this is done, but why it is so difficult. Davis has spina bifida. Just a few years ago, Davis wrote, she was an abortion rights advocate.

> Basically I supported the right to abortion because I did not want to be burdened with unwanted children myself. I did not actually know what an abortion involved, neither did I want to know, but I did know I dreaded being unwillingly pregnant more than almost anything else, and did not feel anyone had the right to tell me I could not have an abortion if I wanted one.

Then she read about a couple who, with the aid of their doctor, starved their baby to death because she had spina bifida.

> [The Doctor] called this "the loving thing to do" because she would
> have been unable to walk, and doubly incontinent and would, he
> deemed, have compared herself unfavorably with her sisters. She
> would, in short, have been exactly as disabled as I am myself.

After two years of brooding, she wrote a letter to the editor, protesting
the killing of handicapped newborns. She was promptly deluged with
unwanted mail from pro-lifers who pointed to the link between abortion
and infanticide:

> I was, admittedly, already faintly uncomfortable with my by now
> modified view that women did have a right to choose to have an
> abortion, but I still desperately wanted to preserve my peace of mind,
> so that if necessary I could have an abortion without a guilty conscience.
>
> I think this blinkered view is quite typical of oppressive situa-
> tions when people are determined not to recognize them as such, and
> of the inconsistencies that such a position produces, particularly in the
> face of an incontrovertible truth, such as the fact that abortion kills a
> human being. So anxious was I that disabled people (i.e., me) should
> be accorded equal rights, I was advocating that we should have more
> rights than anyone else. That the unborn handicapped should be pro-
> tected from abortion, but not the unborn able-bodied. A kind of re-
> verse discrimination if you like, that would not stand up to the slight-
> est examination. The reason for this apparent discrepancy was not
> difficult to understand, though, because my motive for holding it was
> not one of mercy for the unborn, but rather of protecting my rights to
> have an abortion if I wanted one. In retrospect, I believe this feeling
> underlies the attitude of many women to abortion. It is not so much
> that they deny the humanity of the unborn, but because it will so
> profoundly affect them if they do acknowledge it, they choose (and
> choice is taken to be a right, remember) to ignore it. In this way
> liberation becomes an end in itself, and if it means that women be-
> come in turn oppressors of a still more vulnerable group (in this case
> their unborn children), then so be it.

True feminism, Davis concluded, cannot ultimately be based on self
interest:

> I changed my mind about abortion and its place in the liberation of
> women because the facts demanded it. If we want true liberation and
> equality we cannot allow our selfishness to blind us to reality, even

when it is unpalatable. We cannot claim liberation "for me" if it means denying it to others, for eventually the oppression of one group rubs off on us all. True liberation for all will mean accepting a degree of responsibility for each other which maybe we escape now, but liberation and quality "just for me" inevitably means oppression for someone else, which is unfair, inhumane, and, I would maintain, ultimately unworkable.

We need to make it clear that we oppose abortion not because it is a form of discrimination but because it is a form of murder. Opposing abortion is not something we do to help ourselves. A true pro-life ethic calls upon people to accept responsibility for the children they create—and to understand that shelling out $250 for an abortion is not an acceptable definition of "responsibility." This is not easy in our society, where the idea of making sacrifices for the sake of others is rapidly falling by the wayside. I recall reading once that the psychologists and sociologists had done such a good job of convincing people that guilt was unhealthy that we were no longer a nation of neurotics but were verging on becoming a nation of sociopaths. We have become a nation in which doing "what is best for me" is not just one factor in a decision, but often the dominant or sole factor. And it is this very ethic of self-interest that has allowed abortion to become the most common surgical procedure in the United States.

Yes, we can and should catch the ear of the unconverted by appealing to this self-interest. But we must make it clear that this is not the bottom line. For as long as we appeal only to the idea that "abortion is bad for YOU," we reinforce the very ethic that enables people to choose abortion.

Mature people, loving people, are those who are capable of giving up some of their own desires for the sake of another. To the extent that the feminist movement has accepted abortion as a legitimate means of solving problems, it has failed to call women and men to be mature, loving people. It is this ethic of sacrifice for the sake of others that is the greatest strength of the pro-life movement. Let us not fail to call all women and men to live up to it.

—*Sisterlife*, Winter 1991.

Juli Loesch Wiley

Juli Loesch Wiley, whose peace, justice, and prolife activism, writing, and speaking are well known within these movements, is considered by many to be the "Grand Mother" of the organized consistent life ethic movement. As a young woman, she organized boycotts for the United Farm Workers and, after her studies at Ohio's Antioch College in 1972, helped to found the PAX Center, a Pennsylvania Catholic peace and justice community. Through her peace education work in schools and churches, she came to embrace a prolife position concerning abortion. While she was delivering a speech on the effects of radiation on the fetus, a woman in the audience rose and commented that if Wiley thought radiation was harmful to the child in the womb, she should consider the damage abortion wreaks on the fetus. Wiley had to admit that a prochoice stand on abortion was indefensible in terms of her nonviolent values. In 1979, she founded Prolifers for Survival, an activist organization opposed to abortion and the arms race. In 1987, Prolifers for Survival disbanded to invest its resources in the Seamless Garment Network, now Consistent Life, a coalition of groups that embrace a consistent life ethic including opposition to abortion, euthanasia, war, poverty, capital punishment and the arms race. Wiley has served on the boards of JustLife and Consistent Life. Presently she homeschools two sons, cares full-time for her medically dependent father, and, in her words, is "the worshipper of one God and the wife of one husband—and still Catholic after all these years." She continues to champion the rights of women and other oppressed groups while working toward a world without violence.

The Myth of Sexual Autonomy
by Juli Loesch Wiley

Late last year the *Village Voice*, a weekly paper serving New York's Greenwich Village, long a mouthpiece for the cultural avant-garde, devoted an entire issue to the question, "Abortion: Where Are We Now?"[1]

The editors were all agog about something they evidently find quite disturbing: the emergence of *left-wing* anti-abortionists who are now challenging the "prochoice" status quo with particular effectiveness.

Most interesting to me was Ellen Willis' pro-abortion piece, which was notable for what it conceded:

That the left and the media tend to be won over by the "seamless garment" approach, which includes opposition to abortion in the context of opposition to other kinds of sanctioned killing.

That prolife feminists have grasped some "essential feminist truths" which make their arguments against abortion more compelling.

Clearly, for Willis, this is no time to engage in peripheral arguments. With the game beginning to go against her, she folds the rest of her hand and slaps her highest card on the table: *sexual autonomy*.

No matter what else happens, says Willis, and no matter what "utopian" changes may come, there will always be the vagaries of sexual passion and the failures of contraception. Thus, come what may, abortion will always be "necessary" if we are to be free to live "sexually autonomous" lives.

Then she hurls the following challenge: "I have yet to hear any right-to-lifers take full responsibility for that fact or deal seriously with its political implications."

On the contrary. I think that it's the advocates of sexual autonomy who have failed to recognize its political implications.

The opposite of sexual autonomy, or independence, is sexual bondedness, or interdependence. What the autonomous wish to enjoy is precisely unbondedness; and one of the bonds to be rejected is a bond to offspring who were conceived without deliberate choice.

To the defenders of such autonomy I would like to post these questions: Is there such a thing as parental obligation? If so, when and how, and for whom, does this obligation arise?

In the past, people assumed that simply by engaging in heterosexual relations with each other they acquired parental obligations if and when pregnancy resulted. But now, says Willis, this is to be seen as a denial of sexual autonomy. Obligations now arise, not from the decision to have sex, but from the strictly separate decision to bear the child.

But please note: The decision to have sex is a decision made by both partners. The decision to bear the child is made by *only one of them*: namely, the woman.

Thus, the woman's responsibility corresponds to her choice, made at some point during the pregnancy. If she doesn't want to assume any obligation, she can choose abortion and any question of parental responsibility is foreclosed.

But for the man, parental obligation supposedly arises from the woman's choices: her choice to bear the baby, and her choice to name him as the father and even to bring legal action to compel his support, if it comes to that.

The problem here is obvious. You can expect increasingly to hear the sexually autonomous male's just complaint: "How is it that she gets a choice, but I don't? She chose to be a mother. I didn't choose to be a father. I just chose to have sex!"

There will always be men who, at any given moment, want sex but don't want a child; some of these men will get women pregnant. But sexual intercourse now implies for each of them—exactly nothing, no responsibility. It's only the woman's subsequent and separate option that determines everything. That being the case, why should any man feel he's acquired an obligation if the woman decides to give birth? Because he deposited sperm in the woman's vagina? Don't be medieval.

Am I predicting that the elevation of sexual autonomy to the status of a "right," coupled with the availability of abortion, will cut men loose entirely? That paternal responsibility will sink to zero? That men are not only going to take off, but feel justified about it?

Hell, no. I'm not predicting that. I'm *reporting* it. I've done my share of women's shelter work in the last ten years. I see it all the time. A couple has a child. Three years down the line he decides he isn't cut out to be a father.

"But you can't just walk out. This is your child too!"

"Sure, sure. But it was *your choice.*"

Well, the gentleman is right, given that the availability of abortion has made procreation a unilateral female decision.

Most male commitment to the long-term responsibility of child rearing is not obtained through court order. It is obtained voluntarily through a man's sense, bolstered by society, that it's right and fair. Why? Because the choice that obliges both him and the woman is the choice they made together, in the act that made the child.

The vast majority of women and children in this world rely upon webs of interrelation predicated upon a sexually connected man: a man whose sexuality makes him the husband of *this* woman, the father of *this* child. It's sex that binds him, obliges him to another gender and another generation.

If the act of generation loses this weight, this significance—and the abortion culture simply blows it away—then you end up with fathering that never makes a father, mating that never makes a mate, short-circuited sex that dreams of nothing more than being plugged into its own sockets.

Autonomy—in this sense—is as pro-woman as poverty and as pro-sex as an amputation. And abortion—the dismembered offspring—is not only its program, but its most perfect and fitting image.

—1986; publ. as "Dear Ellen," *Sisterlife*, Spring 1987

Toward a Holistic Ethic of Life
by Juli Loesch Wiley

Many of us once looked to feminism as a movement with true change-the-system potential. Disconcertingly, the feminist movement now appears to be composed of a number of strikingly different "teams" all wearing the same jersey. Some feminist factions are actually opponents to each other; others aren't even playing the same game.

For instance: some feminist leaders call the Equal Rights Amendment and abortion the two central goals of the women's movement; on the other hand, Eleanor Roosevelt, credited with having inspired much of the movement, saw abortion as irrelevant to female advancement and opposed the ERA for forty years on the grounds that it would hurt the interests of working women. Some feminists defend the sex-entertainment industry as liberating; Andrea Dworkin of Women Against Pornography denounces it as exploitative. In *The Female Eunuch* (1970), Germaine Greer advocated that women be "deliberately promiscuous" but not have babies; in *Sex and Destiny* (1984), she rejects promiscuity and says the export of contraceptives to the Third World is "evil."

Feminists take such startlingly different stands on economic, sexual, and cultural issues that, although there are many different permutations and combinations, it might be said that there are two fundamentally different approaches in the women's movement.

"Assimilationist feminism" insists that men and women be treated identically in law, in the marketplace, and in social relations. Assimilationists oppose special benefits for women as much as they oppose adverse discrimination. Once the differences between women have been eliminated by equal rights legislation plus reproductive freedom (i.e., the freedom not to reproduce), women will achieve power, money, and satisfaction on the same terms as men.

"Social Feminism," on the other hand, holds that it is not primarily legal inequality or normal fertility that traps women in second-class citizenship, but rather the dual burden women carry in the home and in the work force.

Social Feminists argue that because women are wives and mothers as well as workers, their mother-status needs extra compensation and support if they are to have equal opportunities in the world beyond the home.

In her brilliant book on women in the work place, *A Lesser Life*, Sylvia Ann Hewlett finds that American feminists' single-minded pursuit of formal equality has trapped millions of women in a very unfavorable situation if they happen to have children.

Pregnant workers are routinely fired. Others are defined as "new-hires" when they come back to work after childbirth, losing accumulated benefits, merit raises, and seniority fights. And large numbers of new mothers, unable to find affordable child care, are forced to take a third or fourth part-time job close to home, or quit the work force altogether.

But most American wage-earning women *have* to work: 75% are either single mothers or are married to low-income men. At some point in their lives, 90% of women have—or want to have—children: the market economy severely penalizes such women *precisely because it treats them like men.*

In every other industrial nation in the world, Social Feminists have pushed successfully for guaranteed job-protection and full or partial income replacement when a woman takes time off to have a baby. Throughout Europe, the *average* maternity leave is five months at full pay. In Sweden, both parents can opt for a six-hour work day until their child is eight years old. In Italy, working women receive two years' credit toward seniority every time they give birth to a child.

But in America, where assimilationists have largely set the feminist agenda, 60% of wage-earning women have no right to any job-protected maternity leave whatsoever. Overall, women lose 20% of their earning power each time they give birth.

The practical effect of assimilationist feminism is to redesign women to fit into a male oriented system. Don't get pregnant—or if you do, don't *stay* pregnant—don't make any demands on the system for child care or flextime or maternity benefits ("preferential treatment"), and you'll be treated just like a man.

The practical effect of Social Feminism, on the other hand, is not to redesign women to fit the work place, but to redesign the work place to fit women.

The same contrast between the Assimilationists and the Social Feminists becomes apparent when they address sexual issues.

For example: a sexual culture which is highly favorable to male-pattern, fast access gratification has contributed to the rapid spread of sexually transmitted diseases and untimely pregnancies, especially among the young.

The Assimilationist approach is to *structurally adapt the women*, through gynecological surgery and chemical modification, to conform more easily to the male-pattern system. Thus the goal is short-term damage limitation with notable reliance on the "technical fix": contraception, abortion, and for older-than-teenagers, sterilization.

In contrast, the Social Feminists would see no point in habituating people to sexual patterns which are inherently destructive. They would work instead for behavioral changes in men and women for a more socially constructive, sustainable, and wholesome sexuality. Thus, building self-confidence for adolescent abstinence, resisting date-rape and acquaintance-rape, and promoting fertility awareness are important for Social Feminists. (Interestingly, natural family planning has historically drawn its main support from conservative Catholics and from feminist health advocates.)

Prenatal care, maternity benefits, job-protected parental leave, family allowances, affordable family medical coverage, and more realistic tax deductions for dependents could relieve much of the pressure which tempts even prolife-leaning women to consider abortion. Similarly, strengthening people's ability to resist immature or exploitative sexual encounters would help protect millions from sexually transmitted diseases, callousness, alienation, and abortion. It's exciting to realize that an alliance between traditional prolife and social feminist forces—already begun—could help build a social environment which is much more humane for men and women, and a much safer place for fragile growing children . . .

—from "Social Feminism: Change the System," *Harmony*, Nov/Dec 1987; repub. *Sisterlife*, Spring 1988.

Nat Hentoff

Nat Hentoff confuses many people when he describes himself as a Jewish atheist civil libertarian prolifer. Never one to shy away from controversy, Hentoff has dedicated himself to defending civil liberties, particularly First Amendment rights, and championing his favorite art form—jazz. Growing up in Boston, Hentoff battled anti-Semitism and developed a love for music upon meeting some of the great jazz musicians of the day. He received his B.A. from Northeastern, continued graduate study at Harvard, and started his journalism career as editor of *Down Beat* magazine. From his days as a vigorous civil rights and anti-Vietnam War agitator, he has used his skills as a writer to protest social oppression on multiple levels. Hentoff came to oppose abortion in the 1980s while covering the two infamous "Baby Doe" cases in which the parents sought the "right" to deny routine but lifesaving medical treatment to their infants with Down Sydrome and spina bifida, respectively. Once a bulwark of the American Civil Liberties Union, Hentoff split with the organization over the right to life of unborn children, disabled persons, and others targeted for euthanasia.

A prodigious writer, Hentoff has written on education, social justice and legal issues, jazz, and autobiographies, biographies, novels, and children's and young adult's literature. He has edited several music journals and has written for the *New Yorker, Washington Post, Wall Street Journal*, and *JazzTimes*, and columns for the *Village Voice* and the *Washington Times*. A sampling of his book titles demonstrates the breadth of his social concerns and interests: *Our Children Are Dying* (1966), *Does Anybody Give a Damn? On Education* (1977), *Jazz Life* (1978), *First Freedom: The Tumultuous History of Free Speech in America* (1980), *Peace Agitator: Story of A.J. Muste* (1982), *John Cardinal O'Connor: At the Storm Center of a Changing American Catholic Church* (1988), *Free Speech for Me—But Not for Thee: How the American Left and Right Relentlessly Censor Each Other* (1992, which addresses censorship against Feminists for Life), and *The War on the Bill of Rights—and the Gathering Resistance* (2003). Among his many honors are Guggenheim fellowships, American Bar Association awards for coverage of legal issues, an Honorary Doctorate of

Law from Northeastern, and most recently, a National Endowment for the Arts Jazz Master Fellowship.

Hentoff shows the power of a consistent life ethic message. And it's still easy to get him riled up—just suggest that some lives are less worthy of protection than others.

The Choice to Have Their Babies
by Nat Hentoff

As part of the momentum of the feminist movement, the Los Angeles County Commission on the Status of Women was established in 1975. It advises the Board of Supervisors on issues of particular importance to women and is otherwise actively engaged in breaking down discrimination against women.

For the past three years the commission has given annual Women Helping Women awards to those in the various communities of Los Angeles who have made a difference in the lives of other women. This year the Commission on Women, voting on June 1, declared Rebecca Younger one of the winners. However, a second vote was taken on June 29, and the award was taken away from Younger.

Commission President J. Lindsay Woodard sort of explained what had happened: "I can only say that the commission did not have all the facts when she was nominated."

Soon, however, a staff member of the commission clarified what had gone wrong: "The commission was not apprised of [Younger's] affiliation with the prolife community."

The damning charge was true. The 38-year-old Younger, whose husband runs a family company that rebuilds diesel fuel-injected engines, started a shelter for homeless pregnant women two years in Long Beach. It's called New Beginnings, and the women who stay there receive medical care, clothes, furniture, parenting classes and career counseling. The mothers also have to agree to attend classes at Long Beach City College, two blocks away from New Beginnings.

"Our program," Younger told Valerie Takahama of the *Long Beach Press-Telegram*, "is really geared toward helping them take care of themselves in the future. It's not just a flop-house."

As first, Younger was startled at being rejected for one of the Women Helping Women awards. "I am all for women's rights," she says. "We are not second-class citizens. We can certainly accomplish and achieve anything that we set our minds to. Anything."

But what about this prolife attitude? Well, she says, the idea for the shelter came from meeting women who felt they had no choice other than to have an abortion. "But they didn't want to do that, they wanted help." Some had been beaten up by husbands or sometime lovers. Others were homeless or had very little education.

Younger could not understand why the Commission on the Status of Women held New Beginnings against her. "What we offer women is the choice to have their babies. How can they be against that?"

The more she thought about it, the angrier the former nominee became. "I'm always fighting for something or someone. If it's not fighting the welfare system to get someone on welfare, it's a boyfriend who's battering his girlfriend. I don't think this [award thing] is some place I should have to fight." But she did, and in a way that surprised some people into thinking twice about the conventional wisdom that liberals, including liberal feminists, are invariably open-minded and generous of spirit while prolifers are characteristically crabbed and bigoted.

"It made me angry," Younger told Leslie Bond of *National Right to Life News,* "that prejudice still exists in our country. It would be no different if [the commission had taken away the nomination] because I am a Christian or because I am Hispanic. It's just not right."

On Aug. 10, the commission voted once more. Younger appeared to have won, 6 to 4. But there were three abstentions, and commission president Woodward ruled that the abstentions were to be counted as negative votes.

At this point, the legal counsel for Los Angeles County overruled the magical transformation of abstentions into negative votes, and Younger was finally assured of embattled recognition. Recently, she was one of 17 winners to receive a scroll attesting to the fact that she is indeed an outstanding woman helping women.

A past recipient of the award, renowned feminist lawyer Gloria Allred, remains displeased. Younger should not be considered, Allred says, as "any kind of role model held up to the community as a person whose work should be emulated."

But Susan Carpenter-McMillan, a member of the commission, notes that no previous nominee for the award has done more to help poor women than Younger. And she adds that Younger's victory is a sign that "prolife women will no longer be told to sit at the back of the bus. We are part of the women's movement—like it or not."

—*Washington Post,* 15 Dec. 1987.

Freedom of Speech Under President Clinton
by Nat Hentoff

For too long politicians told most of us that what's wrong with America is the rest of us. Them, the minorities . . . . Them, the liberals . . . . Them, the gays. Them, them, them. But there is no them; there's only us. One nation, under God . . . .

   —Bill Clinton, accepting the Democratic nomination for the presidency

. . . At the anti-free-speech [1992] Democratic convention, there was the dismaying experience of Anne Maloney, a delegate from Minnesota. An assistant professor, she teaches feminist philosophy at the College of St. Catherine's in St. Paul. It is a liberal Catholic college, so liberal that the predominant view on abortion there is pro-choice. Anne Maloney is in the minority. But although most of her students are pro-choice, their evaluations of her teaching are enthusiastically positive. Yet the college will not allow her to teach biomedical ethics. She is also a vice-president of the Minneapolis affiliate of Feminists for Life of America. This is a national organization, based in Kansas City, Missouri—with members in every state and chapters in 35. Many of its members are veterans of—and are still involved in—civil rights work. Many also came out of the anti-war movement.

The lively president of Feminists for Life, Rachel MacNair—who is one of my few heroes—has been arrested at least 17 times. The busts include protesting against nuclear plants and nuclear weapons, once for sitting on the sidewalk holding a sign at an abortion clinic, twice for passing out leaflets on clinic property, and once for sitting in front of an abortion clinic door.

These prolife women on the Left believe in a consistent ethic of life. They are politically active against capital punishment, against the kind of Republican economics that breed large scale poverty, against violence of any kind, including war or preparations for war. They lobby for stiffer laws against sexual and domestic violence, and for a scope and quality of economic justice for women that Clinton can't even imagine—and would discard as too "radical" if he could. As for abortion, Feminists for Life say that "truly liberated women reject abortion because they reject the male worldview that accepts violence as a legitimate solution to conflict."

I know members of the group around the country, and last spring spent time with Minnesota Feminists for Life. They were very pleased at the time, having just stopped a death penalty bill in the legislature. At their meeting, I met several Minnesota Democratic state officials, all of them much farther to the left than Clinton, and all of them pro-life.

So Anne Maloney of Minnesota Feminists for Life, a member of a lifelong Democratic family, took the money she had saved for the family vacation and went, as an elected delegate, to the grand Democratic Convention at Madison Square Garden. This is her report:

"I am confused and upset by what happened to me last night (July 15). Originally I was thrilled to be a delegate to the DNC. My whole family was excited for me. I knew that my anti-abortion position was an unpopular one within the hierarchy of my party, but I honestly believed that I would be allowed to have a voice. I thought this was a party where everybody could have a voice.

"Instead, however, I was screamed at, shoved, pushed, and verbally harassed. I have 21 black-and-blue marks on my legs from the shoving. One large heavyset man attempted to rip my sign from my hand, wrenching my shoulder in the process.

"There has to be room for dialogue and debate in the Democratic Party. *As I was being harassed, the stirring speeches from the podium were reminding us all that everyone deserves a voice. That's all I asked for. I shouldn't be black-and-blue because of that. All we wanted was five minutes. What are they afraid of?*" (Emphasis added.)

I asked a member of the battered and beleaguered pro-life Minnesota delegation where the security guards were. "Oh, they were there. But they didn't do anything." Neither did any official of the Democratic National Committee. All of this could be seen from the stage. Prolifers are *them*. And *them* have no place anymore in the Democratic Party.

"I was told," said Angel Bennett, also a pro-lifer, "to get out of the Democratic Party . . . . I watched, horrified, as a gentle woman was hit in the face with signs, kicked and shoved without any security bothering to remove the perpetrators . . . .

"Another woman pro-life delegate, only a few feet away, was being continually body-pressed by a woman trying to force her out of her chair for almost one-half hour. Later, a large, aggressive male delegate karate chopped at her arms about six times."

Another Minnesota pro-life delegate, Grant Colstrom, of the United Auto Workers, said, "A pro-abortion Minnesota delegate pushed and shoved me until he succeeded in getting me partially out of the spot I had been in for seven hours—in order to keep me from holding any 'STOP ABORTION NOW' signs before the cameras. He threatened to punch me if I attempted to regain my prime spot. He bragged to his cohorts that they did not have to worry—that he had me 'under control.'"

There were other mighty efforts to keep these dangerous heretics from the microphone and the cameras when the roll call came around to Minnesota. But these dissenting democrats would not be moved, and when the time came, they cast 10 votes for the pro-life governor of Pennsylvania, Robert Casey.

Hearing there had been death threats against them, Minnesota Senator Paul Wellstone, who is pro-choice, came to the besieged pro-lifers, and—as he told me later—helped escort them safely out of the midst of the Democratic *[sic]* convention.

Weeks later, Anne Maloney was still horrified at what has happened to freedom of speech in her party. "In the row in front of us while all of this was going on," she said, "there was Walter Mondale. He didn't say or do anything."

In her hotel the morning after, a cameraman from Channel 2 in New York told her that in the editing room, he had seen what had happened to her and the others. It was appalling, he said. But the violence against these elected delegates from Minnesota—elected by people who knew what they stood for—was not on television. Nor in that newspaper of partisan record, the *New York Times*.

—*Village Voice*, 8 Sept. 1992.

The Censoring of Feminist History
by Nat Hentoff

March is Women's History Month, and much attention is being paid in schools and forums to two women who were most influential in creating this nation's feminist movement while combating sexism in all its forms.

Elizabeth Cady Stanton organized the first women's rights convention in Seneca Falls, N.Y., in 1848. Her persistent ally was Susan B. Anthony, a founding officer of the National Woman Suffrage Association in 1869.

Both were the subjects of a Public Broadcasting System documentary last November. It was called *Not for Ourselves Alone: The Story of Elizabeth Cady Stanton and Susan B. Anthony*, and has been repeated since.

Both women were unremitting opponents of abortion. Yet that fundamental element of their lives was omitted from this widely publicized and reviewed, but selective, documentary. It was as if a televised life of Dr. Martin Luther King focused entirely on him as a fighter for civil rights without a word about his lifelong commitment to direct-action pacifism as taught by Gandhi and the American minister A.J. Muste, who first—as Dr. King told me—convinced him of the power of nonviolence.

Ken Burns, who has created deeply illuminating television series on subjects such as the Civil War and baseball, was the director and co-producer of *Not for Ourselves Alone*. He is now completing what will be the most definitive documentary series on jazz in international television history. I have seen some of it; and, judging by the expertise of the person who interviewed me for it, I am sure it will equal Burns' Civil War project.

Why, then, did Ken Burns remove from *Not for Ourselves Alone* Susan B. Anthony and Elizabeth Cady Stanton's passionate descriptions of abortion as "child murder" and "infanticide"? And why did none of the reviews of the documentary I saw in the mainstream press mention this distortion of the record of these original feminists?

I asked Ken Burns if he had known of their pro-life views. "Yes," he said unhesitatingly. "But I thought it really important to show the connection between the women's and the abolitionist movements. How Frederick Douglass, for instance, so strongly stood up for women's right to vote."

"But in your research," I told Burns, "you couldn't have missed how often and fiercely they fought against abortion." Burns did not deny that they did, but he insisted that what he calls "the largest social transformation in American history" should not, in his documentary, have been "burdened by present and past differing views on choice."

I respect Burns a great deal, but his use of the word "choice" indicates to me where he's coming from on the subject of abortion. Both Anthony and Stanton believed unequivocally that in an abortion the unborn child does not have a choice of whether to continue living.

Feminists for Life of America, an organization based in Washington, D.C., has protested this exclusion of a belief that meant so much to Anthony and Stanton. Feminists for Life of America believes in the idea of the "seamless garment." That is, it's pro-life across the board, opposing abortion, capital punishment, assisted suicide and euthanasia. And it works through Congress for the rights of the poor and against domestic violence.

Feminists for Life of America provided Ken Burns—before *Not for Ourselves Alone* was aired—with substantial research documenting the prolife views of Stanton and Anthony... But none of it got into *Not for Ourselves Alone*.

In all of the lectures, newspaper articles, broadcasts, and classroom discussions during Women's History Month this March and beyond, I wonder whether any of the tributes to Susan B. Anthony and Elizabeth Cady Stanton will include their prolife convictions. Were they still here, I think they would have picketed the showing of *Not for Ourselves Alone*.

—*Jewish World Review*, 27 Mar. 2000.

Leslie Keech (1954-1989)

Leslie Keech contributed richly to FFLA, especially as its treasurer and a radio spot project creator, writer, producer, and actor. She served Kansans for Life as president, then public relations director. In the spirit of Elizabeth Cady Stanton, who insisted that pregnant women need not be invalids, Keech was a childbirth instructor who celebrated women's reproductive talents and a service provider to young women facing crisis pregnancies. On September 8, 1989, Leslie Keech died unexpectedly as the result of a blood clot following a hysterectomy. Her funeral was appropriately held at The Lighthouse, a large Kansas City maternity home, and the overflowing crowd testified to her impact on many lives.

Keech was an articulate speaker, a clear thinker, a courageous and witty campaigner, and a strong and loving friend whose convictions stemmed from her deep Evangelical Christian faith and feminism. Her loss reminds us that we have far to go; her life reminds us that, with hope, we may arrive. These two responses to popular-magazine articles exemplify Keech's sharp wit and ability to address even the sober abortion issue with humor.

The Sensitive Abortionist
by Leslie Keech

One of the most incredible nuances of the pro-abortion movement is the ambivalence that occasionally leaks out of it. This was epitomized in the pro-abortion book *In Necessity and Sorrow*.

Possibly the all-time best example of this philosophy, however, is an article which appeared in the October 1987 issue of *Harper's* magazine entitled, "We Do Abortions Here," by Sallie Tisdale. It is written by a registered nurse in an abortion clinic and is as graphic in its description of an abortion as anything I have ever read from the prolife movement. Her conclusions, however, about the need to continue this practice are quite disturbing.

The article must be read in its entirety to completely appreciate the mental gymnastics one must perform in order to work in a place such as she describes, but there are several points crying out for comment.

It seems as if the pro-aborts have decided to admit to hand-wringing, agonizing and having second thoughts about abortion—this apparently makes them "sensitive." Their conclusions, however, are predictable. You may have second thoughts as long as the *second* one is that abortion is acceptable and right, agonizing though it may be.

Ms. Tisdale reaches this conclusion, even though she admits, "I have fetus dreams, we all do here: dreams of abortions one after the other; of buckets of blood splashed on the walls; trees full of crawling fetuses." I'd be willing to bet that other nurses performing legitimate medical procedures don't have similar dreams about tonsils and appendixes.

The abortionists are even ambivalent—"For one physician the 'boundary' is a particular week of gestation; for another, it is a certain number of repeated abortions. But these boundaries can be fluid, too . . ." Why all this wishy-washiness if this is so acceptable and necessary?

The pro-abortion movement has long maintained that abortion is simply a "removal of the contents of the uterus," an allegedly safe procedure with no long-term side effects. Ms. Tisdale explains, "Abortion is so routine that one expects it to be quick, cheap and painless." Why then do we hear her admission, "Abortion is the narrowest edge between kindness and cruelty. Done as well as it can be, it is still violence—merciful violence . . ." This is painless? For whom? The abortionist?

Feminists have long pointed out that violence against weaker members of the human race by stronger ones only perpetuates society's inability to deal with social problems. The chauvinism of men "owning" their wives and children has long contributed to this problem. Abortion is the continuation of this violence by those who should know better—women, who brutalize their own children (property) in the name of gaining control over their own lives. At whose expense? Does this really liberate us, or lower us to the level of the original perpetrators of the violence?

And has the exercise of this "right" improved women's options in life? Apparently not. Tisdale states, "Women who have the fewest choices of all exercise their right to an abortion the most."

Feminists for Life has said all along that abortion takes away real, affirming choices and replaces them with women who have abortions because they feel they have no choice.

Abortion has always seemed to me very much like a rape in reverse. The doctor (usually a male), for a fee, undoes what has already been done. Interestingly, Tisdale relates a dream she has had: "I dreamed that two men grabbed me and began to drag me away. 'Let's do an abortion,' they said with a sickening leer, and I began to scream, plunged into a vision of sucking, scraping pain, of being spread and torn by impartial instruments that only do what they are bidden." I am both fascinated and repulsed by the revelation that even to nurses in the clinics, this supposedly safe, allegedly necessary procedure is subconsciously perceived to be a male-on-female rape.

The rationalization of abortion as a necessary evil, if only you are sensitive enough and wring your hands enough, is where the pro-abortion movement has finally landed. It is an intellectually dishonest position, especially after looking at the facts as Ms. Tisdale obviously has.

"We talk glibly about choice," she admits, "but the choice for what?" We've been telling you, but you haven't been listening, Ms. Tisdale—the choice to kill.

—*Sisterlife*, Spring 1988

Better Living (for men) Through Surgery (for women)
by Leslie Keech

We are all used to it by now: the media establishment portraying prolifers as insensitive, sexist clods, while the noble knights of the proabortion position are the champions of women's rights. But occasionally the hand slips, and even the mass media reveals that the central right abortion grants is the right to be exploited. Two articles that came my attention recently should cause any thinking person to reexamine legal abortion's legacy really is.

In the July issue of *Glamour* magazine an article by Eric Goodman appeared, entitled "Men and Abortion." It is an account of several men's experiences with their partners' abortions. The thread running throughout the article in nearly every instance was that the abortion was *his* idea—and the woman agreed to follow his lead.

For instance, "Walt's" account: Instead of advising her to do what she thought best for her own life, Walt allowed his lover to be guided by her strong desire to "save their relationship." "I said, 'What do you want to do?' She suggested abortion, thinking this would make it possible for me to continue to paint, that that in turn would prolong our relationship . . . She's my age, thirty-five, and it may have been her last chance to have a child. I believe she would be much happier if she'd had it—but I would be unhappy having a child I never saw and didn't live with. I guess I sound like a real cad. Maybe I was." Gee, Walt, I had a *stronger* word in mind . . .

Or how about "Christopher" who got the money for the abortion from his mother, then accompanied his girlfriend to a clinic that he likened to an "abortion factory" (front-alley variety). As he waited for the abortion to be completed, he pondered his predicament. "I think I felt more concerned about her than I really was, because I was there with her?" Kind of amazing what a little trip to the abortion clinic will do for one's conscience, isn't it?

"Jack's" lover had an abortion while he was in law school. They considered themselves too young to have a child, and they were both in the middle of pursuing careers. They broke up some time after the abortion, and he married a woman who was unable to bear a child. He said, "So it turns out my one chance for a biological child was that aborted pregnancy in law school." The article goes on to admit, "If Jack's wife had been able to have children, it's unlikely he would have given much thought to what happened in law school."

"Jeff" has been involved in two abortions, but it took the second one to make him regret his behavior during the first. "I was afraid of getting snarled up in two kids and a house, so I took the refuge of asking, 'What do you want to do?' She was waiting for me to mention marriage, so she opted for abortion."

The selfish, sexist, irresponsible behavior shown by these and many other men is heightened and encouraged by abortion's easy way out. Our society expects that fathers should pay child support for their children, but at the same time we make it very easy for a man to simply use the woman for his pleasure, and then buy his way out of the deal for a couple hundred dollars! Why should a man pay child support for eighteen years if he can "get rid of the problem" so neatly?

"Alex" shared his experience: "From the moment she told me, I wanted her to have an abortion. She knew I would. I'm still paying child support for the first three kids, and I don't make that much. The way things fell out, there's been a kid under four in my life for the past ten years. I'm tired of waking up in the middle of the night." Poor "Alex." It *is* important to get your rest—no matter what the cost.

Finally, an interview appeared in *Penthouse* magazine with George Brett, first baseman for the Kansas City Royals baseball team. The interview is extremely enlightening concerning male attitudes towards abortion—and towards women.

George admits to paying for two women to have abortions, and feels that those decisions were the right ones, since he wasn't ready to get married. (Keep in mind that this is a man who could easily afford to raise a child, marriage or no.) George *was* rather pleased about one aspect of the abortions, however. It "proved" that he was indeed the stud he purports to be. He candidly states, "I know I'm fertile. I've got the checkbook to prove it. But getting a couple of girls pregnant gave me a sense that there's no sweat. I can have kids anytime I want. I've had the security of knowing I'm a proven performer."

What a wonderful service to humanity those two women have contributed; by subjecting themselves to surgery, they have assured us that George Brett is not infertile. That's just swell. Did two children really have to die to prove it?

I wonder if the "prochoice" movement really understands how anti-woman abortion really is? It has certainly not brought us forward in establishing equality with men. We need callous, exploitative men to step up to our level, not drag us down to theirs.

—*Sisterlife*, Fall 1989.

Frederica Mathewes-Green

Sisterlife, the original newsletter for Feminists for Life, reached a peak in quality as well as circulation under the editorship of Frederica Mathewes-Green. Mathewes-Green's articulate and sensitive approach to the abortion issue in her role as FFL Vice President for Communications also gained the organization a good deal of respect from national and local media. An abortion rights advocate in the early 1970s, Mathewes-Green changed her position after reading a description of a second-trimester abortion. Through her work as a childbirth educator, her respect for the child in the womb has only increased and convinced her that the violence of abortion harms the mother as well as the child. Mathewes-Green's writings have appeared in dozens of journals and publications including *Parenting, Policy Review, Human Life Review, Christianity Today, Washington Times, Philadelphia Inquirer, Baltimore Sun, San Francisco Examiner* and the *Phoenix Gazette*. Like that of so many early feminists, her pen has proved a powerful instrument of inspiration and change, one recording a maternal voice of compassion and reason.

Since Mathewes-Green wrote the third selection outlining prolife opposition to euthanasia, the state of Oregon legalized physician-assisted suicide (1997) under much-touted "safeguards" which have not always been followed—something that has also happened in the Netherlands. Over 100 people have since been killed through the "aid" of doctors. Of those who committed suicide in 2000, 63% cited the fear of being a "burden" on loved ones. Only 19% were referred for psychiatric evaluations. Meanwhile Oregon is threatening to cut essential health funding for the chronically ill and working poor, and a memo was recently leaked from a large HMO complaining that too many patients were opting for continued life rather than suicide, which is much better for the bottom line. In good news, other American states have—at least to date—turned down laws like Oregon's, and in 2001 Jack Kevorkian was sentenced to 10-27 years for the murder of Thomas Youk, a man with the degenerative neurological disease amytrophic lateral sclerosis.[1] The growing rejection of doctor-assisted suicide in the U.S. is due in no small part to a decidedly non-"Religious Right" group: disability rights activists, who belong to a growing international movement.[2]

The Bitter Price of "Choice"
by Frederica Mathewes-Green

When I was in college the bumper sticker on my car read "Don't labor under a misconception—legalize abortion." I was one of a handful of feminists on my campus, back in the days when we were jeered at as "bra-burning women's libbers." As we struggled against a hazy sea of sexism, abortion rights was a visible banner, a concrete, measurable goal. Though our other foes were elusive, within the fragile boundary of our skin, at least, we would be sovereign. What could be more personal than our reproductive lives? How could any woman oppose it?

I oppose it now. It has been a slow process, my path from a pro-choice to a prolife position, and I know that unintended pregnancy raises devastating problems. But I can no longer avoid the realization that legalizing abortion was the wrong solution; we have let in a Trojan Horse whose hidden betrayal we've just begun to see.

A woman with an unplanned pregnancy faces more than "inconvenience"; many adversities, financial and social, at school, at work, and at home confront her. Our mistake was in looking at these problems and deciding that the fault lay with the woman, that she should be the one to change. We focused on her swelling belly, not the discrimination that had made her so desperate. We advised her, "Go have this operation and you'll fit right in."

What a choice we made for her. She climbs onto a clinic table and endures a violation deeper than rape—the nurse's hand is wet with her tears—then is grateful to pay for it, grateful to be adapted to the social machine that rejected her when pregnant. And the machine grinds on, rejecting her pregnant sisters.

It is a cruel joke to call this a woman's "choice." We may choose to sacrifice our life and career plans, or choose to undergo humiliating invasive surgery and sacrifice our offspring. How fortunate we are—we have a choice! Perhaps it's time to amend the slogan—"Abortion: a woman's right to capitulate."

If we refused to choose, if we insisted on keeping both our lives and our bodies intact, what changes would our communities have to make? What would make abortion unnecessary? Flexible school situations, fairness in hiring, more flex-time, part-time, and home-commute jobs, better access to prenatal and obstetric care, attractive adoption opportunities, a whole garden of safe family planning choices, support in learning how to handle our sex lives responsibly, and help with child care and parenting when we choose to keep our babies: this is a partial list. Yet these changes will never come as long as we're lying down on abortion tables 1,600,000 times a year to ensure the status quo. We've adapted to this surgical substitute, to the point that Justice Blackmun could write in his Webster dissent, "Millions of women have ordered their lives around [abortion]." That we have willingly ordered our lives around a denigrating surgical procedure—accepted it as the price we must pay to keep our life plans intact—is an ominous sign.

For over a hundred years feminists have warned us that abortion is a form of oppression and violence against women and their children. They called it "child-murder" (Susan B. Anthony), "degrading to women" (Elizabeth Cady Stanton), "most barbaric" (Margaret Sanger), and a "disowning [of] feminine values" (Simone de Beauvoir). How have we lost this wisdom?

Abortion has become the accepted way of dealing with unplanned pregnancies, and women who make another choice are viewed as odd, backward, and selfish. Across the nation three thousand crisis pregnancy centers struggle, unfunded and unrecognized, to help these women with housing, clothing, medical care, and job training, before and after pregnancy. These volunteers must battle the assumption that "they're *supposed* to abort"—especially poor women who hear often enough how much we resent our tax dollars going to feed their children. Prochoice rhetoric conjures a dreadful day when women could be forced to have abortions; that day is nearly here.

More insidiously, abortion advocacy has been poisonous to some of the deeper values of feminism. For example, the need to discredit the fetus has led to the use of terms that would be disastrous if applied to women. "It's so small," "It's unwanted," "It might be disabled," "It might be abused." Too often women are small, unwanted, disabled, or abused. Do we really want to say that these factors erase personhood?

A parallel disparaging of pregnancy itself also has an unhealthy ring. Harping on the discomforts of pregnancy treats women as weak, incompetent; yet we are uniquely equipped for this role, and strong enough to do much harder things than this. Every woman need not bear a child, but every woman should feel proud kinship in the earthy, elemental beauty of birth. To hold it in contempt is to reject our distinctive power, "our bodies, ourselves."

There is a last and still more terrible cost to abortion, one that we have not yet faced. We have treated the loss of our fetuses as a theoretical loss, a sad-but-necessary loss, as of civilians in wartime. We have not yet realized that the offspring lost are not the enemy's, nor our neighbor's, but our own. And it is not a loss of inert, amorphous tissue, but of a growing being unique in history. There are no generic zygotes. The one-cell fertilized ovum is a new individual, the present form of a tall blue-eyed girl, for example, with Grandad's red hair and Great-aunt Ida's singing voice. Look at any family, see how the traits and characteristics run down the generations in a stream. Did we really think our own children would be different?

Like the gypsy in Verdi's opera, *Il Trovatore*, our frustration has driven us to desperate acts. Outraged by the Count's cruel injustice, she stole his infant son and, in a crazed act of vengeance, flung him into the fire. Or so she thought. For, in turning around, she discovered the Count's son lay safe on the ground behind her; it was her own son she had thrown into the flames. In our desperate bid for justice we have not yet realized whom we have thrown into the flames; the moment of realization will be as devastating for us as it was for her.

Until that time, legal abortion invites us to go on doing it, 4500 times a day. And, with ruthless efficiency, the machine grinds on.

—*Tampa Tribune*, 3 Dec. 1989; repub. *Sisterlife*, Spring 1990

Designated Unperson
by Frederica Mathewes-Green

The discipline of ethics draws participants from a wide variety of fields, and never more so than when the most basic ethical question is under discussion: what is human personhood, and when does it deserve protection? When is it permissible to kill another human being? If other ethical questions can seem arcane, this one touches common lives and inspires public debate of a deservedly vehement sort. This ancient riddle is being reviewed on many lively fronts today, as public debate targets or defends our wartime enemies, the vicious criminal, those struggling with hopeless disease. Yet the fiercest debate circles around one who is neither an enemy, nor evil, nor ill. The debate concerns our own unborn offspring.

It is certainly a sign of life-out-of-balance that such a debate should arise at all. In a healthy society, new life is welcomed and women's awesome powers of fertility are respected and accommodated. Yet in our nation over a million and a half women each year find that the continuing of a pregnancy would exact such a grievous price that abortion seems comparatively easier to bear. With alternatives so forbidding, abortion must be right; yet how can it be right if it takes the life of one's own child?

It then becomes necessary to demonstrate that the unborn is not a person. It must not be my child that dies in abortion; it must be something else, something less, not really one of us at all. Although one of the greatest lessons of our age is the value of every human life, regardless of race, age, gender, or any other determinant, a grieving sense of necessity drives abortion defenders to insist that their own offspring are not quite human. Thus the depersonalization of the unborn begins.

The unborn is not a person because she is so small. The charge that "every good argument for abortion is a good argument for infanticide" finds confirmation here. Size remains relative throughout human life. The six-week fetus is very small compared to a newborn, but one could just as justly compare the newborn's size with that of Hulk Hogan. The argument from size is a version of one of human society's most durable, least honorable assertions: might makes right. Big people can throw away small people. As most women are smaller than most men, it is a doubtful assertion for us to champion. Too many of us know in our own bodies what violence at stronger hands is like.

The unborn is not a person because he is unwanted. We speak here women's disabling fear: I'm nothing without a man. If no one wants me, I don't exist. If worth depends on someone else's approval, then we may in turn eliminate our own children who do not please us. Worth based on wantedness, that chimerical achievement, is ominous for children, blacks, women, the disabled, and other living things.

The unborn is not a person because she does not have human form. This is in fact untrue; that "glob of tissue" finds order quickly, and every baby aborted has a face, hands, eyes, gender, and a beating heart. But even if a method were available that could strike during that rush to recognizable form, it would be an ominous precedent to embrace. Discrimination against living human beings because they "look funny" has a long and ignoble history. The truth is that even the earliest embryo has a human form, though it may be an unfamiliar one. We are all "globs of tissue" in changing form from conception until death.

The unborn is not a person because he would be disabled. Our disabled friends may well feel a chill; if we'd only caught them before they were born we would have "spared them" their unhappy, unsightly lives. Killing in the name of compassion has had a tenacious appeal for this ruthless and sentimental age. We stand with Scrooge, with the strong and healthy, and locate the "surplus population" in the weak and sick. It is worthwhile to recall that we are each only temporarily able-bodied, each potential candidates for lovingly-administered death.

The unborn is not a person because she could be abused. Prenatal dismemberment is indeed an effective preventative for postnatal abuse, though the net result to the child may not be what she would have preferred. Implicit here is the assumption that the lives of the abused, like the lives of the disabled, are not worth living; that the rape survivor, the battered spouse, should never have been born. When this future abuse is only theoretical, as in the case of an unborn child, we make a devastating affirmation of the abuser's power, and undermine the hope of those who believe the past can be overcome. The hope that abortion would prevent child abuse has been cruelly mocked by statistics which indicate that, though every child in America could have been aborted during the past eighteen years of legality, reported child abuse has in that time increased 500%. The notion of the disposable child persists even after birth.

The unborn is not a person because he is not sentient. Consciousness, self-awareness, is a trait which gradually emerges and then fades during the course of a normal human life, and is by no means fully present in a newborn; the average house cat is capable of more intelligent interaction than a month-old child. Some would choose six months fetal age as the point that the potential for this future awareness is present; however, potential is a slippery concept, as all the potential abilities of a lifetime are present at the moment of fertilization. To attach increasing value to those of increasing awareness is no doubt flattering to the intelligentsia who developed the standard, but a bit worrisome for the rest of us—especially for our mentally disabled friends, who may grow up to star in their own TV shows for all we know. The unborn child is only temporarily lacking in awareness, in consciousness, and daily moving toward its completion. To rush to kill him before he achieves it is as repulsive as rushing to kill a recovering coma victim before she can open her eyes.

The unborn is not a person because she lives inside her mother's body. The unborn is not a part of her mother's body, any more than an astronaut is part of the space ship. The fact that neither is viable without necessary access to oxygen, food, and shelter does not prove that they are not persons. Both the fetus and the astronaut are tenants, though in the case of the unborn it cannot be denied that she can be an uncomfortable and demanding one. Does this give the mother the right to evict her unwanted tenant? The situation may be like that of a sea captain who discovers a stowaway and considers whether to throw him overboard. The missing factor in the analogy is that the unborn did not take up residence in his mother's body under his own will, but was called into being (in virtually all cases) by a consciously-chosen act that the participants were aware could result in pregnancy. For both parents, undertaking to have sexual relations must be accompanied by a responsible recognition that (even with careful contraception) a child may result. That this result disproportionately taxes the woman, that the man can walk out, abandoning his responsibility to her and his child, does not prove that it is right for the woman to do the same. Choices that lead to greater responsibility, greater accountability, are choices that lead to a stronger society for women and their children, and men as well. Choices that feed the cycle of heedless abandonment hurt us all.

This century has already taught us, in too many bloody lessons, that it is a dangerous thing to designate any human life "unperson." Devaluing, rationalizing, renaming, discarding seem to spread outward in concentric rings of expediency. When women so desperately agree to depersonalize their own children, as a condition of full participation in society, a lot more is at risk than those tiny lost lives. Better check your size, your sentience, your wantedness; there's no telling who is next.

—*Sisterlife*, Spring 1991

The Euthanasia/Abortion Connection
by Frederica Mathewes-Green

On June 4, 1990, Jack Kevorkian attached Alzheimer's patient Janet Adkins to a homemade contraption in his 1968 VW bus, then watched her push the activating button that made her die.

Public reaction was swift and generally negative. Judge Alice Gilbert, in barring Kevorkian from ever again using the device, charged that he "flagrantly violated" all standards of medical practice. She added that through arrogant and self-promoting "bizarre behavior" Kevorkian revealed that "his real goal is self service rather than patient service." Kevorkian's lawyer, Geoffrey Fieger, responded with an admirable non-sequitur: he claimed that Gilbert is "taking up the standard of fanatical anti-abortionists, people who wish to perpetuate suffering." As far as we know, the Kevorkian machine does not perform abortions.

The appearance of prolife activists in the movement against euthanasia has been confusing to many. Opposing euthanasia does not seem to give opportunity for outlawing contraceptives, frowning on sex, keeping women out of jobs, or forced childbearing, goals assumed to be central to the prolife movement. Yet there is a connection. Both abortion and euthanasia make helpless people die. Dying is not, in itself, the activity that prolifers so strenuously oppose. Death naturally occurs along the entire spectrum of life, from the earliest miscarriages to the centenarian's last breath. The objectionable activity is making people die—people who may be small, weak, or disabled, but are not dying; people who cannot defend or speak for themselves. The objection is to the creation of an ever-widening class of unpersons, persons unwanted or imperfect, and imposing on those persons a duty to die.

Consider the following cases. While Nancy Cruzan was dying, the staff at Missouri Rehabilitation Center continued to insist that she was no vegetable. They had seen her smile at funny stories, cry when a visitor left, and indicate pain with her menstrual periods. She was not living on machines: a feeding tube had been inserted years before only to replace spoon feeding and make her care easier. An activist present during those days of dying commented, "It was like one of those horror movies where everybody in the town knows something, but nobody can get word out to the outside world." Information about Nancy's true condition was persistently blacked out, while the staff endured the nightmare of watching her die.

In a horrible déja vû, another disabled woman at the Center has been selected for the same fate. Twenty-year-old Christine Busalacchi's condition is improving: she waves, smiles, objects to having her teeth brushed, vocalizes to indicate TV preferences, and very much enjoys visits from young men. This is not enough for her father, who has visited her seldom in the last two years (and then sometimes accompanied by TV cameras) and, we are told, stands to inherit $51,000 from her estate. Pete Busalacchi does not have the "clear and convincing evidence" necessary to have her starved in Missouri, so he is trying to have her moved to Minnesota where the standard is less stringent.[3]

Dr. Ronald Cranford, the euthanasia advocate who hopes to help Pete Busalacchi take care of Christine when she is brought to Minnesota, had a similar case in 1979. Sgt. David Mack was shot in the line of duty as a policeman, and Cranford diagnosed him as "definitely . . . in a persistent vegetative state . . . never [to] regain cognitive, sapient functioning . . . never [to] be aware of his condition." Twenty months after the shooting Mack woke up and eventually regained nearly all his mental ability. When asked by a reporter how he felt, he spelled out on his letter board, "Speechless!"

Similar stories recur. Cancer patient Yolanda Blake was hospitalized last November 30 after experiencing severe bleeding. Despite the insistence of her sister and of the friend who held her power of attorney, the hospital refused to leave in a feeding tube or a catheter, and on December 14, the county judge ruled in the hospital's favor that Blake should be allowed to "die with dignity." On December 15, Blake woke up. When asked if she wanted to live, she responded "Of course I do!"

Richard Routh, 42, was hospitalized with head injuries after a motorcycle accident. He had learned to signal "yes" and "no," could smile and laugh at jokes, when his parents and doctors decided to have him starved. A nurse's aide says that as they stood by the bedside discussing the starvation decision, Routh shook his head "no." Though the coroner's report says he died of head injuries, he had lost thirty pounds during the hospitalization. The autopsy showed that he had not been given painkillers to ease the pain of starvation.

Washington State Senator Ray Moore represents more clearly than most the views of those who believe the disabled should want to die. He is supporting that state's Initiative 119, which would allow a doctor to give a poisonous injection to a terminally ill patient requesting it; he believes that his mother would have benefited from such a service. He says that many people feel medical professionals profit "indecently" by caring for the dying, and we must grant that patience in the face of natural death can have a detrimental financial effect on the estate. But perhaps Moore is most honest when he says, "there is a growing aggravation with the sights and smells of hospitals and nursing homes."

It has been observed that sick and wounded animals do not commit suicide; when they are "put to sleep," it is to ease the pain of their owners. We may be horrified to contemplate life as a paraplegic, or brain-damaged, or unable to chew our own food. Yet once we are there, who is to say that the bits of life we still hold may not be incomparably sweet? The sound of a loved voice filtering through dim consciousness, the sweet breeze when windows are first opened in the spring, a long afternoon in the sun, may become precious tokens, eagerly held. A generation who once pondered the possibility of "alternate states of consciousness" should be especially sensitive here. Rita Greene has been in an unconscious state for forty years; Claire Norton, the nurse who has cared for her throughout those years, speaks of Rita as "a saint" whose life represents "a tremendous amount of mystery." Who can prove her wrong?

Kevorkian's lawyers misunderstand. Prolifers do not wish to perpetuate suffering. We do not wish to prolong dying. But when people aren't dying—when they are only disabled or recovering or even merely old—we want to offer them loving support till the end. It may not make for a neat, tidy society where everyone is productive and attractive. But it does make for the only kind of humane and just society that we can imagine.[4]

—*Sisterlife*, Spring 1991

Anne M. Maloney

Anne M. Maloney graduated from Mount Mary College in Milwaukee, Wisconsin, in 1980 and obtained her Ph.D. at Marquette University in 1987. She is currently a (very popular) professor of feminist philosophy at the College of St. Catherine (St. Paul, Minnesota), Vice President of Feminists for Life of Minnesota, and board member of the Feminism and Nonviolence Studies Association. She resides in St. Paul with her husband and three children. At the 1992 Democratic National Convention in New York City, Maloney and other prolife Democrats were harassed and silenced while the media looked on, failing to report any of the violence captured by their cameras. Her experience, related in detail by Nat Hentoff in this collection, proved to be the most violent censorship Professor Maloney has experienced, but it was certainly not her first or last. On February 25, 1991, she was scheduled to testify before the Senate Health and Human Services Committee of the Minnesota legislature. At the last minute, the hearing time was cut and testimony was discontinued shortly before Professor Maloney was to have been called. Our second selection comprises her intended testimony.

Cassandra's Fate: Why Feminists Ought to be Prolife
by Professor Anne M. Maloney

In ancient Greek mythology, Cassandra, a daughter of Priani, was so loved by Apollo that he gave her a great gift: the gift of prophecy. Cassandra did not return Apollo's love, however, and the spurned god was enraged. No gift, once given by the gods, can ever be taken back, and so Apollo could not take away Cassandra's vision of the future. Instead, he cruelly twisted it: yes, Cassandra would always have knowledge of what was inevitably to come, but whenever she might try to share this knowledge with fellow human beings, they would disbelieve her. With all of her foresight, Cassandra would be impotent, spurned and laughed at by the very people she would desperately try to save.

In the late twentieth century, we find ourselves in the frustrating and even terrifying situation of Cassandra—seeing so clearly the disastrous consequences of the current abortion ethic, consequences not disastrous just for the unborn women, who are aborted in far greater numbers than men, not just for the women who abort, but consequences disastrous for all of society: all women, all children, all men. When we try to point out what awaits us ahead, we are usually ignored, sometimes laughed at, while our feminist credentials are questioned.

The term "feminist" refers to anyone who is dedicated to the ideal that men and women, although possessed of different sexual natures (and thus, as we shall see, of differing ways of relating to reality), have equally valuable and valid contributions to make to the world, and therefore ought to have equality of opportunity. Furthermore, to be a feminist is to be wholly committed to making this world into one wherein both women and men are equally valued and respected.

The term "prolife" refers to the position that human life is intrinsically valuable; in other words, human life ought to "count" in society, regardless of whether it is useful, convenient or pleasant.

Some women's rights advocates react with incredulity, even anger, when prolife people dare to call themselves feminists. At a "woman-to-woman" conference in Milwaukee, Wisconsin, fifteen years ago, Letty Cottin Pogrebin, co-editor at the time of *Ms.* magazine, told the organizers of a Feminists for Life booth to pack up and go home because they did not belong at a convention dedicated to helping women. What is sorely needed in such situations is an explanation of why anyone would be both prolife and feminist—of why, in fact, a correct understanding of feminism demands that we be both.

Abortion advocates such as Carol Gilligan and Beverly Harrison argue on two basic fronts: First, they claim that women have an absolute, fundamental right to abortion because they have a basic right to control their reproductive lives. Without such control, these authors argue, there can never be social equality for women. On the other front, they argue that abortion is proscribed only because we still inhabit a patriarchal society which seeks to elevate men at the expense of women, and anyone who opposes abortion is either a perpetrator or a victim of this patriarchal ideal. Witness the following: "Many women who espouse the prolife position do so, at least in part, because they have internalized patriarchal values and depend on the sense of identity and worth that comes from having accepted 'women's place' in society."

Entwined in the discussion of these points is usually the conviction (a correct one, I think) that men and women approach reality from two different ethical perspectives: that men tend to focus on the principles involved in making choices, where women tend to view such choices in terms of the persons involved.

I believe (1) that the demand for abortion rights as a necessary prerequisite for a woman's reproductive freedom, for a woman's control over her own body, betrays a decidedly patriarchal, rather than feminist, understanding of both "freedom" and "control"; (2) that, whereas our society is, in many ways, constructed on a model that erects and sustains patriarchal values at the expense of feminine values, the solution to this patriarchal bias does not lie in an abortion ethic, and in fact, an abortion ethic feeds, rather than destroys, this bias; and finally (3) that while men and women do approach reality from different ethical perspectives, one focused on principles and the other on persons, these are not always conflicting perspectives, and an abortion ethic destroys both of them.

In calling for abortion rights as the ultimate guarantee that women can control their own bodies, abortion advocates are viewing a woman's body as a kind of territory to be subdued, interfered with, dominated. This is not a feminist perspective, regardless of how many people maintain that it is.

Abortion, if it is an act of control, is a violent act of control. When a woman is pregnant, be it six days or six months, her body has become inextricably wedded to the body of another living being; the only way out of that relationship for a woman who does not want to be pregnant is a violent one, an act that destroys the fetus and invades the body (and often the mind) of his or her mother. Traditionally, it has always been women who have realized that violence solves nothing and usually begets more violence, that violent solutions often wound the perpetrator as well as the victim. That is why women have historically been opposed to war, to capital punishment, to the rape and destruction of the environment. Why should women's traditional (and quite wise) abhorrence of violence stop at the threshold of their own bodies?

In the male-dominated world we have all inhabited for the last 2500 years, unfortunately power (thus, "control") has been accorded only to those strong enough to seize it, or at least demand it. Furthermore, it has historically been those in power who have set the standard for who gets to "count" as persons. For far too many of those 2500 years, it has been men who have been in power and women who have not been "counted." It is, therefore, particularly chilling to read arguments such as those of theologian Marjorie Reiley Maguire, who says that in order for a fetus to count as valuable, the pregnant woman must confer value upon it; as she puts it: "The personhood (of the fetus) begins when the bearer of life, the mother, makes a covenant of love with the developing life within her to bring it to birth. . . . The moment when personhood begins, then, is the moment when the mother accepts the pregnancy."

The fetus, according to such argumentation, is a person if and only if the pregnant woman decides to invest her with value. How, we ask, does this differ from the long entrenched patriarchal ideal that it is the powerful who determine the value of other human life?

The notions of control and power at work in the abortion ethic, then, are ones that surely ought to give any feminist pause. It is indeed unconscionable that women have, for so many thousands of years, been dominated and victimized by men, whose hold on power was reinforced by the patriarchal structure of society. Thus, it is especially disorienting to hear the argument that the only road away from such victimization is to victimize, in turn, another group of human beings—their completely powerless and voiceless offspring. Their very powerlessness makes them the ideal victims: the question that all women must ask themselves is whether the path away from victimization really lies in joining the victimizers, whether the road to freedom must really be littered with the dead bodies of their unborn children.

In the "March on Washington" in the spring of 1989, women of all colors and walks of life forcefully proclaimed their commitment to the tenet that women will never be truly free or equal to men until they can walk away from their sexual encounters just as men have always been able to do. The feminists who were not marching that day wonder whether the March on Washington was not a march down the wrong road, a road fraught with danger.

Men and women are different, not just in their biological characteristics, but in their sexual natures as well. There are exceptions, of course, but throughout history men have traditionally approached sex differently than women have. No one can deny that women have always had a higher biological investment in sexual union; abortion seeks to undo that tie. Is the ideal to be pursued a world wherein sex can (and often will be) commitment-free? Leaving abortion aside for just a moment, even most forms of contraception invade the woman's body, not the man's—and in more cases than we want to admit, scar and irrevocably damage those bodies. (Even condoms, the one "male" form of contraception, usually ends up being the woman's responsibility—survey after survey shows that it is invariably women, not men, who are responsible for purchasing condoms.)

One of the points on which all feminists agree is that women need to build their self-confidence and self-esteem. In a sexist culture, this can be hard to do. As Carol Heilbrun pointed out in a talk given to the Modem Language Association, a man's traditional experience of selfhood can be summed up in a line from the poet Walt Whitman: "I celebrate myself and sing myself, and what I assume you shall assume," whereas poet Emily Dickinson best sums up how women have, for too long, experienced selfhood: "I'm nobody." Does abortion build a woman's self-esteem? The point is to question whether abortion on demand can ever bring about the condition wherein the feminine perspective is valued as much as the male, or whether, in fact, abortion ultimately robs women of their self-confidence and self-esteem.

Those who acquiesce to the conviction that pregnancy is a form of enslavement and childbearing a burden are adding weight to, not destroying, the yoke of patriarchy. They are letting men be the arbiters of what is valuable and fighting hard for the "right" to have their own bodies invaded and their own children destroyed so that they can get it.

What feminists, all feminists, should be doing is working to achieve a world in which the power to bear children is viewed as a gift to be protected rather than a burden of which to be relieved. That means working for fundamental changes in the structure of society, including, but not limited to, far greater flexibility in the work place for both mothers and fathers, better pre—and postnatal care for impoverished women, and much more stringent enforcement of male responsibility for child support. Such changes would be a true feminization of society. They will occur only when we insist upon them, however, and abortion on demand precludes such insistence. When abortion is easily accessible, society no longer has to take pregnancy seriously. Once a woman decides to continue her pregnancy, society is under no obligation to help her: it is, after all, her choice, her responsibility.

In militating for the right to abortion on demand, abortion advocates are trying to win their game on the same old game board—the patriarchal world view that denigrates what is unique to women as unimportant, trivial, not to be taken seriously.

They are embracing a kind of freedom that uses the female body as an object to be invaded and, if need be, subdued. Feminists who are prolife see that this can lead only to disaster for women and for their unborn children—yet our voices still go unheard and unheeded.

Cassandra's fate was to see the future.

And be disbelieved.

—Sisterlife, Fall 1990

To the Minnesota Senate Health
and Human Services Committee
by Professor Anne M. Maloney

Thank you for giving me this opportunity to speak with you. I come here this evening to offer you what I believe to be the feminist view of abortion.

Women, as I tell my students in my Feminist Philosophy class, should be on the same list as the spotted owl. We are an endangered species. To be a woman in the United States today is to be the potential victim of battering and rape. Pornography eroticizes our victimization and screams it from every newsstand. The majority of families living below the poverty level are headed by women. Women are used as medical guinea pigs, subjected time after time to untested drugs and procedures. Witness DES, the IUD, the early form of the Pill—now acknowledged to be a hormone bomb—and silicone breast implants. When abortions are performed for sex selection purposes—and they are performed for that reason—it is female fetuses who are killed.

Women are 51% of the U.S. population. We are beaten, raped, starved, experimented on, and killed because of our gender. I'm not even going into the rest of the world, where women are routinely sterilized, have their clitorises excised, and are killed as infants in a ritual called "giving the baby a bath" because their lives just aren't valuable enough.

Is abortion any solution to these brute facts of a woman's life? Indeed not. Abortion further victimizes women by giving society an "easy out," a cheap fix for deep, real problems, problems that abortion exacerbates rather than solves. Were you raped? Well, it isn't a safe world for women. But here, it's OK. Have an abortion. Are you the victim of incest? Too bad. Men are powerful, aren't they? But hey, it's OK, have an abortion. Too many kids? Are you in poverty? Trying to finish school or hang on to your job? Being pregnant won't do. Don't expect society to change or help you. But hey, it's OK, have an abortion. This, ironically, is called "choice." In reality, abortion is no choice at all.

Some people will argue that if abortion is not legal, women will be desperate enough to resort to knitting needles and coat hangers. The solution these "prochoice" people offer is *not* to address the cause of such desperation, *not* to root out and destroy the viruses inherent in society that forces women to such measures. Oh, no. To the woman so beaten down by society's callousness that she resorts to killing her own offspring, they offer not food, or a job, or education, or help. They offer her a cleaner knife to abort with, the so-called "safe" legal abortion . . . .

Feminists for Life stands for a different version, a society where women are valued and where their power to give and nurture life is valued. As long as abortion exists as a cheap and easy solution, this society will remain a dream. Abortion exists because it's a man's world. If men got pregnant, they would demand health care, living wages, family leave, child care. They would demand that society value their ability to give and sustain life. But abortion? Having one's body forcibly violated, being told that the price of success is such constant violation? Forget it. Men would never stand for it. It's time for women to stop standing for it, too.

I hope that none of you will stand for it, either.

—*Prolife Feminism, Yesterday and Today*, 1995.

Rachel MacNair

Rachel MacNair was Feminists for Life president from 1984 to 1994. She graduated from Earlham College (a Quaker school) in 1978 with a major in Peace and Conflict Studies, and earned her Ph.D. in psychology and sociology in 1999. Her Quaker heritage places her activism in the tradition of Lucretia Mott and Susan B. Anthony. She first agitated for social justice at age 13 with the antiwar movement during the war in Vietnam. She has vigorously protested nuclear weapons production, nuclear energy use, and U.S. military interventions. She is a vegan and has been active in vegetarian concerns. She has long been committed to the feminist and prolife movements.

MacNair comes from an activist family: her grandfather was arrested in a sit-in in Talladega, Alabama, during the Civil Rights movement of the 1960s, and her mother and grandparents attended the 1963 March on Washington while her father watched the four-year-old MacNair at home. That she would have feminist understandings, like the rest of her family, was an expected development. Her initial reaction to the *Roe v. Wade* decision was that this was a good thing, since fewer women would be killed by back-alley butchers; she changed her mind when she realized what legalization meant instead, as she details below. When she saw that the dynamics of violence, such as the dehumanization of its targets, applied in abortion—not only against the fetal child, but also against the mother—she felt compelled to take a stronger stand.

Since this book's first edition, she has researched a little-studied but critical subject: the psychological effects of killing on those who do the killing, ranging from abortion staff to combat veterans to those who carry out executions. She presents her findings in her book *Perpetration-Induced Traumatic Stress: The Psychological Consequences of Killing* (Praeger, 2002). She has also written the college textbook *The Psychology of Peace: An Introduction* (Praeger, 2003), its middle-school version, *Gaining Mind of Peace: Why Violence Happens and How to Stop It* (Xlibris, 2003), and *History Shows: Winning with Nonviolent Action,* a colorful picture book on successful nonviolent campaigns throughout history (Xlibris, 2004).[1] MacNair's online book, *Achieving Peace in the Abortion War* (www.fnsa.org/apaw), talks about the recent downward trend in U.S. abortion and its creation of a psychologically safer atmosphere for listening to prolife arguments. She currently directs the research arm of Consistent Life, the Institute for Integrated Social Analysis.

Would Illegalizing Abortion Set Loose the Back-Alley Butchers?
No—Legalizing Abortion Did That
by Rachel MacNair

Many people now understand the harm abortion does to women but still think making it illegal will cause more problems than it solves. We need to make it clear why it's in women's interests that abortion be illegal.

It used to be that when abortions were botched, the woman at least had the option of turning her abortionist in. On those few occasions when the woman actually died, at least then the prosecutor would pay attention and maybe put the abortionists out of business. But now, we can cite several instances where women died of legal abortion and the abortionist had only to put up with the irritant of a malpractice suit. We do not protect women by telling back alley butchers they are free to advertise in the Yellow Pages.

For example, when Richard Mucie was convicted of a woman's death by abortion in 1968, his license was revoked. When *Roe v. Wade* came down, he used it to go to court and get his license back. He is back in business. [Now deceased.—Eds.]

In 1983 and 1984, the state of California reported no abortion deaths—but we documented with our amicus brief in the Webster case the incontrovertible evidence that at least four women died in Los Angeles

County alone in those two years. California has not corrected its records. The mother of one of the young women wrote, "I cry every day when I think how horrible her death was. She was slashed by them and then she bled to death . . . I know that other young black women are now dead after abortion at that address . . . Where is [the abortionist] now? Has he been stopped? Has anything happened to him because of what he did to my Belinda? . . . People tell me nothing has happened, that nothing ever happens to white abortionists who leave young black women dead."

We should not be allowing the government to participate in the deception of women. Abortion kills a living human being and mutilates another. Surgery done on a healthy body is mutilation, and such surgery done without adequately informed consent is a battery. Legalized abortion without even minimal informed consent is widespread, epidemic battering of women. Women deserve a straightforward acknowledgement by government of this fact.

Many women wouldn't consider abortion if it were illegal. Others would find many of the unfair pressures for abortion lifted if their families and friends knew this was not a quick way out. Nonviolent solutions to the problem become more attractive when the violent solution is less expedient.

Illegalization would cause the number of abortions to go down dramatically. When Medicaid funding was cut off, studies contrasting one year with funding to the next year without funding found that the number of abortions went down dramatically—and the number of childbirths went down slightly. The abortions that didn't happen weren't replaced by childbirth. They were replaced by greater responsibility in avoiding pregnancy.

Illegalization would cause the number of services to pregnant women to increase dramatically. Not only would the emotional support of friends and family improve in many cases, but volunteers working on alternative services would have more time and resources. Already, crisis pregnancy centers outnumber abortion clinics. More is needed.

Finally, it is the abortionists who will try to get prosecutions of women, not the prolifers; if the abortionist can [give her the legal status of] accomplice, her testimony is less credible and she is less likely to turn the abortionist in.

Let me underscore this point: in practical terms, abortion laws will be enforced by the women who have had abortions.

Women should no longer be denied this power.

—*Sisterlife*, Summer 1989

Parallel Cages: The Oppression of Men
by Rachel MacNair

Abortion defenders say that women must have access to abortion in order to have equality with men. The prolife feminist responds that there is no other oppressed group that requires surgery in order to become unoppressed. Abortion defenders suggest that we now have technology available to fix the inherent biological handicap of women. Prolife feminists believe that Nature was never the source of the idea that our bodies are inferior due to their innate abilities.

We apply that reasoning on a biological basis, and should apply it on a social basis as well. Oppression has not been confined to one sex. For instance, we complain about the playboy mentality that treats a woman's body as a recreational object. Under traditional role constraints, there is also a female parallel: the woman who regards a man as a walking wallet. The gold digger is like the playboy; for each their prey is seen as an object rather than as a real person.

There is also a common strain popular in current anti-feminist rhetoric, which holds that men are basically predators, always on the prowl, and require the virtuous woman to "civilize" them. This is a breathtaking put-down of men.

We complain of the hysterical image of the woman who "finds herself pregnant" and needs her abortion paid for by "the one who did this to you," as if the idea that she is responsible for herself, or in control of her life, were impossible. The predator image of men suggests that a man is not responsible for himself or in control of his life either, but subject to irresistible impulses.

It is striking to set the stereotype of feminist man-haters against this man-hating anti-feminist rhetoric. Likewise, just as some women organized against suffrage, the Equal Rights Amendment, and other matters of benefit to women, men are expounding on this anti-male theme with vigor.

One way this insulting predator image hurts women as well as men is the role assigned to the virtuous woman: to keep men in line. If she fails to do so, if she makes herself sexually available—indeed, if she fails to make herself emphatically sexually unavailable—then she has not done her job. *His* bad behavior becomes *her* fault. This becomes an example of an airtight blame-the-victim strategy.

As this gender theory of man-as-predator gets worked out, a striking paradox emerges. It would seem to be a forceful argument against any form of male domination; she should rather take control of disciplining that conscienceless brute. It's therefore puzzling to see proponents of the theory upholding female submissiveness as virtuous. The philosophy that has women being submissive to husbands—or potential husbands—is in internal conflict with the philosophy that sees women's role as taming the prowling male.

In my frequent radio talk-show interviews on prolife feminism, the subject of male irresponsibility for their own children comes up constantly. It's one of the major causes of abortion, and comes clearly under the heading of abortion as a male-dominated society's oppression of women. But whenever I make this point, I follow up by adding that men are entitled to be nurturing of their children—not just the wallet and spanking paddle of the family, not nurturing confined to an occasional storybook or baseball game, but involved in the whole spectrum of childrearing, just as women are expected to be.

Abortion, then, has another negative effect on the development of healthy, responsible roles for male adulthood. While it rewards rotten fathers by letting them off the hook, making it easier to use women and walk away, abortion can also punish men who would be good, sensitive fathers by telling them to chill their emotions until birth and don't begin bonding: they have no right to care about that "tissue."

Men who engage in exploitative behavior are indeed one of the root causes of abortion, and we should cry that from the rooftops. But it is not properly sensitive to oppression, not really feminist or egalitarian, if we leave it there. Just as you can't help the unborn child without helping the mother, and you can't hurt that child without hurting the mother, it's also true that the very same things that hurt women worst also hurt men.

Equality goes both ways—women becoming equal to men, men becoming equal to women. If it doesn't go both ways, then we are accepting the model of "natural" male superiority at the same time that we rebel against it.

Men get post-abortion syndrome. Men usually have a strong desire, not merely to protect, but to be strongly involved in the raising of their children. Thoroughly right-wing men will often become more sympathetic to feminism when they understand that we value and support such male interests as these.

Making this connection is crucial because otherwise anger at oppression leads merely to different forms of oppression. If feminism is about dispensing with oppression, all of it, we must identify "The Oppressor" not as a set of individuals, but as the attitudes and philosophies that confine both women and men.

—*Sisterlife*, Fall 1991

Schools of Thought
by Rachel MacNair

Every large movement has internal disagreements. Hostile outsiders call these factions. If the movement accepts that designation, the opposition succeeds in making it a divided movement. If they are regarded as schools of thought rather than factions, the movement is strengthened by its diversity.

Among divisions common to every movement:

1. The "purists" vs. the "pragmatists." Purists say compromise is immoral and detrimental in the long run. Pragmatists argue for an "all or something" approach. In the prolife movement, American Life League (ALL) is the largest purist group, and split from the National Right to Life Committee (NRL), the pragmatists, over that point. Among abortion defenders, the National Organization for Women (NOW) springs to mind as purist, and has come under fire from pragmatist groups for it. (Someone in the National Women's Political Caucus was quoted as saying she'd like to take out a contract on Molly Yard for proposing a third political party.)

2. The "straight" people vs. the "street" people. Nonviolent "street" people argue that it's immoral to wait for normal legal channels rather than taking direct action immediately, versus "straight" people who believe respectability is important, and being outside the system is harmful to the cause. In the prolife movement, of course, nonviolent rescuers are "street" people, and NRL emphasizes respectability. This isn't a strict division, of course; both schools of thought are represented in normal legal demonstrations, and large numbers of people will engage in both kinds of activities. NOW tries hard to essentially do both. Still, there are tensions between the points of view.

3. "Single Issue" vs. "Everything's Connected." In prolife circles, the latter school of thought may be the consistent life ethic position, or alternatively the pro-family blanket of issues typically espoused by the right. That shows immediately what people see of value in the single issue approach—people of widely divergent views can still work together on a single problem.

I would argue that, on all the above points, both schools of thought are correct and add strength to the movement.

1. If the entire movement stands ready to compromise, the final goal could get lost, and there is value in the strategy of pursuing the fullest expression of the movement's goal. If you convince people that killing

the child is wrong and hurts the mother even in cases of rape and incest, then you've settled the question on just about everything else as well. On the other hand, an all-or-nothing approach will probably end up achieving too much nothing. Compromise can save lives, and moves us closer to the goal than we were before. In short, let the pragmatists push and the purists pull, and between the two of us, we'll get there faster than either one of us alone.

2. Concerning "street" people vs. "straight" people, I recall an instance in which I was attending my state NOW convention. Outside the conference of 50 people, there were 400 prolifers yelling "Stop the Killing Now!" They were regarded as crazy, of course, but an interesting phenomenon occurred: several of the NOW women attending turned to me as the reasonable person to whom they could come and explain their sincerity, that they really weren't advocating mass murder of children, etc. I enjoyed some of the most productive dialogue that I have ever had at such a convention. If I had not been there, the prolife view would have been entirely dismissed as crazy. If the picketers had not been there, I would have had little opportunity for the matter to come up. In our movement, as in any other, a good balance of respectable people wringing their hands over the tactics, while the people in the street keep the issue hot, results in good progress. That's how women finally got the vote.

3. When I was president of FFL, the single-issue vs. multi-issue question got the most passion. We tried to strike a balance by being single-issue, broadly defined. That got us into related issues like equal male responsibility for children, family leave, child care, and opposing rape, but kept us out of issues like religion or the military. This was important, because the word "feminist" was not a gimmick, but required interest in these other issues. We've also been able to work with other groups in coalition on these issues, which didn't dilute but strengthened the single issue. But we have always had scarce resources, and needed to put the priority on what was unique to us, letting other groups take care of what was unique to them.

Balancing all these different schools of thought is not easy. All are valid, and all have something to contribute. But there is no need for a win-lose battle among them. With some strategic thinking and a good understanding of how well they balance, they can all contribute. As different people take different views of where they want to expend their own energies, we can still all work together in harmony.

—*Sisterlife*, Spring 1991; rev. 2004.

Carol Nan Feldman Crossed

After teaching in Kentucky and Maryland, Carol Crossed extended her talents to peace and justice issues, including feminist prolife work, for which she has become an extraordinary activist and organizer. She got her start in social activism during the civil rights movement and the Vietnam War protests of the sixties, risking arrest on numerous occasions. Her protesting since then has focused on human rights issues in Central America and the rights of women and the unborn, for which efforts she has been arrested on at least 18 different occasions.

As an organizer, Crossed has coordinated, chaired, fundraised, and/or served as a delegate to conferences, commissions, workshops, and community hearings committed to spreading the messages of justice and nonviolence and effecting their reality. Her Cherokee heritage has provided her insight concerning issues of diversity and inclusiveness; and she has applied her expertise to such efforts as Project Roothold, an Indian rights cooperative promoting relations between Native North Americans and indigenous peoples in Latin America, the Third World Visiting Journalist Program, the Women's Peace Encampment, the World Health Organization Conference on Women and Children, and the Soviet Realities Conference.

In May of 1993, she testified before the U.S. Senate Judiciary Committee on nonviolent civil disobedience.

She has served the consistent life ethic movement as Vice President of JustLife, Executive Director of Common Ground of Upstate New York, and Executive Director of the Seamless Garment Network. Her articles have appeared in various feminist and pacifist publications; she was editor of *Seeds of Change* from 1980-1986, a news magazine focusing on justice issues surrounding hunger; and she has been a guest speaker for conferences on world hunger, nonviolence, and various other issues affecting women. She has received numerous awards for her activism including the Reconciliation Network honor (1998), the Susan B. Anthony Award (2000), the Gaudete Medal from St. Bonaventure University (2000), and a National Catholic Press Association Award (2000). Currently she is president of Democrats for Life of America and a Consistent Life board member.

FFL Chapter Declines to Be Silenced
by Carol Nan Feldman Crossed

Gandhi would have been proud of FFL of Western New York on the evening of October 1, 1991. Our chapter decided to participate in the local "Take Back the Night" march and rally, despite the fact that the NOW organization demanded that the Women Acting Against Violence committee take an abortion rights position or they would boycott the event. After all, they claimed, not giving women the right to choose (to be violent?) was a violence against women.

Previously, WAAV had agreed to avoid any pro-abortion expression as a courtesy to FFL of Western New York, and the chapter's participation was welcomed at the first "Take Back the Night" in February 1990. But pressure from NOW caused the position in favor of abortion to be resumed, and our chapter was told we could not be a sponsor in the month-long program, nor could we be promised that abortion would not be promoted at the rally.

The Rochester *Democrat and Chronicle* ran an article on this situation, quoting FFL and WAAV steering committee member Suzanne Schnittman as saying, "this does not feel like our interpretation of feminism. This feels like a gag rule." The paper also editorialized against the foolishness, saying that "the campaign to eliminate violence against women needs all the support it can get. It doesn't need ideological litmus tests that only weaken the effort."

Our chapter grappled with the question of what our response should be. We had participated in last year's march, and we were certainly against violence to women (isn't that why we are prolife?). These women were our friends and co-activists when it came to peace and justice issues. They knew us and we knew them. They were our sisters, weren't they?

Yes, we would march with them. Not protest on the sidelines, but be with them. And so we did, over 60 women walking in silence, composing a fourth of the total number present. We carried signs of the true violence of abortion: symbolic tombstones, each with the name of a different woman who died in a legal abortion. Carrying such a testimony of the horror of abortion affected us each deeply.

One participant, Mary Nicholson, later wrote: "I carried a memorial of a woman who bled to death after she was refused follow-up care at the abortion clinic. There is nothing 'alleged' about a death certificate that states a cause of death: hemorrhage. These are the statistics no one dares to publicize. Abortion is the most anti-woman, anti-feminine violence against women in history. The act of suctioning or scraping the inside of her uterus to intentionally cause the death of her baby can hardly be described as nonviolent or humane."

As we arrived at the place where the rally would be held, we once again asked each other, "Should we go in?" Do we sit here and listen to euphemisms like "choice" and "rights" which mean violence against women? Or could we trust them, in the spirit of unity, to focus on those varieties of violence we all oppose?

After some hesitation we decided to go in and found—you guessed it— that all the seats were taken except the ones in the front rows. We filled in those seats, and listened as the emcee, president of the local NOW chapter, gave the introduction. Within three sentences she had gotten to "the violence against women who are exercising their constitutional right to have an abortion."

As if on cue, we all stood. We had no other alternative. We walked out of the hall.

But wait. As we made our way out through the lobby, a woman ran after us, asking where we were going. We explained that we were women who saw abortion as violence, and so could not in conscience stay. The woman asked us please to stay and to listen.

What happened next was nonviolence in action. The woman happened to be Ester Ostertag, founder of a safe house for prostitutes, and the main speaker for the evening! Ms. Ostertag walked up on stage and asked the group to invite us back in. "We need their vision of what violence is. We need to be united," she said. As we resumed our seats, Ms. Ostertag suggested that the group show us a warm welcome, and led a round of applause. At the conclusion of her speech, she left the stage to join us in the front row, greeting us with hugs. The feeling of exhilaration for our chapter was indescribable!

We had another high point just three weeks later, when our chapter sponsored leftist feminist historian Elizabeth Fox-Genovese in a talk at the University of Rochester entitled, "Feminism Without Illusions: Rethinking Abortion." Fox-Genovese is concerned that insisting on individual rights, without considering responsibility to the community, is leading to a fragmented society, "a multiplicity of unrelated cultures and selves." She feels that feminism has been taken over by white, upper middle class women who expect all women to share their expectations and values, and who deny many women's sense that they have rightful obligations to their children and society. Fox-Genovese is ambivalent on the abortion question, saying that it makes her "queasy" and that it is always a taking of life. However, she feels that this could be justified in the first trimester—but not as a woman's unilateral right. Such an action would have to represent the consensus of the community. While not agreeing with every facet of Fox-Genovese's stand, we were pleased to hear the views of one who is in the process of "rethinking abortion."

All kinds of social change have their origin, one way or another, in similar "rethinking." FFL of Western New York hopes that we've opened some minds to new ideas recently, and we look forward to more such opportunities in the future!

—*Sisterlife*, Winter 1992.

Kay Kemper

Kay Kemper (formerly Kay Castonguay) served as the President of FFL Minnesota, one of FFLA's largest and most active state chapters, for several years and also as the national office's Vice President for Chapter Development. A consummate social activist, she helped keep the death penalty out of Minnesota and she took the lead in persuading her home state to pass the nation's first state parental leave legislation. She played a major role in launching the consistent life ethic movement in Minnesota; she was instrumental in the formation of the Pro-Life Alliance of Gays and Lesbians; and she has been a member of Amnesty International, the Animal Rights Coalition, Minnesota Peace Action (formerly Sanefreeze), World Population Balance (an abortion-neutral environmental group), and Hand-Gun Control.

Kemper's writings have appeared in magazines, newspapers and other local publications; we have included here two selections from the FFL Minnesota newsletter. In the second article, Kemper records her observations concerning two issues of interest to feminists: the Clarence Thomas Supreme Court nomination hearings, during which Anita Hill came forward with her accusations of sexual harassment, and the William Kennedy Smith rape trial. The revelations concerning sexual harassment by Senator Robert Packwood, Oregon, which surfaced after Kemper wrote her article, suggest that some feminists need to reexamine their uncritical view of prochoice legislators as feminist heroes.[1]

Enough Violence, Enough Hatred, Enough Injustice
by Kay Kemper

Recently I took part in a two-day leadership-training course. Continuing education is absolutely essential to good leadership. Apparently, the instructor's curiosity got the better of her, and, during a break, she walked over to my table and asked the inevitable question: "You're really in the heat of things, aren't you? Tell me about Feminists for Life." Everyone at the table turned to look at me expectantly, as I mentally braced myself, and responded.

Few words generate stronger feelings than the words "feminist" and "prolife." Sometimes I know how celebrities feel when they don their sunglasses and try to fade into the background. Every once in a while, it's nice to go incognito, to know that occasionally one can function socially without generating controversy. As I started to go into the history of the early feminists, and progressed into our present-day platform, I could sense a growing awareness and understanding among my listeners.

Just as the early feminists did, we take a consistent life ethic approach to issues. The end result is that we don't think like other people do—in spite of societal conditioning, we reject an either/or approach to life and justice concerns. The rest of the world tends to pit one group of human beings against another, then decides which group gets to survive and which group gets sacrificed (some people refer to that as "choice"). It's either women against their unborn children, blacks against whites, the innocent against the guilty, Americans against foreigners, straights against gays, etc.

The end result of this "lifeboat ethics" philosophy is discrimination, war, abortion, the death penalty, and other assorted forms of violence.

We view human life as a continuum, from conception to natural death, and act accordingly. Unlike most, we don't look at a major human problem and then attempt to decide who gets to live and who doesn't. We look at major problems and attempt to solve them as constructively peacefully as possible.

Violence, too, is interconnected. One of the training session participants shared with us her work in the prison system. She found in the course of her work that most violent offenders were themselves victims of violence earlier in their lives—they never learned any other way of dealing with their problems. I added that the death penalty is part of that pattern of perpetuating violence. Studies have shown that a high percentage of death row inmates were themselves victims of various forms of child abuse.

I went on to explain how violence perpetuates itself—no matter what its form, abortion, sexism, social neglect, abuse, military aggression, the death penalty. All of these things demean us as human beings and invite further abuses. What this society needs is not further abuses nor increases in violence. This society needs real solutions. That's what we're here for.

Instead of placing human beings in either/or situations, our job is to encourage people to see the interconnected nature of human life. The unborn child killed by abortion, the abused child, the battered woman, the homeless man who dies of society's neglect—all are victims of violence. If we write off any group of people because of convenience or our own prejudices, we effectively write off ourselves. It's not a case of either/or, it's a case of "and." We as a society will be judged by future generations on how we treat those among us who are unable to defend themselves. Instead of taking the Hatfield v. McCoy approach to life like most others have taken, FFL, along with other consistent life ethic groups, is willing to stand up and say, "enough violence, enough hatred, enough injustice. It stops here, with us. We will not continue along this path of continuing violence."

One of the key phrases in the leadership training course was the following: "Do not follow where the path may lead. Go instead where there is no path and leave a trail." I believe that we are doing just that. By our actions, our vision of the world, and our direction, we are traveling down a new path.

Hopefully, the rest of the world will follow.

—1995.

Of Clarence and Anita and Willie and the Unknown Woman[2]
by Kay Kemper

Undoubtedly, one of the biggest winter headlines was the William Kennedy Smith rape trial. Following closely on the heels of the Clarence Thomas/Anita Hill controversy, it, too, held most of us captive to our TV sets for several days. Both cases bore a great deal of similarity—a woman claiming mistreatment and oppression at the hands of a powerful male figure—a familiar scenario that has been played out with minor variations throughout history. But there seemed to be a crucial difference between the two cases. I couldn't quite put my finger on it until I received a phone call from a very frustrated woman during the William Kennedy Smith trial. "Where are all the women's groups?" she asked. "I haven't heard of any demonstrations on this poor woman's behalf!"

Of course! That was it! Gone from our TV sets was the omnipresent face of Kate Michelman and other self-proclaimed "feminists" who had repeatedly spoken of their concern for women at the Clarence Thomas Senate hearings. The William Kennedy Smith trial seemed to produce no slogans, buttons, or organized protests. The editorials appearing in major newspapers relating to both cases also markedly differed. During the Thomas nomination hearings, columnists (many of them women) unreservedly threw their hats in Anita Hill's corner: "She's right, he's wrong, case closed."

During the William Kennedy Smith trial, however, many political writers and commentators were singing a far different tune. "Well, she could be telling the truth, but let's not be too hasty. Didn't she fail to prove her case?"

So, why the rush to judgment on Clarence Thomas but not William Kennedy Smith? Some have put forth the theory that since the stakes (meaning the Supreme Court) were higher in the Thomas hearings, more attention was necessarily focused on keeping him out. True, but by the same token, isn't rape a more serious crime than sexual harassment?

And it may have also been a bit harder for the American public to bond with a woman whose name and face were not revealed to them, unlike Anita Hill's.

But I really don't think that either of these theories is the answer. The one glaring difference in both these cases is ABORTION. Think about it. Let's put aside the issue of actual guilt or innocence (we'll leave that can of worms for another time). Just use your imagination for a minute and make a few basic changes: What if Clarence Thomas were suspected of being an abortion supporter instead of an abortion opponent? Would Anita Hill have received the same backing from groups such as NOW and much of the media? And what if William Kennedy Smith were the nephew of Orrin Hatch rather than Ted Kennedy? Get the picture?

This, of course, begs the next question: "Should a plaintiff's or defendant's feelings on abortion determine his or her perceived credibility, the amount of political or organizational support received, even guilt or innocence?"

Of course, it shouldn't. Verbal and physical abuse are serious offenses and both accused and accuser should be entitled to due process and even-handed treatment by groups who purport to speak for women and minorities.

This doesn't seem to have occurred here. Moira Lasch, the plaintiff's attorney in the William Kennedy Smith trial, was lambasted for supposedly being inept and for being either too emotional or too unemotional. No criticism was heard of the female juror who was interviewed on TV's "Inside Edition" after the trial. She was not only blatantly pro-Kennedy (she seemed about ready to confer sainthood on both Willie Smith and Uncle Teddy), she also made an incredibly inept, unprofessional, and anti-woman statement. It seemed that one of the biggest factors that led her to vote for his acquittal was her feeling that Willie Smith was just TOO handsome and TOO charming to have to force himself on any woman!

The case did have its notable exceptions. Anti-pornography crusader Catharine MacKinnon wrote an excellent editorial and didn't allow her feelings on abortion bias her judgment. She referred to the trial as the "second public hanging of a woman who accused a powerful man of sexual violation."

We've said repeatedly that feminism and abortion advocacy are a contradiction. I think we've just proved it.

—*Sisterlife*, 1992.

Benazir Bhutto

Mohtarma Benazir Bhutto, former Pakistani Prime Minister, is the first woman ever elected head of an Islamic nation. She was born in 1952 in Karachi, Pakistan, to a wealthy landowning and political family. Her father, Zulfikar Ali Bhutto, prepared his oldest daughter from girlhood to someday enter national government herself, despite cultural strictures against women in public life. At 16, when she matriculated at Harvard-Radcliffe, she was exhilarated by Americans' relative ease at speaking out against their government in ways that would mean certain prison time in Pakistan. She joined peace marches against the Vietnam War. In 1973, she graduated *cum laude* with a B.A. in Government and then departed for Oxford to study politics, philosophy and economics. The same year, her father was elected Prime Minister as the candidate of the left-leaning Pakistan People's Party (PPP). In 1977, her father was re-elected Prime Minister in parliamentary elections, which his enemies accused him of rigging. Widespread demonstrations broke out. Ten days after Benazir's homecoming to pursue a Foreign Service career, General Zia Ul-Haq declared martial law, placed himself at the head of the government, put her under house arrest, and jailed her father, accusing him of conspiracy to murder a colleague. In 1979, Zulfikar Ali Bhutto was executed by hanging. His colleagues urged Benazir to succeed him at the helm of the PPP.

Benazir Bhutto spent the next seven years under house arrest or exiled in Great Britain. She went back to Pakistan in 1986 and entered an arranged marriage with businessman Asif Ali Zardari. In 1987, after learning of her first pregnancy, General Zia called for the first democratic elections in the country since he had seized power. According to Bhutto, he assumed "a pregnant woman couldn't campaign, I could, I did, and I won."[1] At her swearing-in, she "felt a tremendous sense that Pakistan had showed the way for other Muslim countries, that a woman could be elected as chief executive."

Bhutto's agenda emphasized social concerns: feeding the hungry, reproductive health education and care including voluntary family planning, and relieving gender discrimination through women's development banks and courts and police stations staffed by and for women. Her rationale was that female police officers and judges would, for example, be more sympathetic to female rape victims in a country where they were (and still are) so often considered "disgraces" to their families and justifiable targets for so-called "honor killings." Under Pakistani law, the victim's evidence was not deemed admissible in rape cases, and the testimony of one man was considered equal to the testimony of two women. She remarked to the BBC World Service,

> Above all I want to be remembered for what I did for women . . . I felt that my life has to make a difference to the lives of other women, so in terms of population control or in terms of exposing domestic violence or in terms of permitting women easy access to credit to start business of their own, I have always done my best to allow women to succeed . . . I found that a whole series of people opposed me simply on the grounds that I was a woman. The clerics took to the mosque saying that Pakistan had thrown itself outside the Muslim world and the Muslim *ummah* [community of believers] by voting for a woman, that a woman had usurped a man's place in the Islamic society. I found that my opponents reduced themselves to verbal abuse rather than discuss issues, the very mere fact that I was a woman seemed to drive them into a frenzy.[2]

During each of her three pregnancies, Bhutto felt, her opponents tried to take the most advantage of her:

> I was brought up to believe that a woman can do anything that a man can. But there are certain things that only women can do such as carry a child and I found myself in a very strange position because each time I was pregnant my political opponents somehow thought I would be paralyzed . . . Another time my political opponents had me teargassed at a time I was carrying my youngest child. It was a pretty harrowing experience. I found that the old-fashioned notion that a woman who's expecting a child has to be bedridden was absolutely wrong, a woman can do anything if she's lucky enough not to have morning sickness.[3]

In 1988, Bhutto's opponents accused her of corruption, a common Pakistani political maneuver for ousting rivals from power. As of this writing, the truth of the charges remains undetermined (many Bhutto supporters suspect her spouse of unethical business dealings in his government post). In 1993, Bhutto fought her way back into office when her replacement, Nawaz Sharif, was charged with corruption. In 1996 Sharif again sacked Bhutto, jailed her spouse, and reportedly funded police hit squads and murdered her brother. Bhutto fled to England with her children and awaits a hearing before the Pakistani Supreme Court while investigations continue. Although Bhutto denies all charges, her political troubles reveal the prevalence of corruption and the temptations of power, ambition, and wealth. While the facts are to be determined, they do not call into question the ability of women *per se*—including pregnant women and other mothers—to lead countries, nor the validity of a Muslim feminist vision that embraces both women and the unborn, a vision shared by many other persons.[4] Bhutto's contributions to her country, and particularly Pakistani women and children, have been both positive and remarkable.

Thus we reprint Benazir Bhutto's speech to the 1994 United Nations International Conference in Population and Development, held in Cairo, Egypt. At Cairo, people from the Two-Thirds World for the first time persuaded Americans and Europeans to openly acknowledge that population and quality of life issues could not be remedied apart from overconsumption patterns and the sequestration of economic power in the industrialized, more prosperous nations. And despite the centrality of women's bodies and lives to these very issues, never before had as many as one-third of the delegates been women. For the first time at such a conference, women held leadership roles. The event's Secretary General was Dr. Nasif Sadiq, also of Pakistan, and the keynote speakers were Norwegian Prime Minister (and future World Health Organization head) Gro Harlem Bruntland, and Benazir Bhutto.[5]

Wearing the head-scarf that Muslimahs deem a sign of their devotion to God, she presented an often unrecognized face of her billion-strong faith tradition: the face of a modern feminist woman confidently rooted in her religion even as she challenges what men have made of it.

"We All Have a Right to Dream"
by Her Eminence Mohtarma Benazir Bhutto

Bismillahir-Rahmanir-Rahim
[Arabic, "In the name of God/Allah, the Compassionate, the Merciful"][6]

Mr. President, Secretary General, distinguished delegates, ladies and gentlemen,

I come before you as a Woman; as a Mother; and as a Wife.

I come before you as the democratically elected Prime Minister of a great Muslim nation—the Islamic Republic of Pakistan.

I come before you as the leader of the ninth largest population on earth.

Ladies and Gentlemen,

We stand on the cross roads of history.

The choices that we make today will affect the future of mankind.

Out of the debris of the Second World War arose the impulse to reconstruct the world.

Large communities of people exercised their right of self-determination by establishing nation states of their own.

The challenge of economic development led, in several instances, to group-formation where states subordinated their individual destiny to collective initiatives.

It seemed for a while that these collective efforts would determine the political architecture of the future.

The events of the last few years have, however, made us aware of the growing complexity and contradictions of the human situation.

The end of the cold war should have freed immense resources for development.

Unfortunately, it led to the re-emergence of subregional tensions and conflicts. In extreme cases, there was a breakup of nation states.

Sadly, instead of coming nearer, the objective of a concerted global action to address common problems of mankind seems lost in the twilight.

The problem of population stabilization faced by us today cannot be divorced from our yesterdays.

Ironically enough, population has risen fastest in areas which were weakened most by the unfortunate experience of colonial domination

The third world communities have scarce resources spread thinly over a vast stretch of pressing human needs.

We are unable to tackle questions of population growth on a scale commensurate with the demographic challenge.

Since demographic pressures, together with migration from disadvantaged areas to affluent states, are urgent problems, transcending national frontiers, it is imperative that in the field of population control, global strategies and national plans work in unison.

Perhaps that is a dream. But we all have a right to dream.

Ladies and gentlemen,

I dream of a Pakistan, of an Asia, of a world where every pregnancy is planned, and every child conceived is nurtured, loved, educated and supported.

I dream of a Pakistan, of an Asia, of a world not undermined by ethnic divisions brought upon by population growth, starvation, crime and anarchy.

I dream of a Pakistan, of an Asia, of a world, where we can commit our social resources to the development of human life and not to its destruction.

That dream is far from the reality we endure.

We are a planet in crisis, a planet out of control, a planet moving towards catastrophe. The question before us at this conference is whether we have the will, the energy, and the strength to do something about it.

I say we do. We must.

What we need is a global partnership for improving the human condition.

We must concentrate on that which unites us. We should not examine issues that divide us. Our document should seek to promote the objective of planned parenthood, of population control.

This conference must not be viewed by the teaming masses of the world as a universal social charter seeking to impose adultery, abortion, sex education and other such matters on individuals, societies and religions which have their own social ethos.

By convening this conference, the international community is reaffirming its resolve that problems of a global nature will be solved through global efforts.

Governments can do a great deal to improve the quality of life in our society.

But there is much that governments cannot do.

Governments do not educate our children. Parents educate children. More often mothers educate children.

Governments do not teach values to our children. Parents teach values to our children. More often mothers teach values to children.

Governments do not socialize youngsters into responsible citizens. Parents are the primary socializing agents in society. In most societies, that job belongs to the mother.

How do we tackle population growth in a country like Pakistan? We tackle it by tackling infant mortality. By providing villages with electrification. By raising an army of women, 33,000 strong, to educate our mothers, sisters, daughters in child welfare and population control.

By setting up a bank run by women for women, to help women achieve economic independence. And, with economic independence, have the wherewithal to make independent choices.

I am what I am today because of a beloved father who left me independent means, to make independent decisions, free of male prejudice in my society, or even in my family.

As chief executive of one of the nine largest populated countries in the world, I and the Government are faced with the awesome task of providing for homes, schools, hospitals, sewerage, drainage, food, gas, electricity, employment and infrastructure.

In Pakistan, in a period of 30 years—from 1951 to 1981—our population rose by 50 million.

At present it is 126 million.

By the year 2020, our population may be 243 million. In 1960 one acre of land sustained one person. Today one acre of land sustains 2.5 people.

Pakistan cannot progress, if it cannot check its rapid population growth.

Check it we must, for it is not the destiny of the people of Pakistan to live in squalor and poverty condemned to a future of hunger and horror.

That is why, along with the 33,000 lady health workers and the women's bank, the government has appointed 12,000 community motivators across the country.

To educate and motivate our people to a higher standard of living through planned families, spaced families, families that can be nurtured.

In our first budget, we demonstrated our commitment to human resource development.

We increased social sector spending by 33%. And by the year 2000 we intend to take Pakistan's educational expenditure from 2.19% where we found it to 3% of our Gross National Product.

This is no easy task for a country with a difficult International Monetary Fund structural programme.

With a ban on economic and military assistance from the only superpower in the world.

With 2.4 million Afghan refugees forgotten by the world.

With more Kashmiri refugees coming in needing protection.

But we are determined to do it. For we have a commitment to our people.

A commitment based on principles.

Such a commitment demands that we take decisions which are right, which are not always popular.

Leaders are elected to lead nations.

Leaders are not elected to let a vocal narrow-minded minority dictate an agenda of backwardness.

We are committed to an agenda for change.

An agenda to take our mothers and our infants into the 21st century with the hope of a better future.

A future free from diseases that rack and ruin.

A future free from polio, from goiter, from blindness caused by deficiency in vitamin A.

These are the battles that we must fight, not only as a nation but as a global community.

These are the battles on which history—and our people—will judge us. These are the battles to which the mosque and the church must contribute, along with governments and nongovernmental organisations and families.

Empowerment of women is one part of this battle.

Today women pilots fly planes in Pakistan, women serve as judges in the superior judiciary, women work in police stations, women work in our civil service, our foreign service and our media.

Our working women uphold the Islamic principle that all individuals are equal in the eyes of God.

By empowering our women, we work for our goal of population stabilization and, with it, promotion of human dignity.

But the march of mankind to higher heights is a universal and collective concern.

Regrettably, the conference's document contains serious flaws in striking at the heart of a great many cultural values, in the north and in the south, in the mosque and in the church.

In Pakistan our response will doubtless be shaped by our belief in the eternal teachings of Islam.

Islam is a dynamic religion committed to human progress. It makes no unfair demands of its followers.

The Holy Qur'an says:

Allah wishes you ease, and wishes not hardship for you.

Again the Holy Book says:

He has chosen you, and has not laid on you any hardship in religion.

The followers of Islam have no conceptual difficulty in addressing questions of regulating population in the light of available resources.

The only constraint is that the process must be consistent with abiding moral principles.

Islam lays a great deal of stress on the sanctity of life.

The Holy Book tells us:

Kill not your children on a plea of want.

We provide sustenance for them and for you.

Islam, therefore, except in exceptional circumstances, rejects abortion as a method of population control.

There is little compromise on Islam's emphasis on the family unit.

The traditional family is the basic unit on which any society rests.

It is the anchor on which the individual relies as he embarks upon the Journey of Life.

Islam aims at harmonious lives built upon a bedrock of conjugal fidelity and parental responsibility.

Many suspect that the disintegration of the traditional family has contributed to moral decay.

Let me state, categorically, Mr. Chairman, that the traditional family is the union sanctified by marriage.[7]

Muslims, with their overriding commitment to knowledge would have no difficulty with dissemination of information about reproductive health, so long as its modalities remain compatible with their religious and spiritual heritage.

Lack of all adequate infrastructure of services, and not Ideology, constitutes our basic problem.

The major objective of the population policy of the newly elected democratic government is a commitment to improve the quality of life of the people through provision of family planning and health services.
Mr. Chairman,

We refuse to be daunted by the immensity of the task.

But the goals set by this conference would become realistic only with the whole-hearted cooperation amongst the nations of the world.

Bosnia, Somalia, Rwanda and Kashmir are but a few reminders of how far we have departed from our principles and ideals.

In many parts of the world we witness the nation-state under siege.

The rise of so-called fundamentalism in some of our societies, and emergence of neo-fascism, in some western communities, are symptoms of a deeper malaise.

I believe the nation states might just have failed to meet their people's expectations within their own limited national resources or ideological framework.

If so, the malady is probably none other than a retreat from the ideals of the Founding Fathers of the United Nations.

We can, perhaps, still restore mankind to vibrant health by returning to those ideals the ideals of Global Cooperation.

Given that background, I hope that the delegates participating in this conference will act in wisdom, and with vision to promote population stabilization.

Pakistan's delegation will work constructively for the finalization of a document enjoying the widest consensus.

Ladies and gentlemen,

Our destiny does not lie in our stars. It lies within us. Our destiny beckons us. Let us have the strength to grasp it.

Thank you, President Mubarak, for hosting this Conference on such an important global concern. And thank you Mr. [UN] Secretary General and Dr. Nafis Sadik for making it possible.

Thank you.

—Official statement of Pakistani nation to the United Nations International Conference in Population and Development, 4 Sept. 1994.

Jennifer Ferguson

"Our voices, fortunately, never lie," Jennifer Ferguson often says. Ferguson is one of South Africa's leading creative artists, a music therapist, longtime social justice activist, and former Member of Parliament ("MP," 1994-1997) for the post-apartheid ruling party, the African National Congress (ANC). The truthtelling, healing nature of the voice is a recurrent motif in the musical, dramatic, and poetry pieces she has composed and performed. During the 1980s and early 1990s, the apartheid regime banned most of her work. Ferguson studied English, politics, and drama performance at the University of Cape Town, and learned vocal, instrumental and sound healing methods from many cultures. She expresses deep gratitude for

> The gift of encountering so many extraordinary women and men of the South African Story of liberation, the poets, the philosophers, writers, performers, activists, mothers of the nation . . . the vast landscape of South Africans that have inspired my work and challenged my perceptions . . . And of course, the deeply resonant work of mothering and partnership . . . in many of these aspects I am still a student at the feet of these teachers.[1]

During the 1980s, Ferguson experienced both a legal abortion and an illegal, backstreet attempt at one. During her parliamentary term, she was raising her son Ralph as a single mother when she met and married the Swedish composer and musician Anders Nyberg. She has had two more children since: son Gabriel and daughter Joanna, who has Down Syndrome. Ferguson's journey through abortion and motherhood helped to shape her best-known decision as an MP.

In 1996, the Choice on Termination of Pregnancy Bill proposed the most unrestricted abortion access of almost any law in the world, save that of China or the U.S. It cast the abortion issue in bitterly polarizing terms out of synch with the far more holistic views South Africans of all races and religions tend to have.[2] Despite the fact that most of its rank and file members opposed abortion on "demand," and many others were quite ambivalent, the ANC ordered all its parliamentary representatives to vote "yes" for the bill: a directive that guaranteed passage. About 100 dissenting ANC MPs walked out the day of the vote. Ferguson stayed and cast her lone abstention. Even as Catholic bishops lauded Ferguson, her ANC colleague and sister feminist leader Pregs Govender charged her in an open letter with "self-righteousness and smugness" and a lack of compassion for victims of rape, women in poverty, and other difficult cases. Ferguson publicly responded that she was, in fact, acting with compassion for the vulnerable and oppressed.[3]

Contrary to expectations, the ANC never formally disciplined Ferguson. In 1997, she resigned from Parliament. Even as she and her views evolve, Ferguson stands by her controversial vote.

Abortion Issue Is One of Peace
by Jennifer Ferguson

Dear Pregs,

Thank you for your open letter to me ... I was moved by its power.

This is a response that will clarify my decision to abstain in the vote on the Choice on Termination of Pregnancy Bill.

We have both come from the time of struggle where our common dream was to realise the liberation of all in this country, especially the women. We have worked in different ways, but always aspiring to give voice to the voiceless, power to the disempowered, human dignity for all.

Now we as women sit in the national Parliament, exercising our power, having been given voice by those who voted us in.

It is the time of a new struggle but, true to tradition, our mandate, is still to give voice to the voiceless.

The bill has been given to the women of SA as a step towards our empowerment. If however, we see abortion only as an issue of women's liberation, we have planted a seed of another cycle of oppression one which neglects to hear that most silent voice of all, the voice of the unborn child.

In your letter you list the circumstances under which pregnancy may be terminated, from the 13th up to and including the 20th week. I quote: "The bill is very clear that abortion after 12 weeks will be allowed only under those specific circumstances outlined such as rape, danger to the physical or mental health of the women and so on."

If we look at what's hidden behind "and so on" there's more to it. We find in clause 2(1)(b)(iv), one of the main reasons I abstained from voting:

"A pregnancy may be terminated if the continued pregnancy would significantly affect the social or economic circumstances of the woman."

Every child affects the social and economic circumstances of a woman significantly. At 20 weeks, premature babies have been known to survive.

When does life begin? When is life given value? Who is to decide? The mother, the doctor, the father, the foetus, the MP?

When you list our litany of social ills in the abortion context, the street child, the malnourished, the abused child, would it have been a better solution had they been aborted? Is not the face of the suffering child a cry to humanity for compassion? If our compassion truly encompassed the unborn child, surely the life of the street child would also be affected?

If we see the foetus as the "other", the obstacle, objectified as it is in the terminology of the bill, where the unborn child is defined as "the contents of the uterus of a pregnant woman", we are indeed dehumanising ourselves.

In India, where abortion has been legalised for some time now, there is statistical evidence of a severe shortage of women in the future. Why? The majority of the abortions are girl-foetuses, exposed on the screen of the ultra-sound scan. Is this liberation for women? Is this what we are fighting for?

My problem with the pro-choice position as it stands is that it is not radical enough. We've fallen into the old trap of dualistic perception that positions the right of the mother against the right of "the other," the child. Our bodies, their lives.

On the pro-life side on the other hand, there is a financial and media core that consists of American conservatives trying to buy up the issue to suit their agenda. The banners of these pro-life protesters also proclaim pro-gun, pro-bomb, pro-death penalty. Need I distance myself from them?

We need a new way of seeing! We need to understand with empathy that abortion is a symptom not a solution. We need debate, education, awareness.

Are we as a nation ready to take on the moral challenges that arise out of the bill's implementation?

As an MP I felt unable to reduce the complexity of the issue into a mere choice of two buttons. Surely there is more to it?

I was searching for the third way, the one that could compassionately embrace both mother and child. I know many of my colleagues were in a similar dilemma.

When time came for voting, a neighbourly comrade held my hand and said: "Press the yes-button, my darling, then go home and pray to God."

It wasn't an easy decision. We had been instructed that the vote was to be one of no conscience. I didn't know how I would be able to vote without conscience.

The option of leaving the chamber and going for tea as many of our colleagues did, made little sense to me. I stayed. I abstained.

Pregs, you quoted in your letter "the words of that great being of compassion and love, Let he who is without sin cast the first stone."

The simple and powerful beauty of his words does not end there. There is more to it. Having said this to the teachers of the law, he turned to the accused woman with the words: "I don't condemn you either. Go now and sin no more."

Of course we have a choice. Life is choice. In its deepest sense the abortion issue is a peace issue, maybe the most important one for this country and the world today.

Abortion is a rejection of the innermost, but if we reject the rejectors we reject ourselves.

In order to attain peace in it we must embrace the rejected, true to that being of compassion and love, himself an illegitimate child, significantly affecting the social and economic situation of his mother.

—*Cape Times*, 18 November 1996.

Lorraine Hansberry (1930-1965) and Bernadette Waterman Ward

Playwright Lorraine Hansberry came from a prominent family of African-American activists and intellectuals on Chicago's South Side. Paul Robeson, Langston Hughes, and W.E.B. Dubois were regular visitors to their house. When she was eight, her parents purchased a home in an all-white neighborhood, becoming targets of violence. They won an antisegregation lawsuit before the Illinois Supreme Court. At 20, after dropping out of the University of Wisconsin, Lorraine Hansberry moved to New York to establish herself as a literary author. She worked as a waitress, cashier, and associate editor on Paul Robeson's *Freedom*. In 1953, Hansberry wed Robert Nemiroff, a Jewish songwriter she met on a picket line. After Nemiroff had a hit song, Hansberry concentrated full-time on writing. In 1957, beginning to recognize her lesbian identity, she joined the Daughters of Bilitis, a pioneering, San Francisco-based "homophile" or gay-rights organization, and wrote in the August issue of its magazine *The Ladder*: "Homosexual persecution has at its roots not only social ignorance, but a philosophically active anti-feminist dogma."[1]

In response to the dearth of parts for Black actors and roles portraying "ordinary" people's responses to oppression, Hansberry wrote *A Raisin in the Sun*, based on her family's own confrontation with housing discrimination. In 1959, after several hugely acclaimed runs outside New York, it became the first Broadway-produced drama by an African-American woman. She became the fifth woman and the first African American to receive a New York Drama Critics' Circle Award. Starring Sidney Poitier as Walter Lee, *Raisin* ran on Broadway for over 500 performances and was made into a movie. To mark the Civil War centennial, NBC-TV quickly commissioned Hansberry's next play, *The Drinking Gourd*, then refused production, claiming her "too-controversial" depiction of slavery. *The Sign in Sidney Brustein's Window* enjoyed a moderately successful Broadway run. The same year, 1964, Hansberry and Nemiroff divorced, but remained close friends. When she died of cancer at 34, he became her literary executor. Nemiroff helped to publish and produce *To Be Young, Gifted, and Black* (play, 1969; book,

1970) and *Les Blancs* (1970), and collaborated on the Tony Award-winning musical adaptation of *Raisin* (1973). The musical was revived on Broadway (1981) and the drama produced for television (1991).

Lorraine Hansberry's prophetic work has inspired wide-ranging critical explorations that, in Bernadette Waterman Ward's view, have made a rather curious omission. Here Waterman Ward poses previously unasked (to our knowledge) questions about *Raisin*. Waterman Ward received her Ph.D. from Stanford after a *magna cum laude* A.B. at Harvard. She has authored *World as Word: Philosophical Theology in Gerard Manley Hopkins* (Catholic University of America Press, 2002) and numerous articles on nineteenth- and twentieth-century English and American literature. An associate professor of English at the University of Dallas, she is on the board of the Venerable John Henry Newman Association and a member of University Faculty for Life, Feminists for Life, and the Colloquium on Violence and Religion. The reflections below bring to mind Hansberry's assertion that "all art is ultimately social"[2] and her admirer James Baldwin's image of *Raisin* as "flesh and blood—corroborating flesh and blood—as we say, testifying."[3]

Silencing Lorraine Hansberry
by Bernadette Waterman Ward

A lot of academic scholarship starts with a footnote. "Where did that come from?" you ask, and then chase down the chain of evidence and start to form your own conclusions. That's what annotation is for. But this investigation starts with a footnote that was intended to keep people from forming their own conclusions. This year I was preparing to teach *A Raisin in the Sun* by Lorraine Hansberry, from a very standard textbook, *The Norton Introduction to Literature*, Seventh Edition. Sadly, even after forty years of effort in civil rights, not much in the play really needed explaining. However, towards the end of Act 1 in the Norton edition, there is a footnote. The section and the note are quoted below.

Mama is talking to her son Walter, with his wife Ruth nearby, but, as usual, Ruth is not saying much.

> Mama: Son-how come you talk so much 'bout money?
> Walter: (WITH IMMENSE PASSION) Because it is life, Mama!
> Mama: (QUIETLY) Oh—(VERY QUIETLY) So now it's life. Money is life. Once upon a time freedom used to be life—now it's money. I guess the world really do change . . . .

Walter: No—it was always money, mama. We just didn't know about it.

Mama: No . . . something has changed. (SHE LOOKS AT HIM.) You something new, boy. In my time we was worried about not getting lynched and getting to the North if we could and how to stay alive and still have a pinch of dignity too . . . . Now here come you and Beneatha—talking 'bout things we ain't never even thought about hardly, me and your daddy. You ain't satisfied or proud of nothing we done. I mean that you had a home; that we kept you out of trouble till you was grown; that you didn't have to ride to work on the back of nobody's streetcar—you my children—but how different we done become.

Walter: you just don't understand, Mama, you just don't understand.

Mama: Son—do you know your wife is expecting another baby? (WALTER STANDS, STUNNED, AND ABSORBS WHAT HIS MOTHER HAS SAID) That's what she wanted to talk to you about. (WALTER SINKS DOWN INTO A CHAIR) This ain't for me to be telling—but you ought to know. (SHE WAITS) I think Ruth is thinking 'bout getting rid of that child.

Walter: (SLOWLY UNDERSTANDING) No—no—Ruth wouldn't do that.

Mama: When the world gets ugly enough—a woman will do anything for her family. *The part that's already living.*

Walter: You don't know Ruth, Mama, if you think she would do that. (RUTH OPENS THE BEDROOM DOOR AND STANDS THERE A LITTLE LIMP)

Ruth: (BEATEN) Yes I would too, Walter. (PAUSE) I gave her a five-dollar down payment. (THERE IS TOTAL SILENCE AS THE MAN STARES AT HIS WIFE AND THE MOTHER STARES AT HER SON)

Mama: (PRESENTLY) Well—(TIGHTLY) Well—son, I'm waiting to hear you say something . . . . I'm waiting to hear how you be your father's son. Be the man he was . . . . (PAUSE) Your wife say she going to destroy your child. And I'm waiting to hear you talk like him and say we a people who give children life, not who destroys them—(SHE RISES) I'm waiting to see you stand up and look like your daddy and say we done give up one baby to poverty and we ain't going to give up nary another one . . . . I'm waiting.

> Walter: Ruth—
>
> Mama: If you a son of mine, tell her! (WALTER TURNS, LOOKS AT HER, AND CAN SAY NOTHING. SHE CONTINUES, BITTERLY) You . . . you are a disgrace to your father's memory. Somebody get me my hat.

This is the turning point of the play. This is when mama goes out and buys a house. The footnote to this scene reads, "Abortions were illegal and dangerous at that time."[4]

One of the principles of good scholarly editing is that you don't muscle in between the author and the reader. If something speaks for itself, let it speak. On that principle alone, you can imagine how appalled I was at reading this footnote. One can sometimes excuse an intrusive note on the grounds that social sentiments have undergone such a drastic change that it is necessary to explain them in terms contemporary students will understand; indeed, some noises of that sort come into the editorial head that matter to the play. But this assumes that the disapproval of abortion is something so foreign that it cannot be explained in anything like the terms in which the playwright explains it; moral opposition is presented as a simply incomprehensible relic of the past. For contrast, take another selection in the same book, "Song: To Lucasta, Going to the Wars," by Richard Lovelace:

> True, a new mistress now I chase,
> The first foe in the field;
> And with a stronger faith embrace
> A sword, a horse, a shield.
>
> Yet this inconstancy is such
> As you too shall adore;
> I could not love, thee, dear, so much,
> Loved I not honor more.[5]

Now there's a bit of cultural sentiment that's undergone some change. The Norton editors didn't touch it.

The policy of letting things explain themselves is generally followed even in *A Raisin in the Sun*. The editors leave Walter unchallenged when he says to his sister, who wants to be a doctor, "Go be a nurse like other women—or just get married and be quiet" (I. i., p.1813). Neither do they challenge Mama when she tells Walter: "I'm telling you to be the head of this family from now on like you supposed to be" (II.ii, p.1846) or saying of him, when he has taken charge of their financial affairs on a moral basis, "He finally come into his manhood today" (III, p. 1869). Now, a definition of manhood that depends on making the women's financial decisions is mightily offensive to women under today's cultural conditions,[6] yet the editors present nothing to explain it away.

And so I asked my students, just to ascertain that Hansberry's meaning was clear. "Is Mama horrified about abortion because she's afraid Ruth is going to damage her health? Or because she'd break a law?" Of course, even when there were laws against abortion, the criminal was the doctor—the woman was a witness—but until I told them, my students didn't know that. Still, they could all tell that these were not the sources of Mama's horror or Walter's dumbfoundedness. No, thematically it was all clear. Hansberry mercilessly denigrates Walter's manhood throughout the first two acts. She shows his subordination to his mother, intellectual inferiority to his sister, financial dependence on his wife, and irresponsibility to his employers. Here he is belittled again: he is incapable of protecting his child. When Walter's mother says, "We a people who give children life, not destroys them," my students understood her not as a caricature of a conservative fanatic but as the great moral authority in the play. Opening night critics understood her the same way: "the old lady achieves real stature," said one, and "nobility of spirit," said another; she "teaches self-respect to her willful offspring," said a third and, as another concluded, she is the "solid rock on which a Chicago Negro family is founded."[7] The play was originally titled "The Crystal Stair," after Langston Hughes's poem "Mother to Son," in which a woman who has worked as a housemaid all her life—like Mama—rises to become a figure of heroic nobility as she gives her advice to her discouraged son.[8] My students didn't know that poem, but they knew that the mother in this play wants only, as Brooks Atkinson said, "that her children adhere to the code of honor and self-respect that she inherited."[9] Hansberry herself identified Mama with one of the patron saints of the Civil Rights movement: Mama is "the Rosa Parks sitting in the front of the bus in Montgomery."[10] Mama embodies integrity and self-respect; when abortion appalls her, that moral horror is central.

I asked my students why Hansberry chose to put a pregnancy in the play, and immediately they came up with the most important literary reason: a pregnancy always symbolizes new life and involves the audience's emotions in hopes for that new life (as John Conley has demonstrated).[11] Of course everyone wants the baby to live; of course abortion means a complete social and personal collapse. The visceral power of the symbolism was so obvious as to make my questions seem almost trivial. Mercilessly Hansberry shows us that Ruth acts not out of self-directed desire to improve her life, but for the reasons Frederica Mathewes-Greene heard over and over, from women who procured abortions: because she thinks other people want her to.[12] Ruth is shown from the beginning as a woman running on automatic. She has learned to disregard her husband, as all the other women in the family do, even when he desperately needs to tell her that he loves her and wants a better life for her. Everyone else has plans for how the $10,000 in insurance money ought to be spent; but Ruth's concept of community is so broken that she thinks Mama would leave them behind and serve her own pleasure. Ruth asks and expects nothing; her rights and will do not matter; that's why Hansberry calls her "limp" and "beaten" in the stage directions to the scene where Walter hears of her abortion plans. She simply feels that the world is a conspiracy of death for her and all who belong to her.

American apartheid was not so unlike South Africa's; there, abortion was a deliberate tool of genocide.[13] Hansberry's African political concerns—very evident in the person of Asagai in the play—indicate a political as well as a thematic reason why Hansberry made Ruth pregnant. It was clear why the family had been driven to think of "killing babies" and "wishing each other dead," as Mama puts it. According to some Black scholars, racism is still the driving force behind the promotion of abortion among African Americans.[14]

The Norton footnote made me wonder about blind spots among Hansberry's other critics. They shifted over time. Opening night criticism touched gingerly, if at all, on the racial oppression on which the whole drama turns. One thought that Hansberry began to touch on racial problems when the Younger family buys a house in a white neighborhood halfway through the play, when in fact race is always the main source of the characters' tension.[15] The next wave of critics saw Hansberry as very racially conscious and lauded Hansberry's prophetic stance on housing integration. Early critics found Walter's pan-Africanist sister Beneatha frivolous in her enthusiasm for the politics of the African college student Joseph Asagai. Later, Hansberry was praised for her remarkably clear-eyed look at the realities of newly independent African nations finding their way out from under colonial oppression.[15] First-night critics had kind words for Walter's "patient little wife." Later critics saw the play as fundamentally an ironic feminist manifesto, the forerunner of a number of feminist and lesbian plays by Black women. Yet later critics marveled at her insightful and, again, prophetic interest in the identity crisis of the African American male in the face of matriarchy.[17]

Obviously, early critics had some substantial blind spots, and the play's political implications flowered more fully as the culture's consciousness evolved. Only one matter to which the earlier critics were not altogether blind have later critics conscientiously ignored. Several opening night critics mentioned Ruth's pregnancy, and others hinted at it, speaking of the "worried wife," or the "young wife burdened with problems." One dropped a hint in describing how Mama "bewailed the loss of a new life for her brood." The Jesuit publication *America* noted both the racial dimension of the play and how Ruth is "contemplating desperate measures."[18] In 1965, Arthur France wrote in *Freedomways* of the terror in the play, including the "terror of abortion" and the "pity for an expectant mother with no place to lay her babe."[19] However, once the movement in favor of abortion came to be established in the American intellectual left, no one noticed Ruth's pregnancy anymore, though it plays a more vital role in the plot than Beneatha's feminism and Asagai's African nationalism.

Behind this selective blindness is the mythic stature of Hansberry as social prophet. Born into a prosperous African American family, with educated parents, she was from her childhood acquainted with some of the greatest people in African American cultural history. Paul Robeson had her represent him at an international conference that he was forbidden to attend by the State Department.[20] Her parents successfully challenged the constitutionality of "restrictive covenants" in real estate, by moving into a legally all-white neighborhood. Eight-year-old Lorraine narrowly missed being brained by a brick through the window, and her mother had to pack a gun inside the house. The playwright met her husband at a civil rights protest; the night before they married they demonstrated against the execution of the Rosenbergs. Her second play became a sort of cause célèbre of the New York theatre-going intelligentsia, who raised funds to keep it open until she died at thirty-four in January 1965.[21] Remarkably prescient about politics, Hansberry had opinions that bellwhethered political trends for the next thirty years. Besides racial equality, African liberation, and feminism, she espoused cooperation between Jews and Blacks, anti-nuclear and anti-war causes, and, now coming to the fore in Hansberry studies, gay rights.[22]

But it is not merely that she could find the corner from which the bandwagon was about to set out. Hansberry had a consistent ethic. Racism, for instance, warps everyone in *Raisin*. Hansberry casts a withering eye on the faults of—well, every character except Mama, and even Mama comes off as a bit overbearing with Beneatha. Of course we hate the villains: Bobo and Willie are smalltime crooks; George Murchison is a blind-hearted materialist; and the white man, Lindner, is a hypocrite and coward beneath contempt. But Hansberry gives us something to repel us in even the good guys. Ruth is a doormat and a liar; Beneatha is an unrealistic, frivolous egotist; Asagai is a sweet-talking sexist; even ten-year-old Travis is manipulative. And the hero of the drama, Walter, is an irresponsible drunkard and a selfish fool.

Rather than reverence, we are asked for understanding and compassion. We don't have to accept it when Walter plays hooky from work for three days for aimless drives and time in a jazz bar. Yet Hansberry demands that we see its context, too. It is the self-destructive rebellion of a stunted man hemmed in by an oppressive life. No one applauds his selfish gullibility when he wastes the family fortune; but we understand him well enough to rejoice in his courage and his sense of honor when they emerge at the end of the play. Hansberry promoted a sort of tough compassion that desires to see that another person should flourish, shed faults, gain in real human stature. Such a love must include everyone who can be brought to greater flourishing. Her reluctance to leave anyone out got her into trouble professionally. In her last stage play (other performances were cobbled together from her works posthumously), there are yet more unlovable characters: a lying prostitute; the man who loves her and rejects her when she tells the truth; a politically apathetic Jew; a self-pitying playwright so focused on his homosexuality that he antagonizes nearly everyone. Hansberry demanded sympathies too various for her audiences to exercise in one night. But her consistency is telling; she really does want to include everybody. Her characters struggle to free themselves of the selfishness, which grew from living under crushing injustice. Her recognition that abortion is a manifestation and instrument of oppression follows logically from her well-respected positions on all sorts of other issues. It is her impeccable credentials as a prophet of the American left that make Hansberry's pro-life sentiments so dangerous that they must be sanitized for freshmen. She is dangerous because of the grand consistency of her vision.

It is true that she did not live to see the abortion bandwagon get rolling. Martin Luther King, Jr. could confidently talk about the Civil Rights movement as modeled after the Christian subversion of the evils of Roman infanticide.[23] Given that civil rights has become the excuse for practices that come within seconds of legally being infanticide—and sometimes slip over the line—his innocence seems amazing; and he died years after Hansberry, though she was younger. Abortion proponents could perhaps make something of Mama's line about the "ones that are already living" for whom the unborn might be sacrificed, though Mama clearly considers Ruth's plan a sign of desperation from which the family and community should defend the woman. King's companion Jesse Jackson gave himself over to the proponents of abortion, and who knows if Hansberry would have been among those who also bowed the knee to Moloch?

The fact is, no one knows what she would have been—and, unlike the frightened editors of the Norton Introduction, we must take her for what she was. She was a woman of courage and conscience, passionate for a moral vision of human integrity and compassion. The fact is that she put onto the American stage a play that not only opposes abortion in the strongest terms but shapes those terms as the Feminists for Life would also articulate them ten years after her death. She too understands that abortion is a tool of oppression and an act of desperation; she too understands that the woman should be considered a victim more than a perpetrator; she too recognizes that an inclusive vision of human flourishing cannot banish the unborn. In a culture whose pressures cost a third of the lives of African American children before they even see the light of day, it is good to have a figure of such political, intellectual, and moral stature call upon that community to consider how to be true to itself: "We a people who give children life, not who destroys them." Let us hope that the people of whom Mama speaks will re-awaken to her vision and their own history and make Mama's grand declaration the proud and undeniable truth.[24]

—Life and Learning, 10, 2000, 333-342; archived at
<http://www.uffl.org/resources.htm>

Serrin M. Foster

Serrin Foster is a prime example of a single person who, like Susan B. Anthony and some other feminist foremothers, has no children of her own but feels a deep responsibility towards and compassion for those who do. Foster succeeded coeditor Rachel MacNair as head of Feminists for Life of America in 1994, when the organization moved from Kansas City, Missouri, to Washington, D.C. Foster graduated from Old Dominion University and served 12 years in the nonprofit sector: seven years at St. Jude Children's Research Hospital (Memphis, Tennessee), and five as development director of the Arlington, Virginia-based National Alliance for the Mentally Ill.

The highly mobile, energetic, dialogue-catalyzing Foster once quipped that she was probably the only person on Capitol Hill who ever divided her day between the American Civil Liberties Union and the conservative Heritage Foundation. Under her leadership, FFLA has grown steadily in numbers and in media visibility and has brought celebrities like the actors Margaret Colin and Patricia Heaton on board. Through the College Outreach Program, Foster has committed FFLA to mobilizing and creating pregnancy, parenting, and adoption resources for unexpectedly expectant women who wish to have their babies and continue their educations. Foster's rhetorical gifts have made her a notable prolife feminist spokesperson. In 1995 she spoke at the U.S. Department of State "Bringing Cairo Home" conference, where she drew parallels between the current needs of women in the Two-Thirds World and those faced by early American feminists. In 1996, at the Republican National Convention, the Creative Coalition invited Foster to join Ambassador Alan Keyes and USA Today special correspondent Linda Chavez in an abortion debate with Massachusetts Governor William Weld and Pennsylvania Senator Arlen Specter. Foster appeared on C-SPAN's "The Politics of Abortion" in 1996 with author Naomi Wolf and former U.S. Treasurer Bay Buchanan. In 1998, Foster was a featured speaker at the first prolife-prochoice conference in Dublin, Ireland, which included former Prime Minister John Bruton and members of Parliament. Entitled "5,000 Too Many," after the number of abortions Irishwomen obtain annually in Great

Britain, the meeting addressed abortion alternatives and practical resources for pregnant women in Ireland. It was inspired by FFLA's Pregnancy Resources Forums to marshal support for mothers on college campuses.

In 1998, Foster and FFLA joined with the ACLU to defend Somer Chipman (now Hurston) and Chasity Glass, two accomplished Kentucky teens barred from the National Honor Society after they chose to carry their nonmarital pregnancies to term. The first selection below is excerpted from her affidavit in the case. The young women won their case and shortly before their high school graduations were greatly applauded and cheered as they were inducted into the National Honor Society.[1] Foster later testified before Congress (transcript below) on behalf of the Unborn Victims of Violence Act addressing non-abortion violence against pregnant women and their unborn children.

Eliminate, Through Practical Solutions, the Root Causes
by Serrin M. Foster

. . . Feminists for Life's mission is to eliminate, through practical solutions, the root causes driving girls and women to abortion. FFL has emerged as the link between pro-life and pro-choice organizations, working on legislative efforts in support of the Violence Against Women Act, child-support enforcement, and removal of the child exclusion provisions in welfare reform. FFL also provides pregnancy resource kits to clinic staff, college counselors and student groups on campuses across the country and leads the discussion to develop nationwide practical resources to support pregnant and parenting students on college campuses. As a result of these efforts, FFL has developed significant insight into and expertise regarding the reasons driving girls and women to abortion and infanticide, the factors causing pregnant and parenting girls and women to become welfare recipients, and the relationship between education, poverty, and welfare.

I understand Somer Chipman and Chasity Glass were denied admission to the National Honor Society by the Grant County School District solely because, at the time the decision to exclude them was made, Ms. Chipman was an expectant mother and Ms. Glass was a mother. As Executive Director of FFL, I strongly believe granting preliminary relief in this case is in the public interest for the reasons set forth below.

According to the Alan Guttmacher Institute, Planned Parenthood's research organization, 1 million adolescent girls—12% of all girls aged 15-19 and 21% of those who have had sexual intercourse—become pregnant each year.

Defendants may argue their decision was necessary to send the message unwed motherhood is undesirable. However, in reality, Defendants' actions send student unwed mothers a different, far more dangerous message: choose between education and career plans, on the one hand, and your children on the other hand. Actions such as those of the Grant County School District encourage students to hide their pregnancies and not seek prenatal care (thereby putting them and their babies at medical risk) and instead obtain an abortion or, worst of all, commit neonatal infanticide. Many of such students are teens who are otherwise highly likely to attend and complete high school and college but fear their academic success is threatened by their own children.

If Ms. Chipman and Ms. Glass had had abortions, their sexual activity would not have become known to school officials. Actions such as those of the Grant County School District thus send a message that a decision to carry a pregnancy to term will be punished. According to the Center for Disease Control and Prevention, nearly 4 in 10 teen pregnancies (excluding miscarriages) end in abortion. There were 308,000 abortions among teens in 1992.

Finally, the fear of punishment by powerful adults such as school officials could well play a role in inducing or encouraging teens to commit neonatal infanticide. Although we do not know the real number of newborns killed each year by their parents (usually the mother), approximately 250 cases of neonatal infanticide are reported annually to the Department of Justice . . .

—from "Affidavit of Serrin M. Foster in Support of Plaintiffs' Motion for Preliminary Injunction," *Somer Chipman and Chasity Glass. et al v. Grant County School District et al.*, Civil Action No. 98-180, U.S. District Court, ED Kentucky, 1998.

One Victim or Two?
by Serrin M. Foster

Good afternoon, Mr. Chairman and Members of the Subcommittee. My name is Serrin Foster and I am the President of Feminists for Life of America. Feminists for Life is an education and advocacy organization that continues the work of the early American feminists who championed both the rights of women and legal protection for the unborn.

Feminists for Life is a member of the National Task Force to End Sexual and Domestic Violence Against Women. As a proud advocate of the Violence Against Women Act, we applaud the universal support by Members of Congress for VAWA. I thank the Members of Congress here who have supported VAWA. We can all be proud that statistics show violence against women has decreased since VAWA was enacted. But there is much more work to be done.

Feminists for Life has a track record of getting beyond deadlock on polarizing issues by addressing the root causes of the problems women face. One of the ways we do this is by listening to women and then prioritizing what women really want. Today I am pleased to speak from that perspective about an urgent question: what is the appropriate response to a woman who has lost her unborn child due to an assault that she survived? What is the appropriate response to survivors when an assault takes the lives of both a pregnant women and the child she carries?

Sarah Norton, an early American feminist who was the first woman to seek admission to Cornell University, asked this question more than a century ago.[2] Speaking of the then-common situation in which an unwilling father attempted to kill an unborn child, she asked, "Had the scheme been successful in destroying only the life aimed at, what could have been the man's crime—and what should be his punishment if, as accessory to one murder he commits two?" Today's victims are speaking loudly and clearly on this issue. We need to listen.

According to a recent two-year study by the Center for the Advancement of Women, run by Faye Wattleton, former president of the Planned Parenthood Federation of America, reducing violence against women is the number one priority of women. Women who are pregnant are at particular risk of being targeted for violence. In fact, recent studies by two different state health departments have shown that a leading cause of maternal mortality is not complications during pregnancy or childbirth—rather, it's homicide. For example, according to the *Journal of the American Medical Association*, a Maryland study concluded that "a pregnant or recently pregnant woman is more likely to be a victim of homicide than to die of any other cause."

We are hearing more and more horrible stories via mainstream media of pregnant women who are assaulted by those who do not want them to carry a child to term.

- A doctor was videotaped as he tried to poison his pregnant fiancée.
- Another doctor attacked his girlfriend's abdomen with a needle.
- A number of women have tried to kill the unborn child of another woman who is involved with the same man.
- Unwilling fathers have hired thugs to intentionally kill the unborn child.

For every story we hear, there are countless more that go untold, such as the story of Marion Syversen, a board member of Feminists for Life, who lost her unborn child when her abusive father threw her down a flight of stairs when she was pregnant.

Women who have survived such unthinkable violence are unequivocal: justice demands recognition of and remedy for both their assault and the killing of their unborn baby. The Unborn Victims of Violence Act would support justice for women who lose children as the result of a federal crime of violence.

Many women do not survive such crimes, and their grieving survivors are equally unequivocal: justice demands recognition of and remedy for the killing of both victims, the woman and her unborn child or children.

The gruesome and well-publicized case of Laci Peterson and her unborn baby, Conner, prompted Americans to examine their own convictions on this issue. The American people, too, were unequivocal. They recognize and mourn the loss of both mother and child. According to a Newsweek/ Princeton Survey Research Associates poll released June 1, 2003, 84% of Americans believe that prosecutors should be able to bring a homicide charge on behalf of a fetus killed in the womb. This figure includes 56% who believe such a charge should apply at any point during pregnancy, and another 28% who would apply it after the baby is "viable," i.e., of sufficient lung development to survive outside the mother. Only 9% believe that a homicide charge should never be allowed for a fetus.

Feminists for Life and our partners in the Women Deserve Better® campaign support the Unborn Victims of Violence Act because it would provide justice for the victims of federal crimes of violence. As victims, survivors, and the American people clearly demand, the Unborn Victims of Violence Act would recognize an unborn child as a legal victim when he or she is injured or killed during the commission of a federal crime of violence.

Congresswoman Lofgren has introduced an alternative to the Unborn Victims of Violence Act, called the Motherhood Protection Act of 2003. Instead of recognizing a woman's unborn child as an additional victim, it would "provide additional punishment for certain crimes against women when the crimes cause an interruption in the normal course of their pregnancies."

An "interruption?" That implies something temporary, as if it were possible for the victim's pregnancy to start back up again. Dare we ask: mother of whom? Motherhood is neither protected nor honored through the proposed Motherhood Protection Act. Instead, it tells grieving mothers that their lost children don't count. It ignores these mothers' cries for recognition of their loss and for justice. It is a step backward in efforts to reduce violence against women.

Ten days ago in the Bronx, a 54-year-old man allegedly kicked and punched his 24-year-old girlfriend in the abdomen. Julie Harris was nine months pregnant at the time. She went through labor only to deliver stillborn twins. The Motherhood Protection Act, which some call the single victim substitute, would only recognize one of these three victims.

The family of California murder victims Laci and Conner Peterson is explicitly urging Congress to pass the Unborn Victims of Violence Act, also known as Laci and Conner's Law—not the single-victim substitute. Sharon Rocha, Laci's mother and Conner's grandmother, concluded a letter to Senators DeWine, Hatch, and Graham and Congresswoman Hart:

> I hope that every legislator will clearly understand that adoption of such a single-victim amendment would be a painful blow to those, like me, who are left alive after a two-victim crime, because Congress would be saying that Conner and other innocent unborn victims like him are not really victims—indeed, that they never really existed at all. But our grandson did live. He had a name, he was loved, and his life was violently taken from him before he ever saw the sun.
>
> The application of a single-victim law, such as the [Lofgren] amendment, would be even more offensive in the many cases that involved mothers who themselves survive criminal attacks, but who lose their babies in those crimes. I don't understand how any legislator can vote to force prosecutors to tell such a grieving mother that she didn't really lose a baby—when she knows to the depths of her soul that she did. A legislator who votes for the single-victim amendment, however well motivated, votes to add insult to injury.
>
> The advocates of the single-victim amendment seem to think that the only thing that matters is how severe a sentence can be meted out—but they are wrong. It matters even more that the true nature of the crime be recognized, so that the punishment—which should indeed be severe—will fit the true nature of the crime. This is a question not only of severity, but also of justice. The single-victim proposal would be a step away from justice, not toward it. For example, if Congresswoman Lofgren's legal philosophy was currently the law in California, there would be no second homicide charge for the murder of Conner.

The Unborn Victims of Violence Act would also avoid multiplying the pain of survivors of horrendous federal crimes of violence such as the bombing in Oklahoma City or the terrorist attacks of September 11, 2001.

After years of trying to have a child, Carrie and Michael Lenz, Jr., were overjoyed to learn that she was carrying their son, whom they named Michael Lenz III. Carrying a copy of the sonogram, Carrie went to work early the next morning to show coworkers the first photo of baby Michael. She and Michael were killed, along with three other pregnant women and their unborn children, when the Alfred P. Murrah Federal Building exploded on April 19, 1995. This father's agony was multiplied later when he saw that the memorial named only his wife, not his son, as a victim. In the eyes of the federal government, there was no second victim. Timothy McVeigh was never held accountable for killing Michael Lenz's namesake.

If the legal system does not recognize the loss of the unborn child, it becomes an unwitting agent of the perpetrator who robbed the survivors of the child and the life they would have had together.

Women have a right to have children. When a woman has this right taken away from her due to violence that kills the fetus in her womb, she needs and deserves the support of all those who champion women's rights, including those who support legalized abortion. Columbia Law School Professor Michael Dorf, who is pro-choice, agrees: "Certainly pro-choice activists would oppose government-mandated sterilization. For similar reasons, they should support punishing feticide."

It is also worthwhile to note that outside the context of abortion, unborn children are often recognized as persons who warrant the law's protection. Most states, for example, allow recovery in one form or another for prenatal injuries. Roughly half the states criminalize fetal homicide. Unborn children have long been recognized as persons for purposes of inheritance, and a child unborn at the time of his or her father's wrongful death has been held to be among the children for whose benefit a wrongful death action may be brought. Federal law similarly recognizes the unborn child as a human subject deserving protection from harmful research.

Some have questioned whether it is reasonable to apply this law if the perpetrator is unaware that a woman is pregnant, especially if she is in the earliest stages of pregnancy.

Neither the Unborn Victims of Violence Act nor the Motherhood Protection Act makes a distinction about the age of the fetus. But would anyone seriously suggest—especially those who advocate a right to privacy—that it is a woman's responsibility to disclose her pregnancy to a potential attacker or murderer?

In 1990, the Supreme Court of Minnesota answered that question. In *State v. Merrill*, a man who killed a woman was responsible for two deaths, even though the woman was just 28 days pregnant. The court said: "The possibility that a female homicide victim of child-bearing age may be pregnant is a possibility that an assaulter may not safely exclude."

Knowing this may serve as a deterrent to future attacks on women of childbearing age.

We cannot tell grieving mothers like Tracy Marciniak, who testified here today, that her son Zachariah didn't count. We cannot tell Julie Harris, mother of twins, that there was only one victim when there were three. We cannot tell the families of Laci and Conner, or Carrie and Michael III, that they have only one loss to mourn. The Motherhood Protection Act would deny these victims the recognition and justice they deserve.

Women have spoken. Women want the justice promised by the Unborn Victims of Violence Act.

We are asking our elected Representatives to honestly answer the question in the case of Laci Peterson and baby Conner, was there one victim or two?

Those who support the single-victim substitute would deny women justice.

On behalf of women and families who have lost a child through violence, a father who has lost both his wife and child through terrorism, and Laci and Conner's family, I urge unanimous support for this bill, not the single-victim substitute.[3]

—Testimony before the Committee on the Judiciary, U.S. House of Representatives, Hearing on H.R. 1997: The Unborn Victims of Violence Act, 8 July 2003.

Cheryl Long Feather (Hunkuotawin)

Cheryl Long Feather, whose American Indian name is Hunkuotawin, is an enrolled member of the Standing Rock Sioux Tribe, part of the Great Lakota Nation. The Lakota were buffalo hunters and farmers on the Great Plains for thousands of years. Beginning in the nineteenth century, the U.S. government forced them off their lands onto reservations like the Standing Rock. At Wounded Knee in 1890, U.S. soldiers murdered over 300 unarmed Lakota, including mothers with babies. The genocide of the Lakota and other First Nations continued beyond the nineteenth century through widespread assimilationist government-run boarding schools, sterilization abuse, and heritage-destroying transracial adoption policies, among other practices parallel to the genocide of other indigenous peoples like Australia's Koori.

Long Feather takes part in a movement among the Lakota and other Nations to heal such historical traumas and reclaim traditional culture while living with twenty-first century circumstances. She is the daughter of Joe and Marilyn Kary, the spouse of Wes Long Feather, and the mother of four children, DaLayne, Trevan, Tayson, and Tallon. She holds a bachelor's degree in Communications and a master's in Management from the University of Mary in Bismarck, North Dakota. After working nine years for a tribal college on her reservation, she has been a curriculum specialist and trainer for the Native American Training Institute.[1] This collaboration among North Dakota's tribes helps non-Native professionals do culturally competent work with American Indian children and families around such issues as foster parenting, adoption, and HIV awareness.

Long Feather formerly penned "Four Directions," a column for the *Bismarck Tribune*. In 1999, she joined the national discussion over a controversial study on the U.S. crime rate, an urgent issue for Indians, who are twice as likely as other Americans to experience violent assaults (mostly at the hands of white offenders), yet twice as likely to be involved in the criminal justice system. The researchers postulated a causal relationship between abortion-on-"demand" legalization and a drop in the national crime rate. Critics have identified many methodological flaws in the study, including conclusions that come from a pro-abortion bias. The lowered crime rate came at the same time as a lowered abortion rate. Rather than earlier abortions causing a later drop in crime, one might reasonably conclude that whatever later caused people to resort to the violence of abortion less also caused them to engage in violent crime less. Setting aside that debate, however, Long Feather had a different problem with the conclusion. She asserts that the implied "solution" for crime was criminal itself.

American Indians Regard Abortion As a Crime
by Cheryl Long Feather

A new and controversial study conducted by John Donahue and Steven Levitt to determine reasons for the recent drastic drop in crime rate has created quite a debate over abortion and its ramifications instead. The pair determined that the famous *Roe v. Wade* decision had a significant impact on today's decline in crime. They point to the fact that the women having abortions following the *Roe vs. Wade* decision—teens, minorities, and the poor—were those most likely to raise the criminals of our society. The research conclusions are thought-provoking indeed.

While it is true that there seems to be a link between the legalization of abortion and the decline in crime, it does not necessarily hold true that abortion is a solution to the problem of crime rate (nor do the researchers encourage such an idea). However, proponents of abortion may use this research to hold abortion up as, at best, a desirable solution or even, at worst, a necessary evil. But the reality is that abortion is merely capital punishment before the fact. Abortion allows us to murder the criminals before they have a chance to commit the crimes. How convenient our society makes it.

We would be making a serious mistake if we allowed the findings in this research to tell us abortion is a desirable thing. Long ago, the killing of an unborn child was abhorrent in any culture. Today, we have become hard-hearted in our views of the gift of life.

It would be very difficult to find an American Indian person who truly knows and follows their culture who could be called "pro-choice." In the traditional culture, abortion was a crime against nature. Natural family planning was practiced throughout the social culture. Husbands and wives did not have intimate relations while the mother was nursing. A woman's "choice" was exercised in how long she chose to nurse.

I have always wondered why we call abortion a woman's choice. Abortion is not a woman's choice but a woman's second chance. A woman's true choice in regard to her body is clear; if a woman does not want a baby, she should not take the risk of having sex (or unprotected sex, in today's contraceptive-laden world). When a woman finds she is pregnant, she has already made her choice. An abortion is merely a chance to amend the consequences of her choice.

The problem of unwanted children/criminals will not be solved by abortion. The only way to solve the problem of unwanted pregnancies and the creation of criminals is by doubling, tripling our efforts to teach and model personal responsibility and moral behavior. Although this is not the fast-food, convenient solution some may prefer, it is the only solution that will endure.

—"Four Directions," *Bismarck Tribune,* 18 Aug. 1999.

Cecilia Brown

Cecilia Agnes Brown was born in Clearfield, Pennsylvania, but has lived mostly in Cleveland, Ohio. She is one of eight children, half of whom are gay, and has a daughter, Margaret. Contrary to the stereotype that prolifers hold monolithic views on non-abortion related issues like same-sex marriage, Cecilia tells us that in 1993 she wed her partner Rena even though Ohio did not recognize their marriage. A freelance photographer, Brown currently works as a server and a housckeeper, so she has the flexibility to both take on photography projects and act as Prolife Alliance of Gays and Lesbians (PLAGAL) national president.[1] In 2000, four years after joining PLAGAL's board of directors, she became the group's first female president. Brown works for PLAGAL as part of her consistent prolife ethic, which includes active support for abolition of the death penalty, economic justice, peace, animal rights, and environmental issues. She has also participated in the Silent No More campaign. Brown is a member of the Green Party and a lacto-ovo vegetarian.

My Journey Into the Prolife Movement
by Cecilia Brown

During my teenage years I remember never having the normal talks about sex, birth control, sexually transmitted diseases, relationships and parenthood that most teenagers should have with their parents. My parents did not talk of such matters. Maybe it was because our household was such a dysfunctional mess. Alcoholism and its associated problems took precedence over all other matters. Pregnancy was never mentioned except when my father was in a drunken abusive rage and he would scream at me, "If you ever become pregnant, don't bother coming home!" What my father did not know was that I was attracted to females. I kept that secret to myself because another one of his daily drunken tirades dealt with gays— how "evil" they were, how "perverted," and so on, and so on. My Uncle Dave (now deceased) was gay, and my younger brother Charlie had a very effeminate, "gay-looking" appearance. My uncle was forbidden to come to our home; my brother had to endure daily physical, emotional, and verbal abuse because my father believed him to be gay. For as long as I can remember, my father mistreated Charlie. He mistreated all of us, but his abuse of Charlie was even worse. This was very difficult for me and two of my brothers because we too felt same-sex attractions. However, because we were not stereotypically gay-appearing, we were not targets of my father's drunken homophobic tirades. We did everything we could to hide our sexuality, even going so far as to date and have sex with people of the opposite gender. It would be too easy to put the whole blame of our being closeted on my father. The truth is, we had to pretend to everyone we knew. Society as a whole was not accepting of gays or lesbians at the time. The problem of lying about who you are can lead to unimagined complications.

I had not even been to college one month when I had found out that I was pregnant. I had become pregnant before arriving there; I just had not known it. I only found out because I had developed an infection and had gone to the college infirmary. I was so ignorant about my body and how it worked. I thought the late period was caused by the infection or the medication I was given. What did I know? All my education on such matters came from friends and people that were just as unknowledgeable as I was. The nurse practitioner decided to perform a pregnancy test. When I received the news about my pregnancy, my father's words came to mind. The words telling me I could never come home if I were pregnant. See where pretending to be someone you are not can lead? If I had been who I felt I was on the inside, instead of pretending to be straight for the world and my family, I would not have ended up in this mess. I was a whirlwind of mixed emotions. I did not know what to do. I was scared. I felt that I had nowhere to go and no one to talk to except the baby's father. It was clear that abortion was on his mind. After all, he too was in college. He did not work. The nurse practitioner told me all the reasons I should have an abortion but never once mentioned alternatives. I did not even have the money for an abortion. Funny thing, though: the college had a "special" fund for girls like me. They would "loan" me part of the money for the abortion. I could pay it back in monthly installments. I felt I was being pushed into the abortion. I wanted time to think about everything, but there was no time. A decision had to be made quickly.

November 3, 1981, is etched in my brain forever. It is a day I regret. I wish I could turn back the hands of time. It is the day that I had my abortion. My boyfriend went with me to the clinic for support—or was it obligation? It did not take me long to find that I was being handed a bill of goods, harmful ones. I was told that the abortion would cause little pain, that the baby was just a blob of tissue, that abortion is the best answer because it will make everything better. I soon learned that was a big lie. Part way though the "procedure" I freaked out. The pain was immeasurable. The doctor started yelling at the "counselor" to hold me down. She started yelling things at me like "this is what you said you wanted!" I looked to my right and saw that the so-called "blob of tissue" had fingers and toes. I felt violated. I felt betrayed because I was not told the truth. Because I was so upset, they did not put me in the same recovery room as all the other women; they did not want me upsetting them. It was bad enough that the whole procedure was painful and emotionally traumatic, but then I developed an infection that landed me in the college infirmary for a week. That was the tip of the iceberg.

The whole ordeal put stress on the relationship with my boyfriend and we broke up. I found myself alone with no one to talk to about how I was feeling. I spent weeks crying and withdrew into myself. I felt shame over the abortion. I tried to put it all behind me; instead, I found myself dwelling on what I had done. It was like an open wound that was not going to heal. I found myself in destructive behavior. It took over 10 years before I could talk about my abortion. I discovered that abortion is not a quick fix. It did not change the circumstances that led to it. My father was still a drunken idiot. I still did not have any money and ended up dropping out of school anyway. And worse of all, I was still pretending to be straight.

I did learn something from the whole ordeal. I did not want to experience abortion again. I learned about birth control and I used it—that is, until the night I conceived my daughter. I was drunk and not at home. I never thought to bring my diaphragm with me; after all, sex was not on the agenda that day. On April 1, 1985, I found out I was pregnant again. This time, however, my circumstances were different. I had my own apartment, but I was out of work. I already knew that abortion was out of the question. The only thing that was on my mind was "How will I make it on unemployment?" I had no health insurance. I barely could feed myself. My mother was dying of cancer, and she would not be there to help me. My father was still a drunk and I did not want his help. I was lucky. My dear friend Linda pointed me in the right direction. I began to straighten out my life and shed the destructive behaviors. After all, I had a child on the way who needed me. I found work even while pregnant and everything was looking up. My daughter Margaret was born on December 4, 1985. She was the only good thing to come out of the lies I had spun for the world's sake, the lies about being someone I was not: straight. No one would ever suspect I was a lesbian deep inside. After all, I had a daughter. I felt my secret was safe.

I felt so blessed while holding her in my arms, this tiny life so fragile and beautiful. It was not long before thoughts about the child I aborted began to creep in. I began wondering what that child would have looked like. How old would he or she be now? Why did I not have the support then that I did now? All the pain that I had spent so much time trying to bury was resurfacing. As my daughter grew, the questions continued. At some point I decided that I wanted to help women who were facing the kind of circumstances I had faced. I knew it meant that I had to talk about my abortion. It meant stepping forward and sharing my story. It meant becoming involved with the prolife movement

I first became involved with a group called Greater Cleveland Life Link, attending their prayer vigils and their picketing of abortion clinics and abortionists' homes. But I did not feel comfortable. It was not that I did not share their pro-life convictions. It was because I was a lesbian and they spent a lot of time focusing on the "evils" of people like me. In my mind I questioned my involvement with this group. After all, what does attacking gays and lesbians have to do with the prolife cause? It is only through heterosexual sex that women become pregnant. I knew that. That is how I got pregnant. It certainly was not from sleeping with a woman that I had experienced two crisis pregnancies. I thought about my circumstances. I wondered how many women were like me. How many other lesbians have become pregnant because of trying to be someone they are not? How many of these women have suffered because of abortion? If these pro-lifers were so much against gays, how can these women even contemplate coming to them for help? I knew there had to be an organization where I could fit in. I was no longer living in a closet. I was living as a lesbian with a woman who has since become my life partner. Together my partner and I were raising my daughter. I would continue with Greater Cleveland Life link until I could find something better. It was not until I attended a Cleveland Right to Life annual event that I ran across a Feminists for Life flyer. I figured I would give them a call. I had pictured feminists to be like Molly Yard from the National Organization for Women. I certainly did not fit that profile, but I figured that I could give them a call anyway. I talked to Marilyn Kopp from FFL's Ohio chapter and told her my story. She told me she had the perfect group for me, PLAGAL, The Pro-life Alliance of Gays and Lesbians. Imagine my surprise! I was not even aware of such a group. I immediately gave them a call.

I was so excited to have found a group that shared my pro-life convictions while at the same time allowing me to be who I was without hiding it. I jumped in feet first, without hesitation. It was not until I jumped in that I found out how troubled the waters really were. I certainly knew that groups such as Greater Cleveland Life Link disliked gays. But I figured that since they were a fringe group, they did not share this belief with other, more mainstream groups. Boy, was I wrong! To make matters worse, I received hostility from my own GLBT (Gay-Lesbian-Bisexual-Transgendered) community. I could not help but feel that both sides were hypocrites. The prolife side talked about the love of God while at the same time treating me as a pariah. The GLBT community talked about acceptance and tolerance while at the same time tried to silence my outspoken prolife stance. Both sides have accused me of spying for the other side to disrupt their respective movements. This makes me mad! It makes me more determined than ever to speak out for life as a lesbian who refuses to be shoved into any kind of closet. They will have to learn to work with me, like it or not, because I am not going away. With time and perseverance, PLAGAL members have been able to build bridges. Many times it is not easy, but it needs to be done, and PLAGAL members are willing to step up to the plate and do it. It is not hard to see why I love working with PLAGAL. Our members are so dedicated to the cause. They do not proclaim the prolife message only when it is easy; they will take the chance of being ridiculed by both the prolife and GLBT communities. No fly-by-night prolifers here. That is why I agreed to become their first woman president. I was and am proud to lead such a fine group.

As president, I have found it difficult to build working relationships with people who do not want them. Some people are so close-minded, they would rather cut off their noses to spite their faces. In all the bridge-building work PLAGAL has attempted, we have found only one person who was not even willing to bend a little. That person is Nellie Gray, the President of the annual March for Life in Washington, D.C. PLAGAL has attended the March since 1991. We have always been respectful and have never caused trouble. We carry our banner, pass out our literature, and visit our representatives—just like all the other organizations who participate in the March. Overall, PLAGAL gets a positive response from other attendees. The occasional marcher spouts Biblical verses at us, but most are glad about our presence. It is Nellie Gray who does not want gays in "her" march, so she draws a line in the sand. So what is a good gay prolifer to do? Especially one that is stubborn as I am? We stepped over Nellie's line. In 2002 she had us arrested for doing so. Even with the arrest, we believed so strongly in our message that we came back in 2003. From year to year we do not know if we will be arrested, but we keep coming back.[2] Our message is that important to us. Saving babies and their mothers from the horrors of abortion is so important that I personally would risk arrest over and over again to do so.

Since my arrest, I have made it my personal mission to open the prolife movement to all who are peaceful. I want to see the prolife movement move from a white, heterosexual, Republican and Christian base to one that welcomes people of all religious, racial, social, economic, and political affiliations—not to mention sexual orientations. I want to see the prolife movement willingly set aside differences so that the needs of women and their children are put first and met. I also am committed to the continued outreach within the GLBT community. I want GLBT people to know that we do not have to sacrifice the unborn and their mothers so that we can receive civil rights. Abortion rights and GLBT civil rights are not the same. I want more members of the GLBT community to become involved with the prolife movement. Above all, I am concerned about GLBT youth who find themselves in crisis pregnancies because they are trying to hide who they really are. It is my fear that prolifers will not help them and will turn them away because of their sexual orientation. Even worse, I fear that pro-abortion GLBT individuals may push abortion on them, as if that will solve anything.

—© 2003 Cecilia Brown.

Rus Cooper-Dowda

Reverend Rus Cooper-Dowda has learned firsthand about the dubious meanings of "choice" for disabled women. She has lupus and uses a wheelchair. She is a Unitarian Universalist, minister, liberal, teacher, and freelance writer who has contributed to the disability rights magazines *Ragged Edge* and *Mouth*, the national GLBT newsmagazine *The Advocate*, and Tolerance.org, the website of the Southern Poverty Law Center's "Teach Tolerance" project. Cooper-Dowda outspokenly defended Terri Schindler Schiavo, the brain-damaged woman from Pinellas County, Florida, whose husband succeeded in his legal battles to remove her feeding tube and hydration on the grounds that Terri would not *choose* to continue life-prolonging measures. Terri died March 31, 2005, after almost two weeks without hydration or nourishment. Cooper-Dowda related strongly to Schindler-Schiavo because, she recounts, she was once in a coma at the mercy of people who could not imagine, let alone affirm, her wish to live. During her 1985 pregnancy, Cooper-Dowda found that her desire to give life through bearing and parenting a child was also unthinkable in some people's eyes.

Greetings From Your Mom
by Rus Cooper-Dowda

. . . I was thrilled. In the first three days after the blood test I must have rolled up to at least two dozen people, sharing the news. The grin on my face could not have been wider. There were only three variations on the responses: (1) When are you terminating? (2) Do you want me to go with you when you terminate? (3) Can I pick you up after you terminate? Nobody said "Congratulations!" Nobody said, "You look so happy! I'm happy for you, too!" It all had to do with how they felt about a woman who used a wheelchair also having a baby. All of them went out of their way to explain that. The pressure to abort was so unrelenting that I had to isolate myself until almost the due date to avoid it. But that still didn't entirely take the pressure off.

When I was in delivery, as my son's head was crowning, the medical staff carried on a lively debate over whether women with disabilities should be allowed to have children. Finally, I yelled out between contractions, "Either get out! Or be supportive! Or, *shut up!*" They all stayed. But instead of supportive, they all got very quiet. There was no, "You can do it . . . You're almost there . . . One last push!" My son was born in total silence except the volume of love turned up in my heart . . .

I'm glad you're here, kiddo.

—*Mouth: Voice of the Dislabelled Nation,* Jan.-Feb. 2003.

Cooper-Dowda's son Max is now a college student and fabric artist. He has joined her in defending Terri Schindler Schiavo. Many other currently living disabled persons' rights to nonviolent reproductive choice have been disrespected. In 1986, an obstetrician who feared a "defective" fetus (and perhaps a "wrongful life" lawsuit) tried to pressure multiply disabled coeditor Mary Krane Derr into aborting her daughter. When Derr angrily responded that "defective" people—like her—were not the problem, but attitudes like his, he stammered "Uh—it's your choice" and swiftly backed out of the room.[1] Jackie Malone's recent experience shows that such pressures—however camouflaged as "choice"—have not gone away. Malone, who has publicly challenged her Unitarian Universalist church to offer pregnant women help instead of abortion, is PLAGAL's national secretary. She was happy to see the strong heartbeat and lively limbs of her nine-week-old daughter or son on the ultrasound, but the nurse did not connect with her delight. The nurse kept pressing Malone about her congenital disability, Arnold-Chiari malformation, finally insisting that she should see a genetic counselor as soon as possible. Malone challenged the evasive nurse to name the purpose of this supposed imperative:

> She said that a lot of people would consider a termination if the news were bad. It took me a couple seconds to recover from the shock of her even making the suggestion. Then I looked at her and asked if I deserved to die because I had a birth defect. She started to talk and I said that I wasn't perfect, and I certainly wouldn't kill my child for not being perfect. She got really quiet. I've seen looks that people give me though. I have a 16-month-old son [already] and I walk with a forearm crutch.[2]

Such stories—like many stories about the personal realities of living under oppression—are often dismissed as fabrications or paranoid exaggerations. Yet as *Mouth* editor Lucy Gwin likes to say, "It's not paranoia if people really ARE coming after you!" In addition, there are statistics to back up these three mothers' insistence that they have encountered reproductive coercion. During the late 1990s, the first ever U.S. survey of disabled parents was conducted by the disability rights/independent living group Through the Looking Glass: Parenting With a Disability.[3] A majority reported barriers to exercising their reproductive rights.

- For nearly 80%, transportation issues hindered their participation in a major, daily part of childrearing: "routine parent-child activities."
- 42% encountered one or more "attitudinal barriers."
  - Discrimination (32%)
  - Pressure to be sterilized (14%)
  - Pressure to abort (13%)
  - Difficulties during prenatal care and birth caused by health care workers' ignorance of disability issues (36%)
  - Attempts to have custody of their children taken from them (15%)
  - Obstacles to adopting a child (8%)[4]

Mary Meehan

Since the 1960s and 70s, independent-minded Irish American women like Mary Meehan have been well-represented in the contemporary U.S. prolife movement, whose early members often hailed from the civil rights and anti-Vietnam War movements. Meehan graduated from Trinity College (Washington, D.C.) with a major in history. She worked for Senator Eugene McCarthy in his 1968 antiwar presidential campaign and did research and other work for him in the 1970s. Later she was active in Prolifers for Survival (an early consistent life ethic group), Feminists for Life, and on the steering committee of an anti-death penalty group in Washington, D.C. For the past 25 years, though, Ms. Meehan has focused mainly on writing. Her work has appeared in publications ranging from *Human Life Review* and *Celebrate Life* to *The Progressive* and the *Washington Post*. Her 1980 *Progressive* article, "Abortion: The Left Has Betrayed the Sanctity of Life," caused quite a stir and encouraged others to speak out on behalf of the unborn. Meehan was invited to a pioneering prochoice/prolife dialogue called by writer and psychologist Sidney de Shazo Callahan, an enduring, articulate voice of prolife feminism, and her prochoice spouse Daniel Callahan, founder of the Hastings Center, a prominent bioethics think tank. The Callahans gathered participant contributions into the volume *Abortion: Understanding Differences* (Plenum Press, 1984).

Meehan, now a public speaker as well as a writer, lives in Cumberland, an old pioneer city in the Western Maryland mountains. Not long ago, she researched the archives of the American Civil Liberties Union to learn more about its role in abortion law repeal.

ACLU v. Unborn Children
by Mary Meehan

The right to life underlies and sustains every other right we have. Yet the American Civil Liberties Union fights against it for one class of human beings—unborn children, the smallest and weakest of all.[1]

How and why did this contradiction occur? The organization's own archives, located at Princeton University, tell much of the story. Some files there are not yet open to researchers; but enough information is available at the ACLU Archives, and in other sources, to give depth to this report.[2]

Dorothy Kenyon—lawyer, feminist and veteran ACLU board member—tried unsuccessfully to persuade the organization to fight abortion restrictions in the 1950s. Attorney Harriet Pilpel renewed the effort at a 1964 ACLU conference. An able lawyer and a strong personality, she was devoted to the cause of birth control and population control, including abortion. Her law firm represented the Planned Parenthood Federation of America. Pilpel and the Planned Parenthood president, Dr. Alan Guttmacher, pursued the legalization of abortion in many forums in the 1960s. Guttmacher, who was vice president of the American Eugenics Society from 1956-1963, probably influenced Pilpel toward eugenics.

At the 1964 ACLU conference, Pilpel showed some interest in the right to life—but only the life of the woman. She asked: "Does it not unconstitutionally deny a woman life, liberty and the pursuit of happiness, for example, if despite her wishes and the opinions of concurring doctors she is forced to bear a child she doesn't want and, objectively, shouldn't have?" In a footnote she suggested that a woman shouldn't have a child injured by the drug thalidomide while in the womb.[3] Her eugenic approach to fetal handicaps would be echoed later by other ACLU activists. Singling out the handicapped for destruction contradicted the ACLU's principle of equality and its tradition of fighting for minorities and outcasts.

In her 1964 paper, Pilpel suggested that legislation restricting birth control and abortion "breeds and perpetuates conditions of delinquency and crime" by encouraging "the multiplication of births among low income groups."[4] Ironically, she said this while the ACLU was deeply involved in the civil rights movement, defending the rights of low-income African

Americans. Pilpel's eugenics bent should have raised a warning flag for all ACLU activists.

Apparently it did not, because the 1964 conference called for a study of abortion laws' constitutionality. In 1966 an ACLU staff member said the organization had "farmed this research out to our Southern California affiliate . . . I don't think that we should wait any longer for them, in view of the growing interest and demand for action on this subject."[5]

Pilpel, meanwhile, had recently testified before a New York legislative committee. Speaking on behalf of New York's ACLU affiliate, she suggested that abortion be viewed simply as a health problem and left to doctors' discretion. Severely restricting abortion, she said, placed an enormous economic burden on the country. She estimated that each year's cohort of "unwanted children" could cost the public $17.5 billion—a *huge* sum of money at that time. She acknowledged that viewing "unwanted children solely in monetary terms is simplistic, as well as callous." But her higher ground seemed to be that an unwanted child "suffers from his parents' attitude toward him." Apparently it did not occur to her that the parents should change their attitude.

Pilpel complained that poor women and minorities suffered a disproportionate number of deaths from illegal abortion. But she did not propose positive efforts to help such women obtain prenatal and obstetrical care instead of abortion. She expressed special concern that women be able to obtain abortions if their unborn children "would probably be defective." She acknowledged, but quickly discounted, the argument that the unborn have a right to life.[6]

As the ACLU Due Process Committee developed an abortion policy for consideration by the group's national board, it used heavily-biased working papers collected by ACLU staff.[7]

Two errors in a 1965 paper by William Kopit and Harriet Pilpel misled the ACLU at a critical time and have been widely circulated since then, thus misleading many other people as well. Kopit and Pilpel suggested that there were between one million and 1.5 million illegal abortions in the United States each year—and over 8,000 maternal deaths from those abortions each year. Yet *legal* abortions have ranged between one million and about 1.6 million per year since 1975.[8] Common sense suggests that removal of criminal sanctions, establishment of abortion clinics all over the country, heavy advertising, and public funding of abortion in many states produced a vast increase in abortion after the 1973 *Roe v. Wade* decision. No one knows precisely how many illegal abortions there were before *Roe v. Wade*; but in 1981 three researchers estimated a range from "a low of 39,000 (1950) to a high of 210,000 (1961) and a mean of 98,000 per year."[9]

The number of maternal deaths actually reported by the U.S. government was far lower than the number given by Kopit and Pilpel. Better post-abortion medical treatment apparently caused a fairly steady decline in maternal deaths. According to researcher Cynthia McKnight, government figures showed 1,313 maternal deaths from illegal abortions in 1940, trending down to 197 in 1965 (the year Kopit and Pilpel wrote that there were over 8,000 such deaths each year!). McKnight attributes the mortality decline to antibiotics, blood transfusions, and improved surgical techniques. She cites two major abortion advocates, contemporaries of Kopit and Pilpel, who made far lower estimates than they did. One apparently accepted government figures; the other suggested about 500 deaths per year.[10]

The highly-inflated figures on illegal abortions and maternal deaths are still in circulation and still influence the abortion debate. They lead many people to believe that legalizing abortion saved thousands of women's lives each year, yet did not greatly increase the number of fetal deaths.

Most abortion opponents probably did not know that the ACLU was about to enter the abortion fight, but the organization did hear from a few opponents. Michael Gask of New York warned that civil libertarians "must oppose selectivity with regard to rights—some human life which is protected, and some which is not—or some more equally than others." He also suggested many ways to reduce pressures leading to abortion—including prenatal and postnatal care and improving the status of unwed mothers and "illegitimate" children. An ACLU staff member thought that Gask's point about positive solutions "may have some merit," but doubted "that society is ready to take on the kinds of financial costs involved." Later he suggested that Gask "does not adequately deal with the impact of the unwanted child" and questioned whether changes needed "to provide wide-spread care for unwanted children are within the proper scope of civil liberties concern."[11]

Here we see the "unwanted child" consigned to a lower tier of humanity—precisely what Gask had warned against. And, given their stress on the evils of illegal abortion, ACLU staff and board members seemed markedly indifferent to positive alternatives. If they thought such solutions were outside "the proper scope of civil liberties concern," they did not have to undertake such work themselves; but they at least could have encouraged private foundations and charities to do it.

Benjamin DuVal, a lawyer active in the New York Civil Liberties Union, submitted a paper arguing that anti-abortion laws "do not violate any provision of the United States Constitution." DuVal apparently favored some exceptions to the anti-abortion laws of his day. But he made two crucial points often overlooked by civil libertarians: 1) The fact that wealthy women could obtain abortions when poor women couldn't did not result from discrimination in the laws themselves but, rather, from "the failure of the prosecuting authorities to enforce the law" when illegal abortions were done in hospitals; and 2) Enforcement of anti-abortion laws did not "conjure up visions of police officers invading the bedroom."

DuVal's paper apparently influenced Due Process Committee members. According to a staff memo, they concluded that laws restricting abortion were "not unconstitutional on their face" and that society could "place such value on the life of the unborn child as to render abortion possible only in a narrow range of circumstances." As a matter of *policy*, though, the committee wanted abortion to be legal up to twenty weeks of pregnancy provided that the husband—"if any, if he is available"—consented.[12]

When the ACLU board considered the issue in February 1967, board member Harriet Pilpel was ready to pounce. The committee, she felt, had not gone nearly far enough. Using the New York anti-abortion law as an example, she said it was unconstitutional for five different reasons: it was "unconstitutionally vague"; denied equal protection of the laws to poor women; infringed upon rights to decide about childbearing and to have marital privacy; impaired doctors' right to practice medicine; and deprived women of lives and liberty "without due process of law." Pilpel did not consider equal protection of the laws or due process for the child. She felt that a husband's consent to abortion should *not* be required and that abortions should be allowed *after* twenty weeks in some cases. Her broad exceptions included cases where the mother was "mentally ill or a mental defective."

Dorothy Kenyon, still on the board, thought that Pilpel's approach was not radical enough. Some board members, though, were concerned that late abortions could harm women's health, so the board reduced the proposed abortion period from five months (twenty weeks) to three months. It sent the question of abortion after three months back to the committee "for further clarification."[13]

The board had been wrestling with legal questions, but had not shown much interest in philosophy or ethics. There was a tendency to dismiss such concerns as religious (and particularly Catholic) matters. But when Thomas Shaffer, a University of Notre Dame law professor and activist in the Indiana Civil Liberties Union, wrote the ACLU to protest that the group was coming down "on the wrong side," he did not make the religious arguments the ACLU might have expected from a professor at a Catholic university. Indeed, he said that one "of the weaknesses of the defense [of life] is that it is associated with Roman Catholicism—which, because of its medieval attitude on birth control and divorce is least competent to carry it out." But Shaffer also declared: "If any group defends secular ethics in our society, it is the ACLU. The first principle of secular ethics is that life is an absolute value. The Union's defense of pacifism is an ancient example of that; its statement on capital punishment is a more recent example." He added: "Abortion is a betrayal of secular ethics because it solves human problems by the destruction of life . . . ."

Shaffer enclosed a letter he had just written to a newspaper, in which he said that: "It is not true that abortion is merely an extension of medical science to the pregnant, any more than the careful antiseptic administration of cyanide would merely extend medical science to the aged. The question in either case is whether doctors should be healers or executioners."[14]

By late 1967, Shaffer apparently had lost hope of reversing an increasingly radical ACLU trend; now he was just trying to prevent open season on the unborn throughout pregnancy. He charged that: "The reform movement is morally irresponsible because it will not face the possibility that this particular form of birth control is infanticide, that it shatters, therefore, the only certain unity mankind has—its unity against death. You and I both know that the standard debater's answer to this challenge is that "of course" no human life is involved. That sort of evasion makes the reform movement morally indistinguishable from Treblinka and Buchenwald . . . ."[15]

Shaffer's strong words made some board members worry about late abortion as possible infanticide; but the stampede toward a hardline, pro-abortion position was so strong that it overrode a specific time limit. In March 1968, the ACLU reached a radical position that it still holds today. It qualified its statement that "a woman has a right to have an abortion" by defining abortion as "a termination of pregnancy prior to the viability of the fetus." A footnote suggested that this was "sometime after the twentieth week of pregnancy" and, practically speaking, "not until several weeks later."

Yet even this vague limit seemed to be negated by the next sentence, which asked that "state legislatures abolish all laws imposing criminal penalties for abortions." This meant that "any woman could ask a doctor to terminate a pregnancy at any time." Dr. Christopher Tietze—a population controller, abortion advocate and eugenicist—apparently had convinced ACLU staff that late abortions were rarely done and would not be a serious problem if abortion were legalized.[16]

ACLU staff had been champing at the bit for some time, anxious to fight for abortion in court. "I think we should get hot on abortion . . .," staff member Eleanor Holmes Norton had written in December 1967. "The Legal Department will, of course, be wanting to get involved in litigation wherever it can be found."[17] When the board passed the 1968 policy, she and other staff were off to the races. They looked especially to Hugh Hefner's Playboy Foundation for money to finance abortion lawsuits—a strange position for people who were supposed to be fighting for women's rights. Norton (who is now the District of Columbia's non-voting delegate in Congress) even asked, "Are there some bunnies we can get who have particular influence with the management?" The Playboy Foundation, possibly at that time and certainly later, did support ACLU abortion activity; so did many other foundations, especially ones with strong interests in population control.[18]

Soon the ACLU was deeply involved in litigation to strike down abortion restrictions. It helped win a partial victory in the 1971 case of *United States v. Vuitch*, which blasted large holes in the District of Columbia's anti-abortion law. Texas lawyer Sarah Weddington was the lead attorney for abortion forces in *Roe v. Wade*, but ACLU lawyers handled *Roe's* companion case, *Doe v. Bolton*.[19] Those 1973 cases led to a situation close to abortion on demand.

ACLU staff have been deeply involved in abortion cases ever since. They fight tenaciously against every restriction on abortion, and they try to obtain public funding for it. Ironically, they often see themselves as champions of the poor and of minorities in these battles. Finding solutions to help both mothers and children has seemed beyond their ability or interest. With their ideological view of a woman's making the abortion decision in a detached and sovereign way, they have overlooked women in desperate financial straits, women under heavy pressure from boyfriends or husbands, and scared teenagers who are afraid to tell their parents that they have become grandparents.

The eugenicists and population controllers must have been delighted to see the ACLU put the gloss of rights and freedom on abortion. It made their effort to suppress the birthrates of poor people and minorities so much easier.[20] Did ACLU leaders know or care about that kind of agenda? Aryeh Neier, ACLU executive director from 1970-1978, later referred to some African Americans' "feeling that there were whites who were eager to eliminate or limit the number of welfare mother babies out of an anti-black feeling and [that] that's why they were supporting abortion." In a 1979 interview with one of his law students, Neier added that "there's no question that I dealt with some supporters of abortion who are very much in favor of abortion for exactly that reason . . . . There was a foundation in Pittsburgh that was willing to provide support for litigation efforts on behalf of abortion because of that feeling."

He said that was also "certainly the ideology" of a Missouri foundation that had supported ACLU litigation. Was Neier bothered by taking that kind of money? "I don't regard it as dirty money," he said, "so long as people don't try to impose conditions on what you can do with the money." He added that if you tried "to go back and find out where people made their money and what all their other beliefs are . . . you'd go crazy. So as long as they don't try to impose restrictions, I will always take the money."[21]

Why should they have imposed restrictions when the ACLU already was doing precisely what they wanted done?

Taking *chutzpah* to new heights, ACLU activists suggested that it was not they, but rather the defenders of life—and of the unborn poor—who were really anti-poor. In a fundraising letter, ACLU leader Norman Dorsen charged that "those who are trying to force compulsory parenthood on poor women have little regard for our Constitutional freedoms." Yet Dorsen also realized that cranky taxpayers were among his potential supporters. "Financing abortions for the poor is far less expensive than the cost of childbirth and welfare support for unwanted children," he wrote. "So the government is actually paying out your tax dollars to force poor women to become mothers."[22]

In 1974 the ACLU had established a Reproductive Freedom Project to defend and expand its court victories. In 1977 staff member John Shattuck remarked: "Since the abortion issue is so controversial outside the ACLU, our 'pro-choice' campaign should be conducted in the context of a larger effort to defend human rights." Later, when the ACLU board discussed and approved the campaign: "It was pointed out that the Right-to-Lifers are the only group educating on abortion at the grass roots level, and it was suggested that such reactionary groups are representative of some of the most anti-civil libertarian forces in the country."[23] What was the basis for the second statement? The record does not show any ACLU effort to meet right-to-life leaders or to discuss civil-liberties issues with them. ACLU leaders, moreover, knew that *some of their own activists* opposed abortion.[24]

At a board meeting months later, eugenics raised its ugly head again when a member "felt that a way to turn around the tide against us [on abortion] would be to assert the right of women who suffer health defects or whose fetuses would be so defective as to be a hardship on the parents." But another board member, although reliably pro-abortion, "observed that it would be difficult to obtain the support of parents of retarded children in a lobbying effort which works against the creation of retarded children."

She thought that the parents "would not be in a position psychologically to defend a pro-choice stand on this ground."[25]

As noted earlier, official ACLU policy defines abortion as occurring "prior to the viability of the fetus." ACLU lawyers devised a way to make this limit meaningless: In the late 1970s, they argued that "the decision as to fetal viability must be left to the good faith medical judgment of an attending physician." The Supreme Court was all too eager to protect abortionists in this fashion.[26]

The 1968 policy—with its vague viability limit—appears to be still in effect, technically speaking. But the limit means little or nothing. The ACLU fiercely resists efforts to ban even the gruesome D & X or "partial birth" abortion.[27]

Organizations, especially ones as old as the ACLU, are notoriously difficult to turn around on major policy questions. Yet it is possible to imagine appeals to reason and conscience that would reinforce dissenters within the ACLU ranks and encourage others to review their policy. Such appeals might also alert liberals in general—including liberal judges—to the profound contradictions in ACLU policy.

—Condensed by the author for this volume, 2004; originally appeared in *Human Life Review*, (Spring, 2001); complete article available on "Meehan Reports" (www.meehanreports.com).

Mary Krane Derr

Mary Krane Derr is an American descendant of Irish *An Gorta Mor* survivors, working-class Polish laborers like the one on this book's cover, Alsatian war refugees, and a Separatist minister driven from England by religious persecution. As a scholarship student, she achieved a bachelor's degree in biology from Bryn Mawr, a nineteenth-century women's college, and a master's from the University of Chicago school of social work, cofounded (she discovered later) by her distant cousin Julia Lathrop. Derr practiced as a reproductive counselor for five years until retiring because she could not find a job that accommodated her multiple disabilities. She is now a freelance writer and activist whenever possible for various nonviolence causes. She has served on the boards of Consistent Life, the Feminism and Nonviolence Studies Association, and Feminists for Life of America. She has published her poetry in small-press magazines like *Many Mountains Moving*, anthologies like *Hunger Enough: Living Spiritually in A Consumer Society* (ed. Nita Penfold, Pudding House, 2004), and such websites as Poets Against the War (www.poetsagainstthewar.org). She has read it at the Chicago Cultural Center and the 1999 Parliament of the World's Religions, Cape Town, South Africa. Her nonfiction has been published by *Utne Reader,* the disability rights magazines *Mouth* and *Ragged Edge,*[1] and the independent Turkish news agency BIAnet. She lives on Chicago's South Side with her English teacher wonder-spouse, vocal music scores (she is a mezzo soprano), lots of fragrant houseplants, and an organic community garden plot. Their only child, who came from an unplanned pregnancy of truly crisis proportions, is now almost grown, living well with her learning disabilities, working as a home health aide to a severely disabled young friend, and preparing to become a special education teacher.

Pro-Every Life, Pro-Nonviolent Choice
by Mary Krane Derr

Every woman knows that if she were free, she would never bear an unwished-for child, nor think of murdering one before its birth.
—Victoria Woodhull, USA (1875)[2]

371

> Abortion for the masses . . . does not represent a conquest for civilization, because it is a violent and death-dealing answer to the problems of pregnancy, which, moreover, further culpablizes the woman's body . . .
> —Via Cherubini Feminist Collective, Milan, Italy (1975)[3]

My vision for peace in the abortion war could be called "pro-every life, pro-nonviolent choice." As a devout believer in religious pluralism and the separation of "church" and state, I would not presume to bother others with it if it imposed exclusively sectarian morality, no more than I would insist on public policy dictating that everyone say the Buddhist refuge prayer every day. But respect for all lives is a basic value that can be shared by people of all faiths and none.[4] I oppose abortion because I cannot—though I have certainly tried!—get around its "violent, death-dealing, culpablizing" character for *both* women and unborn children.

The contemporary prochoice movement has long publicly emphasized the fetus as a clump of tissue removable through minor surgery. It now more openly grapples with increasing scientific knowledge that, along with many women's reproductive intuitions and experiences, make this argument seem less credible. An anonymous abortionist reflects on a former Planned Parenthood president's words:

> Faye Wattleton said recently, "I think we have deluded ourselves into believing that people don't know that abortion is killing. So any pretense that abortion is not killing is a signal of our ambivalence, a signal that we cannot say yes, it kills a fetus, but it is the women's body, and therefore ultimately her choice." I believe that very firmly. You look at the ultrasounds and there's a fetus with a heartbeat and then after the procedure, there's the fetus, usually in pieces, in a dish. It was alive one moment and it's not the next.[5]

Like Wattleton and this unnamed abortionist who quotes her, more prochoicers are acknowledging out loud that a fetus is indeed alive and (at least biologically) human. For many, the decisive matter remains: "What does the fetus mean to the pregnant woman?" Laury Oaks writes:

> Fetal identity is open to a variety of interpretations at the personal as well as social, cultural, religious, and political levels . . . Feminists and women's health advocates should increase efforts to expose the prolife fetus—which feeds fetal rights and fetal abuse ideologies—as just one of many versions of the fetus.[6]

It is indeed important to discover and understand the multiplicity of fetal interpretations and their practical effects. It is vital to challenge sensationalistic prolife imagery and rhetoric that depict the fetus as an already-born infant trapped within a feckless, lethal shirker of "maternal destiny," as simply floating around in the air somewhere, or contained within some inert, insensate, unseen vessel that has no purposes other incubating than his/her overblown life. Such depictions deny pregnant women their full complexity as human beings and their indispensable contributions to fetal life and well-being. In other words, they are visual images of the maternal-fetal conflict itself. They also turn fetuses into adult anthropomorphic projections, rather than seeking an openhearted, openminded knowledge of what it is like to actually *be* a fetus—just as mawkishly cute depictions of already-born children or of animals can get in the way of compassionately discerning and respecting what it is like to exist on *their* terms.

On the other hand, does the multiplicity of fetal interpretations in and of itself mean that all carry the same ethical and political weight? After all, there are multiple interpretations of *women*, many of which feminists have quite rightly challenged, including the abovementioned defacement of pregnant women. Feminists do have some criterion for evaluating the ethical and political validity of a particular interpretation—perhaps the same one that runs through so many other social justice movements, religious and secular/interfaith alike: the recognition that above and beyond any phenomenal interpretation of him/her, every human being has an innate value that ought not to be violated through lifetaking and other acts of violence—simply because s/he exists. Interpretations are ethically and politically sound (not simply existent as human phenomena) to the degree that they honor this innate value. (As a devout environmentalist and vegetarian, I by no means wish to restrict innate value to human lives; I merely limit this particular essay's scope to the human species.)

The twentieth-century Jewish philosopher Emmanuel Levinas was a survivor of both Russian pogroms and the Nazi holocaust. Mindful that war combatants often cannot shoot "enemies" who look straight at them, he had a beautiful, moving way of expressing human beings' innate value.

> The relation with the face can surely be dominated by perception, but what is specifically the face cannot be reduced to that.... [T]he face is meaning all by itself... the first word of the face is "Thou shalt not kill."... However, at the same time, the face of the Other is destitute; it is the poor for whom I can do all and to whom I owe all. And me,

whoever I may be, but as a first person, I am he [sic] who finds the resources to respond to the call.[7]

Does it make any sense to say that the fetal face is among those that issue such a call? The utter dependence of the fetus upon the pregnant woman *does* matter, and greatly—but in a sense quite other than rendering the biologically human and alive fetus devoid of equal innate value and the ethical and political claims that flow from it. Honestly, what is it that makes fetal dependence—or any other kind of dependence—appear the unquestionable hallmark of mattering *less than*? Could it be the same false paradigm of domination and submission that kills and maims women and other oppressed groups daily, and results in ecocide? *All* biologically human (not to mention other) lives are embryos in the womb of the Earth. Some even describe the global environmental crisis as "ecoabortion." Even as we cannot live and thrive apart from these ecological bonds of dependence/ interdependence, we humans are each at the same time on our own equally valuable, uniquely embodied life courses.

It is neither ethically, politically, nor biologically absurd to speak of the fetus as having a face. I refer readers to Alexander Tsiaris's *From Conception to Birth: A Life Unfolds*, a factual and sensational (but not sensationalized), richly detailed visual trip through prenatal development on the parallel but different scales of both the pregnant woman and the unborn child. At 21-23 days after conception—when many women verge on the suspicion of pregnancy—the embryo is still smaller than a grain of rice. In addition to a beating heart and a fledgling nervous system, s/he has already sprouted the neural crest cells that are the start of the face and skull. By 40 days, the embryo is the size of a small adult's fingerprint. S/he has developed recognizable eyes and is about to have detectable brainwaves.[8] In the brief time before the literal, biological face has clearly emerged, the fetus is not ethically or politically faceless—no more than an already-born human being with missing or impaired facial features would be. "Of all circumstances biasing the judgment or restricting the sympathies," noted Matilda Joslyn Gage, "none have shown themselves more powerful than physical differences."[9] Women have all too often known this reality in their own flesh, for they, along with their unborn children, have been cast—and cast out—together as inferior, insensate "merely biological" entities without "souls," even as their respective partisans have pitted them against each other to the point of death.

Abortion violates the innate value of already-born as well as unborn human lives—especially women who undergo it—and decidedly *not* because it hinders some purported "One True Godly Purpose of Procreation." Nor do individual women all have the same emotional and spiritual responses to abortion, just as military personnel do not all react alike to combat. Yet recurrent themes do connect the wide range of abortion stories to which many others and I have borne witness, especially the wish that there could have been another way, but there wasn't one in sight. No little girl sits around exclaiming, "When I grow up, I want to have an abortion!" Unfortunately, her circumstances may someday shove her against a wall, with no other evident prospect of escape.

It's been said that if men got pregnant, abortion would be a sacrament. On the contrary: if men got pregnant, *pregnancy* would be treated as the sacrament; abortion would be considered blasphemy against their sacred bodies and lives and those of their children; and pregnant humans would finally, finally receive the alternatives they deserve instead of what one social activist calls, from bitter experience, the "choice" between "abortion or else."

Some healing professionals respect and work with the body's honesty and wisdom which may or may not be conscious—about everything that has happened in a person's life.[10] According to one sex therapist, the deepest part of the vagina, the part around the cervix, stores up the pain of rape, traumatic childbirth (often caused by inadequate prenatal care and/or undue medical interference in labor and delivery), and abortion. Often this pain needs to be released and resolved before a woman is free to enjoy sexual pleasure and have orgasms as she deserves.[11] As prochoice feminist psychologist Sue Nathanson lamented after her abortion: "Instead of feeling free, sensuous, sexual, I feel like a 'thing,' a piece of meat, existing only for the pleasure of my husband, deadened to any possibility of pleasure for myself."[12] Though denial and silencing of women's pain certainly persists on a global scale, rape and the most common causes of childbirth trauma are now consciously recognized—at least among feminists—as acts of violence, of sexual/reproductive coercion that women would choose not to experience if they were free not to. Now why would women's bodies respond in the same way to abortion as to these more acknowledged violations?

Dreams and visceral sensations in the waking state can both express the body's deep intelligence.[13] In this volume, Leslie Keech discusses an abortion clinic nurse's dream of abortion as a male-on-female rape. The same nurse says that her "belly flip-flops with sorrow" each time the vacuum aspirator machine enters the woman on the table and begins its work. A dedicated employee of a different clinic names her most frightening work-related dream: "going into labor alone on a high open hill, and looking down to see that what was emerging from her body was not a baby, but twisted pieces of metal, like something from a junkyard." She interprets this nightmare as "about the whole idea of abortion . . . the personal sorrows that enveloped them every working day at the clinic."[14] Is even the body-wisdom of persistently committed, prochoice-feminist abortion providers signaling that abortion is violence against fetuses, caused by violence against women?

These clinic staff members both feel they must set aside their profoundly unsettling insights about their work, rather than follow through these insights to the point that they disarm. They explain their work as submission to "necessity" arising from the fact that they "see women" who take priority over anything they see of fetuses. However impeccably intended, however meant as a corrective against long injustice, this too is a truncated vision of the two intertwined lives and bodies that make up each and every pregnancy, a vision that requires annihilative sacrifice—just like the antiabortion vision of fetuses without women. Here, too, is an example of the maternal/fetal conflict.

Prochoice feminists have powerfully, rightfully critiqued the equation of feminine compassion and goodness with the utterly destructive "duty" of unquestioned, limitless self-sacrifice that women have been conditioned to obey. They have particularly exposed it as it figures in certain antiabortionist perspectives, such as revivals of the adoption mandate as "atonement" for (female) nonmarital sex. Yet few prochoicers have openly identified and questioned this conditioned imperative of female sacrifice as it figures in the *practice* of abortion. Might this very "duty" explain why some clinic staff, and other prochoicers as well, feel obligated to hold at bay their profound misgivings about the procedure? Why they may fear betraying the very cause of women simply for having and voicing such thoughts? And why so many women feel—most tragically and understandably so—that they have no recourse but abortion?

Prolife feminists have long thought and said this, and now our conclusions overlap with those publicly voiced by at least one prochoice feminist, Rebecca Ann Parker.

> I have seen that women sometimes choose abortion in ways that are heartbreaking—and unnecessary. For example, a woman will believe that aborting her pregnancy is the divinely sanctioned punishment she deserves for having gotten pregnant. Or, like me, she will abort a pregnancy in order to save a man from something he fears. Feminists need to discuss how the decision to abort can reflect women's obedience to life-denying ideas and reinforce women's subordination and entrapment in abuse.[15]

Parker breaks the silence surrounding such abortion experiences with a courageous, poignant offering from her own life. When she conceived, her spouse immediately squashed her joy with his decree that he did not want to be a father and their marriage stood no chance unless she had an abortion. She "felt his words as if they were a physical blow—swift, precise, unexpected." In isolation and silence, fearing (inaccurately, she concluded later) that no one would help her bear and raise the child, she agonized over what to do. Finally, in springtime, "when the lilacs were heavy with purple blossoms," she had the pregnancy ended. She and her spouse did not speak of it, and he soon left her.

Parker now feels she did the best she knew how at that time, in those circumstances. She remains prochoice, out of laudable concerns for women's safety and moral agency. At the same time, she concludes that her abortion came from obedience to a deeply inculcated ideology of love as unlimited sacrifice, rather than from moral discernment and freedom.

> I felt keenly the loss of the child whose beginning I had welcomed with joy. I was left with grief and shame, and hid these feelings from my family, friends, and religious community. During the day I did my job, but at night, I wrestled with anguish. I wanted to die. I was troubled that the choice to sacrifice came so easily. It was clear to me that in choosing the abortion I was choosing to make a sacrifice. The pregnancy was a blessing. Letting it go was a loss. The gesture of sacrifice was familiar. I knew the rubrics of the ritual by heart: you cut away some part of yourself, then peace and security are restored, relationship is preserved, and shame is avoided . . .

Parker began to deeply question and explore why she and the women she knew were so prone to enacting this ritual, even though it was "clearly a horror" and "futile." She realized that it had thwarted her from articulating and asserting moral claims of responsibility upon her spouse and from trusting that her communities would aid her in caring for the child. The sacrifice of the child and "the desires of my heart" resulted in "sorrow. Nothing was redeemed or saved. I felt bereft . . . The abortion made me aware of an interior vacuity—an absence of self-possession, of self-protection, of freedom . . . I had no inner sanctuary."[16]

Parker eventually connected her abortion and the ritual behind it to a much earlier hurt: repeated childhood sexual abuse by an adult male neighbor she had trusted. A history of abuse is another common thread to the biographies of many who have directly experienced abortion. For example, as many as 75% of clients in one post-abortion counseling project have described histories of sexual abuse.[17] This is much higher than the reported global average of one in three women. Parker recognized that her husband, too, had incurred sexual abuse, although his response to it, in the context of the pregnancy and abortion, was aggression and withdrawal. The repercussions of child/youth abuse upon men as well as women need to be better understood, prevented, and alleviated, in abortion-related contexts and elsewhere.[18]

It is indeed heartbreaking and unnecessary for human beings to suffer like this. If only the culture had not censored the likes of Matilda Joslyn Gage, instead of taking to heart her warnings from over a century ago. Noting that woman's "training has ever been that of self-sacrifice," Gage declared: "She must no longer be the scapegoat of humanity upon whose devoted head the sins of all people are made to rest."[19] (This dynamic does not tend to foster well-being in the scapegoaters, either.)

Not that sacrifice is *never* a good or responsibility. I am simply calling attention to the deeply entrenched, pernicious ideology of *unlimited* female-*only* sacrifice as a primary reason why women are denied better options than abortion and inhibited from even searching for whatever alternatives might actually exist for them now. Then they are expected to suffer, in silence, the brunt of the whole setup. As a former pregnancy counselor, and as a veteran, with my boyfriend (now spouse), of an unplanned pregnancy in a context of ongoing medical crisis, poverty, disrupted life plans, and others' harsh judgmentality, I am well aware of all that it takes to sustain and birth an unborn child, then carry out a decision to parent or place for adoption, especially in a culture of gender inequality. While unborn children should generally not have to sacrifice their lives, taking parts of their mothers with them, I vigorously protest some antiabortionists' dismissal and trivialization of what women so frequently undergo in pregnancy and beyond. Indeed I have long railed against blithe, uncomprehending or downright hostile references to "convenience abortions." I do suspect, again as witness and veteran of crisis pregnancy and its aftermath, that decent health care and cultural support can greatly reduce any element of sacrifice, far more thoroughly than U.S. culture in particular has ever dared to imagine.

But what if there is some irreducible element of sacrifice for women in carrying pregnancy to term? Does this necessarily mean that one cannot possibly reject the "duty" of feminine self-sacrifice-without-boundaries and still oppose abortion on "demand"? No; after all, if a pregnancy endangers a woman's literal life, I think abortion is an option—although of course if women and unborn babies received adequate health care, such horrible dilemmas could be largely prevented, as they generally are now in the more prosperous nations. And the value of any responsibility to carry a pregnancy to term in other less dire but still difficult circumstances does not lie in some inherently ennobling, redemptive quality realized when women are forced to submit to endless self-effacement and self-injury, especially in obedience to some "ovarian destiny" decree. It lies quite elsewhere: in (at the very least) the fact that (with current technology) carrying the pregnancy to term is the sole means by which the lethal sacrifice of another, even more vulnerable human being can be prevented—and that within one's own sentient, remembering flesh.

Especially in the Two-Thirds World and in the castoff sectors of America, I have seen enough of human and particularly female resilience, resourcefulness, courage, and strength to trust that women can survive and even flourish—along with, not in opposition to, their children—as they meet the challenges of carrying pregnancies to term—not to mention the challenges beyond!! At the same time, it is immensely cruel to scapegoat and revile women who have felt too disempowered to take it on. They deserve nothing less than empathy and determined commitment to alleviate the social problems that put them in such a hard place to begin with. Partners, families, communities, governments, and humankind as a whole all have the responsibility to do whatever they can through nonviolent means to prevent and alleviate suffering for *all* lives involved in a crisis pregnancy, before, during, and ever after birth. It is just plain *wrong* to dump upon pregnant women the entire responsibility of struggle and sacrifice—most of which is unjust, unnecessary social construction masquerading as "God's will," "nature," "survival of the fittest," "practical necessity," or "just the way things are" anyway! Not because women are weaklings or eternal victims. (Whoever dubbed us "the weaker sex" was probably just smitten with womb envy, breastfeeding envy, multiple-orgasm envy . . .) Because *all* human beings, no matter how independent-minded—and rightfully so— are social animals who cannot make it alone.

In practical and political terms, what might it mean to see both female and fetal faces simultaneously? A general turn away from fetal lifetaking— legal or illegal—as a way to "resolve" very real human problems—and *at the very same time* complete respect, in deed as well as word, for women's right to nonviolent sexual and reproductive choice. Support at all levels of society for the exercise of this fundamental right is simultaneously a matter of justice and mercy for women, the surest protection for children before and after birth, and the lifting (free at last!) of the grotesquely oversized burden of sacrifice imposed upon both. Within this right, at least as I have described it here, there are likely significant areas of common ground between prolife and prochoice.

Women 's ethical and political right to nonviolent choice encompasses (at least) the following.

- Comprehensive, scientifically accurate, culturally competent sexual/reproductive health education—throughout the entire life cycle, well ahead of the questions and dilemmas that generally characterize each phase of it. Its success depends on both "the facts" and the skill and social power to apply them according to one's own preferences, circumstances, and ethical or spiritual values.

- Freedom to choose one's own consenting adult partner, or to not have a partner.

- Freedom from such bodily/psychic assaults as child abuse, hate crimes, domestic violence (which, incidentally, often escalates during pregnancy), "honor killings," "dowry murders," all degrees of sexual harassment and coercion, from lack of protection against HIV and other sexually transmitted infections, from poverty that leaves no survival recourse but sex work, from female genital mutilation, sterilization abuse, excessively medicalized and aggressive obstetrical "care," abortion (illegal or legal), and the punitive denial of postabortion health and social service care.

- Freedom to minimize the possibility of conception through whatever scientifically safe method(s) accord with one's personal preferences, ethical/religious/spiritual values, health needs, and circumstances. One's choice(s) may or may not include celibacy/abstinence, masturbation, heterosexual outercourse, same-sex relationship, natural family planning/fertility awareness, or "artificial" methods like condoms, diaphragms, and surgical sterilization.

- Greater responsibility and reciprocity from men in the making and carrying out of sexual and reproductive decisions. Men should not simply be discouraged from irresponsibility and domination, but actively encouraged to be equal partners and/or parents.

- In the event of unplanned pregnancy, freedom of choice among parenting, adoption, or some other mother- and child-safe care arrangement, and the right to whatever nonstigmatizing assistance is needed to carry out the decision, before, during, and ever after birth. This freedom requires accommodations for pregnant and parenting women in workplaces, schools, and everywhere else, as well as access to open adoption and other services that may ease adoption for the birth mother.

- Freedom to deliberately seek parenthood, through efforts to conceive, nonharming infertility treatment, adoption, and/or foster care. This, too, requires accommodations in schools, the workplace, and everywhere else, regardless of the means by which a child comes to one's family.

- Conditions that promote the greatest maternal/child (and indeed over all human) health possible. These include safe workplace, home, local, and global environments free of pollutants that, for example, cause miscarriage as well as other maternal and/or fetal harms; contaminate breast milk; and cause fertility-impairing diseases like endometriosis and possibly lethal gynecological cancers. Safe, competent prenatal care and childbirth alternatives from midwives and/or physicians who do not treat pregnancy as a state of health rather than disease, while taking a vigilant, prevention-oriented approach towards any medical problems that may arise. Prompt, nonpunitive substance abuse treatment. Ready, free/affordable access to antiretrovirals and other HIV/AIDS-related services. Encouragement and support of breastfeeding, including workplace accommodations, without stigmatizing mothers who bottle-fed.

- Freedom to forego biological and/or social parenthood through means other than abortion. Freedom from stigma whether one's nonparent status is due to choice or infertility.

- An overall cultural climate of support not only for all nonviolent forms of family and parenting, but *generativity*, which may or may not involve biological and/or social parenthood.

- Equality of access to sexual/reproductive health-related education, care services, and all other nonviolent options, whatever one's race/ ethnicity, nationality, socioeconomic status, occupation, parent/ nonparent status, disability/health condition, marital status, or sexual orientation.

As far as abortion itself is concerned, ought there be a law? Mere legal bans may in fact sabotage their stated purpose of respect for life unless and until they have *generous* provision for women's right to nonviolent choice *written right into them*. I challenge prochoice legislators to likewise write this into their bills, so that whatever abortion's legal status is, human beings can hope to have other and better ways open to them. I do have an idea of the least imperfect way to deal with the complexities of the legal-or-illegal question: something like the Western European model Mary Ann Glendon praised almost two decades ago, in great contrast to *Roe v. Wade* and its emphasis on autonomy, separation, and isolation in the war of all against all . . . The European laws not only tell pregnant women that abortion is a serious matter, they tell fathers that producing a child is serious, too, and communicate to both that the welfare of each child is a matter in which the entire society is vitally interested.[20]

Of course many women already know abortion is serious, but many are not fully informed, and at any rate, it can only help for the law to affirm, rather than ignore or undermine, women's knowledge and need to gain knowledge. The European landscape has of course changed greatly since the 1980s, but Western social welfare democracies like France and the Netherlands have essentially held to this model. Despite their poverty, the fledgling democracies of the East have overall moved towards similar models, instead of retaining the entrenched, optionless Soviet-era "abortion culture."

In one of my ancestral homelands, Poland, the Soviet-controlled regime had imposed, against the largely silenced wishes of many citizens, state-funded abortion-on-request since 1956. After the regime's 1989 fall, Nobel Peace Prize winner Lech Walesa and the 10-million-strong independent trade union and political party Solidarnosc (Solidarity) came democratically to power, with great support from women. Solidarnosc and President Walesa almost immediately moved to craft abortion-reducing legislation. In 1993, Walesa signed a new law into effect, with the backing of Solidarnosc, most other political parties, much of the Sejm (parliament), and the general populace, as well as Hanna Suchoka, Poland's first female prime minister. This law did not simply limit abortion to a small range of circumstances; it offered "a comprehensive program of assistance to pregnant women and their unborn children," family planning services that encompassed both contraceptives and natural family planning, and sex education in the public schools. It stipulated that illegal abortionists would receive a maximum of two years in prison, and women none at all.

Since the law's passage, reported legal abortion and maternal mortality rates have dropped steeply in Poland.[21] It is difficult to say just why; the same obscuring, silencing woman-vs.-fetus construct gets in the way. U.S. and other prochoice partisans attribute the drop to a secret, dangerous abortion "underground" and travel abroad for the procedure. Some feel betrayed and baffled that the change in the law was initiated and led by Walesa and Solidarnosc: the courageous nonviolent resisters to the old regime; the eloquent defenders of "ordinary" workers and their right to self-determination; the outspoken critics of environmental degradation, the death penalty, anti-Semitism, and ultranationalism. Must be some nasty, masculinist sectarian quirk, right? They, like some prolife partisans, miss the whole constellation of "life" issues and collective social welfare responsibilities to which the Polish policy is deeply connected. Such prolife partisans conclude that more women are completing rather than aborting their crisis pregnancies—as if that in and of itself means everything is just fine and dandy!

Personally I suspect that both "sides" are onto something. If so, why do women feel compelled to take such risks for self-induced, "underground," or foreign abortions? Do women not feel that available alternatives empower them to successfully prevent and complete difficult pregnancies and live bearable lives afterwards? Has Poland, as a poor, long-devastated nation—and one now beset with its own all-or-nothing abortion-war partisans—had difficulty implementing the hope of prevention and pregnancy aid embedded in the law? If so, how can the international community, especially the richer nations, and most of all Poles themselves cooperate in alleviating the situation? Simply inveighing against "punitive misogyny" or lauding "the triumph of family values" will not help anyone to understand, let alone meet, the needs of Polish women and babies—or any others.

All over the world, the faces of millions of women and children, born and unborn, are calling. Who will see and hear, and in a "pro-every life, pro-nonviolent choice" spirit "find the resources to respond to the call"? What will happen next?

—Adapted from "Reproductive Choice: A Prolife Ecofeminist Affirmation," speech to Consistent Life's "Nonviolence In a Time of War" conference, San Francisco, CA, 2 November 2002.

Wangari Maathai

Wangari Muta Maathai, globally acclaimed environmentalist, human rights campaigner, feminist, and 2004 Nobel Peace Prize recipient, was born in 1940 to a farming couple in a rural area of Nyeri, Central Province, Kenya, near wildlife-rich Mount Kenya. The young Maathai was already sensitive to the start of disturbing changes in the landscape she loved deeply: the replacement of small, eco-friendly farms and forests with commercial monoculture plantations, the drying up of clean, abundant water, soil erosion, the disappearance of familiar plants and animals. Over the past 150 years, possibly 75% of Kenya's forest cover has been destroyed, first by Anglo colonialists, then wealthy plantation owners and the poor Kenyan farmers they have squeezed out and made desperate for fuel, arable land, food, and water.

In 1960, Maathai was awarded scholarships to study in the United States. She earned a B.S. and M.S. in biology (Mount Saint Scholastica College, 1964, and University of Pittsburgh, 1966, respectively). Her Ph.D. in anatomy (University of Nairobi, 1971) made her the first East African woman to achieve a doctorate. From 1973 to 1980, she directed the Kenyan Red Cross. In 1976, she was appointed chair of the Department of Veterinary Anatomy, University of Nairobi. During the late 1970s, as a leader of the National Council of Women of Kenya, she was deeply affected by the laments of rural women over the countryside's accelerating degradation, which deprived them more and more of healthy diets, farming income, drinking water, firewood, shelter, and kinship with the living world and one another. In 1977, Maathai founded the Green Belt Movement (GBM), which has pioneered a home-grown approach to overcoming these threats against poor women and their families, and against the ecosystem at the same time: hiring the women to plant and nurture trees.[1]

During the early 1980s, Maathai's husband left her and their three children, Waweru, Wanjira, and Muta. A judge granted him a divorce on the grounds that she was "too educated, too strong, too successful, too stubborn and too hard to control."[2] Maathai told the judge that he was incompetent, and he sentenced her to a night in jail. She persisted as leader of the Green Belt Movement despite this and numerous other run-ins with Kenyan authorities, especially the heavy-handed, thoroughly corrupt regime of President Daniel arap Moi. Moi and his associates derided her as a "national menace" and an "un-African"—because outspoken and unsubmissive—woman. The nonviolent Maathai endured further arrests as well as death threats and injuries from beatings. Moi has since fallen from power, but the Green Belt women can now celebrate three decades of accomplishment. Within Kenya, over 600 GBM community groups have planted over 30 million trees in both rural and urban settings, in the process schooling "ordinary" citizens, especially women, in political advocacy skills and inspiring parallel activism in other Two-Thirds World nations. Most recently the GBM has ventured into personal and community empowerment through sexual and reproductive health education in the facts and decision-making skills surrounding abstinence, voluntary family planning, and HIV/AIDS prevention.

Maathai continues to serve on GBM's board, and those of the National Council of Women of Kenya, the United Nations Advisory Board on Disarmament, the Earth Charter Commission, Green Cross International, and the Women and Environment Development Organization, among others. In 2002, Moi's abdication made free democratic elections possible, and Maathai resigned as GBM leader to run for office. From 2002 to the present, Maathai has served as Member of Parliament for her hometown district, and since 2003 as Kenya's deputy environment minister.

The list of Maathai's honors grows ever longer: the Goldman Environmental Prize (1991), the United Nations Environment Programme Global 500 Hall of Fame (1991), the UN Africa Leadership Prize (1991), the Jane Addams Leadership Award (1993), the Golden Ark Award (1994), the Kenyan Community Abroad's Excellence Award (2001), the Republic of Kenya's Eldership of the Burning Spear (2003), the Conservation Scientist Award (2004), the Petra Kelly Environmental Prize (2004), and the J. Sterling Morton Award of the National [U.S.] Arbor Day Foundation (2004), to name only some. In late 2004, Maathai was granted the Nobel Peace Prize, becoming the first African woman ever to achieve a Nobel of any kind. On hearing the news, Maathai planted a Nandi flame tree at the foot of Mount Kenya. She asked admirers around the world to celebrate this honoring of the GBM women and to "secure the future for our children" by planting trees also.[3]

Maathai often says: "What we do to the Earth, we do to ourselves." These words express her wisdom—drawn from both modern scientific and ancestral knowledge—about many issues, including abortion and its relationship to female disempowerment. The article below comes to us from Lifesitenews (www.lifesite.net), affiliated with Canada's Campaign Life Coalition.

"Abortion Is Wrong," Says Nobel Peace Prize Winner
by Lifesitenews

OSLO, NORWAY—Kenyan Nobel Peace Prize winner, Mrs. Wangari Maathai, said "abortion is wrong" in a conversation with Norway's *Dagen* newspaper reporter Jostein Sandsmark Tuesday. Professor Maathai is Kenya's deputy minister of the environment.

"But I am trying to avoid condemning the victim," she said, referring to the pregnant mother who seeks an abortion. She sees both mother and child as casualties: "Both are victims. There is no reason why anybody who has been conceived, shouldn't be given the opportunity to be born and to live a happy life. The fact that a life like that is terminated, is wrong," said Maathai.

"When we allow abortion, we are punishing the women—who must abort their children because their men have run away—and we are punishing the children whose life is terminated," she continued. "But it is because we are not willing to put the men where they should be, and that is taking up the responsibility."

"I want us to step back a little bit and say: Why is this woman and this child threatened? Why is this woman threatening to terminate this life? What do we need to do as a society? What are we not doing right now as a society? A part of that answer lies in this House," Maathai said, pointing at the Kenyan Parliament building.

While abortion is still illegal in Kenya, Maathai suggests going further—
that the 1960s law making fathers financially responsible for any children
they conceive be re-instated.

"That law was removed by men in this Parliament," she emphasized.
"Now I think we are too lenient on men. We have almost given them a
license to father children and not worry about them. That is part of the
reason why women abort, because they do not want to be burdened with
children whose fathers do not want to become responsible."

Maathai will be awarded the Nobel Prize in Oslo Friday for her
involvement in fighting for the environment, human rights and women's
rights.

See link to the full interview with Mrs. Wangari Maathai (in Norwegian):
<http://www.dagen.no/show_art.cgi?art=6832>.

—Lifesitenews e-mail release, 7 December 2004.

Linda Naranjo-Huebl

Linda Naranjo-Huebl grew up in a large family in northwest Denver, Colorado (the "North Side"). She became involved with Denver's first crisis pregnancy center in 1981 and shortly afterward joined Feminists for Life, actively serving its Denver chapter as a writer and speaker. With much help and support from her family, she returned to college and continued her education at the University of Colorado, where she obtained a Ph.D. in English specializing in Women's and American Ethnic Literature. Currently an assistant professor at Calvin College in Grand Rapids, Michigan, she also maintains a part-time residence in Denver, Colorado. She still cannot believe that she makes a living at what she loves most—reading books and talking about them (incorporating music at every opportunity). She has come to learn that the most powerful form of resistance against oppression is celebrating life; and echoing a passage in one of her favorite books, she "has seen beauty and it has burdened [her] with responsibility" (Rudolfo Anaya, *Bless Me Última*).

Room for One More
by Linda Naranjo-Huebl

When our daughters were small, we would read a delightful book called *Always Room for One More*. It was the illustrated text of a Scottish folktale and song about Lachie MacLaughlan and "his wife and ten bairns," who had a gift for hospitality. Lachie would stand at the front door of his wee abode and invite passersby in for a bit of food and fellowship, each time declaring that there was always room for one more. There was a song score at the end, so we learned the melody and sang it as we viewed the book's illustrations. Perhaps we liked it so much because it was quickly becoming our own family motto.

In 1981, I learned about a pregnancy center opening in the Denver area designed to help women experiencing crisis pregnancies. I had always been prolife and prowoman; it never occurred to me that some people might think these two positions were incompatible until NOW made abortion rights central to its platform. When I learned about the right-to-life movement as a young teen, I quickly identified with its principles; but I also had an emerging feminist consciousness and family experience that made me look at the issue from the woman's point of view. I knew the most significant struggle for life takes place not in the philosophy and rhetoric of the prolife or prochoice movements, but with each individual woman deciding whether she will carry or abort her child; and I also knew that many women feel like they have no choice at all. If the choice is between bearing a child and continuing one's education, or between a child and one's career, or between a child and the support of one's family and friends, then the rhetoric of choice is a mockery. So when the new pregnancy center opened up in our community, we signed on to be a "Shepherding Home," that is, we hosted in our home young women who were experiencing crisis pregnancies.

We were good candidates for the job—coming from a large, working class family, I was used to having lots of people around, and my husband, Scott, is one of the most laid back people I know. We had very little income, but our house was large; and the pregnancy center, our church community, friends, and family all helped out with food, time, and moral support. The pregnant women, mostly very young and lacking the support of friends and family, each became part of our household, attending family and community events, holidays, birthdays, and other special celebrations. Our church hosted baby showers for the young women, and many church members became close to them and still maintain those relationships. All of this is not to suggest that our lives were not turned upside down with each new arrival.

The crisis, or crises, leading to the need for emergency housing during pregnancy became our own upon each woman's arrival, and I found myself increasingly angry and frustrated at those social forces that make pregnancy so difficult in the first place. Many people believe that as a society we have progressed from those days when a single woman's pregnancy was cause for ostracism or even punishment. We no longer send women off to "homes" where they can have their babies in secret, place them for adoption, and return home as if nothing had happened, do we? With each new arrival, we were astounded to observe the hardships and discrimination most of these young women face as a result of their pregnancy.

While it is true that immature teens often romanticize childbearing and the attention that comes with it, sometimes leading to intentional pregnancies, such idealization is quickly dispelled by real life circumstances. Women facing unplanned or inopportune pregnancies are subjected to all kinds of insults, censure, discrimination, and abandonment. They are aware of a continual undercurrent of judgment against them, including negative assumptions about their morals, their intelligence, their judgment, their self-discipline and sense of responsibility. They also face more overt discrimination. We have witnessed, and vigorously protested, substandard treatment of these women by medical establishments, schools, and various social service agencies, not to mention their personal friends, family, and even their church communities. They are also routinely discriminated against in the workplace, if they can even get a job. Most desire to work through their pregnancy, but not even those employers of minimum-wage workers will give a pregnant woman a job. I used to laugh when well meaning friends would say, "but discriminating against a pregnant woman is illegal." How silly to think that making something illegal would put an end to the practice (which isn't to say that it *shouldn't* be illegal—just that a law alone cannot solve a social problem—an important lesson for prolife activists). Most traumatically, the young women who were placed in shepherding homes all experienced abandonment at some level; they came to live with us because they lacked the support of family and friends.

Our years of experience also taught us that reactions to unplanned pregnancy are frequently influenced by class and ethnicity. Middle- and upper-class Anglos tend to react more negatively to an unplanned pregnancy than working class people and ethnic minorities. Penny Salazar, who helped found the Center and served as its Executive Director for over twenty years, has shared with me how she has encountered some panicky middle- and upper-class white parents who would almost prefer their teenage daughter die than have a baby. Contrastingly, while aware that unplanned pregnancies come with a financial burden, the Latino, African American, and working class communities less often regard the situation as a major crisis.[1] In my own extended Latino family, those most likely to consider an unplanned pregnancy a serious problem are those who are rising on the economic ladder. We can see how these different cultural and economic perspectives extend beyond our borders. Women in the Two-Thirds World frequently criticize American feminists for their emphasis on abortion rights instead of equal educational and economic opportunities for women. They tell us that children are not the problem; it's the systems into which they are born.[2]

Many feminists believe that as a society we have also progressed from the days when a woman measured her value only in relationship to a man. We imagine that young women today are more liberated, intelligent, and assertive than their mothers. Unfortunately, with each new generation of women, the lessons must be taught anew because we still live in a culture that undervalues the female. As a professor of women's studies, I am frequently reminded with each new class how our culture bombards young women with negative messages about their self worth. Pregnancy help centers are filled with clients suffering from very low self-esteem—young women who enter into sexual relationships as a means of establishing intimacy and gaining affirmation and recognition from the more dominant sex.

In the worst cases, these young women have suffered abuse by their boyfriends, husbands, or their parents and family, and, finding themselves pregnant, reach out to the pregnancy center staff in an attempt to save not only their baby's life, but their own. While cases involving dangerous situations are referred to the more experienced women's shelters, several women who have lived with us suffered milder, but still pernicious, forms of psychological and verbal abuse. One controlling boyfriend, having lost the immediate target of his wrath, would call his girlfriend in our home and berate her over the telephone. "What a strange thing—to tolerate abuse when all one need do is hang up the phone," I thought as I hung it up for her. Another young woman, before coming to our home, lived with a substance abuser and drug dealer, but his attentions were so flattering (he was considered very attractive), she stayed with him even after she caught a bullet that was intended for him in a drug deal gone awry. In the saddest cases, even after being rejected by their boyfriends, young women would continue to lie and steal on their behalf. In such relationships, the pregnancy center counselors and we would frequently hope that the baby's father would just leave, disappear from the situation. What a sad commentary that experience caused us to prefer the father's abandonment of the woman and her child! Nevertheless, it was frequently easier to work on building or shoring up a young woman's self esteem without abusive parties in the picture.

Such experiences, of course, underscore what every feminist knows— that young women need to build their identities separate from recognition from men; but these women taught me how fiercely and unconditionally women can love. When a controlling man (or parents) orders his girlfriend to get an abortion and she chooses otherwise, she is frequently motivated by a growing unconditional attachment and loyalty to her child *and also to herself*. Psychologists tell us that the "good enough" mother has a healthy sense of self and that her love for her child is an extension of her love for herself.[3] Abortion, then, can be interpreted, at one level, as an act against oneself, against one's own identity. By contrast, the young woman who defies boyfriend, husband, parents, friends, or authorities in carrying her child to term performs a heroic act that affirms and builds up her own sense of self while at the same time acknowledges the equally valuable life of her child. And it is appropriate that we too affirm those equally valuable lives evidenced by her self-and-other decision and step up to help her overcome the obstacles she faces.

And there are good stories to tell: of little DeShawn, who decided he liked our house enough to be born there instead of the hospital; of his mother Cynthia, the card sharp, whose country cooking will long be fondly remembered; of sweet Kris and Josh who have found a permanent place in our extended family and in our hearts; of Ruby and Laura, whose quiet spirits and courage continue to inspire—too many names to mention, but all of whom became part of our family, big sisters to our daughters, Micaela and Maura. And there is so much fun to remember. The birthday celebrations, card and board games, picnics, dinners, singing, dancing, even the bathroom cleaning competition (was that a good idea or what?) will always make us laugh. The laughter, tears, joy, and hope changed us forever.

Over the years, the pregnancy center grew quickly, serving more and more women and having more help in doing so—from staff, volunteers, churches, contributors, school systems, and both governmental and non-governmental service organizations. Several of the public school systems instituted programs aimed at keeping teen mothers and fathers in school and providing parenting classes, daycare, and vocational education. Unfortunately, funding for such programs is unreliable and fluctuates with the vicissitudes of the economy. Unlike a few pregnancy centers across the country, Alternatives Pregnancy Center has enjoyed a good working relationship with prochoice service organizations that do not share our prolife or faith perspectives. APC frequently gets referrals from Planned Parenthood and even abortion providers. In one case, the staff workers at an abortion facility in the same medical building secreted a client out the back door of their office and brought her to the Center because she was being pressured by her father (in their waiting room) to get an abortion she did not want. An APC counselor went and spoke with the father and, after presenting to him the help available to both his daughter and his family, he apologized to his daughter and made an appointment with the Center.

One of the reasons the Center has been so effective is because it is staffed largely by qualified, compassionate women who have firsthand experience with crisis pregnancy and, in many cases, abortion. They understand that women do not need laws to guide them as much as they need hope and help in dealing with all the issues surrounding unplanned pregnancy. While the Center unabashedly opposes abortion, it is not involved in political lobbying or policymaking except to the extent that it promotes a pro-woman perspective. It is perhaps because of this perspective that one of the services of the center that has experienced the most demand is its post-abortion counseling.

Many women suffering the psychological effects of earlier abortions have found themselves attracted to the pro-woman, prolife philosophy of crisis pregnancy centers, and many of them come to receive counseling and/or to volunteer to help women whose problems they understand firsthand. While the center was originally opened with the intention of focusing primarily on the needs of pregnant women, it soon became evident that there was an urgent need to develop a post-abortion counseling program. Starting with referrals from local psychologists and counselors who were not familiar enough with post-abortion issues to adequately serve their clients but who knew Penny Salazar's work, the program now constitutes a major aspect of the Center's services. Ms. Salazar's work has helped advance the field, in which there is now a growing body of research on post-abortion syndrome. Her book, *A Season to Heal*, co-written with the director of a sister center in Kentucky, is used by dozens of faith-based centers and counselors throughout the U.S. and abroad, and in support groups and workshops.[4]

The effectiveness of the programs at the Alternatives Pregnancy Center has placed its training directors in demand throughout the international community. In Africa, where AIDS exacerbates the crisis of unplanned pregnancy, pregnancy help centers are quickly springing up. At the invitation of various community groups in Uganda, Kenya, South Africa, and other African nations, Salazar and other pregnancy center staff have helped establish and maintain new facilities, and train staff and volunteers. Our African sisters have likewise inspired us with their hope, their faith, and their deep respect for life in countries that are ravaged with death to a degree that we can only struggle to understand. By coming together as an international community committed to helping women and children, by opening our lives to each other, we are all making a difference.

Going back to the story of the hospitable MacLaughlan family, one evening the wee house gets so full that it bursts at the seams. Everyone "wail[s] for a while in the heather" until they decide to "raise up a bonny new house" for the MacLaughlans that will hold even more than the old one. In the end, the story is not only a celebration of the MacLaughlan hospitality; it illustrates how their hospitality is really a community effort. And Lachie knew something important—that inviting others into our lives enriches us immeasurably. This has certainly been affirmed by the more than 50 young women who graced our home with their hope, their determination, and their lives. May each of us, in our hearts, our homes, our communities, and our lives, always have *room for one more.*

—Written for this volume, 2005.

Further Resources for Thought and Action

Appendix A—Prolife Feminist/Consistent Life Ethic Groups and Reading Materials

Groups

- Feminists for Life of America, <http://www.feministsforlife.org> (some Spanish content), 733 15th Street NW, Suite 1100, Washington, D.C. 20005, USA, phone 202-737-FFLA, email <info@feministsforlife.org>. *Oldest and largest group entirely dedicated to prolife feminism. Primarily action-oriented. College Outreach Program marshals empowering resources for pregnant and parenting students.*

- Consistent Life, <http://www.consistent-life.org/>, P.O. Box 187, Columbia, MO 65205-1087, phone 573-875-1128, email <info@consistent-life.org>. *Formerly the Seamless Garment Network. International coalition of individuals and organizations for peace, justice, and life. Opposes all forms of violence, seeing them as interconnected. Contact Rachel MacNair, director of CL's research arm, the Institute for Integrated Social Analysis, at <drmacnair@hotmail.com> or phone (816) 753-2057.*

- Feminism & Nonviolence Studies Association, <http://www.fnsa.org>, 811 East 47th Street, Kansas City, MO 64110, USA, phone 816-753-2057. *This book is a project of FNSA, an electronic and print publisher of scholarly works on prolife feminism. Website features this volume's online enhancements and the online* Feminism and Nonviolence Studies Journal *(see below).*

- *Harmony Magazine*, Sea Fog Press, P.O. Box 210056, San Francisco, CA 94121-0056. *Editors: Rose Evans and Carol Crossed. Important forum since 1988.*

Books Supporting Prolife Feminist Perspectives

- Kennedy, Angela, ed. *Swimming Against the Tide: Feminist Dissent on the Abortion Issue*, Dublin, Ireland: Open Air/Four Courts Press, 1997. *Powerful essays from Eireann/Ireland and Great Britain. Foreword by Mary McAleese, currently President of the Irish Republic.*

- Sweet, Gail Grenier, ed. *Pro-Life Feminism: Different Voices.* Toronto: Life Cycle Books, 1985. *The pioneering anthology.*
- Foster, Serrin, ed. (forthcoming) *Women Deserve Better. Planned Feminists for Life anthology; publication to be announced at* <http://www.feministsforlife.org>.
- Liagin, Elizabeth. *Excessive Force: Power, Politics, and Population Control.* Washington, D.C.: Information Project for Africa, 1996.
- MacNair, Rachel. *Achieving Peace in the Abortion War.* Online only: <http://www.fnsa.org/apaw> 2000.
- Ring-Cassidy, Elizabeth, & Gentles, Ian. *Women's Health After Abortion: The Medical and Psychological Evidence.* Toronto: The deVeber Institute for Bioethics and Social Research, 2002.
- Brennan, William. *Dehumanizing the Vulnerable: When Word Games Take Lives.* Chicago: Loyola University Press, 1995.

FNSA Journal Articles

In 1995, the quarterly academic print journal *Studies in Prolife Feminism* began publication. (Paper copies may still be available from drmacnair@hotmail.com). In 1998, the journal went online at <www.fnsa.org> and was renamed *Feminism and Nonviolence Studies.*

- Number One—Winter 1995~~Feminism, Self-Estrangement and the 'Disease' of Pregnancy (Mary Krane Derr)~~What Politicians Don't Say About the High Costs of the Death Penalty (Richard C. Dieter)~~The Politics of Breast Cancer Research (Rachel Mary MacNair)~~Amicus Brief in *Bray v. Alexandria* (Christine Smith Torre, et al.)
- Number Two—Spring 1995~~Rethinking Abortion in Terms of Human Interconnectedness (Elizabeth Fox-Genovese, Ph.D.)~~The Greatest Modern Threat to Genuine Reproductive Freedom (Elizabeth Liagin)~~Abortion and Rights: Applying Libertarian Principles Correctly (Doris Gordon)~~Compassion and Concentric Circles of Support (Frederica Mathewes-Green, M.A.)~~Amicus Brief in *Webster v. Reproductive Health Services* (Christine Smith Torre, et al.)
- Number Three—Summer 1995~~Great Britain's Debate Over the Utilization of Fetal Ova (Angela Kennedy)~~Female Objects of Semantic Dehumanization and Violence (William Brennan, Ph.D.)~~Studies Suggesting That Induced Abortion May Increase the Feminization of Poverty (Thomas Strahan, J.D.)~~Citizen Petition to the Food and Drug Administration on RU-486 (Americans United for Life)
- Number Four—Fall 1995~~You Say You want a Revolution? Pro-Life Philosophy and Feminism (Anne Maloney)~~A Feminist Case Against

Self-Determined Dying in Assisted Suicide and Dying (Sidney Callahan)~~Similar Principles: The Animal Rights Movement, Feminism, and Abortion Opponents (Vasu Murti)~~Commentary: Beyond Beijing's Cue Cards (Ruth Enero)~~From Peek-a-Boo to Sarcasm: Women's Humor as a Means of Both Connection and Resistance (Linda Naranjo-Huebl)

- Special Issue on Spiritual Diversity—Fall 1998~~*Abortion Isn't Always A Spiritually Divisive Matter* (Mary Krane Derr)~~*Religion and the Prolife Movement* (Tom Sena)~~*Feminist, Prolife and Atheist* (Kathryn Reed)~~*Prolife, Prochoice: Buddhism and Reproductive Ethics* (Karma Lekshe Tsomo)~~*Christianity Requires Gender Equality and Respect for Life* (Monnica Terwilliger [now Williams])~~*Abortion Is Bad Karma: Hindu Perspectives* (Vasu Murti and Mary Krane Derr)~~*Mercy, Lovingkindness and Peace: A Jewish Affirmation of Respect for Life* (Janet Podell)~~*"Mommy Let Me Live": Judaism Confronts Abortion* (Rabbi Jacob Neusner)~~*Our Religion Teaches Equality and Peace:* (The Muslim Women's League USA)~~*I Believe: An Orthodox Christian's Profession of Faith* (Frederica Mathewes-Green)~~*Radical Roman Catholics Affirm A Seamless Garment Position* (Pax Christi USA)~~*A Lively Concern: The Religious Society of Friends (Quakers)* (Rachel MacNair)~~*Six Songs for the Unborn* (Poetry by Joan Baranow)~~*"Our Struggle Is For All Life:" The Theosophist/Unitarian Feminist Pioneer Matilda Joslyn Gage (1826-1898 CE)*~~*The Sword Was Not With the Goddess: A Spiritual Midwife Seeks to Heal Abortion* (Jeannine Parvati Baker)~~*If Your Religious or Philosophical Perspective Is Not Represented Here: An Invitation*

Appendix B—Nonviolent Choice

A more comprehensive directory is forthcoming at <http://www.fnsa.org>. It, too, will address nonviolent options from diverse ethical and religious/ spiritual perspectives.

Crisis Pregnancy Help

*   Birthright International, <http://www.birthright.org> (English, Spanish), 777 Coxwell Avenue, Toronto, Ontario M4C 3C6 Canada, email <info@birthright.org>. *Motto: "Every baby has a right to be born, every woman has a right to give birth." Search website for nearest center. In U.S. and Canada, call 1-800-550-4900; Colombia, +57.2435.570490.477811; South Africa, Ghana, Nigeria, and Cameroon, call the Durban, Kwa Zulu Natal, SA office: +27.31.202.6528. Toronto headquarters can advise on starting or volunteering for a center.*
*   Heartbeat International, <http://www.heartbeatinternational.org>, 665 East Dublin-Granville Road, Suite 440 Columbus, OH 43229 USA, toll-free phone 1-888-550-7577, fax (614) 885-8746. *Online, searchable Worldwide Directory of Pregnancy Help. In the U.S. and Canada, call the 24-hour Option Line, 1-800-395-HELP. Outside the U.S., email <answers@optionline.org>, consult the Worldwide Directory, or contact the Columbus headquarters. Training and consultation for starting and running pregnancy resource centers.*
*   VBOK, <http://www.vbok.nl> (Dutch), Arnhemseweg 23 Postbus 559 3800 AN Amersfoort, Netherlands, phone +33.460.50.70, fax +33.461.59.01, email <info@vbok.nl>. *Member of Consistent Life. Pregnancy aid to women in Holland, in concert with the country's generous social benefits.*
*   The Nurturing Network, <http://www.nurturingnetwork.org>, P.O. Box 1489, White Salmon, WA 98672 USA, phone (509) 493-4026, fax (509) 493-4027, email <tnn@nurturingnetwork.org>. Client helpline: 1-800-TNN-4MOM. *Founded by Mary Cunningham Agee after 90% of 100 abortion clinic clients surveyed said they would have preferred another alternative. Volunteers in 25 countries. Will assist any pregnant woman. Specializes in assisting those who fear for their educational and career goals.*
*   Epigee Pregnancy Resource, <http://www.epigee.org>. *Long-time crisis pregnancy center counselor Monnica Williams puts her expertise online for women facing difficult pregnancies.*

Health
*   Sandra Steingraber, *Having Faith: An Ecologist's Journey to Motherhood*, Berkley/Penguin, 2003. *Poet/ecologist lyrically narrates her unfolding*

pregnancy in the context of a global environment now full of threatening pollutants. An eloquent call to action; includes environmental health resource directory.

- The Vegetarian Resource Group, <http://www.vrg.org/index.htm>, P.O. Box 1463, Baltimore, MD 21203, (410) 366-8343, email <vrg@vrg.org>. *Materials for starting and sustaining the health, environmental, culinary, and financial benefits of vegetarian/ vegan lifestyles. Covers veg nutrition during pregnancy and breastfeeding, and raising veg kids.*

- Sidelines High Risk Pregnancy Support, <http://www.sidelines.org/index.html>, National Office, P.O. Box 1808 Laguna Beach, CA 92652, toll-free phone 1-888-447-4754 (HI-RISK4), fax: (949) 497-5598, email <sidelines@sidelines.org>.

- British Columbia Reproductive Mental Health Program, <http://www.bcrmh.com/index.htm>, BC Women's H214—4500 Oak Street Vancouver, B.C. V6H 3N1 Canada, phone (604) 875-3060 or (604) 875-2025, fax (604) 875-3136, email <info@bcrmh.com>. *In-person help (for BC women) and online information (for women everywhere) dealing with depression, anxiety, or other psychiatric concerns around pregnancy, the postpartum period, infertility, pregnancy loss, menstruation, or menopause.*

- Association for Pre—& Perinatal Psychology and Health, <http://www.birthpsychology.com/>, P.O. Box 1398, Forestville, CA 95436, <apppah@aol.com>.

- Jacquelyn Campbell, Claudia García-Moreno, & Phyllis Sharps, "Abuse During Pregnancy in Industrialized and Developing Countries," *Violence Against Women*, July 2004. *Domestic violence often begins or escalates during pregnancy, endangering both mother and child. A serious global health issue.*

- Lundy Bancroft, *Why Does He Do That? Inside the Minds of Angry and Controlling Men*, New York: G.P. Putnam, 2002. *A counselor of men who mistreat women discusses their methods of manipulating partners. Addresses how women can detect potential abusers, assess dangers to themselves and their children, and make decisions to facilitate their safety.*

- National Coalition Against Domestic Violence, <http://www.ncadv.org>, P.O. Box 18749, Denver, CO 80218, USA, phone (303) 839-1852, fax (303) 831-9251. *National network of shelter, service, and advocacy groups.* Advises: **"If you need immediate assistance, dial 911."** *To locate local battered women's shelters and programs, call the National Domestic Violence Hotline, toll-free phone 1-800-799-SAFE; TTY for the Hearing Impaired, 1-800-787-3224.*

- Coalition For Improving Maternity Services, <http://www.motherfriendly.org>, P.O. Box 2346, Ponte Vedra Beach, FL

32004, toll-free phone 1-888-282-CIMS or (904) 285-1613, fax (904) 285-2120, email *<info@motherfriendly.org>. Global coalition in support of The Mother-Friendly Childbirth Initiative.*

- La Leche League International <http://www.lalecheleague.org/> (some Spanish content), 1400 N. Meacham Road, Schaumburg, IL 60173-4808, (847) 519-7730. *"To help mothers worldwide to breastfeed through mother-to-mother support, encouragement, information, and education."*
- MaterCare International LifeSaver Program, <http://www.matercare.org>. *Click-for-free-donation site. Makes surgery for repair of painful, devastating birth injuries possible for West African women.*

Parenting/Childrearing
- HOPE Network for Single Mothers <http://www.hopenetworkinc.org/index.html>, P.O. Box 531, Menomonee Falls, WI 53052-1531, USA. *Founded by prolife feminist Gail Grenier-Sweet. Creative, self-help-oriented ways to address local single mothers' needs. Interested persons from the Milwaukee area only: call (262) 251-7333 (weekdays). For information on starting a similar organization, email <generaldelivery@hopenetworkinc.org> with "General Information" in subject line and snail-mail address in the body of the message.*
- Family Pride Coalition, <http://www.familypride.org>, P.O. Box 65327, Washington, D.C. 20035-5327, USA, phone (202) 331-5015, fax (202) 331-0080. *GLBT persons as parents.*
- National Fatherhood Initiative, 101 Lake Forest Boulevard, Suite 360, Gaithersburg, MD 20877 USA, phone (301) 948-0599, fax (301) 948-4325, <http://www.fatherhood.org>.
- National Child Support Enforcement Association, <http://www.ncsea.org>, 444 North Capitol Street, Suite 414, Washington, D.C. 20001-1512 USA, phone (202) 624-8180, fax (202) 624-8828, <ncsea@sso.org>.
- Prevent Child Abuse America, < http://www.preventchildabuse.org/>, 200 S. Michigan Avenue, 17th Floor, Chicago, IL 60604-2404, USA, phone (312) 663-3520, fax (312) 939-8962, email <mailbox@preventchildabuse>.
- Take Back Your Time, <http://www.simpleliving.net/timeday/>, The Simplicity Forum, P.O. Box 9955, Glendale, CA 91226, USA, toll-free phone 1-877-UN-STUFF, email <contact@simplicityforum.org>. *"Major U.S./Canadian initiative to challenge the epidemic of overwork, overscheduling and time famine."*

- The Clearinghouse on International Developments in Child, Youth and Family Policies at Columbia University, <http://www.childpolicyintl.org/policies.html>.
- Mary Krane Derr, "Making Abortion Rare: A Tale of Two Countries," *Harmony Magazine*, November 2004. *Why does the U.S. have almost four times the abortion rate of the Netherlands?*

Adoption and Foster Care
- AdoptUSKids Together, <http://www.adoptuskids.org>, c/o Adoption Exchange Association, 8015 Corporate Drive Suite C, Baltimore, MD 21236, USA, toll-free phone 1-888-200-4005, email <info@adoptuskids.org>. *In the U.S. alone, thousands of "special-needs" children wait for adoption. The federal Children's Bureau (Julia Lathrop's own) started this photolisting site to help them find families.*
- Adoptive Families of America, *Adoptive Families Magazine*, <http://www.adoptivefamilies.com>, 39 West 37th Street, 15th Floor, New York, NY 10018, USA, phone (646) 366-0830, fax (646) 366-0842, subscription/customer service toll-free phone 1-800-372-3300, email:<letters@adoptivefamilies.com>. *Information on every kind of adoption, throughout the life cycle. By and for all parties in the adoption process.*
- National Foster Parent Association, <http://www.nfpainc.org/index.cfm>, 7512 Stanich Ave. #6, Gig Harbor, WA 98335, USA, phone (253) 853-4000 or toll-free 1-800-557-5238, fax (253) 853-4001.
- Concerned United Birthparents (CUB), Inc., *www.cubirthparents.org*, P.O. Box 503475, San Diego, CA 92150, USA, email <info@cubirthparents.org>. *Promotes choice and openness in adoption. For birthparents/families, adoptees, adoptive parents/families, and professionals.*

Other Ways to Nurture Children
- Human Rights Watch—Children's Rights Division, <http://www.hrw.org/children> (English, Portuguese, Russian, German, Spanish, Chinese, Arabic, among other languages), 350 Fifth Avenue, 34th Floor, New York, NY 10118-3299, USA.
- Alliance for Youth Achievement, 534 Commons Drive, Suite 100, Golden, CO 80401, USA, phone (303) 526-5219, fax (303) 526-2922, <http://www.allforyouth.org/index.htm>. *Many bright, motivated children—many of them girls and/or AIDS orphans—in the Two-Thirds World cannot afford any school fees. Consider sponsorship.*

- Room to Read, <http://www.roomtoread.org>, The Presidio, P.O. Box 29127, San Francisco, CA 94129, phone: (415) 561-3331, fax: (415) 561-4428. *16% of the world's adults are illiterate—as many as 70% in the rural Two-Thirds World. This nonprofit comprehensively seeks to boost child literacy in Nepal, Vietnam, Cambodia, and India. Gives girls long-term scholarships.*

Pregnancy Prevention/Voluntary Biological Motherhood

- Men Can Stop Rape, <http://www.mencanstoprape.org>. P.O. Box 57144, Washington, D.C. 20037 USA, phone (202) 265-6530, fax (202) 264-4362, email info@mencanstoprape.org.
- *Network*, Spring 1998 issue on "Men and Reproductive Health," archived at <http://www.fhi.org>.
- EngenderHealth: Family Planning, <www.engenderhealth.org/wh/fp/index.htm>.
- Epigee Birth Control Guide: Conscientious Contraception and Sensible Sexuality, <http://www.epigee.org/guide>. *Another Monnica Williams production.*
- YouthHealthNE (Ireland): Sexual Health: Contraception: Outercourse, <http://www.nehb.ie/youthhealthne/index.htm>.
- *The Garden of Fertility: A Guide to Charting Your Fertility Signals to Prevent or Achieve Pregnancy—Naturally—And To Gauge Your Reproductive Health,* <http://www.gardenoffertility.com/index.htm>.
- Abstinence Clearinghouse, http://www.abstinence.net, 801 East 41st Street, Sioux Falls, SD 57105, USA, phone (605) 335-3643, toll-free order line 1-888-577-2966, email <info@abstinence.net>, (some Spanish content). *Works in the U.S. and with 350+ organizations in the Two-Thirds World.*

Sexual/Reproductive Health Education

- *You Are A Masterpiece* (video, Human Development Resource Council, 2001); Sheila Kitzinger, *Being Born*, Dorling Kindersley, 1990; Lory Freeman, *It's My Body!* Parenting Press, 1984 (Spanish ed., *Mi Cuerpo Es Mio*) and its companion, *Loving Touches*, Parenting Press, 1985. *Teaching young children about prenatal development, protecting themselves against sexual abuse, and enjoying appropriate touch.*
- Advocates for Youth, 2000 M Street NW, Suite 750, Washington, D.C. 20036 USA, phone (202) 419-3420, email <questions@advocatesforyouth.org>, <http://www.advocatesforyouth.org>. *Promotes "comprehensive" (in contrast to "abstinence-only") sex ed. Affiliated with <http://www.youthresource.com> (by/for*

GLBT/questioning youth), *<http://ambientejoven.org> (GLBT/questioning Latino/a youth)*, *and <http://www.mysistahs.org> (young women of color).*

- TeenSTAR International, c/o Hanna Klaus, MD, Natural Family Planning Center of Washington, D.C., 8514 Bradmoor Drive, Bethesda, MD 20817 USA, phone (301) 897-9323, fax (301) 571-5267, <http://www.teenstar.org>. *Trains abstinence and NFP curricula instructors.*
- Disability Resources: Sexuality, <http://www.disabilityresources.org>.
- World Health Organization, "Sexual Health," <http://who.int/topics/sexualhealth/en/>, and "Reproductive Health," <http://www.who.int/topics/reproductive_health/en/>; UNAIDS, <http://www.unaids.org>.

Appendix C—Free & Low-Cost Internet & Computing Resources

For all the talk of the Internet's ability to make the world more connected, a mere 6% (about 429 million) of Earth's 6 billion-plus people have access. This book seeks to open global conversation, debate, and action to largely unheard voices. Here are some resources to help (at least some of) the other 94% to join in.

- *The Bridges.org Toolkit: Guide to Free IT.* Booklet (in print, on CD, or online) from the nonprofit information technology group Bridges, <http://www.bridges.org>. P.O. Box 715, Cape Town 8000 South Africa, Tel: +27.21.465.9313, fax +27.21.465.5917. Where to find donated, or low-cost computers, technology-savvy volunteers, and free email accounts, website development/hosting, electronic mailing lists/ discussion groups, training manuals, and software.
- Gerald E. Boyd, "Accessing the Internet by E-mail: Guide to Offline Internet Access," <http://www.faqs.org/faqs/internet-services/access-via-email/>. Fifteen million Internet-connected people have email alone. They can now use it to explore the World Wide Web. Retrieve this guide's latest version by sending an email as directed to the following auto-responders. (If busy, keep trying).

English version:
  o To: <mail-server@rtfm.mit.edu> (for U.S., Canada, & South America).
  o Enter this line only in the BODY of the note: send usenet/ news.answers/internet-services/access-via-email
  o To: <jiscmail@jiscmail.ac.uk> (for Europe, Asia, Africa, Oceania)
  o Enter only this line in the BODY of the note: get lis-iis\e-access-inet.txt
  o Send blank e-mail To: <accmail-faq@expita.com>

Translated versions:
  o To: <accmail.xx@expita.com>, where "xx" is the country, as follows: Chinese is gb, Dutch nl, Farsi ir, Italian it, Romanian ro, Russian ru, German de, Spanish sp, Hungarian/Magyar hu, Swedish se, Indonesian id, Urdu pk

Endnotes

Introduction, Part One:

[1] "Man's Inhumanity to Woman, Makes Countless Infants Die," *Revolution* 1(18): 279 (May 1868).

[2] A few pre-1960s feminists unequivocally endorsed a general moral and legal right to abortion, notably French physician/abortionist Madeleine Pelletier (Felicia Gordon, *The Integral Feminist: Madeleine Pelletier, 1874-1939*, Univ. of Minn. Press, 1991, and Madeleine Pelletier, "The Right to Abortion," in *Feminisms of the Belle Epoque: A Historical and Literary Anthology*, Waelti-Walters and Hause, eds., Univ. of Nebraska Press, 1994); her countrywoman Simone de Beauvoir (*The Second Sex*, 1949); the Canadian-born Stella Browne (Sheila Rowbotham, *New World for Women: Stella Browne—Socialist Feminist*, Pluto Press, 1978); and some in Weimar and Nazi Germany ("Reproductive Wrongs," Part One).

[3] Works omitting the early feminist stand are ubiquitous. One example appears in Hentoff, Part Two. Attacks on present-day prolife feminists and/or our invocations of this history include Ruth Rosen, "Feminists for No Choice," *San Francisco Chronicle* (6 Nov. 2003); Frances Kissling, "Trust Women" (letter), *National Catholic Reporter* (19 May 2000); Amy Richards, "Ask Amy: Reproductive Rights," Feminist.com, <http://www.feminist.com/askamy/repro/>, [17 Sept. 2004]; Barbara Finlay, Carol Walther, and Amy Hinze, "What the Founders of Feminism Really Thought About Abortion," *Touchstone* (Summer 2000); Jane A. Ussher, letter, *Utne Reader* (Sept/Oct 1990); Cynthia Bogard, letter, *Utne Reader* (Nov/Dec 1990); and Kristen J. Leslie, letter, *Daughters of Sarah: The Magazine for Christian Feminists* (Nov/Dec 1990).

[4] In her "Teaching the U.S. Women's History Survey at a Catholic University," (*Radical History Review*, Winter 1996, archived at <http://chnm.gmu.edu/rhr/rhr.htm>), Gail Bederman, who is prochoice, shows a commendably open heart and mind towards her prolife feminist (and other) students. Although many prolife feminists are not Catholic, we recommend this article for anyone wishing to get past abortion-debate stereotypes.

[5] Rosalind Pollack Petchesky, *Abortion and Woman's Choice*, Boston: Northeastern UP, 1985, 44; James Mohr, *Abortion in America*, Oxford UP, 1978, 109-113; Terry Cosgrove, "Distorted History" (letter), *Chicago Sun-Times*, 8 Feb. 1991; Robin

Orlowski, "Ignores Historical Realities," Amazon.com review of *Prolife Feminism Yesterday and Today*, 1st ed., 14 June 2001. Petchesky and Cosgrove do not delve into primary sources. Mohr finds the early feminist stance "ironical" and attributes it to distaste for nonprocreative sex. Orlowski asserts that feminist foremothers in our book were "ingrained [sic] with the idea that good girls did not talk about anything sexual period." She suggests that we long to return to the Victorian double standard despite its added perils in the era of HIV/AIDS. Mary Krane Derr, who has done her share of HIV/AIDS work, emailed Orlowski about these interpretations but never received a response.

6   Carl Degler, *At Odds: Women and the Family in America From Revolution to the Present*, Oxford UP, 1980, 243.

7   Sally Roesch Wagner, *A Time of Protest* (Sky Carrier Press, 1998) concerns early feminist nonviolent civil disobedience, like many life stories in this volume. Early feminist support for legal restrictions on abortions is documented in, for example, "Revolution Will Discuss . . .," *Revolution*, 15 Jan. 1868; "What the Press Says of Us," *Revolution*, 5 Feb. 1868; "Important Movement," *Revolution*, 8 April 1868; Lozier and Duffey, Part One. In "My Word on Abortion, and Other Things" (*Woodhull and Claflin's Weekly*, 23 Sept. 1871), Tennessee (Tennie C.) Claflin did despair that "abortion cannot be put down by law" because "it is one of the fixed institutions of the country . . . the marked characteristics of the age . . . the indicative symptoms of the ripening and rottening of our age!" Claflin was hardly defending a right to abortion here; she was simply observing that deeper measures than law were needed to abolish it.

8   See, for example, Hooker, Part One; and the cartoon made famous by the Women's Trade Union League (*Life and Labor*, March 1917). Under the words "$acred Motherhood," a harried, gaunt woman struggles to breastfeed her baby while sewing garment-industry piece work.

9   Reproductive health educator Frederick Hollick insisted, "Those who suppose that sexual enjoyment is altogether immoral and unworthy of rational beings . . . are in error." He frankly described the clitoris, noting women's ability for "considerable excitement" (*The Marriage Guide*, NY: TW Strong, 1850, 333, 356, Chapter 9.) Elizabeth Cady Stanton chided Walt Whitman, whose poetry and sexual frankness she otherwise loved, for being "apparently ignorant of the great natural fact that a healthy woman has as much passion as a man" (*Elizabeth Cady Stanton as Revealed in Her Letters, Diaries, and Reminiscences, Vol. 2*, Theodore Stanton and Harriet Stanton Blatch, eds., NY: Harper & Bros., 1922, 210.) Against prevailing medical "wisdom" about women's purportedly constitutional lack of sexual desire, Elizabeth Blackwell publicly asserted that women's lack of pleasure was not innate, but a self-protecting response to realistic fears of traumatic pregnancy and pain from men's inadequate sexual skill or outright violence (John S. and Robin

M. Haller, *The Physician and Sexuality in Victorian America*, NY: WW Norton, 1977, 99). Victoria Woodhull thundered, in no uncertain terms, for men to fully reciprocate the sexual pleasure they routinely expected from women: "[H]e shall not, either from ignorance or selfish desire, carry her impulse forward only to cast it backward with its mission unfulfilled . . ." (qtd. in Emanie Sachs, *The Terrible Siren*, NY: Harper, 1928, 223-224).

[10] William Leach, *True Love and Perfect Union: The Feminist Reform of Sex and Society*, Basic Books, 1980, 39.

[11] One outspoken "Alphaism" advocate was freethinking writer Elmina (Elizabeth) Drake Slenker (1827-1908) who believed it "as a rule" the "safest, wisest, and best" pregnancy prevention method (Elmina Drake Slenker, "Contraceptics," *Lucifer the Light-Bearer*, 23 July 1886, in Linda Gordon, *Woman's Body, Woman's Right: A Social History of Birth Control in America*, Penguin Books, 1977, 106-107). In 1887 anti-vice crusader Anthony Comstock raided the aging Slenker's confidential sexuality counseling letters and left her to a cold prison cell with no bed and a jeering, nationally sensationalized "obscenity" trial. Readers of the freethought newspaper *Truth Seeker* raised money for her legal defense. The jury found Slenker guilty, but the judge freed her ("Elmina D. Slenker (1827-1908)," in *Women Without Superstition*, *"No Gods—No Masters," The Collected Writings of Women Freethinkers of the Nineteenth and Twentieth Centuries*, ed. Annie Laurie Gaylor, Freedom from Religion Foundation, 1997). As Linda Gordon notes, twentieth-century birth controllers were much "less aware than the nineteenth-century voluntary motherhood advocates of the importance of other forms of sexual expression, both genital and nongenital." They also "isolate[d] sexual and reproductive problems from women's overall position," thus leaving the power imbalance within intimate relationships essentially unaltered (Gordon 1977, 381, 389-390). For contemporary feminist (prolife and prochoice) appraisals of Alphaism, now called "outercourse," see Judith A. Baer, Introduction, *Historical and Multicultural Encyclopedia of Women's Reproductive Rights in the United States*, Greenwood Press, 2002, xviii-xix; Karyn Milos, "Feminism and 'Choice': The Sexual Issues," *Feminists for Life of Minnesota Newsletter*, Jan. 1991; *Italian Feminist Thought: A Reader*, Paola Bono and Sandra Kemp, eds., Cambridge, MA: Basil Blackwell, 1991; and Derr, Part Two.

[12] Historians have pondered the role/nonrole of same-sex erotic attraction and expression in Boston marriages. In *Women of Hull House: A Study of Spirituality, Vocation, and Friendship* (State Univ. of New York Press, 1997), Eleanor J. Stebner acknowledges and reviews the question's complexities, while emphasizing that a homophobic culture feels less threatened if these relations are deemed asexual, and that it is more just and accurate to characterize couples like Jane Addams and Mary Rozet Smith as lesbian, in the present-day sense of the term (160-

166). Lillian Faderman's *To Believe in Women—What Lesbians Have Done for America—A History* (Houghton Mifflin, 1999) makes this point even more strongly, mentioning pregnancy prevention as *one* motive for Boston marriage (Chapter 2).

13 See, for example, Matilda Joslyn Gage, *Woman, Church, and State*, Chicago: Charles Kerr, 1893, Chapter V, and Baker and Lathrop, Part One.

14 Regina G. Kunzel, *Fallen Women, Problem Girls: Unmarried Mothers and the Professionalization of Social Work, 1890-1945*, New Haven: Yale UP, 1993, 66-68, 199n10; Marvin Olasky, *Abortion Rites: A Social History of Abortion in America*, Wheaton, IL: Crossway Books, 1992 (colonial cases); Addams, Part One.

15 Janet Farrell Brodie, *Contraception and Abortion in Nineteenth-Century America*, Cornell UP, 1994, 274.

16 Cartoon by Robert Minor, *The Masses* (Sept. 1915), in Miriam Reed, *Margaret Sanger: Her Life in Her Words*, Barricade Books, 2003.

17 Freethought publisher D.M. Bennett documents Comstock's boast that Madam Restell was the fifteenth person he had driven to suicide. Bennett adds "to this number a large list . . . of those who by his persecutions and prosecutions . . . have been driven to an untimely grave, as effectually and with far greater mental suffering than if he had assassinated them with a knife or pistol. What a reflection it must be to a man, with human feelings in his breast, that he has caused the death of more than thirty persons" (D.M. Bennett, *Anthony Comstock, His Career of Cruelty and Crime*, NY: Liberal and Scientific Pub. House, 1878, 1070-1071). Ida C. Craddock would one day join them (Severance, Part One). Comstock was no more "prolife" than today's clinic violence supporters.

18 Mohr, Chapter 7, concerns the secondary to nonexistent role of "orthodox" sects in the nineteenth-century antiabortion campaign.

19 The era's new religious movements and religious revivals often preached and practiced female equality to an unusual degree (see, for example, Ann Braude, *Radical Spirits: Spiritualism and Women's Rights in Nineteenth Century America*, Boston: Beacon Press, 1989). Note also the questioning stand that writers in Part One (and Two) take towards justice-sabotaging dogmas.

20 Susan Wells, *Out of the Dead House: Nineteenth-Century Women Physicians and the Writing of Medicine*, Wisconsin UP, 2001.

21 Degler, *At Odds*, 247. A poem about Mary Ann Hunt, a pregnant woman whose execution was stayed until after her baby's birth, shows this holistic mindframe. Why, the poet wonders, is the baby's life spared but the same compassion not extended to the mother? ("A Cry From the Condemned Cell," *Water Cure Journal and Herald of Reform*, Sept. 1848).

22 *Feminism and Nonviolence Studies Journal*, Special Issue on Prolife Feminism and Spiritual Diversity (Fall 1998), online: <http://www.fnsa.org>.

Mary Wollstonecraft:

1   Biographies include Diane Jacobs, *Her Own Woman: The Life of Mary Wollstonecraft* (Simon & Schuster, 2001) and Janet Todd, *Mary Wollstonecraft: A Revolutionary Life* (Columbia UP, 2002).

2   A.D. Farr, "The Marquis de Sade and Induced Abortion," *Journal of Medical Ethics* (March 1980). See also Germain Kopaczynski, *No Higher Court* (Scranton UP, 1995), 47, 51, 195. Was any feminist enamored of de Sade before the early abortion-rights supporter Simone de Beauvoir (1908-1986)? At least she grasped far more than de Sade what was at stake in an abortion:

> Some women will be haunted by the memory of this child which has not come into being . . . Men tend to take abortion lightly . . . [Man] commits the fault, but he gets rid of it by putting it off on her . . . [Women] learn to believe no longer in what men say when they exalt woman or when they exalt man; the one thing they are sure of is this rifled and bleeding womb, these shreds of crimson life, this child that is not there. (*The Second Sex*, 1949, Chapter XVII)

3   EngenderHealth: Family Planning, <http://www.engenderhealth.org> [5 Feb. 2005].

4   Kay Redfield Jamison, *Touched With Fire: Manic Depressive Illness and the Artistic Temperament,* Free Press, reissue ed., 1996, discusses Mary Wollstonecraft. Jamison (bipolar herself) contemplates the social and artistic impoverishment resulting from any future prenatal diagnosis and abortion of people with mood disorder genes. Her concerns resonate with those of Not Dead Yet, a disability-rights group opposed to killing of already-born persons with disabilities (see "The Value of Life With a Disability," <http://www.notdeadyet.org> [16 Aug. 2004]).

5   "'Mary Wollstonecraft,' (n.d.) Spartacus Educational," <http://www.spartacus.schoolnet.co.uk/Wollstonecraft.htm>, [7 Feb. 2005]; Henry Salt, Preface, *Animals' Rights: Considered in Relation to Social Progress* (1892), International Vegetarian Union's History of Vegetarianism, <http://www.ivu.org/history/> [18 Aug. 2004].

6   William Godwin, *Memoirs of Mary Wollstonecraft*, London: Constable and Co. Ltd., 1928, Chapter X; Mary Krane Derr, "Herstory Worth Repeating: Mary Wollstonecraft, 1759-1797," *The American Feminist*, Winter 1998-1999.

Ganeodiyo (Handsome Lake):

1   Sally Roesch Wagner, *Sisters in Spirit: Haudenosaunee (Iroquois) Influence on Early American Feminists*, Summertown, TN: Native Voices Book Pub. Co., 2001, 37, 41. Available from Matilda Joslyn Gage Foundation, 210 East Genesee Street, PO Box 192, Fayetteville, NY 13066 USA, telephone (315) 637-9511, email <gagefoundation@earthlink.net>, <http://www.matildajoslyngage.org/>.

2   Roesch Wagner, 30-31, 46-47, 48.

3   Haudenosaunee Environmental Task Force, <http://www.hetfonline.org>.

4   Roesch Wagner, 53; Sally Roesch Wagner, *The Untold Story of the Iroquois Influence on Early Feminists*, Aberdeen, South Dakota: Sky Carrier Press, 1996, 39-40.

5   Without naming this herb, Parker notes that he was shown it. It may have caused permanent infertility as well as abortion.—Eds.

6   "Woman Movement Typified by Indian Mother," *Life and Labor,* March 1917. Early twentieth-century European Americans saw Sacajawea as a "good Indian maiden" submissive to imperialist schemes. Small wonder that many Native Americans have deemed her traitorous. According to her great-great niece, Lemhi Shoshone oral tradition and the expedition's journals exonerate her as deeply faithful to her culture (Rozina George, "Agaidika Perspective on Sacajawea" (n.d.), TrailTribes.org, <http://www.trailtribes.org/Lemhi/culture.htm> [7 Feb. 2005]

7   Faye D. Ginsburg, *Contested Lives: The Abortion Debate in an American Community*, Berkeley: Univ. of California Press, 1989.

Slavery: Violence Against Lives and Choices:

1   On the Weld-Grimké family, see Robert H. Abzug, *Passionate Liberator: Theodore Dwight Weld & the Dilemma of Reform*, Oxford UP, 2004; *The Feminist Thought of Sarah Grimké*, ed. Gerda Lerner, Oxford UP, 1998; *The Grimké Sisters from South Carolina*, ed. Gerda Lerner, Oxford UP reprint, 1998; *Walking by Faith: The Diary of Angelina Grimké*, ed. Charles Wilbanks, South Carolina UP, 2003; Bruce D. Dickson, Jr., *Archibald Grimké: Portrait of a Black Independent*, Louisiana State UP, 1993; *The Journals of Charlotte Forten Grimké*, Brenda Stevenson, ed., Oxford UP, 1989; *Selected Works of Angelina Weld Grimké*, ed. Carolivia Herron, Oxford UP, 1991.

2   Theodore Weld, *American Slavery As It Is: Testimony of a Thousand Witnesses*, NY: American Anti-Slavery Society, 1839; online <http://www.iath.virginia.edu/utc/abolitn/amslavhp.html>.

3   Harriet Jacobs, *Incidents in the Life of a Slave Girl, Written by Herself*, Boston, 1861 (repub. Jean Fagan Yellin, ed., Harvard UP, 1988; available online through the Digital Schomburg African American Women Writers of the 19th Century at <http://digilib.nypl.org/dynaweb/digs/wwm97255/@Generic__BookView>).

4   Weld. The original table of contents and the index identify reports of these (and other) specific atrocities.

5   Jacobs, Chapter 12. Janet Farrell Brodie (*Contraception and Abortion in Nineteenth Century America*, Cornell UP, 1994, 53-54), is unsure if Flint/Norcom means contraception or abortion (53-54). Jacobs promptly follows his assertion about saving her from exposure with words Brodie does not note: "Could he have offered wormwood more bitter?" Jacobs perhaps speaks literally as well as metaphorically here. Wormwood (*Artemisia* spp.) is an ancient, enduring folk abortifacient, and Jacobs was likely familiar also with Biblical references to wormwood or "gall" to symbolize truncated lives.

[6] Levi Coffin, *Reminiscences of Levi Coffin*, Cincinnati: Robert Clarke & Co., 1880, 557-567.

[7] *Ibid.*, 567. Coffin states that boat hands rescued Garner, but her infant drowned.

[8] *Ibid.*, 557.

[9] Sarah M. Grimké, "Marriage," in Gerda Lerner, *The Female Experience: An American Documentary*, Oxford UP, 1992, 90-91.

[10] Dorothy Roberts, *Killing the Black Body: Race, Reproduction, and the Meaning of Liberty*, Pantheon Books, 1997, 39-47.

Elizabeth Blackwell:

[1] Elizabeth Blackwell and Emily Blackwell, "Medicine as a Profession for Women," in *The Feminist Papers*, ed. Alice Rossi, Columbia UP, 1973; Elizabeth Blackwell, *Pioneer Work In Opening The Medical Profession To Women: Autobiographical Sketches*, Humanity Books, 2005; Elizabeth Blackwell, *Essays in Medical Sociology*, Arno Press reprint, 1972; Elizabeth Cazden, *Antoinette Brown Blackwell*, Feminist Press, 1983; Alice Stone Blackwell, *Lucy Stone*, Virginia UP, 2001; and *Growing Up in Boston's Gilded Age: The Journal of Alice Stone Blackwell, 1872-1874*, Yale UP, 1990.

[2] Elizabeth Blackwell diary entry, quoted in Ishbel Ross, *Child of Destiny: The Life Story of the First Woman Doctor*, NY: Harper and Brothers, 1949, 88. Ross personally knew surviving family members, including Alice Stone Blackwell. They granted her "full and free access" to family diaries, letters, and other papers, shared memories, and anecdotes.

[3] Janet Farrell Brodie, *Contraception and Abortion in Nineteenth Century America*, Cornell UP, 1994, 228; "Planned Parenthood Acquires Elizabeth Blackwell Center's Name" (press release), Planned Parenthood Southeastern Pennsylvania, <http://www.ppsp.org/> [11 March 2004].

[4] Ross, 88. On Zakrzewska and her colleagues, see "Changing the Face of Medicine: Celebrating America's Women Physicians," <http://www.nlm.nih.gov/changingthefaceofmedicine/> [23 Aug. 2004]; and Mary Roth Walsh, *Doctors Wanted: No Women Need Apply: Sexual Barriers in the Medical Profession, 1835-1975*, Yale UP, 1977.

[5] On preventive medicine pioneer Rebecca J. Cole (1846-1922), see National Association for the Relief of Destitute Colored Women and Children Home, *Thirty-Seventh Annual Report for the Year Ending January, 1900*, Washington, DC: Smith Bros., 1900, online: American Memory Collection, Library of Congress, <http://memory.loc.gov> [23 Aug. 2004]; Harriet Sigerman, *Laborers for Liberty: American Women 1865-1890*, Oxford UP, 1998, 79; and "Changing the Face of Medicine."

[6] Elizabeth Cushier, "Autobiography," in *Medical Women of America*, ed. Kate Campbell Hurd-Mead, NY: Froben Press, 1933.

[7] Ross, 88.

[8] Leslie J. Reagan, *When Abortion Was a Crime: Women, Medicine, and Law in the United States, 1867-1973*, California UP, 1997, 6, Chapters 1 and 2.

9   In John S. Haller and Robin M. Haller, *The Physician and Sexuality in Victorian America*, W.W. Norton, 1977, 117, 215, 224.

Henry Clarke Wright:

1   Henry Clarke Wright, quoted in "Free Convention at Rutland, Vermont," *Banner of Light*, 10 July 1858. Lewis Perry, *Childhood, Marriage, and Reform: Henry Clarke Wright* (University of Chicago Press, 1980) lists this reformer's prolific but often hard-to-find works on such matters as nonviolent conflict resolution (345-350).

Susan B. Anthony:

1   Ida Husted Harper, *The Life and Work of Susan B. Anthony* Volumes One and Two, Indianapolis: Hollenbeck Press, 1898; Kathleen Barry, *Susan B. Anthony: Biography of a Singular Feminist*, New York UP, 1988; and Lynn Sherr, *Failure Is Impossible: Susan B. Anthony in Her Own Words*, Times Books, 1996.

2   Sherr, 249.

3   Sherr, 5, 9-10; Barry, 123-124.

4   Sherr, 4, 338. Gestation length estimated with data from Elisabeth Griffith, *In Her Own Right:* Elisabeth Griffith, *In Her Own Right: The Life of Elizabeth Cady Stanton*, Oxford UP, 1984, 229.

5   Susan B. Anthony, Diary Entries (4 and 7 March 1876), reprinted in *The Selected Papers of Elizabeth Cady Stanton and Susan B. Anthony, Volume Three*, ed. Ann Gordon, New Brunswick, NJ: Rutgers UP, 2003, 213-214. Thanks to Suzanne Schnittman, who alerted us to these items.

6   Sherr, 9, 166-167, 170-171.

7   Frances E. Willard, *Glimpses of Fifty Years: The Autobiography of an American Woman*, Chicago: Woman's Temperance Pub. Assoc., 1889, 598.

8   Masthead, *Revolution*, 8 Jan. 1868; "Important Movement," *Revolution*, 8 April 1868. Marvin Olasky, *The Press and Abortion, 1838-1988*, Hillsdale, NJ: Lawrence Ehrlbaum, 1988, discusses abortion as an advertising revenue source.

9   Sherr, 200-201; Susan B. Anthony, "Social Purity" (lecture, first delivered Chicago, Spring 1875), reprinted in Harper 1898, Vol. 2, 468ff.; "May 11— Sister Irene Fitzgibbon," in Mary's Pence, *Calendar of Women Companion Booklet*, Metuchen, NJ: Author, n.d., available at <http://www.maryspence.org/mp/May.htm> [16 Sept. 2004]; "History," New York Foundling Hospital, <http://www.nyfoundling.org/history.htm> [9 Sept. 2004]; "Sister Irene Fitzgibbon," Orphan Train Riders Historical Association, <http://www.orphantrainriders.com/otm11.html> [16 Sept. 2004].

10   Harper, Vol. 2, 843-844; Louise W. Knight, "Harriet Alleyne Rice," and Brigid Lusk, "Sarah Hackett Stevenson," in *Women Building Chicago 1790-1990: A Biographical Dictionary*, Rima Lunin Schultz and Adele Hast, eds., Indiana UP, 2001.

11   This piece was signed "A." Anthony was often called "Miss A.," and staff often initialed their pieces. The opinions expressed here cohere with those Anthony expressed elsewhere; "Marriage and Maternity" and Anthony's "Social Purity" have textual similarities.—Eds.

12   Voice attributed to the Biblical Eve in John Milton, *Paradise Lost* (1667 edition), Book 4, Lines 635-37.—Eds.

Elizabeth Cady Stanton:

1   Elizabeth Cady Stanton, *Eighty Years and More: Reminiscences 1815 to 1897*, Kessinger Pub., 2004; Elisabeth Griffith, *In Her Own Right: The Life of Elizabeth Cady Stanton*, Oxford UP, 1984; Elizabeth Cady Stanton, *The Woman's Bible*, Dover Pubs. Rpt., 2003; *Elizabeth Cady Stanton as Revealed in Her Letters, Diaries, and Reminiscences Volumes One and Two*, Stanton and Blatch, eds., NY: Harper & Bros., 1922; *The Elizabeth Cady Stanton-Susan B. Anthony Reader: Correspondence, Writings, Speeches*, ed. Ellen Carol Dubois, Northeastern UP, rev. ed., 1992.

2   Elizabeth Cady Stanton, "Address at the Decade Meeting on Marriage and Divorce," in Paulina Wright Davis, *A History of the National Women's Rights Movement*, NY: Journeymen Printers' Cooperative Association, 1871, 63; Alma Lutz, *Created Equal*, NY: John Day, 1940, 236.

3   Stanton and Blatch, Vol. 2, 44-45.

4   "A Girl as Good as a Boy," *Woodhull and Claflin's Weekly*, 30 Sept. 1871.

5   Sally Roesch Wagner, *Sisters in Spirit*, Summertown, TN: Native Voices Book Pub. Co., 2001, 48.

6   Elizabeth Cady Stanton, address to New York State Legislature, Feb. 1854, reprinted in *History of Woman Suffrage Vol. 1*, Stanton, Anthony, and Gage, eds., NY: Fowler and Wells, 1881, 597-598.

7   Elizabeth Cady Stanton, "Hester Vaughan," *Revolution*, Nov. 19, 1868; Ida Husted Harper, *The Life and Work of Susan B. Anthony Vol. 1*, Indianapolis: Hollenbeck Press, 1898, 309-310.

8   Elizabeth Cady Stanton, "Child Murder," *Revolution*, 12 March 1868.

9   Stanton did not sign "Child Murder" or "Infanticide," but we infer her authorship from their appearance in her newspaper and their similarities to known Stanton texts. See William Leach, *True Love and Perfect Union*, Basic Books, 1980, 147, for a Stanton passage that strikingly resembles "Infanticide"'s conclusion. Brinkerhoff, Part One, credits to Stanton *Revolution's* insistence on "the true education and independence of woman" as the solution to "child murder."—Eds.

10 "Infanticide and Prostitution" reveals Stanton's eugenicist, racist anxieties about increasing immigrant and African American populations. These anxieties are not central to Stanton's abortion stance, and we certainly condemn them today. Unfortunately, the anti-progressive strain in her thought and that of other prosperous Anglo feminists worsened ("Reproductive Wrongs Unto Death," Part One).—Eds.

414 Mary Krane Derr, Rachel MacNair, Linda Naranjo-Huebl

Dr. Anna Densmore French and a Teacher:

1   William Leach, *True Love and Perfect Union*, Basic Books, 1980, 56-57, 59, 183-185; Virginia Drachman, *Women Doctors and the Women's Medical Movement: Feminism and Medicine 1850-1895*, Ph.D. dissertation, State Univ. of New York at Buffalo, 1976, 207.

2   "Respecting Maternity," *Revolution*, 14 Jan. 1869 (excerpt), in Lana F. Rakow and Cheris Kramarae, *Revolution in Words: Righting Women 1868-1871*, Routledge, 1990, Chapter 3, "Hester Vaughanism."

3   Elizabeth Cady Stanton, "Child Murder," *Revolution*, 12 March 1868.—Eds.

Matilda Gage:

1   *History of Woman Suffrage Vol. One*, Stanton, Anthony, and Gage, eds., NY: Fowler and Wells, 1881, 466.

2   Stanton, Anthony, and Gage, 528-530; Sally Roesch Wagner, Foreword and Introduction to Matilda Joslyn Gage, *Woman, Church, and State*, Humanity Books rpt., 2002. See also Leila R. Brammer, *Excluded from Suffrage History*, Greenwood Press, 2000, and Sally Roesch Wagner, *A Time of Protest*, Sky Carrier Press, 1998.

3   Stanton, Anthony, and Gage, 18.

4   Matilda Joslyn Gage, *Woman, Church, and State*, Chicago: Charles Kerr, 1893, 14, 43 (original edition of *WCS*).

5   Wagner in Gage.

6   Lynne Spender, "Matilda Joslyn Gage: Active Intellectual," in *Feminist Theorists: Three Centuries of Key Women Thinkers*, ed. Dale Spender, Pantheon Books, 1983.

7   The phrases "voluntary motherhood" and "enforced motherhood" were formerly *not* invoked to justify abortion, but women's right of choice in pregnancy *prevention*. "Enforced motherhood" meant conception and pregnancy resulting from sex in which the woman did not, in Sarah Grimké's words, "control all preliminaries." Once conception occurred, early feminists like Gage believed a woman was already a mother and her child's life, once started, should not be forcibly stopped.

8   Gage seems to equate abortion with other thefts of female creativity. Victorian English-language slang words actually constructed abortion as such a theft. "Lock picker" meant "abortionist" (Mary Krane Derr, "Olive Schreiner's 'All-Embracing Charity,'" *Feminism and Nonviolence Studies Journal*, forthcoming; Helen Bradford, "Olive Schreiner's Hidden Agony: Fact, Fiction, and Teenage Abortion," *Journal of Southern African Studies*, Dec. 1995).

Eleanor Kirk:

1   *History of Woman Suffrage Vol. 2*, Stanton, Anthony, and Gage, eds., Rochester, NY: Susan B. Anthony, 1881, 390.

2   HWS Vol. 2, 379.

3   Eleanor Kirk (Nellie Ames), *Up Broadway*, New York: Carleton, 1870.

4   Ida Husted Harper, *The Life and Work of Susan B. Anthony Vol. 1*, Indianapolis: Hollenbeck Press, 1898, 309. For more on Kirk, see "Mrs. Nellie Ames," in *Woman of the Century*, F. Willard and M. Livermore, eds., Buffalo, NY: C.W. Moulton, 1893.

Mattie H. Brinkerhoff:

1   Louise Noun, *Strong-Minded Women: the Emergence of the Woman Suffrage Movement in Iowa*, Iowa State UP, 70, 97, 99; "Mrs. Brinkerhoff," *Revolution*, 31 Dec. 1868; Mattie H. Brinkerhoff, "The Lecturing Field," *Revolution*, 12 Nov. 1868; *History of Woman Suffrage Vol. 3*, Stanton, Anthony, and Gage, eds., Rochester, NY: Susan B. Anthony, 1886, 614.

Dr. Charlotte Denman Lozier:

1   Dr. Augustus K. Gardner, quoted in Graham J. Barker-Benfield, *Horrors of the Half-Known Life: Male Attitudes Toward Women and Sexuality in Nineteenth Century America*, Harper & Row, 1976, 87. Male doctors also argued that women should not enter the profession because their unique physical functions were disease processes that impeded public achievement ("Female Practitioners of Medicine," *Boston Medical and Surgical Journal*, 2 May 1867).

2   New Yorker Clemence Sophia Harned Lozier (1818-1888) had a flourishing homeopathic OB/GYN practice. She drew crowds of women for her weekly physiology, anatomy, and hygiene lectures; organized a popular medical library; and founded her homeopathic medical college (1863) despite efforts to deny her state charter. A graduate of Lozier's school, Maria Augusta Generoso Estrella (1861-1946), became Brazil's first woman physician. Consequently, by 1881, Brazil was moved to admit women to higher education. (Sylvain Cazalet, "History of the New York Medical College and Hospital for Women" [n.d.] <http://www.homeoint.org/cazalet/histo/newyork.htm> [15 Aug. 2004]). Clemence Lozier became a leader in the NY Suffrage Association, Moral Education Society, and Moral Reform Society (one of the first organized American movements to protest male sexual exploitation and its role in abortion; Carroll Smith-Rosenberg, "Beauty, the Beast, and the Militant Woman," in *Disorderly Conduct: Visions of Gender in Victorian America*, Oxford UP, 1985). See also Jessica Lozier Payne, "The Life Story of Dr. Clemence Sophia Lozier," in Bertha L. Selmon, M.D., "History of Women in Medicine," *Medical Woman's Journal*, April 1946; Elizabeth Cady Stanton, *Eighty Years And More: Reminiscences 1815-1897*, Schocken Books reprint, 1971, Chapter 28; Barbara Payne Citron, *Dr. Clemence Sophia Harned Lozier—Notable Women Ancestors*, <http://www.rootsweb.com/~nwa/clemence.html> [15 Aug. 2004]; and Gena Corea, *The Hidden Malpractice*, NY: Harper, 1985, Chapter 2.

3   Mohr recounts the Fuller-Moran case, citing "Restellism Exposed" (*Abortion in America*, Oxford UP, 1978, 113), but confuses Charlotte with Clemence. "Restellism Exposed" and other *Revolution* articles show that Charlotte was the physician

involved, as does Abraham W. Lozier's *In Memoriam: Mrs. Charlotte Denman Lozier, MD, Died January 3, 1870*, N.Y.: Press of Wynkoop and Hollenbeck, 1870 (Library of Congress copy donated by Susan B. Anthony).

4   Barbara Payne Citron (Jessica's granddaughter, Charlotte's great-granddaughter—Eds.), "The Short Life and Times of Charlotte (Denman) Lozier, M.D.—1844-1870," Rootsweb: Notable Woman Ancestors, <http://www.rootsweb.com/~nwa/charlotte.html> [6 Feb. 2005].

5   Parker Pillsbury, "Charlotte Denman Lozier, MD," *Revolution*, 13 Jan. 1870. Pillsbury, a distinguished suffragist, fiery anti-slavery activist, vegetarian, and Congregationalist minister turned freethinker, considered foundling hospitals a necessary alternative ("Foundling Hospitals Again," *Revolution*, 30 April 1868). See also Stacey Robertson, *Parker Pillsbury: Radical Abolitionist, Male Feminist*, Cornell UP, 2000.

Paulina Wright Davis:

1   Elizabeth Cady Stanton, "Reminiscences of Paulina Wright Davis," *History of Woman Suffrage Vol. One*, Stanton, Anthony and Gage, eds., NY: Fowler & Wells, 1881, 283-289. See also *The Radical Women's Press of the 1850s*, Ann Russo and Cheris Kramarae, eds., NY: Routledge, 1991.

2   Paulina Wright Davis, *History of the National Woman's Right Movement*, NY: Journeyman Printer's Cooperative, 1871, 32.

3   Olive Banks, *Faces of Feminism*, London: Basil Blackwell, 1986, 39.

Dr. Juliet Stillman Severance and A Mother:

1   "Juliet Stillman Severance," in *Woman of the Century*, Willard and Livermore, eds., Buffalo, NY: C.W. Moulton, 1893.

2   Qtd. in Ann Braude, *Radical Spirits*, Beacon Press, 1989, 153. Contemporary vegan/vegetarian ecofeminists argue too that male abuse of women is tied to animal consumption. (Carol J. Adams, <http://www.triroc.com/caroladams/>).

3   Qtd. in Braude 1989, 198.

4   Juliet Stillman Severance, "Thoughts on the Death of Ida Craddock," *Truth Seeker*, Oct. 1902; Shirley J. Burton, "Ida C. Craddock," in *Women Building Chicago 1790-1990*, Schultz and Hast, eds., Indiana UP, 2001.

5   Juliet Stillman Severance, "Is the Present Marriage System a Failure?," *Universe*, 28 August 1869.

6   A Mother, "Where the Blame Belongs," *Universe*, 28 August 1869.

Dr. Rachel Brooks Gleason:

1   Jane B. Donegan, *"Hydropathic Highway to Health": Women and Water-Cure in Antebellum America*, Greenwood Press; 1986; "Rachel Brooks Gleason," in *Woman of the Century*, Willard and Livermore, eds., Buffalo, NY: C.W. Moulton, 1893.

2   Rachel B. Gleason, *Talks to My Patients: Hints on Getting Well and Keeping Well*. NY: Wood & Holbrook, 1870, vi; Donegan 1986, 48.

Sarah F. Norton:

[1] Sarah F. Norton, "Notes From the Lecturing Field," *Revolution*, 4 March 1869 and 1 April 1869, and "Dr. Bushnell Again," *Revolution*, 15 July 1869; *History of Woman Suffrage Vol. 2*, 390; William Leach, *True Love and Perfect Union*, Basic Books, 1980, 190.

Victoria Woodhull and Tennessee Claflin:

[1] Biographies include Lois Beachy Underhill, *The Woman Who Ran for President: The Many Lives of Victoria Woodhull*, NY: Penguin Books, 1996, and Mary Gabriel, *Notorious Victoria: The Life of Victoria Woodhull, Uncensored*, Algonquin Books of Chapel Hill, 1998.

[2] Victoria Woodhull and Tennessee Claflin, "What Will Become of the Children," *Woodhull and Claflin's Weekly*, 24 Jan. 1874.

Laura Cuppy Smith:

[1] Emanie Sachs, *The Terrible Siren*, NY: Harper, 1928, 207; *History of Woman Suffrage Vol.2*, Stanton, Anthony, and Gage, eds., Rochester, NY: Susan B. Anthony, 1881, 379, 390; and *History of Woman Suffrage Vol. Three*, Stanton, Anthony, and Gage, eds., Rochester, NY: Susan B. Anthony, 1886, 755. On Smith, see also Ann Braude, *Radical Spirits*, Boston: Beacon Press, 1989, 120, 170-172, 174, 193.

Isabella Beecher Hooker:

[1] On the Beechers, see Samuel A. Schreiner, *The Passionate Beechers: A Family Saga of Sanctity and Scandal That Changed America*, Wiley, 2003; *The Limits of Sisterhood: The Beecher Sisters on Women's Rights and Women's Sphere*, Jeanne Boydston, Mary Kelley, and Anne Margolis, eds., North Carolina UP, 1988; "Isabella Beecher Hooker," in *Woman of the Century*, Willard and Livermore, eds., Buffalo, NY: C.W. Moulton, 1893.

[2] Reprinted in *Womanhood: Its Sanctities and Fidelities*, Boston: Lee and Shepard, 1874, 33-37.

[3] Willard and Livermore.

[4] On John Todd, see Graham J. Barker-Benfield, *Horrors of the Half-Known Life*, Harper & Row, 1976, Part 3. Todd, like Frank Harris, panicked that he would lose "control" of his sperm.

Elizabeth Edson Evans:

[1] Elizabeth Edson Evans, *The Christ Myth*, NY: The Truth Seeker Co., 1900, Preface.

[2] "Elizabeth E. Evans Dead," *New York Times*, 15 Sept. 1911; "Edward Payson Evans," in *Appleton's Cyclopedia of American Biography*, James Grant Wilson and John Fiske, eds., NY: Appleton and Co., 1887-1889; "Edward Payson Evans," in *National Encyclopaedia of American Biography*, NY: James T. White, 1907.

[3] Edward Payson Evans, *Evolutional Ethics and Animal Psychology*, NY: Appleton, 1898, 221.

[4] Carl Degler, *At Odds*, Oxford UP, 1980, 234.

[5] "Obscene Literature" (editorial), *Albany (New York) Law Journal*, 17 July 1875.

Eliza Bisbee Duffey:

1   Dr. Edward H. Clarke, *Sex in Education*, Boston: Osgood, 1873; Eliza Bisbee Duffey, *No Sex in Education*, Philadelphia: JM Stoddart, 1874. Mary Roth Walsh, *Doctors Wanted: No Women Need Apply*, Yale UP, 1975, 119-132, summarizes the debate.

2   Owen originally published *Moral Physiology* in 1831, after his friend, Scottish American feminist and anti-racist Francis (Fanny) Wright (1795-1852), became pregnant by a man she did not love. She felt her only choice was to give up her activism, marry the man, and live abroad in obscurity and poverty. Wright had raised Americans' consciousness of Mary Wollstonecraft and contributed her own visions (Janet Farrell Brodie, *Contraception and Abortion in Nineteenth Century America*, Cornell UP, 1994, 119-125).

Dr. Alice Bunker Stockham:

1   "Feminine Enterprise: Chicago Women Who Have a Business of Their Own," *Chicago Tribune*, 14 Sept. 1890.

2   "Alice Bunker Stockham," in *Woman of the Century*, Willard and Livermore, eds., Buffalo, NY: C.W. Moulton, 1893; Alice Bunker Stockham, *Tolstoi, A Man of Peace*, Chicago: Stockham & Co., 1900; Alice Bunker Stockham, *Karezza: Ethics of Marriage*, Chicago: Stockham & Co., 1898; Beryl Satter, "Alice Bunker Stockham," in *Women Building Chicago 1790-1990*, Schultz and Hast, eds., Indiana UP, 2001; and John C. Spurlock, *Free Love: Marriage and Middle-Class Radicalism in America, 1825-1860*, New York UP, 1988, 229.

3   Alice Bunker Stockham, *Tokology: A Book for Every Woman*, Chicago: Sanitary Pub. Co., 1887.

4   Stockham likely refers to the effects of syphilis. The double standard and disempowerment have long rendered women and their children vulnerable to STDs. Whether or not an infected woman is symptomatic, untreated syphilis is transmissible to her baby ("Facts & Answers About STDs: Information to Live By—Syphilis," American Social Health Association, <http://www.ashastd.org/stdfaqs/syphilis.html>, P.O. Box 13827, Research Triangle Park, NC 27709, (919) 361-8400, fax: (919) 361-8425; National STD Hotline: English—1-800-342-2437, TTY—1-800-243-7889, Español—1-800-344-7432). In wealthier countries, prevention and treatment services have relieved much, but not all, harm from syphilis. These services are rare and sporadic elsewhere, even though the HIV/AIDS pandemic makes them even more critical (*Bulletin of the World Health Organization*, June 2004, maternal and congenital syphilis issue, <http://who.int>).—Eds.

Lucinda Banister Chandler:

1   "Mrs. Lucinda Banister Chandler," in *Woman of the Century*, Willard and Livermore, eds., Buffalo, NY: C.W. Moulton, 1893.

2   Alice Bunker Stockham, *Tokology*, Chicago: Stockham and Co., 1888, 158.

3   Sarah Margaret Fuller (later Ossoli) (1810-1850) was, like Ralph Waldo Emerson, a key figure of American Transcendentalism. She edited the Transcendentalist magazine *The Dial*, in which she argued for women's equality, as in her book *Woman in the Nineteenth Century* (1845).

4   William Leach, *True Love and Perfect Union*, Basic Books, 1980, 85-92.

5   Leach, 81.

6   See Leach, 85-92, 293; Willard and Livermore 1893; and Elizabeth Cady Stanton, *The Woman's Bible*, NY: European Pub. Co., 1898; online at Internet Sacred Text Archive, <http://www.sacred-texts.com/index.htm>.

7   Lucinda B. Chandler, *Non Flesh Eating From a Moral Education Standpoint*, Chicago Vegetarian Society, 1890, 6.

8   Lucinda B. Chandler, "Legal Murders Condemned," *Lucifer the Light Bearer*, 18 Oct. 1889.

9   Qtd. in Kristin Hoganson, "'As Badly Off as the Filipinos': U.S. Women's Suffragists and the Imperial Issue at the Turn of the Twentieth Century," *Journal of Women's History*, Summer 2001, online at <http://iupjournals.org/jwh/jwh13-2.html> [07 Feb. 2005].

10   Carroll Smith-Rosenberg, *Disorderly Conduct*, Oxford UP, 1985, 243, 372n75. Smith-Rosenberg cites Chandler's *Divineness of Marriage*, NY: Great American Pub. Co., 1872.

11   Qtd. in Sally Roesch Wagner, *Sisters in Spirit*, Summertown, TN: Native Voices Book Pub. Co., 2001, 20.

Reproductive Wrongs Unto Death: Eugenic Strictures:

1   Mary Krane Derr, "Margaret Sanger's Insufficiently Recognized Debt to Victorian Feminism," unpublished paper accepted by 1990 National Women's Studies Association Conference.

2   William Leach, *True Love and Perfect Union*, Basic Books, 1980, 85, 150-151.

3   Daniel J. Kevles, *In the Name of Eugenics: Genetics and the Uses of Human Heredity*, Knopf, 1985, 84.

4   Lara Foley, "Eugenics," in *Historical and Multicultural Encyclopedia of Women's Reproductive Rights in the United States*, ed. Judith Baer, Greenwood Press, 2002.

5   Carroll Smith-Rosenberg, *Disorderly Conduct*, Oxford UP, 1985, 40-41, 266-269.

6   Erika Lee, "Exclusion Acts: Chinese Women During the Chinese Exclusion Era, 1882-1943," in *Asian/Pacific Islander American Women*, Shirley Hune and Gail M. Nomura, eds., New York UP, 2003; Edwin Black, *War Against the Weak*, Four Walls Eight Windows, 2003, 22-23, Chapter 10; Kevles, 94-97.

7   Black, Chapter 19; Michael Sullivan DeFine, "A History of Governmentally Coerced Sterilization," unpublished paper, University of Maine Law School, 1 May 1997; online at <http://www.geocities.com/ CapitolHill/9118/mike2.html> [8 Sept. 2004].

[8] Black, 108-122, 400; Kevles, 329-330n48; Carlos Santos, "Historic Test Case: Wrong Done to Carrie Buck Remembered," *Charlottesville Times-Dispatch*, 17 Feb. 2002, archived at JUSTICE FOR ALL, <http://www.jfanow.org> [13 Sept. 2004], free e-news service, American Association of People with Disabilities, <http://www.aapd-dc.org>. Josie Byzek, "Kenneth Newman Says," *Mouth Magazine*, March 2000, rptd. at <http://www.mouthmag.com/says/kennethsays.htm> [8 Sept. 2004], honors another voice of experience.

[9] Black, Chapter 13.

[10] Linda Gordon, *Woman's Body, Woman's Right*, Penguin Books, 1977, 174; Marvin Olasky, *Abortion Rites*, Wheaton, IL: Crossway Books, 1992, 235; Craig Buettinger, "Antivivisection and the Charge of Zoophil-Psychosis in the Early Twentieth Century," *Historian*, Winter 1993. Neurologist Charles Dana invented the diagnosis of "zoophil psychosis" so Rational Men of Science could protect themselves from challenging voices (mostly female) and simultaneously preserve their image as "beneficent" champions of human progress.

[11] Black, 308-312, Part Two; Robert Jay Lifton, *The Nazi Doctors: Medical Killing and the Psychology of Genocide*, Basic Books, 1986; U.S. Holocaust Memorial Museum. *Nazi Persecution of the Disabled: Murder of the "Unfit,"* <http://www.ushmm.org/museum/exhibit/focus/disabilities_02/> [8 Sept. 2004].

[12] J. Enamorado Cuesta, "Porto [sic] Rico's Real Problem," (letter), *Birth Control Review*, May 1932; Gordon 1977, 336-339.

[13] Gordon, 416-417.

[14] Gordon, 395-398.

[15] Cynthia Gorney, *Articles of Faith: A Frontline History of the Abortion Wars*, Touchstone/Simon and Schuster, 1998, 220-223.

[16] *Ibid.* 49-54.

The Woman Movement and Irish Catholic America:

[1] Hasia R. Diner, *Erin's Daughters in America: Irish Immigrant Women in the Nineteenth Century*, Johns Hopkins UP, 1983, particularly Chapter 7.

[2] Irish Famine Curriculum Committee, *The Great Irish Famine* <http://www.nde.state.ne.us/SS/irish/irish_pf.html> [9 Sept. 2004].

[3] Diner, 137; Lisa Lipkin, "The Child I've Left Behind," *New York Times Magazine*, 19 May 1996. See also Anthony, Part One.

[4] Linda Gordon, *Woman's Body, Woman's Right*, NY: Penguin, 1977, 249; *Emma Goldman, Living My Life* Volume One, NY: Knopf, 1931, Chapter 15. Though besieged with pleas, Goldman refrained from performing abortions: "It was not any more consideration for the sanctity of life; a life unwanted and forced into abject poverty did not seem sacred to me. But my interests embraced the entire social problem, not merely a single aspect of it, and I would not jeopardize my freedom for that one part of the human struggle." She feared, too, for the women's health and

lives. In taking abortion as a symptom of despair and desperation, and in prioritizing birth control and labor causes as means of prevention, Goldman was closer to predominant early feminist views than to some present-day abortion-rights opinions. Hasia Diner and Beryl Lieff Benderly (*Her Works Praise Her: A History of Jewish Women in America*, Basic Books, 2003, 216-218, 260) attribute Jewish women's support of contraception, sex education, and other maternal/child health and welfare measures to this horrific picture of repeated abortions.

5   Gordon, 274-290.

6   Margaret Sanger, An Autobiography, 1938/Dover 1971, 89-92.

7   Sanger, *An Autobiography*, 55.

8   Margaret Sanger, *Woman and the New Race*, Truth Pub. Co., 1920, 79.

9   Margaret Sanger, *My Fight for Birth Control*, NY: Farrar and Rinehart, 1931, 133.

10 Miriam Reed, *Margaret Sanger: Her Life in Her Words*, Fort Lee, NJ: Barricade Books, 2003, 316-317n19.

11 Gordon, 216-219.

12 On Jacobs, see Hamilton, en4.

13 Kathleen Tobin, *The American Religious Debate Over Birth Control, 1907-1937*, Jefferson, NC: McFarland & Co., 2001, 143-145; Jacob Z. Lauterbach, "156. Birth Control," Central Conference of American Rabbis Responsa/American Reform Responsa, Vol. XXXVII, 1927, 369-384, archived at <http://ccarnet.org> [3 Feb. 2005]. Lauterbach concludes that the Talmudic-Rabbinic law "does not forbid birth control, but it forbids birth suppression."

14 Tobin, 85-87, 110-112; Mary Ware Dennett, "Catholic Discretion," *Birth Control Herald*, 15 May 1924.

15 John Augustine Ryan, "Family Limitation," *Ecclesiastical Review*, June 1916.

16 Diner 1983, 49-50; Tobin 2001, 177-178, 195-197; Leo J. Latz, *The Rhythm of Sterility and Fertility in Women*, 6d, Chicago: Latz Foundation, 1932/1944, 146-148.

17 Carl G. Harman, "Catholic Advice on the 'Safe Period,'" *Birth Control Review*, May 1933.

18 "She's Got Rhythm? A Safe Period for Sanger and the Church," *Margaret Sanger Papers Newsletter*, Fall 2002, <http://www.nyu.edu/projects/sanger/article_list.htm> [9 Sept. 2004].

Jane Addams and Hull House:

1   *The Jane Addams Reader*, ed. Jean Bethke Elshtain, Basic Books, 2002.

2   Eleanor J. Stebner, *Women of Hull House*, State Univ. of New York, 1997, 34.

3   Stebner, 70.

4   Eleanor J. Stebner, *Women of Hull House*, State Univ. of New York, 1997, 34.

5   Stebner, Chapter 6; Rima Lunin Schultz, "Mary Rozet Smith," in Schultz and Hast 2001.

6   Jean Bethke Elshtain, *Jane Addams and the Dream of American Democracy: A Life*, Basic Books, 2002, 160.

7   Mark Regan Essig, *Edison & the Electric Chair: A Story of Light and Death*, Walker & Co., 2003; Richard Moran, *Executioner's Current: Thomas Edison, George Westinghouse, and the Invention of the Electric Chair*, Knopf, 2002 Edison; "BAD ELEPHANT KILLED. Topsy Meets Quick and Painless Death at Coney Island," *The Commercial Advertiser*, NYC, 5 Jan. 1903, online <http://www.railwaybridge.co.uk/topsy.html> [14 Sept. 2004]. Martin Pernick, *The Black Stork: Eugenics and the Death of "Defective" Babies in American Medicine and Motion Pictures Since 1915*, Oxford UP, 1999, 24; Elshtain 2002b, 161.

8   Pernick, 96.

9   Jane Addams, "The Home and the Special Child," in Elshtain, ed.

10   Joint Committee of Hull House and the Chicago Medical Society, "The Midwives of Chicago," *Journal of the American Medical Association*, 25 April 1908.

11   *Ibid.*

12   Jane Addams, *Twenty Years at Hull House*, Macmillan, 1910, Chapter 13.

13   Qtd in Marvin Olasky, *Abortion Rites*, Crossway, 1992, 228.

14   Qtd. in Olasky, 216.

15   Hull House ran clinics affiliated with the Illinois Birth Control League (later Planned Parenthood). Another IBCL affiliate was the Jewish organization Chicago Woman's Aid. See Bernice J. Guthmann, *The Planned Parenthood Movement in Illinois*, Chicago, Planned Parenthood Assoc. Chicago Area, 1965; Hamilton, Part One. Hull House's Dr. Rachelle Slobidinskaya Yarros directed this network of clinics until the early 1940s (Diane C. Haslett, "Rachelle Slobindinsky Yarros," in *Women Building Chicago 1790-1990*, Schultz and Hast, eds., Indiana UP, 2001). IBCL's initial clinic founding committee (1923) expressly sought "to prevent in every manner rational and proper, recourse to abortion, now too prevalent" (Mary Ware Dennett, *Birth Control Laws: Shall We Keep Them, Change Them, or Abolish Them?* Frederick H. Hitchcock/The Grafton Press, 1926, 16).

16   Jane Addams, *A New Conscience and an Ancient Evil*, Macmillan, 1912, Chapter 5; Jane Addams, *The Long Road of Women's Memory*, NY: Macmillan, 1916, Chapter 3.

17   Jane Addams, *My Friend Julia Lathrop*, Macmillan 1935/Illinois UP, 2004, 37-38.

18   Addams 1916, Chapter 3.

Frances E. Willard and the Anchorage Mission:

1   *Twenty-First Annual Report of the Erring Women's Refuge*, Chicago: Knight & Leonard, 1883, 6.

2   Julie Beardsley, "Dr. Sarah Vasen: First Jewish Woman Doctor in Los Angeles, First Superintendent of Cedars-Sinai Hospital," *Roots-Key: Newsletter of the Jewish Geneaological Society of Los Angeles*, Summer/Fall 2003, archived at <http://home.earthlink.net/~nholdeneditor/contents.htm>, [31 Jan. 2005]; Hasia Diner and Beryl Lieff Benderly, *Her Works Praise Her*, Basic Books, 2002, 231-232.

3   George J. Kneeland, "Preventive Agencies," in *Commercialized Prostitution in New York*, NY: Bureau of Social Hygiene/The Century Co., 1913; Regina G. Kunzel,

Fallen Women, Problem Girls, New Haven: Yale UP, 1993; Frances E. Willard, *Address Before the Second Biennial Convention of the World's WCTU*, Chicago: World's Columbian Exposition, 1893, 37; *Report of the National Women's Christian Temperance Union, Twenty-Second Annual Meeting*, Chicago: Women's Christian Temperance Union Pub. Assoc., 1895, 298-299; and Charles N. Crittenton, *The Brother of Girls*, World's Events Pub. Co., 1910.

4   Frances E. Willard, "How the Chicago WCTU Was Founded, What It Has Accomplished, and Who Have Assisted," *Union Signal*, 5 Dec. 1895; Rickie Solinger, *Wake Up Little Susie: Single Pregnancy and Race Before Roe v. Wade*, Routledge, 1992, 67-68, 71-72, 74; National Association for the Relief of Destitute Colored Women and Children, *Thirty Seventh Annual Report for the Year Ending January, 1900*, Washington, D.C.: Smith Bros. Printers, 1900; online at the American Memory Collection, Library of Congress, <http://memory.loc.gov> [23 Aug. 2004]; Kunzel, Chapters 3 and 4.

5   Ruth Bordin, *Frances Willard: A Biography*, North Carolina UP, 2001; *Writing Out My Heart: Selections from the Journal of Frances E. Willard, 1855-96*, ed. Carolyn De Swarte Gifford, Illinois UP, 1995; Frances E. Willard, *A Wheel Within a Wheel: How I Learned to Ride the Bicycle*, Applewood Books reprint, 1997; *Woman of the Century*, Willard and Livermore, eds., Buffalo, NY: C.W. Moulton, 1893; Frances E. Willard, *Glimpses of Fifty Years*, Chicago: Women's Christian Temperance Union Pub. Assoc., 1889; Frances E. Willard, Helen Winslow, and Sallie White, *Occupations for Women*, NY: Success Co., 1897; and Frances E. Willard, *Woman in the Pulpit*, Chicago: Women's Christian Temperance Union Pub. Assoc., 1888.

6   Sara Boudin Edlin, *The Unmarried Mother in Our Society*, Farrar, Straus, and Young, 1954, 36.

7   Kunzel, 33-34; Solinger 1992, Chapter 5. Pathological secrecy and denial also covered up the needs of the birth father, birth relatives, infertile adoptive couples, other adoptive relatives, and adoptees. Many felt *they themselves* had been cruelly rubbed out. The adoption mandate was "justified" as necessary "rehabilitation" for the birth mother's future heterosexual wifehood. Yet many women suffered deep, enduring injuries. Adam Dickter ("As Agency Closes, Emotions Spill Out," *The Jewish Week*, Metro New York City, 6 Feb. 2004) documents women's poignant stories showing how unmoored the Lakeview Home had become from its original, tragically forgotten feminist intentions. By compounding stigma upon nonmarital childbearing, the adoption mandate *encouraged* abortion and gave impetus to calls for social and legal sanction of it. Adoption is sometimes the least problematic solution, but *only* as the woman's own choice. See, for example, Jessica O'Connor-Pitts, "A Birthmother's Cherished Memories," *The American Feminist*, Winter 2004-2005.

8   Rosalind Pollack Petchesky, *Abortion and Woman's Choice*, Boston: Northeastern UP, 1990, 209.

⁹   Title from a Chicago Historical Society-held brochure about the Mission.—Eds.

A Businesswoman's World-Mending Invention:

1   Qtd. in the *Dubuque Times*, 3 Feb. 1874.

2   Louise Klaber, "Lane Bryant Malsin," in *Jewish Women in America: An Historical Encyclopedia, Vol. 2*, Paula E. Hyman and Deborah Dash Moore, eds., Routledge, 1997; Richard W. and Dorothy C. Wertz, *Lying-In: A History of Childbirth in America*, Yale UP, 1989, 148-149.

Dr. Caroline Hedger:

1   "Industrial Supremacy" [transcript], A Biography of America: Companion Website to the Video Series and Telecourse, WGBH-Boston and Annenberg CPB, 2000, <http://www.learner.org/biographyofamerica/prog14/transcript/page04.html> [24 Aug. 2004].

2   *Ibid.;* Emily Clark, "Caroline Hedger," in *Women Building Chicago 1790-1990*, Schultz and Hast, eds., Indiana UP, 2001; Caroline Hedger, M.D., *The School Children of the Stockyards District*, Washington, DC: GPO, 1913. Alison Comish Thorne (*Leave the Dishes in the Sink: Adventures of an Activist in Conservative Utah*, Logan, UT: Utah UP, 2002, 4-5) documents Hedger's style of caring.

3   Hedger likely means sexual harassment and exploitation.—Eds.

Dr. S. Josephine Baker:

1   S. Josephine Baker, *Fighting for Life*, Macmillan, 1939; Marsha Lakes Matyas, "Sarah Josephine Baker, Physician and Public Health Worker" (n.d.), Notable American Unitarians, <http://www.harvardsquarelibrary.org/ Unitarians/ index.html>, [27 Aug. 2004]; and "Changing the Face of Medicine," <http:// www.nlm.nih.gov/ changingthefaceofmedicine/> [23 Aug. 2004]. Baker's partner IAR Wylie penned *My Life With George: An Unconventional Autobiography* (Random House, 1940) about their relationship.

2   S. Josephine Baker, *Child Hygiene*, Harper & Brothers, 1925, Chapter 2.

3   Richard W. Wertz and Dorothy C. Wertz, *Lying-In*, Yale UP, 1989, 228.

Julia Lathrop and the Children's Bureau:

1   Jane Addams, *My Friend Julia Lathrop*, Macmillan 1935/Illinois UP, 2004, 140.

2   Addams, Chapters 5 and 6, 114; Clifford Whittingham Beers, *A Mind That Found Itself*, 2d ed., NY: Longmans, Green, & Co., 1910, online, Disability History Museum, <http://www.disabilitymuseum.org>, [31 Aug. 2004]; and Robyn Muncy, "Julia Clifford Lathrop," in *Women Building Chicago 1790-1990*, Schultz and Hast, eds., Indiana UP, 2001.

3   Julia Lathrop, *First Annual Report of the Chief, Children's Bureau, Dept. of Labor*, U.S. GPO, 1914, 6.

4   Edwin Black, *War Against the Weak*, Four Walls Eight Windows, 2003, 252-258; "Julia Lathrop Fights Decision on Baby's Death," *Chicago Tribune*, 18 Nov. 1915; Addams, Chapter 7. The *Tribune* piece and others on Allan Bollinger's killing are

part of the online Disability History Museum, <http://www.disability museum.org> [31 Aug. 2004]. See also Martin Pernick, *The Black Stork*, Oxford UP, 1999.

5   Julia Lathrop, *Sixth Annual Report of the Chief*, Children's Bureau, Dept. of Labor, U.S. GPO, 1918, 12-13.

6   Richard W. Wertz and Dorothy C. Wertz, *Lying-In*, Yale UP, 1989, 206-210; Kathleen Tobin, *The American Religious Debate Over Birth Control, 1907-1937*, Jefferson, N.C.: McFarland & Co., 2001, 60; Eleanor J. Stebner, *Women of Hull House* State Univ. of N.Y., 1997, 111. Lathrop's friend Grace Abbott, also single and without biological children, although her young niece's preferred guardian, responded to such insults with similar wit. On Abbot and her sister Edith, see Joan R. Rycraft, "Edith Abbott" and Robyn Muncy, "Grace Abbott," in *Women Building Chicago 1790-1990*, Schultz and Hast, eds., Indiana UP, 2001; Lela B. Costin, *Two Sisters for Social Justice* Illinois UP, 2003; Grace Abbott, *Immigrant and the Community*, Ozer Publishers reprint, 1971.

7   Wertz & Wertz, 208-210.

8   Grace Abbott, *Seventeenth Annual Report of the Chief, Children's Bureau, Dept. of Labor*, U.S. GPO, 1929.

9   Wertz & Wertz, 208-210.

10   Trude Bennett, "Carol S. Weisman. *Women's Health Care: Activist Traditions and Institutional Change*" [book review], *Journal of Health Politics, Policy, and Law*, June 2000; online <http://www.jhppl.org> [4 Sept. 2004].

11   Anne Firor Scott, Introduction to Addams, xxi.

12   Qtd. in Kriste Lindenmeyer, *"A Right to Childhood": The U.S. Children's Bureau and Child Welfare, 1912-1946*, Illinois UP, 1997, 69; Letter from Mrs. F.S., Cincinnati, Ohio, 31 July 1922, and response (n.d.) from staffer Ethel Watters, reprinted in Molly Ladd-Taylor, *Raising a Baby the Government Way: Mothers' Letters to the Children's Bureau 1915-1932*, Rutgers UP, 1986, 65-66.

13   Grace Meigs, *Maternal Mortality from All Conditions Connected with Childbirth in the U.S.*, U.S. Children's Bureau Pub. No. 19, Washington, D.C.: U.S. GPO, 1917; Abbott 1929; *Maternal Deaths: A Brief Report of A Study Made in Fifteen States*, Children Bureau Pub. No. 221, Washington, D.C.: U.S. GPO, 1933.

14   Lindemeyer, 257; Wertz and Wertz, 127-128, 161-164.

15   Addams, 150-153.

The Women's Cooperative Guild:

1   Olive Banks, *Faces of Feminism*, Basil Blackwell, 1988, 124, 149, 191-194.

2   Sheila Rowbotham, *A New World for Women*, Pluto Press, 1978.

Dr. Alice Hamilton:

1   Alice Hamilton, *Exploring The Dangerous Trades*, Little Brown, 1943; reprint OEM Press 1995; Barbara Sicherman, "Alice Hamilton," in *Women Building*

Chicago 1790-1990, Schultz and Hast, eds., Indiana UP, 2001. Many aspects of Hamilton's life and work merit even further attention, such as her warnings about tetraethyl lead. This gasoline additive became (and remains, despite some phaseouts) Earth's greatest source of lead pollution/ poisoning. Pregnant, unborn, and young postnatal humans are most vulnerable. In the 1920s, profit-hungry corporations brushed aside and for decades covered up the already damning evidence—thus injuring and killing countless plants, animals, and humans, particularly in the Two-Thirds World. (Bill Kovarik, "Overview: Leaded Gasoline History and Current Situation," <http://www.radford.edu/~wkovarik/ethylwar/overview.html> [27 Feb. 2005]).

2   Alice Hamilton and Harriet Hardy, *Industrial Toxicology, 2d*, Paul B. Hoeber/Medical Book Dept. of Harper & Brothers, 1949 (now in its fifth edition).

3   Hamilton 1943/1995, 184-187.

4   *Bulletin of the Chicago Medical Society*, 4 Dec. 1915. Feminists often stressed this distinction. Dr. Aletta Jacobs (Gerritsen) (1854-1929) was Holland's first woman physician, an improver of barrier contraception, and founder of the world's first birth control clinic. Jacobs took offense at men's false accusations that she was an abortionist (Aletta Jacobs, *Memories: My Life As an International Leader in Health, Suffrage, and Peace*, ed. Harriet Feinberg, Feminist Press, 1996, 48-50). Mary Ware Dennett (1872-1947), National Birth Control League (US) founder, observed,

> . . . The laws link contraceptive knowledge so closely with instruction for abortion that in some of the statutes, there is not even a comma between them . . . Of course the two ideas are actually separated by an abyss that has no bottom . . . [Birth control] does not mean interference with life after conception has taken place . . . (*Birth Control Laws*, Frederick H. Hitchcock/The Grafton Press, 1926, 12.)

See also Marie Stopes, *Married Love*, A.C. Fifield, 1919; "Marie Stopes," in *Encyclopedia of Women Social Reformers*, ed. Helen Rappaport, ABC CLIO, 2001; and Greta Jones, "Marie Stopes in Ireland: The Mother's Clinic in Belfast, 1936-1947" [excerpt], in *The Irish Women's History Reader*, Alan Hayes and Diane Urquhart, eds., Routledge, 2001.—Eds.

Rose Pastor Stokes:

1   On Rose, see "I Belong to the Working Class": *The Unfinished Autobiography of Rose Pastor Stokes*, Herbert Shapiro and David L. Sterling, eds., Georgia UP, 1992; Arthur Zipser and Pearl Zipser, *Fire and Grace: The Life of Rose Pastor Stokes*, Georgia UP, 1989; Linda Gordon, *Woman's Body, Woman's Right*, Penguin Books, 1977, 226, 232-235, 240, 241, 368.

2   Zipser and Zipser; 79-81.

3   Zipser and Zipser, 122-125; Judith Schwartz, *Radical Feminists of Heterodoxy: Greenwich Village, 1912-1940*, New Victoria Publications, 1986.

4   Gordon, 234-235; Zipser and Zipser, 146, 156-157. On Weber and Blaché, see Alison McMahan, *Alice Guy Blache: Lost Visionary of the Cinema*, Continuum International, 2003, and Anthony Slide, *Lois Weber—The Director Who Lost Her Way in History*, Greenwood, 1996.

5   Zipser and Zipser, 137-140; Gordon, 232, 367-368.

6   Zipser and Zipser, 176-177, 181-182, 186-187.

7   Shapiro and Sterling, xxviii-xxix; Zipser and Zipser, 131-142.

8   Shapiro and Sterling, xxx.

Hayes, Mary, Unborn Baby Turner, and Angelina Weld Grimké:

1   *Southern Horrors and Other Writings: The Anti-Lynching Campaign of Ida B. Wells, 1892-1900*, ed. Jacqueline Royster, Bedford/St. Martin's, 1996; Kathleen A. O'Shea, *Women and the Death Penalty in the United States, 1900-1998*, Praeger Publishers, 1999; William D. Carrigan and Clive Webb, "The Lynching of Persons of Mexican Origin or Descent in the United States, 1848 to 1928," *Journal of Social History*, Winter 2003; Valerie Jenness, "Hate Crimes Law and Policy," *Encyclopedia of Lesbian Gay Bisexual Transgendered History in America Vol. 2*, ed. Mark Stein, Scribner's/Thomson Gale, 2004; Laura Hershey, "Researcher Uses Knowledge to Fight Hate: An Interview with Mark Sherry," *Disability World*, June-August 2003, <http://www.disabilityworld.org/06-08_03/gov/sherry.shtml>. Eugenics and lynching/hate crimes, yesterday and today, have targeted identical or parallel groups (Edwin Black, *War Against the Weak*, Four Walls Eight Windows, 2003, 23, 84). In the U.S., lynching and the death penalty's institutionalization are historically linked (Michael J. Pfeifer, *Rough Justice: Lynching and American Society, 1874-1947*, Illinois UP, 2004, and Eliza Steelwater, *The Hangman's Knot: Lynching, Legal Execution, and America's Struggle with the Death Penalty*, Westview Press, 2003).

2   Anti-Lynching Crusaders, "The Lynching of Women" (leaflet, 1922); reprinted in Angelica Mugarro, Karen Anderson, and Marian Horan, "How Did Black Women in the NAACP Promote the Dyer Anti-Lynching Bill, 1918-1923?" in *Woman and Social Movements in the United States, 1600-2000*, Kathryn Kish Sklar and Thomas Dublin, eds., Alexander Street Press and the Center for the Historical Study of Women and Gender, SUNY Binghamton, n.d., online <http://womhist.binghamton.edu/index.html> [3 Aug. 2004].

3   The Turner lynchings still resonate with African Americans; see Kim Mayhorn profile in Asha Bandele and Dawn M. Baskerville, "30 Women to Watch—African American Women," *Essence*, May 2000.

4   *Selected Works of Angelina Weld Grimké*, ed. Carolivia Herron, Oxford UP, 1991.

5   Angelina Weld Grimké, "The Closing Door," *Birth Control Review*, Oct. 1919 (Part 2; continues Part 1 from Sept. 1919's issue).

Ethel Sturges Dummer:

1   Robyn Rosen, "Ethel Sturges Dummer," in *Reproductive Health, Reproductive Rights: Reformers and Maternal Welfare*, 1917-1940, Ohio State UP, 2003.

2   Rosen, 40; Jennifer Platt, "Ethel Sturges Dummer," in *Women Building Chicago 1790-1990*, Schultz and Hast, eds., Indiana UP, 2001.

3   Ethel Sturges Dummer, *Why I Think So: The Autobiography of an Hypothesis*, Chicago: Clarke-McElroy, 1937, 113.

4   Platt, in Schultz and Hast.

5   Platt in Schultz and Hast; Estelle B. Freedman, *Maternal Justice: Miriam Van Waters and the Female Reform Tradition*, Chicago UP, 1996. Miriam Van Waters (1887-1974) was innovative and compassionate in her approaches to pregnant and other female prisoners. A single, adoptive lesbian mother, anti-eugenics birth control advocate, and prominent death penalty abolitionist, Van Waters opposed abortion as a destruction of life, while showing great kindness towards "Carolyn Cook," a troubled woman imprisoned for doing abortions.

6   Julia Lathrop invited psychiatrist William J. Healy to start the Juvenile Psychopathic Institute alongside the Chicago Juvenile Court. Healy wrote: "What may we think of punishment or even of neglect of the unmarried mother when we contemplate the essential fact that, whereas most infraction of laws coincides with destructive results, here we have a law-breaker as a constructive agent, giving as concrete evidence of her 'misbehavior' nature's highest product, a human being . . . A child that is fashioned the same as the rest of us . . . A society that does not properly care for this individual, born or unborn, callously sins against its own moral and physical welfare" (Introduction to Percy Gamble Kammerer, *The Unmarried Mother: A Study of 500 Cases*, Little Brown, 1926, x, xii).

7   Rosen; "Kankakee River State Park—History," n.d., on Illinois Department of Natural Resources website, <http://dnr.state.il.us/lands/landmgt/PARKS/R2/KANKAKEE.HTM> [21 Aug. 2004].

8   Committee on Family Limitation, "Family Limitation Centers In Chicago," *The Survey*, 5 May 1917.

9   Addams, Part One discusses the IBCL.

10 Platt in Schultz and Hast.

11 Dummer, 54.

12 *Ibid.*, 64.

Bertha Pappenheim:

1   Melinda Given Guttmann, *The Enigma of Anna O: A Biography of Bertha Pappenheim*, Moyer Bell, 2001, 67-68.

2   Atina Grossmann, "Abortion and Economic Crisis: The 1931 Campaign Against Paragraph 218," in *When Biology Became Destiny: Women in Weimar and Nazi Germany*, Renate Bridenthal, Atina Grossmann, and Marion Kaplan, eds., New York UP, 1984.

3   Qtd. in Guttmann, 260-261.

4   Qtd. in Guttmann, 292.

5   Qtd. in Guttmann, 321. Pappenheim's writings largely vanished during WWII. Guttmann and Dora Edinger (*Bertha Pappenheim, Freud's Anna O*, Highland Park, IL: Congregation Solel, 1968) reprint some surviving pieces (in translation).

Estelle Sylvia Pankhurst:

1   On the other Pankhursts, see, for example, June Purvis, *Emmeline Pankhurst*, Routledge, 2002; and Timothy Larsen, *Christabel Pankhurst: Fundamentalism and Feminism in Coalition*, Boydell Press, 2002.

2   Qtd. in Patricia Romero, *E. Sylvia Pankhurst: Portrait of a Radical*, Yale UP, 1987, 115.

3   E. Sylvia Pankhurst, *Save the Mothers*, Knopf, 1930, 122.

4   Romero, 37, 185.

Alice Paul:

1   Cynthia Lunardini, *From Equal Suffrage to Equal Rights: Alice Paul and the National Woman's Party, 1910-1928*, iUniverse, 2000; Amy E. Butler, *Two Paths to Equality: Alice Paul and Ethel M. Smith in the ERA Debate, 1921-1929*, New York State UP, 2002; Kathryn Kish Sklar and Jill Dias, "How Did the National Woman's Party Address the Issue of the Enfranchisement of Black Women, 1919-1924?" *in Woman and Social Movements in the United States, 1600-2000*, Kathryn Kish Sklar and Thomas Dublin, eds., Alexander Street Press and the Center for the Historical Study of Women and Gender, SUNY Binghamton, n.d., <http://womhist.binghamton.edu/index.html> [5 Sept. 2003].

2   Cynthia Harrison, *On Account of Sex: The Politics of Women's Issues*, Univ. of Calif., 1988, 205.

3   Robert S. Gallagher, "'I Was Arrested, Of Course': An Interview With Miss Alice Paul," *American Heritage*, Feb. 1974.

4   Evelyn K. Samras Judge to Mary Krane Derr (letters), 12 and 21 Sept. 1989, archived at Feminists for Life of America.

5   Alice Paul Chapter, National Organization for Women, <http://www.apnow.org> [21 Aug. 2004].

6   Bette Duganitz, "Alice Paul: Reality Versus Propaganda," *Feminists for Life of Minnesota Newsletter*, April 1992.

Dorothy Day:

1   Jim Forest, "The Living Legacy of Dorothy Day," *Salt of the Earth* (1996); online *Salt of the Earth*/Claretian Publications <http://salt.claretianpubs.org/issues/DorothyDay/legacy.html> [4 Aug. 2004]; Jim Forest, "A Personal Remembrance of Dorothy Day" (n.d.), online In Communion, <http://www.incommunion.org> [4 Aug. 2004].

2   Dorothy Day, *The Eleventh Virgin*, NY: Albert and Charles Boni, 1924.

3   *Ibid.*

4   Dorothy Day, *From Union Square to Rome*, Silver Spring, MD: Preservation of the Faith Press, 1938, Chapter 5. Most of Day's works, including those cited here, are archived online: Dorothy Day Library on the Web, <http://www.catholicworker.org/dorothyday/> [4 Aug. 2004].

5   Dorothy Day, "Having a Baby—A Christmas Story," *Catholic Worker*, Dec. 1977.

6   Dorothy Day, "Month of the Dead, *"Catholic Worker*, Nov. 1959.

7   Dorothy Day, "On Pilgrimage," *Catholic Worker*, June 1971.

8   Rickie Solinger, *Wake Up Little Susie*, Routledge, 1992, 206.

Laborers of Love:

1   Debra Anne Susie, *In the Way of Our Grandmothers: A Cultural View of Twentieth Century Midwifery in Florida*, Georgia UP, 1988, 30.

2   Qtd. in Susie, 31.

3   Ina May Gaskin and the Farm Midwives, *Spiritual Midwifery*., Summertown, TN: Book Pub. Co., 1975, 31; Louis J. Kern, "Pronatalism, Midwifery, and Synergistic Marriage," in W.E. Chmielewski, Louis J. Kern, and M. Klee-Hartzell, *Women in Spiritual and Communitarian Societies in the United States*, Syracuse UP, 1993.

Introduction to Part Two:

1   The Dalai Lama, keynote speeches, 1993 and 1999 Parliaments of the World's Religions; The Dalai Lama, "Hope for Tibet's Environment," speech at the Endangered Tibet Conference, Sydney, Australia, 28 September 1996; archived at <http://www.tew.org> [7 Nov. 2004].

2   The Dalai Lama, "Greetings from His Holiness the Dalai Lama to Buddhist Women," *Sakyadhita Magazine* (Spring 1996). Since 1959 the Chinese have killed and brutally oppressed millions of Tibetans, laying waste to their environment and culture and subjecting Tibetan women to forced sterilizations and abortions. (Tibetan Women's Association, Central Executive Committee, Bhagsunath Road, P.O. Mcleod Ganj, Dharamsala-176219, Kangra, Himachal Pradesh, India, Tel: 91-1892-221527,221198, Fax: 91-1892-221528, email <tibwomen@yahoo.com>, <http://www.tibetanwomen.org>).

3   At a panel discussion in 1990, I spoke in favor of informed consent legislation which would include providing abortion-seekers with a packet prepared by a bipartisan group (of both prochoicers and prolifers) providing information about the abortion procedure, reproduction and fetal development, and community and governmental assistance available, a Planned Parenthood representative protested the "patronizing" assumption that young women do not know how their own bodies work. When the discussion later turned to sex education, she described some of her young clients who "don't even know where their vagina is." I pointed out the inconsistency of her position concerning the education of these young women. To say that all young women are fully informed about reproductive issues is to

suggest that they have all had equal access to education, which, unfortunately, is not the case. [Linda Naranjo-Huebl, Ed.]

4   Adrienne Rich, *Of Woman Born: Motherhood as Experience and Institution*, New York: Norton, 1971.

5   Germaine Greer, *New Republic*, 5 October 1992.

6   Catharine MacKinnon, "Abortion: On Public and Private," *Toward a Feminist Theory of the State*, Cambridge: Harvard UP, 1989.

7   *Ibid*. 186.

8   Elizabeth Fox-Genovese, "Feminist Theory to Feminist Politics," *Feminism Without Illusions*, Chapel Hill: University of North Carolina Press, 1991.

9   *Ibid*. 84.

10   Faye Wattleton and Pamela Carr, "Which Way Black America—Anti-Abortion, Prochoice," *Ebony*, October 1989.

11   Doctors at a Bureau of Indian Affairs hospital forcibly sterilized Mary Crow Dog's sister just after the sister had given birth to a baby who died from inadequate medical care (*Lakota Woman*, Grove Weidenfeld, 1990, 78-79, 158-159).

12   In the 1970s, Redbird, the first Native American woman lawyer-physician, publicly exposed sterilization abuse of First Nations. She began gathering stories after a hysterectomized patient asked her for a womb transplant. Her efforts led to federal regulations (1979) against sterilization abuse. Redbird challenged another kind of violence in the womb: "The whiteman's solution to the Indian Woman's poverty is to kill her unborn" (qtd. in Indian Women United for Social Justice, *Voices of the Indian Women*, Los Angeles: Author, 1979, 1). On Redbird, see Arlon Benson, "Connie Redbird Pinkerman-Uri," in *Native American Women: A Biographical Dictionary*, Routledge, 2001.)

13   Juan Esparaza Loera, "Huerta Leaves UFW Speechless," *Fresno Bee*, 20 September 2004.

14   Chávez' mother, a lay midwife and curandera (herbal healer) who aided pregnant migrant workers, likely inspired his consistent life ethic. His own concern for pregnant women and their children encompassed challenges to domestic violence and to the use of pesticides that cause prenatal and postnatal disability and death. His ecological concern also expressed itself in vegetarianism ("Eulogy for Juana Estrada Chávez, San Jose, December 18, 1991," and "Wrath of Grapes Boycott Speech, 1986" in César Chávez, *The Words of César Chávez*, eds. Richard J. Jensen and John C. Hammerback, Texas A&M UP, 2002; Dorothy Day, "On Pilgrimage," *The Catholic Worker*, December 1972.)

15   "Bobbi Sykes," in *Women Who Do and Women Who Don't Join the Women's Movement*, ed. Robyn Rowland, Routledge & Kegan Paul, 1984. Many thanks to Angela Kennedy for bringing this material to our attention in the conclusion to her superb anthology *Swimming Against the Tide* (see Appendix A). At 18, Sykes became

pregnant after a gang rape. Her white mother arranged for a court-sanctioned abortion without notifying or consulting her. Yet Sykes birthed her child and grew to love him (*Snake Cradle*, Allen & Unwin, 1997). Sykes later earned a doctorate from Harvard University. The mentor whom she mentions, Mumshirl, is well known among those familiar with aboriginal human rights work ("Bibliography: Mumshirl (1924-1998)," Australian Women Published Sources <http://www.womenaustralia.info/bib/IMP0092p.htm> [12 Jan. 2005]).

16 Vivian Loyola Dames, "Chamorro Women, Self-Determination, and the Politics of Abortion in Guam," in *Asian/Pacific Islander American Women*, Shirley Hune and Gail M. Nomura, eds., New York UP, 2003.

17 *Ibid.* During the 1990s, garment industry labor abuses were systematically exposed on Saipan, another U.S.-occupied Pacific Island with a Chamorro population. Legal loopholes permitted multinational companies to produce clothing under near-slavery conditions and label it "Made in the USA." The companies denied maternity benefits to expectant garment workers, threatening to fire them unless they obtained clandestine abortions. Later, when the U.S. government interpreted the law to permit abortion, contrary to Saipan's constitution, the people of the island resisted. Edith G. Alejandro, "Community Marches for Life," *Saipan Tribune*, 27 January 2003.

18 Vandana Shiva, "Women's Rights Reduced to Reproduction Issue, Part 1" (email release) Penang, Malaysia: Third World Network, 1 Sept. 1994.

19 Stephen Mbogo, "Africans Debate Merits of Anti-Abortion Restrictions in U.S. AIDS Funding," Cybercast News Service release (2002), archived at <http://www.crosswalk.com> [26 Oct. 2004]; USAID, UNAIDS, WHO, UNICEF, and the Policy Project, *Coverage of Selected Services for HIV/AIDS Prevention, Care and Support in Low and Middle Income Countries in 2003*, Washington, DC: POLICY Project, June 2004.

20 Elizabeth Liagin, "Choices: Reproductive Rights and Population Control in the Twenty-First Century," in *Excessive Force*, Information Project for Africa, 1995.

21 Lucy Gwin, "They Call It Therapeutic," *Mouth*, January/February 2003.

22 "Screening Tied To Fall In Down Syndrome Births," Reuters Health wire release, 10 December 1998.

23 "Family Structure Contributes to Selective Abortion of Female Fetuses in China and India," *Kaiser Daily Reproductive Health Report*, 7 May 2001, archived at <http://www.kaisernetwork.org>, [11 Nov. 2004].

24 See Breast Cancer Prevention Institute <http://www.BCPInstitute.org> and "The Politics of Breast Cancer Research and Abortion" <http://fnsa.org/v1n1/bcancer.html>.

25 See Ring-Cassidy and Gentles, Appendix A.

26   Prolife researchers, even the many who have published in peer-reviewed journals, have been discounted because they identify themselves as prolife (for example, Anne C. Speckhard and Vincent M. Rue, "Postabortion Syndrome: An Emerging Health Concern," *Journal of Social Issues*, 48:3, 1992, 95-116; David Reardon and Philip Ney "Abortion and Subsequent Substance Abuse," *American Journal of Drug and Alcohol Abuse*, 26:1, 2000, 61-75; David C. Hanley, Rachel L. Anderson, David B. Larson, Harry L. Piersma, D. Stephen King, and Roger C. Sider, *Posttraumatic Abortion-Related Stress in Psychiatric Outpatients*, New York: Pine Rest Foundation, 1995, 12). Yet some of their conclusions resemble those of researchers who identify as prochoice or who do not disclose their abortion stance (for example, Henry P. David, Niels K. Rasmussen, and Eric Holst, "Postpartum and Postabortion Psychotic Reactions," *Family Planning Perspectives*, 13:2, 1981, 88-92; Dennis A. Bargarozzi, "Identification, Assessment and Treatment of Women Suffering from Post Traumatic Stress After Abortion," *Journal of Family Psychotherapy*, 5:3, 1994, 25-54). Prochoice researchers who have reached opposite conclusions are frequently cited and addressed without charges of political bias (for example, JoAnn Rosenberg, "Emotional Responses to Therapeutic Abortion," *American Family Physician*, 45:1, 1992, 137-140, and Nada Stotland, "The Myth of the Abortion Trauma Syndrome," *JAMA*, 286:15, 1992, 2078-2079). Clearly, further research is necessary. The American Psychiatric Association's *Diagnostic and Statistical Manual of Mental Disorders—IV—Revised* (DSM-IV-R) categorizes miscarriage and death of a child, but not abortion, as "psychosocial stressors" (1993, 18). DSM-III-R (1987, 20) did recognize abortion as one.

27   *Ibid.* We believe it is harmful and inaccurate to claim that abortion *inevitably* dooms women to victimhood or psychological disability. It is particularly objectionable to deploy this claim in order to exploit women's experiences for self-serving, expedient, shallow political agendas. By the same measure, it certainly does not help the thousands of women who have named their abortions as traumas arising from choicelessness to berate and silence them with statements like "grow up," "abortion can't be causing this," or "you've been brainwashed by patriarchal religion." It does help women to *listen* to them.

28   Rachel MacNair, "Position of Mastery," in *Achieving Peace in the Abortion War*, <http://www.fnsa.org/apaw/ch7/html>; Amy Silverman, "The Terminator," *Phoenix New Times*, June 17, 1999, archived at <http://www.phoenixnewtimes.com>; and Paul Rubin, "No Choice: Scenes from a 'Clown Show'—The Finkel Trial," *Phoenix New Times*,8 January 2004, archived at <http://www.phoenixnewtimes.com>.

29   See MacNair, <http://www.fnsa.org/apaw/ch17/html>, on why knowing about a dramatic drop in abortions makes people more open to the case against abortion by making it psychologically safer to hear.

30   In the early years of crisis pregnancy outreach, some centers disguised themselves as abortion referral offices to draw unsuspecting women and bombard them with antiabortion ideology. Prolife pregnancy workers have overwhelmingly rejected such dishonest, unethical tactics, which are now rare.

31   Feminists for Life of America, "MTV Makes Women the Losers" (press release), 29 September 2004.

Fannie Lou Hamer:

1   June Jordan, "1977: Poem for Mrs. Fannie Lou Hamer," *No More Masks! An Anthology of Twentieth-Century American Women* Poets, ed. Florence Howe, New York: HarperCollins, 1993, is a dear friend's tribute to Hamer's daily courage.

2   Fannie Lou Hamer, "It's In Your Hands," in *Black Women in White America*, Gerda Lerner, ed., New York: Vintage Books/Random House, 1972, 607-614.

3   Kay Mills, *This Little Light of Mine: The Life of Fannie Lou Hamer,* New York: Dutton, 1993, 274.

4   Erma Clardy Craven, "Abortion, Poverty, and Black Genocide," in *Abortion and Social Justice*, Thomas W. Hilgers and Dennis J. Horan, eds., New York: Sheed & Ward, 1972.

5   Mills 260-261.

6   Mills 274.

7   African American teen Jo Etha Collier, who showed great promise in both athletics and academics, never used her college scholarships. The night she graduated from high school, a group of white men fatally shot her. Hamer gathered financial and emotional support for her family.—Eds.

8   Keady, a disabled person from a poor Irish background, ruled, "Human experience refutes the dogmatic attitude inherent in such a policy against unwed parents ... While obviously aimed at discouraging premarital sexual relations, the policy's effect is apt to encourage abortion ..." (371 F. Supp. 27, D.C. Miss. 1973).—Eds.

Graciela Olivarez:

1   Francisca Flores, "Conference of Mexican Women in Houston—*Un Remolino* [A Whirlwind]," in *Chicana Feminist Thought: The Basic Historical Writings*, ed. Alma M. Garcia, New York: Routledge, 1997.

2   Bradley M. Patten, *Foundations of Embryology*, New York: McGraw-Hill, 1964, 2.

Cindy Osborne, Pat Goltz, and Catherine Callaghan:

1   Reverend Jesse Jackson, Black civil rights leader; Dolores Huerta, United Farm Workers cofounder and organizer; and Dick Gregory, African American civil rights activist and comedian. Huerta has also reversed her stance.—Eds.

Daphne Clair de Jong:

1   Weininger (1880-1903), an Austrian Jew, renounced his own people as "cowardly" and responsible for "cultural decay," that is, "feminine." He committed suicide.— Eds.

Jo McGowan:

[1] "Family Structure Contributes to Selective Abortion of Female Fetuses in China and India," *Kaiser Daily Reproductive Health Report*, 7 May 2001, archived at <www.kaisernetwork.org>, [11 Nov. 2004].

[2] *Ibid.*

[3] "Shakuntala," qtd. in Viola Roggencamp, "Abortion of a Special Kind" in *Test Tube Women: What Future for Motherhood*, Rita Arditti, Renate Duelli Klein, and Shelley Minden, eds., Boston: Pandora Press, 1984.

[4] V.G. Julie Rajan, "Will India's Ban on Prenatal Sex Determination Slow Abortion of Girls?," *Hinduism Today*, April 1996, <http://www.hinduismtoday.com/1996/4/ #gen241> [1 Jan. 2005].

Grace Dermody:

[1] Dr. Robert Jay Lifton, an expert on the psychology of nuclear war and Nazi medicalized killings, praised Gould's "bold nitty-gritty focus on issues and the people involved in them" ("Robert Gould," Associated Press obituary, 27 February 1998.)

Jane Thomas Bailey:

[1] Aaron Patrick, "Abortion Justified for 'Better Babies,'" *The Age* (Melbourne, Australia), 6 July 2003, archived at <http://www.theage.com.au>. Watson advocates infanticide of disabled newborns ("Children from the Laboratory," *AMA Prism*, May 1973) and has designs on "stupidity" and (female) "ugliness." He does not disavow the apt label of "eugenicist," and even dismisses critics who refer to history's most notorious eugenicist: "We must not fall into the absurd trap of being against everything Hitler was for." (Ralph Brave, "James Watson Wants to Build a Better Human," AlterNet, <http://www.alternet.org/story/16026 >, 29 May 2003 [1 Jan. 2005]).

[2] Simone Apsis, "Anya Souza Talks Back to Genetics," *Mouth*, July/August 2003.

[3] "Jane Roe" (Norma McCorvey) has since disclosed that she constructed the rape story to get help (Introduction, Part Two). This disclosure does not invalidate the hardships of her pregnancy, let alone those of women who have been raped.—Eds.

[4] See Mathewes-Green, n2.—Eds.

[5] Davis' memoir is *From Where I Sit*, SPCK, 1989. In 1995, Davis and Colin Harte started the British charity Enable, which sponsors and supports disabled children in Andhra Pradesh State, South India <http://www.enable-india.org.uk/>.—Eds.

Juli Loesch Wiley:

[1] Wiley was responding to Ellen Willis, "Putting Women Back Into the Abortion Debate," *Village Voice*, 16 July 1985.—Eds.

Frederica Mathewes-Green:

[1] Pertinent resources include the International Task Force on Euthanasia and Assisted Suicide, P.O. Box 760— Steubenville, OH 43952, phone (740)282-3810, <http://

www.internationaltaskforce.org>; Rita Marker, *Deadly Compassion*, William Morrow, 1993/ HarperCollins, 1994/Avon, 1995; and Eric Chevlen and Wesley J. Smith, *Power Over Pain: How to Get the Pain Control You Need*, International Task Force, 2002.

[2]   For disability rights-oriented coverage of medicalized killing, see *Mouth Magazine*, P.O. Box 558, Topeka, KS 66601-0558, <http://www.mouthmag.com>; *Ragged Edge Magazine* (formerly *The Disability Rag*), now online only at <http://www.ragged-edge-mag.com>; and Not Dead Yet, <http://www.notdeadyet.org>, c/o Progress CIL, 7521 Madison St, Forest Park, IL 60130, voice/TTY (708)209-1500, fax (708)209-1735, TTY (708)209-1826.

[3]   Although initially blocked in his legal attempt to move Christine Busalacchi, her father ordered her feeding tubes removed after the Missouri Supreme Court dismissed the case. Christine died of starvation and dehydration March 7, 1993. See <http://humanlife.net/euthanasiaarticles/courtcases.html>.—Eds.

[4]   After Janet Adkins, Jack Kevorkian killed at least 109 people—mostly women, mostly persons with chronic rather than terminal conditions. In 2001, he was convicted of murdering Thomas Youk and sentenced to 10-27 years.—Eds.

Rachel MacNair:

[1]   See <http://www.rachelmacnair.com/books> for updated list and availability.

Kay Kemper:

[1]   In 1995, U.S. Senator Robert Packwood, a lauded abortion-rights advocate since his 1969 election, resigned after the Senate recommended expulsion. Seventeen women, including an abortion-rights lobbyist, had come forward with sexual harassment accusations spanning his senatorial career.

[2]   By custom, and in some jurisdictions law, journalists have withheld names of alleged sexual assault victims. Most did this during the Smith trial. NBC News and the *New York Times* released the "Unknown Woman"'s name early in the case. Both subsequently reverted to customary practice.—Eds.

Benazir Bhutto:

[1]   "Benazir Bhutto—Former Prime Minister of Pakistan." BBC World Service, <http://www.bbc.co.uk/worldservice/people/features/wiwp/dyncon/bhutto.shtml#>, n.d. [1 Jan. 2005].

[2]   *Ibid.*

[3]   *Ibid.*

[4]   Muslim Women's League USA, "Our Religion Teaches Peace and Equality," *Feminism and Nonviolence Studies*, Fall 1998, <http://www.fnsa.org>.

[5]   Rev. Doug Hunt, "Women and Religion Are Major Players at Cairo Conference," *Earthkeeping News*, Nov/Dec. 1994, <http://www.nacce.org/1994/cairo.html >.

[6]   *Bismillah* is a prayer that opens almost every chapter of the Qur'an. It is often recited before reading the Qur'an and starting a daily activity.—Eds.

[7] Islam has been widely interpreted to proscribe homosexuality. Some Muslims feared the Conference would pressure a different stance. Islamic cultures have varied widely in their actual treatment of GLBT persons, from execution to *de facto* tolerance. One group, the Al-Fatiha Foundation <http://www.al-fatiha.org>, asserts that GLBT persons can be faithful to Islam and calls upon Muslims to stop violence against them.—Eds.

Jennifer Ferguson:

[1] Personal communication with Mary Krane Derr, Fall 2003.

[2] In contrast to the ANC leadership, South Africans largely continue to oppose abortion on "demand"-73% of urban dwellers with access to a landline telephone, according to a 2004 survey. Among those whose monthly household income was under R6000, opposition ran over 80%, dropping to roughly 60% for those in the over R15000 category. Although a clear majority of whites, Indians, and Coloureds (racially mixed persons) disagreed with a general right to abortion, Africans (those from Black ethnicities such as Xhosa and Zulu) were most opposed at around 77% (South African Press Assoc., "Abortion Survey: 24% in Favour," 4 Nov. 2004, <http://www.SABCnews.com>, [10 Jan. 2005].

[3] Pregs (Pregaluxmi) Govender, "Abortion: Open Letter to Ferguson," *Cape Times*, Cape Town, South Africa, 6 Nov. 1996.

Lorraine Hansberry and Bernadette Waterman Ward:

[1] Qtd. in David Bianco, "Playwright Lorraine Hansberry," Planet Out: Queer History, <http://www.planetout.com/news/history/archive/08161999.html>, [9 Jan. 2005].

[2] Qtd. in Philip Uko Effiong, "History, Myth, and Revolt in Lorraine Hansberry's 'Les Blancs,'" *African American Review*, Spring 1998.

[3] James Baldwin, *The Devil Finds Work: Essays*, NY: Delta, 2000 (1976), 63.

[4] (The following notes are Waterman's, except where noted.—Eds.) Jerome Beaty and J. Paul Hunter, *The Norton Introduction to Literature*, 7d, NY: W.W. Norton & Company, 1998, 1832.

[5] Norton 1172.

[6] See the comments from Anthony Bethelmy, 92, and Steven R. Carter, 94, in *African American Women Playwrights: A Research Guide*, NY: Garland, 1999.

[7] Richard Watts, Jr., "Honest Drama of a Negro Family," *New York Post*, 12 March 1959; Brooks Atkinson, "Negro Drama Given at Ethel Barrymore," *New York Times*, 12 March 1959; Robert Coleman, "Raisin in the Sun a Superior Play," *Daily Mirror*, 12 March 1959; Walter Kerr, "A Raisin in the Sun," *New York Herald*, 12 March 1959. All are reprinted in *New York Theater Critics' Reviews*, 1959, vol. 20, ed. Rachel W. Coffin.

[8] Cheney 65. Cf. Langston Hughes, "Mother to Son," ed. Paul Molloy, *100 Plus American Poems*, NY: Scholastic, 1970, 24.

[9] Atkinson 345, in Coffin, ed.

[10] Cheney, Ann. *Lorraine Hansberry*, NY: Twayne, 1994, 60.

[11] John J. Conley, S.J., "Abortion as a Metaphor," *Life and Learning VIII: Proceedings of the Eighth Annual Conference of the University Faculty for Life Conference, June 1998, at the University of Toronto*, ed. Joseph Koterski, S.J., Washington, DC: University Faculty for Life, 1999.

[12] Frederica Mathewes-Green, *Real Choices—Listening to Women; Looking for Alternatives to Abortion*, Ben Lomond: Conciliar Press, 1997, 14.

[13] Sally Guttmacher, et. al. "Abortion Reform in South Africa: A Case Study of the 1996 Choice on Termination of Pregnancy Act, *International Family Planning Perspectives* 24:4, Dec. 1998. <http://www.agi-usa.org/ pubs/journals/2419198.html>.

[14] Dorothy Roberts, *Killing the Black Body*, NY: Vintage, 1997.

[15] Watts, op. cit.

[16] Jewelle Gomez, "Lorraine Hansberry: Uncommon Warrior," in *Reading Black, Reading Feminist*, ed. Henry Louis Gates, NY: Penguin, 1990, 311.

[17] Frank Aston, "Raisin in the Sun is Moving Tale," *New York World-Telegram*, 12 March 1959, in Coffin 345. See Jeanne-Marie Miller in *Black American Women Playwrights*, 74.

[18] Theophilus Lewis, "Raisin in the Sun," *America* 51/5 (2605) 286-87.

[19] Q. in the article "Hansberry" in *Contemporary Literary Criticism*, vol. 17, ed. Sharon Gunton, Detroit: Gale, 1981.

[20] Cheney 19.

[21] Steven Carter, "Lorraine Hansberry," *Dictionary of Literary Biography*, Vol. 38: *Afro-American Writers after 1955: Dramatists and Prose Writers*, Detroit: Gale, 1985, 120-26.

[22] Gomez 315.

[23] Martin Luther King, Jr., "Letter From The Birmingham Jail," *The Borzoi College Reader*, 6th ed., Charles Muscatine and Marlene Griffith, eds., NY: Knopf, 1988, 664.

[24] When she saw the 2004 Broadway revival of *Raisin*, Peggy Noonan felt "stunned" by audience reaction to Ruth's abortion plan:

> [W]hen this play came out in 1960 it was received by the audience as a painful moment—a cry of pain from a woman who's tired of hoping that life will turn out well. But this is the thing: Our audience didn't know that . . . didn't understand it was tragic . . . [T]hey applauded. Some of them cheered . . . The reaction seemed to startle the actors on stage, and shake their concentration . . . I can't tell you how much that moment hurt. To know that the members of our audience didn't know that the taking of a baby's life is tragic . . . the taking of your own baby's life is beyond tragic . . . But our audience

didn't know . . . They thought that the fact that the young woman was considering abortion was a sign of liberation . . ." ("'Raisin' and Falling: A 40-year-old Play Reveals Something Awful About Today's Culture," *Wall Street Journal*, 29 April 2004).—Eds.

Serrin Foster:

[1] At last word, Chipman, who had married Shawn Hurston by the time of the case, was raising their daughter Cheyenne with him. Glass was raising her daughter Shelby as a single mother. Both young women were going ahead with their plans to attend college and become helping professionals—Chipman a nurse, and Glass a teacher.

[2] Norton did not herself seek admission to Cornell, but she campaigned for Cornell to change its men-only policy. See *Woodhull and Claflin's Weekly*, 19 Nov. 1870 (Part One).—Eds.

[3] The Unborn Victims of Violence Act (H.R. 1997, S. 1019) came into effect April 1, 2004. On November 2, 2004, a jury found Scott Peterson, Laci's husband and Conner's father, guilty on one count of first-degree murder and (for the baby's death) one count of manslaughter.—Eds.

Cheryl Long Feather:

[1] Native American Training Institute, 4007 State Street, Suite 110, Bismarck, ND 58503, phone (701)255-6374, fax (701)255-6394, <http://www.nativeinstitute.org>.

Cecilia Brown:

[1] PLAGAL, P.O. Box 16753, Alexandria, VA 22302 USA, voicemail: 202-223-6697, email <plagal@plagal.org>, <http://www.plagal.org>.

[2] In 2004, PLAGAL returned to the March for Life without incident, carrying a banner with their symbol: a rainbow triangle holding the image of an unborn child and the words "ABORTION = DEATH," after the anti-AIDS slogan "SILENCE = DEATH."—Eds.

Rus Cooper-Dowda:

[1] Mary Krane Derr, "Pregnancy Is No Mere Inconvenience, Abortion Is No Solution," in *Prolife Feminism Yesterday and Today*, 1 ed., Sulzberger & Graham, 1995.

[2] Jackie Malone, "Abortion Issue Hits Home," *Memorandum (from the Pro Life Alliance of Gays and Lesbians)*, Summer 2004.

[3] Through the Looking Glass, 2198 Sixth Street, Suite 100, Berkeley, CA 94710-2204, toll-free phone (voice) 1-800-644-2666, (TTY) 1-800-804-1616, local (510) 848-1112, fax (510) 848-4445, email <TLG@lookingglass.org>, <http://lookingglass.org/index.php>. Assists disabled parents and others dealing with disability in the family.

[4] Linda Toms Barker and Vida Maralani, *Challenges and Strategies of Disabled Parents*, Berkeley, CA: Through the Looking Glass, 1997.

Mary Meehan:

1   [All notes are Meehan's.—Eds.] ACLU officials might object to my use of the term "unborn children"; yet some ACLU activists used this term in their early debates over abortion. But when Association for the Study of Abortion staff coordinated friend-of-the-court briefs for *Roe v. Wade* and *Doe v. Bolton*, "they kept careful watch over the language used in the briefs; for example, they substituted 'fetus' for 'baby.' They also coined the phrase 'pro-choice' rather than the more value-laden 'pro-abortion.'" Lee Epstein and Joseph F. Kobylka, *The Supreme Court and Legal Change: Abortion and the Death Penalty*, Chapel Hill, N.C.: North Caroline UP, 1992, 171.

2   I am most grateful to the staff of the Seeley G. Mudd Manuscript Library, Princeton University, Princeton, N.J., for their assistance with my research in the ACLU Archives (ACLUA) and for permission to quote from archives documents.

3   Harriet F. Pilpel, "Civil Liberties and the War on Crime," Paper presented at ACLU Biennial Conference, Boulder, CO, 21-24 June 1964, 7-8, 2 & 2n., ACLUA, box 409, folder 15, Seeley G. Mudd Manuscript Library, Princeton University, Princeton, N.J. This and other documents from the ACLUA are quoted with permission of the Princeton University Libraries. See David J. Garrow, *Liberty & Sexuality: The Right to Privacy and the Making of Roe v. Wade*, (NY: Macmillan, 1994) on the role of Pilpel and Guttmacher in legalizing abortion. On Guttmacher's eugenics involvement, see *Eugenics Quarterly*, 1955-1966. Pilpel apparently spoke at a 1970 conference cosponsored by the American Eugenics Society and a division of the Population Council. See her "Family Planning and the Law," *Social Biology* 18, supp. (Sept. 1971), S127-S133.

4   Pilpel, "Civil Liberties and the War on Crime" (n3), 12.

5   Alan Reitman, memo to Eleanor Norton, 7 July 1966, ACLUA, box 87, folder 15.

6   "Testimony of Harriet F. Pilpel, Esq. for the New York Civil Liberties Union," before Committee on Health, New York State Assembly, 7 March 1966, 2-7, ACLUA, box 1143, folder 25.

7   "The office," memo to Due Process Committee, 9 Dec. 1966; and "The office," memo to Due Process Committee, 7 Dec. 1966, incorporating William Kopit and Harriet F. Pilpel, "Abortion and the New York Penal Laws" [1965], ACLUA, box 1145, folder 2. The Kopit-Pilpel paper made five statistical assertions—including the one about numbers of illegal abortions per year—that were cited only to outlines prepared by Pilpel but apparently not published. This was peculiar citation practice, to say the least.

8   U.S. Census Bureau, *Statistical Abstract of the United States, 1999* (Washington, 1999), 91, Table 123.

9   Barbara J. Syska and others, "An Objective Model for Estimating Criminal Abortions and Its Implications for Public Policy," in Thomas W. Hilgers and others, eds., *New Perspectives on Human Abortion* (Frederick, Md., 1981), 164-181, 178.

10   Cynthia McKnight, *Life Without Roe: Making Predictions About Illegal Abortions* (Washington, 1992), 10-15. McKnight's study was published by the Horatio R. Storer Foundation, an affiliate of the National Right to Life Committee. The study is thoroughly documented.

11   Michael M. Gask to Alan Reitman, 25 Sept.1966, 2 & 5; and Joel Gora, memos to Mr. Reitman, 2 & 19 Oct. [1966], ACLUA, box 1145, folder 1.

12   "The Office," memo to Due Process Committee, 6 Jan. 1967, incorporating paper by Benjamin S. DuVal, Jr., 1, 6 & 9; and "The Office," memo to Board of Directors, 8 Feb. 1967, 3-4, ACLUA, box 88a, folder 4.

13   ACLU Board of Directors, 14 Feb. 1967 minutes, 3-7, *ibid.*

14   Thomas L. Shaffer to John de J. Pemberton, 21 March 1967, and to editor of the *Indianapolis Star*, 20 March 1967, reprinted in "IV. Some Arguments Against Abortion," ACLUA, box 1145, folder 2.

15   Thomas L. Shaffer to Alan Reitman, 6 Nov. 1967, 1-2, *ibid.*

16   ACLU, "Abortion," *1976 Policy Guide of the American Civil Liberties Union*, 230-231 (citing 25 Jan. 1968 board minutes & 25 March 1968 news release), Microfilming Corporation of America, "The American Civil Liberties Union: Update, 1974-1978," Reel 2; Will Lissner, "A.C.L.U. Asks End to Abortion Bans," *New York Times*, 25 March 1968, 35; Alan Reitman and Trudy Hayden, memo to Board of Directors (citing Dr. Tietze), 31 Oct. 1967, 7 ff., Microfilming Corporation of America, "American Civil Liberties Union Records and Publications, 1917-1975," Reel 25. Tietze was a member of England's Eugenics Society; see Eugenics Society, "List of Fellows and Members as at August 1957 (London, 1957), [16].

17   Eleanor Norton, memo to Alan Reitman, 5 Dec.1967, ACLUA, box 1145, folder 1.

18   Eleanor Norton, memo to John Fordon, 3 July 1968, ACLUA, box 1145, folder 2; Playboy Foundation, "Grant Allocations for Fiscal Year 1980-81 at 6/30/81" (Chicago, 1981), 3, and 1983 annual report, 8; Foundation Center.

19   Samuel Walker, op. cit. (n. 2); Epstein & Kobylka, op. cit. (n. 6); Garrow, op. cit. (n. 8); Nadine Strossen, "The American Civil Liberties Union and Women's Rights," *New York University Law Review* 66, no. 6 (Dec. 1991), 1940-1961. On ACLU lobbying at the national level, see <http://www.aclu.org>. On ACLU success in guaranteeing public funding of abortion in ten states, see "The ACLU Reproductive Freedom Project," *ibid.*

20   Mary Meehan, "The Road to Abortion (II): How Government Got Hooked," *Human Life Review* 25:1, Winter 1999, 68-82 (especially 69-70 & 78-79 on race).

21   Aryeh Neier, interview by Thomas J. Balch, 3 Nov. 1979, in Balch's "Convincing the Courts on Abortion," Appendix,12-13, Paper for Prof. Neier's "Litigation and Public Policy" course, [New York University School of Law] Fall, 1979.

22   Brief for Appellees at 185, Harris v. McRae, 448 U.S. 297 (1980); and Norman Dorsen, ACLU Campaign for Choice fund-raising letter to "Dear Friend," n.d. [received by the writer on 29 Sept. 1979].

23   Samuel Walker, op. cit. (n. 2), 303-304; John Shattuck, memo to Executive Committee and Board of Directors, 14 Sept. 1977, 2, ACLUA, box 32, folder 6; ACLU Board of Directors, 24-25 Sept.1977 minutes, 3, ACLUA, box 32, folder 1.

24   Jay G. Sykes, "Farewell to Liberalism," *Insight* (Sunday magazine of the *Milwaukee Journal*), 8 Sept. 1974, 30-32; and ACLU Executive Committee, 30 July 1977 minutes, 3, ACLUA, box 117, folder 1. For other examples of dissent within the ranks, see the ACLU publication *Civil Liberties*, April 1970, 6; Nov. 1974, 7; Winter 1986, 2; Spring 1986, 2; Summer/Fall 1986, 13. See, also, Nat Hentoff, "A Heretic in the ACLU," *Washington Post*, 16 Aug. 1985, A-23.

25   ACLU Board of Directors, 4-5 March 1978 minutes, 15-16, ACLUA, box 33, folder 2.

26   Brief for American Public Health Association, American Civil Liberties Union and others as Amici Curiae at 4 & 31, Colautti v. Franklin, 439 U.S. 379 (1979). See the Colautti opinion at 388-389 on this point.

27   Nadine Taub, letter to "Dear Abortion Policy Committee Member," 15 March 1988, with attached excerpt from ACLU board minutes of Jan. [1988], 3-17, ACLUA, box 166, folder 1; Emily Whitfield (ACLU Media Relations Director), memo to the writer, 24 Jan. 2001; <http://wwww.aclu.org>.

Mary Krane Derr:

1   See Mathewes-Green, n2.

2   Qtd. in the *Wheeling (WV) Evening Standard*, 17 Nov. 1875, reprinted in Victoria Woodhull, *The Human Body the Temple of God*, London: privately printed, 1890, 470.

3   Feminist Collective of Via Cherubini, Milan, "We are working on a different political approach," in *Italian Feminist Thought: A Reader*, eds. Paola Bono and Sandra Kemp, Oxford, UK/Cambridge, MA: Basil Blackwell, 1991, 223-225.

4   *Feminism and Nonviolence Studies Journal: Special Issue on Prolife Feminism and Spiritual Diversity*, Fall 1998, <http://www.fnsa.org>.

5   Camille Peri, "Birth Doctor, Mother, Abortionist," *Salon Magazine*, 23 June 1997 <http://archive.salon.com/archives/1997/mwt_feature.html>, [8 Jan. 2005].

6   Laury Oaks, *Smoking and Pregnancy: The Politics of Fetal Protection*, Rutgers UP, 2000, 207. She illuminates the deficiencies of individualistic, entirely fetus-centered antiabortion viewpoints. She does not examine communitarian, holistic prolife approaches here.

7   Emmanuel Levinas, *Ethics and Infinity*, transl. Richard A. Cohen, Duquesne UP, 1985, 89.

8   Alexander Tsiaris, *From Conception to Birth*, Doubleday, 2002.

9   Matilda Joslyn Gage, *Woman, Church, and State*, Charles Kerr, 1893, Chapter X.

10   See, for example, Christiane Northrup, *Women's Bodies, Women's Wisdom*, Bantam, 1994.

11   Margo Anand, *The Art of Sexual Ecstasy*, Los Angeles: J.P. Tarcher, 1992.

12   Sue Nathanson, *Soul Crisis* (Signet, 1990), 168.

13 Karen A. Signell, *Wisdom of the Heart: Working With Women's Dreams*, New York: Bantam, 1990.

14 Cynthia Gorney, *Articles of Faith: A Frontline History of the Abortion Wars*, Touchstone/ Simon & Schuster, 1998, 306.

15 Qtd. in Jessica Jernigan, "Interview: A Theology of Presence" n.d., <http://www.bordersstores.com/features/feature.jsp?file=brockparker> [1 Dec. 2004].

16 Rebecca Ann Parker, "Away From the Fire: Rebecca's Story," Chapter One in Rita Nakashima Brock and Rebecca Ann Parker, *Proverbs of Ashes: Violence, Redemptive Suffering, and the Search for What Saves Us*, Beacon Press, 2001.

17 Vicki Thorne, speech at "Abortion Healing" conference, Marquette University, Milwaukee, WI, 3 November 1993.

18 Male abuse survivors and mental health professionals are raising consciousness about the long-term effects (MaleSurvivor, <http://www.malesurvivor.org>). Stereotypical gender roles and expectations take a tremendous toll on many men, especially the pressure to disavow vulnerabilities (Fredric Rabinowitz and Sam Cochran, *Deepening Psychotherapy With Men*, APA Press, 2001). Abuse compounds the harm.

19 Matilda Joslyn Gage, *Woman, Church, and State*, Charles Kerr, 1893, Chapter X.

20 Mary Ann Glendon, *Abortion and Divorce in Western Law: American Failures, European Challenges*, Harvard UP, 1987, 58.

21 Patrick J. Flood, "Life After Communism: Democracy and Abortion in Eastern Europe and Russia," *Life and Learning* 10, 2000, archived by University Faculty for Life, <http://www.uffl.org>.

Wangari Maathai:

1 Green Belt Movement, P.O. Box 67545, Nairobi, Kenya, Africa, phone: +254.20.573057 / 571523, email <gbm@wananchi.com>, <http://www.greenbeltmovement.org>; Maathai's official site, <http://wangarimaathai.or.ke>; and Wangari Maathai, *The Greenbelt Movement*, rev. Lantern Books, 2004.

2 Priscilla Sears, "Wangari Maathai: 'You Strike the Woman . . .,'" *In Context*, Spring 1991 <http://www.context.org/ICLIB/IC28/Sears.htm> [9 Jan. 2005].

3 To plant trees, see the GBM website and initiatives of such groups as the National Arbor Day Foundation (100 Arbor Avenue, Nebraska City, NE 68410 USA, toll-free phone 1-888-448-7337, <http://www.arborday.org>; 10 trees sent free to each new member) and the Global Releaf (1 tree replanted per $1 donated) and California Wildfire Relief (2 trees per $1) campaigns of American Forests (P.O. Box 1200, Washington, DC 20013 USA, phone (202) 737-1944, <http://www.americanforests.org>).

Linda Naranjo-Huebl:

1 Elizabeth Fox-Genovese documents similar observations in her book, *"Feminism is Not the Story of My Life": How Today's Feminist Elite Has Lost Touch with the Real Concerns of Women*, Doubleday, 1996.

2   Classicist and racist tendencies drive much social concern over unplanned pregnancy rates. Latinos in particular are much more likely to oppose abortion than other ethnic groups (Fox-Genovese, 1996), and yet abortion advertising in Latino and other minority communities is obviously much stronger than in white communities. Likewise, much American neoliberal concern for "reproductive rights" in the Two-Thirds World stems from a thinly disguised eugenicism (Introduction, Part Two).

3   The "good enough" mother is a term used by object relations psychologist D.W. Winnicott to describe the mother who is attuned enough to the needs of the child to meet his or her basic physical and psychological needs.

4   Penny Salazar and Luci Freed, *A Season to Heal*, Nashville, TN: Cumberland House Publishing, 1996.

Index

Made in the USA
Las Vegas, NV
27 September 2021